W9-CCZ-438

THE OXFORD BOOK OF LEGAL ANECDOTES

THE OXFORD BOOK OF LEGAL ANECDOTES

EDITED BY
MICHAEL GILBERT

Oxford New York
OXFORD UNIVERSITY PRESS

Oxford University Press, Walton Street, Oxford OX2 6DP
Oxford New York Toronto
Delhi Bombay Calcutta Madras Karachi
Petaling Jaya Singapore Hong Kong Tokyo
Nairobi Dar es Salaam Cape Town
Melbourne Auckland
and associated companies in
Beirut Berlin Ibadan Nicosia

Oxford is a trade mark of Oxford University Press

First published 1986
Reprinted 1986, 1987 (with corrections)

British Library Cataloguing in Publication Data
The Oxford book of legal anecdotes.
1. Law—History—Anecdotes, facetiae, satire, etc.
I. Gilbert, Michael
340'.09'03 K183
ISBN 0-19-214112-0

Library of Congress Cataloging in Publication Data
The Oxford book of legal anecdotes.
Includes index.
1. Law—Anecdotes, facetiae, satire, etc.
I. Gilbert, Michael Francis, 1912– .
K183.095 1986 340'.0207 85-13857
ISBN 0-19-214112-0

Printed in Great Britain by
Richard Clay Ltd.
Bungay, Suffolk

CONTENTS

INTRODUCTION

THIS book is a collection of extracts from the published reminiscences of judges, barristers, solicitors, magistrates, and also of a variety of people who have viewed the operation of the law not from the eminence of the Bench or counsel's seats, but from the witness stand, the spectators' gallery, and even from the dock. The source of each extract is noted at the back.

A limiting factor in selection has been the meaning of the word 'anecdote'. It will be readily understood that this is not a collection of jokes. But the format does demand some observance of the dramatic unities of time, place, and theme. Each extract describes an incident in the life of the character principally concerned. It has been necessary in some cases to set the scene. The curious experience of Sir Patrick Hastings in the military court in the Ruhr would be incomplete without some account of the difficulties he experienced in getting there; as would the tribulations of poor Mr Stokes on his visit to Brixton. On the whole, however, shortness is the essence of an anecdote.

I have used a minimal amount of editing. The notes at the head of an anecdote are mainly designed to identify the speaker where the text does not make this clear. I noted that the American editor of a similar compilation wrote: 'In quoting, as I do throughout, I have frequently used ellipses, brackets, paraphrases, and other sly means to avoid repetition and technicality and to achieve brevity.' I have not followed this the whole way. I have added nothing of my own without making it clear by the use of italics in headnotes, or square brackets within an extract, that I am commenting rather than quoting. On the other hand, I have not hesitated to leave out words, sentences, or even complete paragraphs if they seemed to encumber rather than assist the point of the story. Also, in the shorter passages, when it may not be clear who is being talked about I have sometimes substituted actual names for expressions such as 'the plaintiff', 'the defendant', or 'the accused'.

It will be seen that the anecdotes are not confined to Great Britain. It was Professor Jacques Barzun, the Dean of Faculties at Columbia University, who encouraged me to cross the Atlantic in search of examples from America and who added to my indebtedness by making me free of the Library of the New York Society, of which he is a

Trustee. To the correspondent of the Oxford University Press in Australia, also, my thanks for referring me to a number of books and sending me a copy of that hilarious compilation *The Judge Who Laughed* by A. S. Gillespie-Jones.

But if the field of selection has been wide enough to cover three continents it is deliberately more restricted in the scale of time. No doubt research would produce any number of repeatable pleasantries from the tribunals of Rome and Athens or from the medieval courts of England; though the exchanges there would be likely to be in bastard Latin or that peculiar dialect known as Law French. But I felt that this obeisance to History would have been at the expense of the unity which resulted from confining the extracts to the English-speaking countries and to the last 250 years.

The field was rich enough. Whether it has been reaped to good effect the reader must judge. No doubt some will be grieved to find a favourite story omitted. I can only hope they will discover others which have previously escaped them.

I have myself been a devourer of legal biography since being introduced, at an early age, to Marjoribanks' classic *Life of Edward Marshall Hall.* Since I undertook the present collection, some six years ago, I have sustained an almost undiluted diet of such works.

There are a few lawyers in every age who catch the eye to such an extent that they become public property. The growth of the popular press in the second half of the nineteenth century brought the names and the fame of F. E. Smith, Marshall Hall, Rufus Isaacs, and Edward Carson to the sort of public attention that is currently accorded to Lord Denning. It was the same forces that promoted Clarence Darrow, Sam Leibowitz, and Earl Rogers in America.

I came to realize, however, that there was a different sort of fame. There were lawyers' lawyers as opposed to public lawyers. The line of distinction was not always clear. Many people outside the law recognize the names of Rigby Swift and Curtis-Bennett, but for Charlie Bowen and Theo Mathew and Peter Edlin and William Maule the bells of memory ring fainter and fainter. Yet these were men who delighted or infuriated a whole generation at the Bar.

A second, and a rather sad, discovery was that it was by no means the most eminent who were the most quotable. There were exceptions, of course. Lord Russell of Killowen breaks all the rules, as he did throughout his tempestuous career. Others were less fortunate. They had biographers who were over-conscious of the gravitas and position of their subjects. At its worst this would produce the traditional 'two volumes of filial piety'. Sometimes, ploughing through them with a despairing hope that there must surely have been occasions when the author took his subject a little less seriously, I found my eye drifting to the bottom of the page. There, tucked away in smaller type, a glint of humanity could sometimes be found. It was as though the biographer faced with some flippant triviality which he hesitated to insert in the text thought he might slip it inconspicuously into a footnote. An oasis in the desert.

There was another side to the coin. No man (as they used to say when such functionaries existed) can be a hero to his own valet. Barristers and judges have clerks. The relationship between them would merit a full-length study. The clerk may be anything from office boy and typist, friend and adviser, to landlord and, virtually, employer of the barristers in his charge. And when a barrister was elevated to the High Court Bench his clerk might go with him, often to the detriment of his own pocket. The books of Arthur Smith and A. E. Bowker, Sydney Aylett, and F. W. Ashley provided very welcome relief. These were men who saw the judges and barristers without their wigs. Their affection for their masters was clear, but it was far from being reverential.

When considering these men, eminent and, in some cases, truly formidable, there is another comforting reflection—lawyers, as Charles Lamb reminds us, were children once. And not only were they children. They all had to start somewhere.

'When I read the biography of a well-known man', says A. A. Milne, 'I find that it is the first half of it that holds my attention. I watch with fascinated surprise the baby, finger in mouth, grow into the politician, tongue in cheek.'

The moment of truth for lawyers comes when they first rise to their feet to address the court. 'First Time Up' is a moment which the most self-possessed of them never seem to forget. Geoffrey Dorling Roberts, a tough extrovert who, in his youth, played Rugby football for England, writes 'the importance of the occasion, the presence of my father, seated beside the Deputy Recorder, of my mother, sister and hosts of friends in the gallery, having come to "hear Geoffrey doing his first case" all conspired to bring on an attack of nerves which deprived me of the power of speech. I was completely tongue-tied, and could only produce animal noises making not a grain of sense.' His shame and mortification, as he says, could be better imagined than described, but he derived some comfort when he read in the autobiography of Sir

Patrick Hastings (another robust character who had survived two years as a trooper in the South African war) the description of *his* first appearance in court: 'my mouth was strangely dry. Even my opening words, which I had learned by heart had left me. I wanted to get out—to run away—but my legs refused to act.'

Procedure in the English court of law, unlike the continental, is based on the adversary system. The theory is that in the heat of the battle the truth will be forged. It is in such contests that the character of the lawyer appears, honest or devious, forthcoming or cold-hearted, likeable or detestable, and it is the record of such contests which seemed to me to be the legal anecdotes most worthy of preservation. A white-wigged Bowen standing up to Chief Baron Pollock: Mathew pulling the almost unpullable leg of the old ogre, Otto Danckwerts: Bottomley outfacing Lush and defeating Avory: Birkett putting down Muir: Abinger, nobly seconded by Frank Lockwood, standing up to Mr Justice Chitty for two punishing rounds after which, 'I did not sit down. My legs gave way and I fell down': or (a prevision of the future), young Charles Russell gradually overcoming the initial hostility of Mr Justice Crompton. It was entertaining, too, to note that when the same Charles Russell was at the plenitude of his power, overbearing judges, paralysing witnesses, and terrifying counsel and solicitors, the only person who defeated him in a personal encounter should have been a solicitor's articled clerk.

Another occasion on which the character of the lawyer, and of his victim, the witness, becomes, sometimes painfully, apparent is in the course of the bout of legal fisticuffs which is known as cross-examination. Some of the questions and answers have become enshrined in the mythology of the law. Carson asking Oscar Wilde 'Did you kiss him': Birkett, in the Burning Car Case, requesting the unhappy metallurgical expert to oblige them with the coefficient of expansion of brass: Inskip's deadly 'Can you explain to me *why* it was you closed the door?', which hanged the murderer Fox. But such small samples are inadequate to assay the whole seam.

Max Beerbohm expresses the true addiction: 'The greatest of all delights that a law court can give us is a witness who is quick witted, resourceful, thoroughly master of himself and his story, pitted against a counsel as well endowed as himself . . . I doubt whether I shall have a day of such acute mental enjoyment as the day of that cross-examination.'

Two points stand out. It was not an hour, not even a few hours. It was a day of cross-examination. It is only in works of fiction that counsel demolishes a witness with half a dozen well-chosen questions. The process, in its highest examples, can be as lengthy and as complex as a great musical composition, with its introductory passage, its *largo*, its *accelerando* and *marcato*, and its artfully devised climax.

There are exceptional cases—two or three examples will be found here—when the questioning is brief. The batsman is stumped in the first over. But the real thing, as Max points out, is a fight between equals. It is not hard to understand that such contests are rare. Counsel is the case-hardened professional, armed with his brief, and the course of the questioning is under his control. If there are surprises to be sprung, he will have the springing of them. The witness is the amateur, normally nervous, and on the defensive. He can only try to anticipate and counter each different attack as it develops.

I did, as it happens, have access to one example of a level contest. The book in which it occurs (*What I said about the Press* by Randolph Churchill) is not easy to get hold of since a number of booksellers refused to handle it. A pity, because it is a gem. Randolph, eminently 'quick-minded, resourceful and master of himself' is being cross-examined by Mr Gilbert Paull QC (the extract will be found under the name of the latter). It is no more than a tiny fraction of the whole, but it seemed to me to encapsulate the essence. One can hear the blades meeting and withdrawing. One can see the duellists shift their feet, withdraw for a new opening, or guard against an unexpected thrust. Max would have been entranced.

The arrangement of the extracts was cause for some thought. Normally, with poets and prose writers, it would have been chronological. Such an arrangement has the merit of allowing the reader to observe changes in style, and see how the Elizabethan school develops into the Classical, the Romantic into the Modern. There are, however, no schools of legal behaviour and utterance. The comments of Mr Justice Maule (who was born in 1788) on the unfortunate result of hearing too many sermons, on the use of four- and six-letter words, or on the defence of consent in cases of rape, seem totally contemporary in style and spirit.

An alternative might have been to collect into sections all the stories dealing with certain recurrent topics—obstinate juries, unsatisfactory witnesses, overbearing judges—but this carried corresponding disadvantages. A single dish may be palatable. No one wants a dinner of it.

A distracted judge once said to a barrister who was rambling in his discourse, 'Could we not have *some* arrangement of your facts, Mr X? Logical, chronological, or even alphabetical.' The advice was intended satirically, but it seemed to present a possible solution. An alphabetical arrangement would produce an agreeable *melange*: and have the additional advantage of enabling a reader to locate his favourite lawyer more easily.

In each case the extract has been headed by the subject of the episode. Where the subjects are on record in the *Dictionary of National Biography*, *Who's Who*, or similar standard works of reference in their country the dates of their birth and death (or birth only if still alive) appear against the name in question. Most of the remaining subjects can be traced through the Law List. This gives only the date on which a barrister is 'called' or a solicitor admitted. (It is an assumption only that their disappearance from the list coincides with their death.) In these cases, therefore, the years given are those in which they were active performers. One curious exception was the author of *Secrets of a Solicitor*, Edward Maltby; the extract here given certainly suggests that he was in active practice in 1880 but search of the Law List reveals no record of a solicitor of this name in the decade in question, or in the surrounding decades. Possibly the book was written under a pseudonym?

I have reserved to the last some thoughts on a difficult topic: is a Court of Law an appropriate place for levity?

For the parties most intimately concerned—the plaintiff and defendant in a civil case, the accused in a criminal case—it may be the most traumatic occasion in the whole of their lives. The conclusion of the judge or the verdict of the jury, even if it did not lead to death, could be the prelude to ruin or disgrace. This is a point of view which has recommended itself to many people, inside and outside the law.

Sir Gervais Rentoul writes: 'Courts of Law do not lend themselves to facetiousness. For the most part the matters dealt with are too serious. And, not unnaturally, there is nothing the parties to them resent more than that they should be treated with levity.'

George A. Macdonald, a solicitor and a rhymester, speaks bitterly of a judge:

> Laying Law down with impatient force
> Jesting, no matter how ill-timed or coarse

and Evelyn Waugh, writing to his friend Nancy Mitford about the witticisms of Mr Justice Stable, says: 'The jury were not at all amused by the judge. All the £300-a-day barristers rocked with laughter at his sallies. They glowered. This was not what they paid a judge for, they thought.'

Nor must it be supposed that this attitude is confined to the sardonic and serious minded. Theobald Mathew was a lawyer who delighted all who knew him. He was, said Patrick Hastings, 'a man with a mind that saw humour in everything', and his clerk, Sydney Aylett, described him as 'a sunny wit, with a unique and delightful sense of the ridiculous'. *But this was out of court.* 'In court', adds Aylett, 'he never attempted humour. Judicial joking and jesting was a habit he abhorred.'

Is the truth of the matter, then, that whilst anyone else may, in suitable circumstances, make a joke, the one person who must never do so is the judge? It is a not unreasonable interdiction. The judge is in a privileged position. He has an audience as pre-sold as the headmaster with schoolboys or the Colonel in the mess with a respectful group of junior officers; a privileged position which should not be abused by the purchase of cheap laughter.

'Quite small jokes go well in solemn surroundings', says Balfour-Brown, 'and that is why there is more laughter in court over a crippled witticism than would welcome it elsewhere.' It was failure to appreciate this that destroyed the reputation, otherwise a deservedly high one, of Mr Justice Darling.

Counsel are in a somewhat different position. If a joke will deflate a hostile witness or will advance the cause of their client by winning the smiles of the jury then they are fully entitled to make it. Even then, a seemly moderation should be the rule. Witnesses, who are the only other people who speak much in court, are not encouraged to joke. If they try, they will be sat on at once. 'Pray remember, sir, that this is no matter for levity. Serious issues are at stake.' They can score points, but very rarely. Few witnesses have the wit of Whistler.

Perhaps the most balanced judgment on this question was given by Judge Edward Parry in *The Seven Lamps of Advocacy* and the last word shall be with him.

> Nor can 'Laughter in Court' (a derogatory parenthesis unknown in the Official Law Reports) be wholly condemned. Laughter may be derisive, unkind, even cruel; or it may be used as a just weapon of ridicule wherewith to smite pretension and humbug. It may be gracious and full of kindliness, putting a timid man at ease, or instinct with good humour, softening wrath or mitigating tedious irrelevancy.

I have mentioned the help given me by Professor Barzun. I would also like to thank particularly Judge Edward Clarke, Judge Stephen Tumim, and Mr F. P. Richardson FLA, the very co-operative librarian of the Law Society, who have helped me with books and suggestions; Jonathan Goodman for his *Old Scottish Judges*; and last, but not least, Wilfrid Picton-Turbervill who introduced me to the delights of the Old Munster Circuit.

MICHAEL GILBERT

A NOTE ON NOMENCLATURE AND FUNCTIONS

MOST of the people quoted and described here started as barristers. Their names head the relevant extract without further description other than the addition, where appropriate, of King's Counsel (KC) or Queen's Counsel (QC). There was also an old-fashioned dignity, long abolished, of Serjeant-at-Law, at one time the highest rank at the English Bar. Serjeant Sullivan, who features here, was the last to hold this title.

It is when a barrister acquires judicial or administrative rank that further distinctions have to be made. He can take one of several routes upwards. He may become a 'Stipendiary Magistrate', in charge of what are commonly, but incorrectly, called Police Courts. He may preside in the Crown Court (successor of the old Quarter Sessions), in which case he takes the title 'Judge'. Finally he may be elevated to the High Court in which, by tradition, he is referred to as 'Mr Justice So and So'. But since he also becomes a knight it has seemed appropriate to refer to him as such. He may go even higher and become a Law Lord, in which case he will be referred to by the title of his peerage.

Specific and higher posts are set out in full when they occur: e.g. the Lord Chief Justice, the Master of the Rolls, the Attorney-General, or the Solicitor-General (who, a further source of confusion, is in fact a barrister).

Non-barristers (except for a few who are too well known to need introduction) are briefly described as, for example, Solicitor, Probation Officer, Barrister's Clerk, or laymen of all sorts who have taken part in or have commented on the rituals of justice, not forgetting the occasional involuntary spectator in the dock.

There are some particular points on function which might puzzle readers who are not familiar with the British system. The first is the difference between solicitors and barristers. Shortly, the solicitor is the man of business to whom a client first comes. He can deal with most difficulties himself, but if his client is destined to end in front of the High Court, a barrister will have to be briefed, since he alone has the right of audience in this and in higher tribunals.

The Introduction mentions that procedure in the English Courts is based on the adversary system. It is gladiatorial. The barrister on one side (or, in a lower court, the solicitor) fights for his client against the equally professional champion on the other side. The judge acts as referee. This is in contrast to most European systems in which it is the judge who has the conduct of the matter. He questions the witnesses, examines the prisoner, listens to any legal submissions that counsel may wish to make, and arrives at a conclusion. A curious offshoot of the British system is that barristers are free to appear on either side. They are not (as, for example, in Italy) trained to operate throughout their careers as prosecutor or defender. This freedom extends even to those who have taken office. There are a number of earlier occasions when an Attorney-General, put out of office by a change of government, is found defending prisoners whom when in office it was his duty to prosecute.

I add, by courtesy of Professor Jacques Barzun:

The American system has a simpler and shorter nomenclature. Any lawyer qualified by the Bar of his state may perform any of the duties that the English system divides between barristers and solicitors. The term 'attorney-at-law' is only a formal synonym for 'lawyer'. The federal government and the several states have an Attorney-General, who supervises the work of a staff for bringing or defending suits. He himself does not prosecute.

The judicial system consists of Federal Courts, State Courts and County or City Courts, independent from one another in appointive (or elective) procedure, but appeal from one level to the next is possible, the highest court of review being the (Federal) Supreme Court. Its nine members are known as 'Justices', one being the 'Chief Justice'. The same titles are used in states that call their highest court of appeals 'Supreme Court.' In other courts, at each level, the presiding officer is known simply as 'Judge'. In the lower courts the prosecutor is (usually) the District Attorney.

EDWARD ABINGER (*fl.* 1887–1927)

I

SWINFEN EADY, afterwards Lord Swinfen, the Master of the Rolls, then a junior, appeared on a Motion for a Writ of Attachment for Contempt of Court [a writ which, if sustained, would lead to arrest] committed by a lady, a Mrs Large, for parting with some property, as she alleged, to a man named Sheppard contrary to his lordship's order. I appeared for the lady.

Sitting in front of me was Frank Lockwood, QC, afterwards Sir Frank Lockwood, Solicitor-General, and other well-known Queen's Counsel.

There was really no defence to the Motion other than that I was armed with an affidavit of a medical man stating that my client suffered from aneurism of the heart and that if arrested the shock might kill her.

I read my affidavit to the Judge (Mr Justice Chitty). Swinfen Eady argued that this was a mere friendly affidavit to avoid the lady being committed to prison for breach of the injunction granted by his lordship on a previous motion.

I protested, and pointed out to the Judge that a person could not be sentenced to death for a mere contempt of court, which might result if the lady were arrested.

Chitty: 'Are you trying to teach me the Criminal Law?'
Myself: 'No, my lord, I am only trying to induce your lordship not to allow this Writ of Attachment to go.'
Chitty: 'Well, now you can sit down!'

Lockwood, sitting in front of me, whispered: 'Don't you sit down. Read your affidavit again.'

'My lord,' I said, 'I am afraid your lordship has not fully appreciated the full weight of my affidavit, and I will read it to you again.'

Once more I read the whole affidavit through, putting great emphasis on the words 'the shock might kill her'.

Chitty: 'Have you done?'
Myself: 'Yes, my lord.'
Chitty: 'Well, then, the Writ will go.'
Lockwood (whispering): 'Stick to the judge. Read your affidavit again.'

Then I got up and said: 'My lord, I have a solemn duty to perform to my client, and I am afraid I cannot have performed it properly, or your lordship would never have ordered the Writ to go. I must read the affidavit again.'

Chitty: 'If you don't sit down, Mr Abinger, I will commit you to Holloway.'*

Lockwood (sotto voce): 'Don't be frightened, he won't send you to prison. Stick to him.'

So I stood erect.

Chitty: If you don't sit down, Mr Abinger, I will send for a tipstaff.'

I still remained standing.

'Usher!' roared the Judge, 'send for a tipstaff.'

A tipstaff arrived, I still standing.

'Come up here', said the Judge to the tipstaff, pointing to the witness box.

'Now,' said Chitty to me, in a terrible voice, 'if you won't sit down I will give you into custody of the tipstaff.'

Lockwood (very, very quietly): 'He won't commit you.'

I did not sit down—my knees gave way and I fell down.

'You may go', said the Judge to the tipstaff.

Chitty (taking a deep breath): 'Usher, bring me a Law List.'

He then, no doubt, discovered that I had not yet been called two years.

'Mr Abinger,' he remarked pleasantly enough, 'I see you have only recently been called to the Bar, and I am going to give you a piece of advice. If you want to win your case do not put the Judge's back up. I have no doubt you thought you were doing your duty, but you should have obeyed my order.'

Then, turning to Swinfen Eady, the learned judge remarked: 'Mr Eady, upon the whole I will adjourn this Motion until the next Motion day. In the meanwhile you had better have the lady examined by a competent doctor and let me have his views on the present affidavit.'

The following week the Motion came on again, and Eady frankly said: 'On the face of my medical evidence which I have now before me, I think it would be injurious to this lady's health if she were arrested.' And no order was made upon the Motion.

* This is not an example of judicial ignorance (cf. Inskip on Roulette). Holloway prison, at that period, housed both male *and* female prisoners (not, as now, female only).

This great judge, instead of taking umbrage at my impudence afterwards treated me with the greatest kindness and consideration, until he died.

SIR EDWARD ACTON (1865–1945)

2

I REMEMBER hearing a case in which a solicitor had done some work for a client to the latter's entire satisfaction, but when the solicitor sent in his account the client found it inconvenient to pay and the solicitor sued him in the County Court.

The client's defence was that the bill was not a sufficient compliance with the Solicitors Act 1843. The County Court judge did not take kindly to this defence and gave judgment for the solicitor. The client appealed to the High Court. There was nothing to be said in his favour except that, unfortunately, he was right and the solicitor was wrong.

In those days County Court appeals were heard by a Divisional Court consisting of two judges of the Kings Bench Division. This one was heard by Mr Justice Acton, who, though one of the kindest hearted of men was not a specially acute lawyer, and the present Lord Chief Justice (Goddard) who had then only been recently appointed to the Bench and was, of course, junior to Acton. From the synopsis I have given it will be seen that the case was of the dreariest description imaginable. However, it was unexpectedly enlivened by Acton.

The Counsel engaged I shall call Brown and Green. Green was addressing the court when Acton interrupted, and the following dialogue ensued.

Acton: I quite understand, Mr Green. You are relying on Section 37 of the Act of 1843, and Mr Brown is saying that the case is covered by Paragraph 2(c) of the Remuneration Order of 1882.

Green: I must apologise to your Lordship; I am afraid I have expressed myself very badly. It is my contention that paragraph 2(c) of the Order applies in this case, and it is my learned friend who is seeking to invoke section 37.

Acton: But I thought . . .

Goddard: No, no. You've got it the wrong way round.

(Followed a whispered conference. I suppose Acton was a bit deaf, anyway, most of the whispers penetrated to the corners of the court.)

Acton: But surely Green's relying on the Act, and . . .
Goddard: No. It's Brown who's relying on the Act and Green's relying on the Order.
Acton: Then why did Green say he was relying on the Act?
Goddard: He didn't. He said Brown was.
Acton: But when Brown opened he said *he* was relying on the Order.
Goddard: No. He said the County Court judge must have relied on the Order, but he ought to have held himself bound by the Act.
Acton: But I thought Green said he *was* bound by the Act.

(Next few exchanges not audible, but they ended with:)

Acton: Ah! So it's Green who's relying on the Order and Brown who's relying on the Act.
Goddard: That's right. You've got it.
Acton: Well. I'm with Brown anyway.

RICHARD ADAMS (1846–1908)

Judge

3

OF all the County Courts, that presided over by Richard Adams, who became Judge of the County of Limerick, was the most remarkable. What might happen in it at any moment was beyond the wit of man to forecast. At times the proceedings were those of a wise and shrewd tribunal. At times they were a pantomime in which the rules even of decency were not strictly observed. The judge had all the genius and the defects of Swift. In the midst of sober and erudite phrases there would flame forth wild outbursts of scathing wit clothed in fantastic and morbid garb.

A typical case in his Court arose out of the rabies scare at the end of the last century. An order was issued to destroy all cattle suffering *or suspected of suffering* from this complaint. If the animal was afflicted beyond doubt, no compensation was payable. But if it was slaughtered on suspicion the owner had to be paid for the value of the beast. Now a number of experts had given testimony that the only way to establish beyond doubt that a cow had rabies was by microscopic examination of the spinal cord. Since this could not be done while the beast was alive she was necessarily slaughtered *on suspicion*.

This imposed a severe financial burden on the local authorities who found themselves condemned to pay for cattle that turned out, in fact, to be rabid. At last one council determined to challenge the theory of the experts and produced in the witness box an ancient 'cow doctor', whose testimony was to shatter veterinary science.

He was not quite sober, but that was rarely noticed in that court.

'The cow she had rabies and before she died I proved it.'

'How did you prove it?'

'By d'infallible test.'

'Did you examine the spinal cord while she was still alive?'

'I did not, but I brought a dog into the stable where she was in her stall and this cow barked. Dat's d'infallible test.'

'Was that the only test?'

'No. In this case there was another infallible test.'

'What was that?'

'Dare was the sudden death of the cow.'

'Describe what happened. Did she die very suddenly?'

'Most suddenly. I shot her.'

Adams burst into a fit of rage. He shouted abuse at the foolish witness, threatened to send him to gaol for daring to come into court in a state of intoxication, and for five minutes there was a most painful scene that reduced the poor cow doctor to a state of actual collapse. Adams at once pulled himself up for, with the exception of his ungovernable tongue, he was all kindness. He resumed his seat, pronounced the usual decree, and had the victim brought to his room for attention and amends.

JAMES EVERSHED AGATE (1877–1947)

4

DINED last night with an old Manchester friend. He vouches for the authenticity of this letter from a native of Lagos to the owners of the vessel which he was helping to load:

Sir,

My statement to you about my speech to my lawyer when he came to demand as per legal orders the sum of £50 for my poor damaged body by falling in Company's lighter while doing my honest due on account of which I might have gone to heaven that day. Praise the Lord I did not go. But, Sir, when you said to my legal adviser:

1st that I was drunken

2nd that cause of drunkenness was stealing gin from lighter

Well, Sir, those two speeches, 1st and 2nd, proved that you are a son of the father of lies i.e. Devil because said gin had been freely drunk at 8.00 a.m. prompt. I fell headlong into lighter at 11.00 a.m. prompt. At 11.00 a.m. gin had passed through body, so cause of top-heaviness had finished. Therefore you are the very first-born of the father of lies, to wit the Devil. Because 2nd charge of stealing gin is libel. Beware Sir do not take away my poor character beside thousand pounds are often lost legal by libel, as legals cost plenty money. Now Sir, for God's sake try and sign for £50 for damage to poor frame of mortality as follows:

Fell down in lighter on tons of metal
One head splitten
One nose useless (very grave)
One shoulder broken (blood extracted)
One arm bent (blood ditto)
One thick leg dashed (ditto ditto)
One private member damaged (slightly bent)
One half leg broken (blood freely)
General conditions (breakings—dashings—all blood freely etc)

Now Sir this hurts are cheap at £50. . . . I will come for book re £50 to morning meantime may God watch and protect over your slumbers tonight so as to keep you safe till morning and I get my £50.

Yesufu Illorin

5

THE *Daily Express* asked me to do an impression of the Rattenbury trial at the Old Bailey. The facts were very simple and hardly disputed. Mrs Rattenbury, aged 38, wife of an architect aged 67, had been the mistress of her eighteen year old chauffeur named Stoner. Somebody had hit the husband over the the head with a mallet.

It was all very like the three major French novelists. The way in which the woman debauched the boy so that he slept with her every night with her six year old son in the room and the husband, who had his own bedroom, remaining cynically indifferent—all this was pure Balzac. In the box Mrs Rattenbury looked and talked exactly as I have always imagined Emma Bovary looked and talked. Pure Flaubert. And last there was that part of the evidence in which she described how, trying to bring her husband round, she first accidentally trod on his false teeth, and then tried to put them back into his mouth so that he could speak to her. This was pure Zola.

The sordidness of the whole thing was relieved by one thing and one only. This was when Counsel asked Mrs Rattenbury what her first thought had been when her lover got into bed that night and told her what he had done. She replied, 'My first thought was to protect him.' This is the sort of thing Balzac would have called sublime; and it is odd that, so far as I saw, not a single newspaper reported it.

SIR EDWARD HALL ALDERSON (1781–1857)

Baron of the Exchequer

6

IN the Assize Court at Chelmsford a barrister was retained to defend a man for stealing a sheep. The principal evidence against the man was that the bones of the deceased animal were found in his garden.

Counsel for the defence, instead of insisting that there was no evidence, since no one could swear to the sheep bones, endeavoured to explain away the cause of death and thus, by a foolish concession, admitted their actual identity. He suggested that sheep often put their heads through gaps or breakages in the hurdles and rubbed their necks against the projecting points of the broken bars; and that being so why should the jury not come to a verdict in favour of the prisoner on that ground? It was quite possible that the constant rubbing would ultimately cut the sheep's throat.

'Yes,' said Baron Alderson, 'that is a very plausible suggestion to start with, but having commenced your line of defence on that ground, you must continue it, and carry it to the finish. And to do this you must show that not only did this sheep commit suicide, but that it skinned itself and then buried its body, or what was left of it, after giving a portion to the prisoner to eat, in the prisoner's garden, and covered itself up in its own grave. I don't say the jury may not believe you; we shall see. Gentlemen, what do you say. Is the sheep or the prisoner guilty?'

The sheep was instantly acquitted.

GILCHRIST GIBB ALEXANDER (1871–1958)

7

UNDERNEATH us (in No. 2 Plowden Buildings) lived an Irish barrister called Counsel, reported to be a cousin of the famous Carson. This gentleman, we were given to understand, bore in Ireland the sobriquet of 'Judge and Jury Counsel'. He was afflicted with a tremendous squint which—so the knowing said—enabled him simultaneously to keep one eye on the judge and one on the jury.

Counsel was once concerned in a most amazing breach of promise case. He appeared for the plaintiff, and having opened with an impassioned appeal to the jury to award heavy damages to his client for the dastardly wrong which had been done to her, he called the plaintiff.

While Counsel, with the aid of the natural advantages already spoken of, was examining the lady, he was amazed to observe that his opponent appeared to be treating the case with levity.

'This is no laughing matter', he observed: but his opponent, who took no notice laughed in his face.

Presently Counsel finished his examination and his opponent rose to cross-examine.

His first question startled everyone in Court.

'Are you married?' he asked the plaintiff.

'Yes.'

'To whom?' was his next question.

'To the defendant' she answered. He sat down and smiled.

'Whaat the divil is the meaning of this? spluttered Counsel to his Solicitor.

Consternation and alarm prevailed. Judge, jury and spectators looked on while Counsel and his clients engaged in loud and heated recriminations.

The explanation was simple.

The whole proceedings had been initiated and carried on by the plaintiff's mother. The girl herself had taken little interest in them. She and the defendant had evidently made it up and had married, but they had not informed her mother, or anybody connected with her.

JAMES BARR AMES (1846–1910)

American Jurist

8

FELIX FRANKFURTER says 'If ever there was a scholar and a gentleman it was James Barr Ames. He was a wonderful teacher, an original mind, and he illustrated, to a degree unexcelled by anyone I knew, the conception by Socrates of a teacher, that of a midwife. Ames was the midwife of minds.

He was never too tired to give a student all the time he wanted. In those days the professors didn't have offices. They had a desk in the stacks. You would go in there and talk with them. You would sort of walk off on clouds as a result of a talk with Ames. Or in the classroom he would try to find the kernel of truth in a heap of sand of nonsense, error and foolishness. Classes are conducted in the Socratic method, at least the best of them are, at the Harvard Law School. Anyone would chip in. If the question wasn't very clear, Ames had a way of holding his elbow on the desk and resting his chin in the palm of his hand, and he would then think a little bit. Then he would say, 'If I understand what you mean, you're asking whether so-and-so.'

The fellows would always say, 'Yes, that's what I mean.'

Ames would always make beautiful and penetrating sense out of a jumble of words. It was a standing procedure. There was a fellow in my class, a man named Williamson from Iowa, a great big husky, a kitchen knife mind. One day he got off some stuff. We thought it was stuff. Dean Ames thought hard over that one. He said, 'Mr Williamson, I suppose what you have in mind is a case of an equitable easement.'

That's a very abstruse conception in law. Williamson said, 'That isn't what I meant, but I'm ready to adopt it.'

Well, the whole class just roared with joy that at least here was one man who was honest and recognised what Jimmy Ames was doing.

ANONYMOUS

9

The Will of a well-known Wall Street broker.

To my wife, I leave my lover, and the knowledge that I wasn't the fool she thought I was. To my son, I leave the pleasure of earning a living. For thirty-five years he thought the pleasure was mine. He was mistaken.

To my daughter I leave $100,000. She will need it. The only good piece of business her husband ever did was to marry her.

To my valet I leave the clothes he has been stealing from me for the past ten years. Also the fur coat that he wore last winter at Palm Beach.

To my chauffeur I leave my cars. He almost ruined them and I want him to have the satisfaction of finishing the job.

And lastly, to my partner, I leave the suggestion that he take some other man in with him if he expects to do any business.

10

A RAILROAD company was being sued for personal injury. The experts for the plaintiff contended that, as a result of the injury, the plaintiff was a confirmed and hopeless victim of neurasthenia, or nervous prostration, and their evidence tended to show that one so afflicted had deteriorated mentally and would rapidly decline. A pitiful picture was painted.

On cross-examination the attorney for the railroad developed from the expert doctor that the main ground for his opinion that the plaintiff was suffering from neurasthenia was the fact that he appeared to suffer no pain when pricked with a pin on top of the head.

The Lawyer for the defendant was an ex-judge, somewhat advanced in years and exceedingly resourceful. Incidentally he was as bereft of hair as the oft-cited billiard ball. When it came time to argue the case to the jury he proceeded to expound the facts with clearness and vigor for a considerable length of time, and finally approached the subject of neurasthenia.

After paying his respects to the learned experts he took up the subject of the final test in the examination the experts had made of the plaintiff. He assured the jury of his great personal regret, and in fact his surprise and astonishment, at the discovery, which the examination of these learned men had disclosed, namely that one who did not experience pain by the prick of a pin on the top of the head was a neurasthenic and rapidly progressing to complete mental decline. He assured the jury that he was a man of reasonable physical vigor, and had always supposed that he was still possessed of his normal mental faculties, but to his great distress he now discovered that he himself was a hopeless neurasthenic and would demonstrate to the jury that he had no business trying lawsuits, but should be preparing rapidly to meet his Maker.

Thereupon he turned back the lapel of his coat and extracted a good sized needle which he promptly stuck in the top of his head. He kept this up until he had some ten or twelve needles sticking in the top of his bald head and looked like an animated pin cushion. He finished his argument and a verdict was returned in favour of the defendant.

In later years he confided to the judge that the last needle got outside the area of the cocaine which his physician had hypodermically injected into his scalp just before he began his argument and had almost unmasked the hoax. As Judge Faville said to me 'If I could picture to you the scene of this venerable old war horse prancing up and down before the jury, with his bald head full of needles, and haranging them at the top of his voice. I should be very happy indeed.'

II

COUNTRY juries are wonderful, and they know more about their neighbours than judges, barristers and policemen give them credit for.

The classic story of a jury was at Dubbo [in New South Wales] where a man was on trial for stealing some heifers. When the jury returned with their verdict the Associate said, 'Do you find the accused guilty or not guilty of cattle stealing?' To which the foreman replied 'Not guilty, if he returns the cows.'

The judge read the jury the riot act and concluded by saying 'Go out and reconsider your verdict. You swore that you would try the issue between our Sovereign Lady, the Queen, and find a true verdict according to the evidence.'

The jury retired again, and when they returned they had a belligerent air about them. The Associate said, 'Have you decided on your verdict?' The foreman said 'Yes, we have. We find the accused not guilty—and he doesn't have to return the cows.'

12

WE assume that today it is comparatively easy to publish a blasphemous or seditious, but not an indecent book. But what is an indecent book? The definition given by the Irish Free State a year ago is 'any book which has a tendency to excite sensual passion'. Now this corresponds with an interesting custom which was alleged to prevail in the nineteenth century. A Scotland Yard detective was sent into Holywell Street and that neighbourhood to inspect books and to read them *after supper*: and if, on reading a book, he experienced anything in the nature of an unbecoming sensation *after that supper*, the book was prosecuted. Nobody worried what he had for supper.

Of course one must always remember (and I have some sympathy with Scotland Yard) the impulse to prosecute a book because it contains a repulsive passage. We all like to preserve our illusions. When I was connected in 1911 with a paper called *The Free Woman* I was always expecting prosecution, because some of the contributions (including my own) elicited letters fom many abusive readers; but nothing really stimulated Scotland Yard until somebody wrote a silly poem about having taken a woman of the town back to her home, and it was stated that she had dirty feet. The Scotland Yard inspector who came to see me on the subject said that he quite approved of various articles which had been written on the prevention of venereal disease and other kindred subjects, but finally remarked: 'In the Yard we don't like pomes about 'ores with dirty feet.' I said that I sympathised, and that if we destroyed these last illusions of the populace we might have a revolution.

13

Justice in the West.

'MR GREEN,' began the Judge addressing the prisoner, 'the jury in their verdict say you are guilty of murder, and the law says you are to be hung. Now I want you and all your friends down on Indian Creek to know that it is not I who condemn you, but the jury and the law. Mr

Green, the law allows you time for preparation, so the Court wants to know what time you would like to be hung.'

The prisoner 'allowed' it made no difference to him, but his Honor did not appreciate this freedom of action.

'Mr Green, you must know it is a very serious matter to be hung', he protested uneasily. 'You'd better take all the time you can get. The Court will give you until this day four weeks', he added tentatively.

The prisoner made no response, but Mr James Turney, the prosecutor, apparently thinking the scene lacked impressiveness, rose and addressed the bench.

'May it please the court,' he began, 'on solemn occasions like the present it is usual for the Court to pronounce formal sentence, in which the leading features of the crime shall be brought to the recollection of the prisoner, and a sense of guilt impressed upon his conscience, and in which he shall be duly exhorted to repentance and warned against the judgement in a world to come.'

'Oh, Mr Turney,' the judge interrupted testily, 'Mr Green understands the whole matter as well as if I had preached to him a month. He knows he's got to be hung this day four weeks. You understand it that way, Mr Green, don't you?' he added, appealing to the prisoner.

Mr Green nodded, and the court adjourned.

W. ST JULIAN ARABIN (*fl.* 1830–40)

Serjeant-at-Law

14

SERJEANT ARABIN had come down from the dining-room with the alderman on the rota, and they took their seats upon the Bench, the countenances of both bearing testimony that their afternoon's carouse had not been a light one. The prisoner first upon the list was in the dock, and the prosecutor was in the witness-box, so that all was ready for the trial. There was no counsel in the case, and, that being so, the judge always examined the witnesses from the written depositions which were taken by the magistrate and returned to the court by him. Now Arabin was very short-sighted, and also very deaf. On this occasion he unluckily took up a set of depositions which had no reference to the prisoner at the Bar; the charge against him being that of stealing a pocket-handkerchief, while the judge's attention was fixed upon a charge of stealing a watch. Holding the abortive writing close to the light, and peering at it through his spectacles, he began his examination.

Judge: 'Well, witness, your name is John Tomkins.'

Witness: 'My lord, my name is Job Taylor.'

Judge: 'Ah! I see you are a sailor, and you live in the New Cut.'

Witness: 'No, my lord, I live at Wapping.'

Judge: 'Never mind your being out shopping. Had you your watch in your pocket on the 10th of November?'

Witness: 'I never had but one ticker, my lord, and that has been at the pawn-shop for the last six months.'

Judge: 'Who asked you how long you had had the watch? Why can't you say yes or no! Well, did you see the prisoner at the Bar?'

'Yes, of course I did,' said the witness, in a loud tone of voice, for he began to be a little confused by the questions put to him.

Judge: 'That's right, my man, speak up and answer shortly. Did the prisoner take your watch?'

Witness (in a still louder tone): 'I don't know what you're driving at; how could he get it without the ticket, and that I had left with the missus?'

Arabin, who heard distinctly the whole of the last answer, threw himself back in his chair, adjusted his glasses, and glared at the witness-box with a look of disgust. At last he threw down the depositions to an elderly counsel, who was seated at the barrister's table, and said, 'Mr Ryland, I wish you would take this witness in hand and see whether you can make anything of him, for I can't.'

Now Ryland had been dining at the three o'clock dinner too, and he was never behind-hand in doing honour to the civic hospitality. He stood up, stared ferociously (for he had a countenance that could do it to perfection) at the unlucky witness, and, turning round and looking up at the Bench, observed, 'My Lord, it is my profound belief that this man is drunk.'

'It's a remarkable coincidence, Mr Ryland,' said the judge, 'that is precisely the idea that has been in my mind for the last ten minutes. It is disgraceful that witnesses should come into a sacred court of justice like this, in such a state of intoxication.' Then, leaning over his desk to the deputy-clerk of arraigns, who was seated below him, he said, 'Mr

Mosely, don't allow this witness one farthing of expenses. I'll put a stop to this scandal if I can.'

ARMSTRONG (*fl.* 1875)

Serjeant-at-Law

15

Serjeant Armstrong (cross-examining a so-called handwriting expert): 'And what about the dog?'

Witness: 'I do not understand.'

Armstrong (slowly and deliberately): 'What–about–the–dog?'

Witness: 'My Lord, I do not understand what the Serjeant means.'

The Judge: 'Neither do I.'

Armstrong (taking not the least notice of either witness or Judge, but repeating the question yet more slowly and deliberately): 'What—about—the—dog?'

Witness (losing all patience and bursting out angrily): 'WHAT DOG?'

The Serjeant: 'The dog that Chief Baron Pigott said he would not hang on your evidence.'

SIR HORACE EDMUND AVORY (1851–1935)

16

R. v. Austin Smith.

JOHN DERHAM was shot in a struggle with Alfonso Austin Smith whose wife Derham had endeavoured to steal. The defence was that Smith was trying to commit suicide.

During his cross-examination another most moving incident occurred. The prisoner was wearing a little sprig of white heather in his button-hole, but the real significance of this only became apparent when a letter was put to him in which he had written to his wife—'For the children's sake send him away. Chappie won't want to have fingers pointed at him as the son of the murderer of an unfaithful wife and her lover, and a suicide. Come back to me, my girl, my little white heather.'

Marshall Hall's speech was superb and he concluded with this passionate appeal. 'He begged his wife not to withdraw the life-belt, which she had thrown him as he was struggling in the water. That life-belt has been withdrawn once, members of the jury. It is for you to say whether you will throw him that life-belt once more, give him the chance of grasping it and being pulled ashore to resume his old happy life with the woman he loves, which has been so long denied him.'

In strong contrast to this emotional and deeply moving speech was the cold and analytical summing-up of Mr Justice Avory. The learned judge made some scathing references to the 'unwritten law'. He said, 'The law you have to administer in this case is the law of this country and not of any other, and, above all, not that which is erroneously called the "unwritten law"). That is merely a name for no law at all. It is the name given to the proposition that every man and woman is a law unto himself or herself, and that reverts us to a state of barbarism. I have told you the law of this country, as it must be applied. If you apply any other law or notions of your own you are violating the oaths you have taken.'

The jury were away from the court for more than two hours deliberating their verdict and when they returned the tensity of the atmosphere in court was almost unbearable. They found Alfonso Smith 'not guilty' of either murder or manslaughter. Everyone waited for the judge to discharge the prisoner. Instead of doing so Mr Justice Avory said sternly, 'There is another charge on the calendar against the prisoner.' This was a charge of possessing firearms and ammunition with intent to endanger life. The judge held that this applied, as prisoner had admitted that he intended to take his own life. The prisoner pleaded guilty to this charge and the judge passed sentence of twelve months' imprisonment with hard labour, an unusually severe sentence.

17

The narrator is 'Khaki' Roberts

THE last scene was enacted in the Court of Criminal Appeal on July 11th, 1927. I argued the point of law with regard to the exact crime in question, and punishment, for some hours. Travers Humphreys then replied for the Crown, and Avory J. proceeded to give the judgment of the Court dismissing the appeal. I hope I may be forgiven for repeating a compliment which fell from the learned judge when he referred to 'the argument which Mr Roberts has presented with admirable lucidity and succinctness . . . '. Avory J., thin and precise, with a reputation of being a 'hanging judge', did not throw bouquets about!

Remorselessly his cold, clear judgment continued. The court became dark. The five appellants gripped the rails of the dock, their faces deathly white, as they listened to the voice of doom.

A flash of lightening illumined the court. Then crash! a monstrous clap of thunder. Avory's voice stopped. Once more he began, only to be interrupted by further celestial roars.

The judge looked angrily aloft. Travers whispered to me: 'If this goes on, Avory will commit God for contempt of court!'

SYDNEY AYLETT (1901–)

Barrister's Clerk

18

I HAD a junior clerk called Catt, a likeable enough chap, but with an over-developed sense of fun. He took nothing seriously. He had a collection of 'joke-props', imitation mice and spiders, that frightened the daylights out of Mrs Hayden, our launderess; tin blots of ink, which found their way into every room, and a variety of things which made rude noises when sat upon. He wouldn't have lasted in Chambers in ordinary times, but I tolerated him because of the (wartime) shortage of manpower. His cheekiness made him an unpopular figure at the Royal Courts of Justice, and particularly in the barristers' robing room. One day he came back from the Courts with a swollen eye. When I questioned him it appeared that he had exasperated one of the counsel to such an extent that he'd taken a swipe at him. Today I suppose someone in Catt's position would bring an action for assault. He took it philosophically. He felt he could afford to since he was a law unto himself. 'Don't you worry, Mr Sydney,' he said, 'I'll get even with him, and with the others who took against me.' He did. During one lunch break he went into the robing room and mixed up all the barristers' wigs and gowns. When they returned, with only enough time to get dressed and into Court, they were in absolute confusion. It must have been a glorious sight. All the cases were delayed and there were red faces a plenty as counsel were berated by judges and unable to give acceptable reasons for their lateness.

Catt would have to go. I was able to be lenient; he had received his calling-up papers and was leaving in a month's time. I felt that by passing him over to the tender mercies of a sergeant-major I would be doing both him and myself a favour.

19

MANY judges took time to come to terms with the new attitude towards the Divorce Law. It had become accepted among Lawyers that there was collusion in many cases, and that the Law was being used as a convenience. Some more enlightened and practical judges realised this, and played along with it, but others still continued rigidly to stick to the conventions. It thus became a matter of great importance which particular judge's list a matter was to be heard in and there were either cheers or groans from the clerks when the lists were examined. The King's Proctor remained a feared figure, for if he found, or had evidence of, inchastity between the granting of a decree *nisi* and a decree absolute, the divorce could become null and void. We had occasion to warn one of our clients who was cohabiting with the lady who was to become his wife after his marriage had been dissolved, that he would have to cease living with her during this period. 'Good heavens, what on earth am I going to do?' 'I suggest you buy a goat' said our barrister. 'If that's your advice, then I will' replied the client. The day the decree *nisi* was made absolute I was instructed to send the following telegram 'You can now kill the goat'.

JOHN HUTTON BALFOUR-BROWNE (1845–1921)

King's Counsel

20

AT Sessions besides getting what was called 'soup', because the prosecution briefs at Leeds were 'ladled' out all round, I had some important 'dockers'. Dockers are, or were—for I am speaking of a time long ago—instructions from a criminal in the dock without the intervention of a solicitor. I confess it went against the grain to take the one pound three shillings and sixpence—sometimes in quite miscellaneous coins—from the accused person over the dock rails. It might be wrapped up in some dirty piece of paper. But I had several of these and did my best for the poor accused persons, who might, I daresay, have said, like the convict who when asked whether he had anything to say why sentence should not be passed remarked: he hoped the Court would take into consideration the extreme youth of his counsel.

21

TALKING of witnesses, I may say it is not often the good fortune of Parliamentary counsel to have lady witnesses to examine or cross-examine. Once, however, I was exceedingly fortunate. A great Water Company promoted a Bill to enable it to purchase land and construct works for the further supply of the important town it served. Amongst the lands to be purchased for the purpose of constructing a large reservoir it was proposed to purchase a shooting-box and about sixty acres, which were situated near the pure source of a north-country river. It was the property of a gentleman who, besides the shooting-box and the sixty acres, was the owner of two large hill-farms close to the lodge which extended to about 5,000 acres. He was also possessed of a wife who was so attractive as to make a most excellent witness. I had the honour to appear for the owner, but I claim none of the credit for the result.

The Water Company made out a case for their Bill. They required more water; the upper waters of the river which they proposed to appropriate were excellent in quality, for they came from the 'hills of sheep', and there was an excellent site for a reservoir near the lodge. It was not likely that a single landowner, however good looking his wife might be, would succeed in throwing out the Bill. Still, we did our best. We put the lady into the witness chair. The Bill trembled! But she did even better than her looks. She said she had a great affection for the shooting-lodge. It was there she had spent her honeymoon. The place was dearer to them than their big house at S—. She had planted most of the shrubs which led a struggling existence against the high winds which came blustering down from the hills.

The Bill was before a Committee of the House of Lords, and their lordships were certainly sympathetic and very much impressed by such compelling evidence. When it was counsel's turn to speak on his case, with his client's consent, of course, nay, with her eager approval, he admitted that a case had been made for the Bill—candour is often useful—but he appealed to their lordships to protect his clients. He told them that under the general law, when a company took part of a house or a manufactory they were compelled, if the owner wished it, to take the whole, and he asked them not to allow this Company to come and pluck out the eye of the estate and leave the bleak farms on his clients' hands, but on the analogy of the section he had mentioned to make them take the whole. As I say, I claim no credit for the result. The battle was won by the witness, and the Lords passed the Bill with a clause in it compelling the Company to take the whole 5,000 acres—which, of course, they did not want.

The question as to what the Company was to pay for the estate went before a well-known arbitrator—who was still young—and you may be certain that counsel for the claimant led off with his best trump card, and called the lady! Again the result of the arbitration was eminently satisfactory, and that shows what can be done by a really good witness.

22

I REMEMBER in the inquiry into the Regent's Canal Railway Bill I was 'put up' to be impertinent by Mr James Staats Forbes, who had a 'spice of the devil' in him. Sir Frederick Bramwell ('Hogshead' Bramwell) was the witness and, as I have said before, he was a most admirable witness. But although he was excellent as a witness he had done very little as a constructive engineer. Afterwards, no doubt, he and his partner, Mr Harris, were engineers for some important Power Bills, and for one sewage scheme, at least; but Bramwell's real forte was evidence. He was very often an Umpire in arbitrations, especially in arbitrations under Section 43 of the Tramways Act. Upon the occasion in question Mr Forbes suggested that I should ask him what works he had designed or constructed, and being young I acted upon his somewhat cruel suggestion.

'We all know', I said, 'your eminence as a witness, but would you tell me what you have done as an engineer? What works have you designed or constructed?'

'Not very much', he answered.

'Can I help you? You designed a floating dock for Bermuda, did you not?'

He assented with a 'Yes' that sounded like a grunt.

'And it would not float?'

Again he grunted.

'And you also designed, if I am not mistaken, the Caterham Lunatic Asylum?'

But, as I say, it was Mr Forbes' doing.

WILLIAM BALLANTINE (1812–87)

Serjeant-at-Law

23

BALLANTINE was one day prosecuting a case before the Common Serjeant, and the counsel who defended was a wild Irishman, who had never shown his face in the court before, and whose manners were very blustering and uncouth. At length, while examining one of his witnesses, the defending counsel put to him an outrageously irregular question.

Ballantine hastily rose, saying, 'My lord, I object to this mode of examining a witness.'

'You object, do you, sor?' said the Hibernian, turning round, and gazing at Ballantine with a threatening air. 'I was tould, when I came here, that what I said would be sure to be objected to; but I am not to be put down, sor, and will prove to my lord judge that it is as genteel a question as ever was put by a counsellor to a deponent, and that, in spite of your objection.'

Meanwhile, Ballantine turned to O'Brien, who was seated next to him, and said, 'Who is this fellow? Do you know him?'

'Oh, yes,' said O'Brien. 'His name is O'Flaherty. He is a regular fire-eater, and has killed one man, and winged two or three others.'

'You don't say so,' said Ballantine; and he immediately rose, and said, 'My lord, I withdraw my objection.'

24

IT would be an exaggeration to class Serjeant Parry and Serjeant Ballantine as great Lawyers, but they knew their briefs and human nature and each other, and sometimes made up in finesse what they lacked in knowledge of the nicer points of Law.

In one case Parry, for the plaintiff, found himself in a tight corner from which there appeared to be no escape until it occurred to him that there was always Ballantine's ignorance of the Law of which advantage could be taken.

'Doubtless my learned brother has overlooked the well-known case of *A* v. *B* which decided the very point he had raised' said Parry, with a well-simulated sympathy, obviously born of superior legal attainments.

Ballantine was equal to the occasion. There might be a well-known case of *A* v. *B* and if his opponent knew about it, the probability was that it was all he did know.

'I am obliged to my learned brother for the reminder' he said in his usual suave and convincing tone, 'but I assure him that I know all about it. In the circumstances, however, it is surprising that my learned brother is ignorant of the fact that the decision in *A* v. *B* was over-ruled quite recently in Exchequer Chambers in the case of *C* v. *D*.'

Both cases were entirely fictitious.

25

BALLANTINE was a great cross-examiner. In the Boston (Election Petition) case Ballantine and Hawkins appeared in the same interest. A lying witness was cross-examined by Hawkins, who made no impression. Ballantine turned to me and said, 'How about the famous Hawkins? I'm going to have a turn next.' When he rose to cross-examine he assumed that diabolical glare which I have more than once seen on his countenance. He stared at the witness for at least a minute before asking a question, and having completely hypnotised him, ended by turning him inside out and tearing his evidence to shreds. As he sat down he said to me, 'Well, who is the greatest cross-examiner? Hawkins or Ballantine?'

26

WHEN Ballantine was blackballed at the Reform Club, Horton, the Master of the Crown Office, said, 'Right! be Jasus! And if Jasus Christ himself had been an Old Bailey barrister they would have blackballed him too!'

JOHN GORELL BARNES (LORD GORELL) (1848–1939)

27

THE mention of Lord Gorell (as he became) tempts me to record a story that was told to me by Lord Mersey. The President of the Probate, Divorce and Admiralty Division wears, for full dress, the black and gold gown, like that of the Lord Chancellor and the Lords Justices. When, as Sir John Bigham, he was appointed to succeed Lord Gorell as President, he bought his gown from him for £50. In course of time he resigned, and Sir Samuel Evans was his successor. Bigham gave the gown to Evans. But meeting Lord Gorell, he said to him, with characteristic and impish humour: 'I say, Gorell, I have done a stroke of business. You remember you sold me that gown for £50. Well, I have got £100 for it from Evans.' Lord Gorell looked at him with grave solemnity, and said: 'Really, Bigham, that's very interesting. You see, Jeune gave it to me.'

SIR GARFIELD BARWICK (1903–)

Australian Barrister

28

Sir Garfield Barwick often appeared before the English Privy Council on appeals from Australia. He noted both the informality of the Law Lords, who were dressed in lounge suits, and the courteous nature of the proceedings. He recorded an unusual exchange.

THE Law Lords, during a hearing, are most polite to those appearing before them, and usually, if asking a question, would preface it by saying to counsel 'Do you mind if I ask a question?' And counsel would say 'Of course not, please ask' (and probably pray that they could answer it).

This particular appeal had been going for five days and for the first four days Lord Symonds (*sic*) had been wearing a blue shirt. On the fifth day he had on a white shirt.

Lord Simonds said to Sir Garfield, who was addressing the Court, 'May I ask a question?'

Sir Garfield said, 'Of course, what is it?'

Lord Simonds said, 'It is addressed to my Lord Symonds. Washing day, my Lord?'

SIR HENRY MAXIMILIAN (MAX) BEERBOHM (1872–1956)

29

THE greatest of all delights that a Law Court can give us is a disingenuous witness who is quick-minded, resourceful, thoroughly master of himself and his story, pitted against a counsel as well endowed as himself. The most vivid and precious of my memories is a case in which a gentleman, now dead, was sued for breach of promise and was cross-examined throughout a whole hot day in midsummer by the late Mr Candy. The lady had averred that she had known him for many years. She called various witnesses who testified to having seen him repeatedly in her company. She produced stacks of letters in a handwriting which no expert could distinguish from his.

The defence was that these letters were written by the defendant's secretary, a man who was able to imitate exactly his employer's handwriting, and who was, moreover, physically a replica of his employer. He was dead now; and the defendant, though he was a very well known man, with many friends, was unable to adduce anyone who had seen that secretary, dead or alive.

Not a soul in court believed the story. As it was a complicated story, extending over many years, to demolish it seemed child's play. Mr Candy was no child. His performance was masterly. But it was not so masterly as the defendant's; and the suit was dismissed. In the light of common sense, the defendant hadn't a leg to stand on. Technically, his case was unshaken. I doubt whether I shall ever have a day of such acute mental enjoyment as was the day of that cross-examination.

30

I SUPPOSE that the most famous cross examination in our days was Sir Charles Russell's of Pigott. It outstands by reason of the magnitude of the issue, and the flight and suicide of the witness. Had Pigott been of the stuff to stand up to Russell and make a fight of it, I should regret far more keenly than I do that I was not in Court. As it is, my regret is keen enough. I was reading again, only the other day, the verbatim report of Pigott's evidence in the series of little paper volumes published by *The Times*; and I was revelling again in the large perfection with which Russell achieved his too easy task. Especially was I amazed to find how vividly Russell, as I remembered him, lived again, and could be seen and heard, through the medium of that little paper volume. It was not merely as though I had been in court and were now recalling the inflexions of that deep, intimidating voice, the steadfast gaze of those dark, intimidating eyes, and were remembering just at what points the snuff-box was produced, and just how long the pause was before the pinch was taken and the bandana came into play. It was almost as though these effects were proceeding before my very eyes—these sublime effects of the finest actor I have ever seen. Expressed through a perfect technique, his personality was overwhelming.

SIR RICHARD BETHELL (LORD WESTBURY) (1800–73)

31

Sir Richard Bethell, the Attorney-General, and Lord Campbell, then Lord Chief Justice, but destined to be Lord Chancellor, spent much of their professional life quarrelling.

THE sparring of the two law lords was the severest ever known to pass between persons who persisted in calling one another 'friend'. The noble and learned 'friends' said the most astonishing things of, and to, each other without ever coming to blows.

When the first rumours became current that Campbell was to be elevated to the Chancellorship Nash records a meeting between the rivals in Westminster Hall. 'The day being cold for the time of year, Lord Campbell had come down to the House of Lords in a fur coat and Bethell, observing this, pretended not to recognize him. Thereupon Campbell came up to him and said, "Mr Attorney, don't you know me?" "I beg your pardon, My Lord," was the reply, "I mistook you for the Great Seal." '

GILBERT HUGH BEYFUS (1885–1960)

Queen's Counsel

32

DONALD WOODS was working in his long, narrow office when Beyfus came slowly through from his book-lined room overlooking the gardens of the Inner Temple. His face now had the grey, weary pallor of constant ill-health but his eyes had a twinkle. Woods had seen it before. He laid down his pen.

'I've been working on the Duchess of Argyll case', Beyfus announced. 'I think I've found a very good phrase.' He paused then told him what he intended calling her. 'What do you think of that?' he demanded, staring at Woods over the top of his begrimed spectacles.

Beyfus had put so much venom into the words that Woods realised with what impact they would hit the jury in the expectant quiet of the courtroom. He hesitated, then said, 'Well, she is a member of the aristocracy. You know what people are.' Beyfus, he knew, did not want his advice, only his reactions to gauge if his phrase would have the effect desired.

Beyfus was satisfied, his eyes lost their twinkle and took on an air of self-satisfaction. 'Anyway, that's what I'm going to call her.' He turned and walked back across the corridor.

Mrs Yvonne Macpherson, formerly the Duchess' social secretary, accused her of both libel in a forged telegram and slandering her good name and reputation in two conversations with a friend and doctor. In court that morning they sat less than three yards from each other, Mrs Macpherson, tall, dressed in black, rather severe beside the Duchess' furred elegance, the first time they had been so close since they parted at the Duchess' Mayfair home after an attempt by the Duke of Argyll to get his wife to apologise. Not only had the Duchess then refused to retract her accusation that it was Mrs Macpherson who told newspaper gossip columnists that she and the Duke had parted, and thus betrayed her trust as a confidential secretary, but added that she was a paid newspaper informer. Lord Rothermere, head of the Daily Mail newspaper group, had told her that Mrs Macpherson got £20 every time she gave them a titbit of information, even it it were not published, she declared.

'Come downstairs. You're acting like a yellow-belly', cried the Duke, when with that parting shot, the Duchess ran to her room. But the Duchess stayed where she was.

Although Mrs Macpherson was the widow of a brigadier-general, Beyfus was to call her a comparatively humble person and use the grey background he created as a contrast to the rich, glowing phrases with which he depicted the Duchess, daughter of a Scots millionaire. 'A dazzling figure . . . high in rank, the possessor of great wealth and famous beauty', he declared grandiloquently.

'As one contemplates her,' he continued, and the eyes of the ten men and two women jurors followed the expressive wave of his hand to the fine, delicately drawn features of the Duchess, 'one thinks back to the fairy stories of one's youth when all the good fairies assembled for a christening and showered their gifts upon the infant.'

His voice, jerky, unmusical yet demanding, drew their attention back to him. 'In some of the fairy stories there is a bad fairy who is not invited to the christening', he continued. 'One can imagine that the bad fairy said. "I can't withdraw the gifts showered upon you but I will give you my own gift. *You shall grow up to be a poisonous liar!*" '

He almost spat the words out. The jury jerked forward. It had all the effect Beyfus had hoped for.

'There imagination ceases and reality begins', he went on ominously. If Mrs Macpherson's witnesses were telling the truth then that was what had happened.

'The Duchess has distilled and distributed her poison about Mrs Macpherson partly by word of mouth and partly by the use—or rather the abuse—of the telegraph office. Mrs Macpherson has brought her to book in this court.'

Those connoisseurs of advocacy, who consider the Royal Courts of Justice a legal theatre, spending their day in its 'Gods', the hard, wooden benches of the public seats, had long ago made Beyfus one of their favourite actors. He shared his enjoyment at getting the answer he wanted with the court, looking round and chuckling, wrote one reporter, almost like a demon king in pantomime. He had his own following, almost a fan club, which went with him from court to court. 'If Mr Beyfus was appearing then the public seats were full', says an attendant at the High Court. His following never spoke nor clapped but they enjoyed each legal nicety and sometimes, sitting on the sidelines, appreciated better his plan of battle than others more immediately involved. They had never heard him give a better opening speech.

JOHN CHARLES BIGHAM (LORD MERSEY) (1840–1929)

33

HE was a native of Liverpool, and took as his title the famous river of which Liverpool men are so justly proud. This title gave rise to some jests. According to one wag, when Bigham was asked why he took the title of 'Mersey' the reply was: 'Well, you see, I thought I would leave the Atlantic for F. E. Smith.'

WILLIAM NORMAN BIRKETT (LORD BIRKETT) (1883–1962)

34

Birkett v. Muir. In the Jubilee Cotton Mills Case Ernest Terah Hooley was on trial with, among others, Thomas Fletcher, on a charge of conspiring to defraud. The Senior Treasury Counsel, Sir Richard Muir, was in charge of the prosecution.

BIRKETT recorded his impression of Hooley in a letter which he wrote to his wife at the time.

Hooley *is* a charming man, and I like him very much. He smiled now and then with quite a *radiant* smile. I can well understand how he got his money from susceptible people.

And sometimes when Muir (who is a silly, pompous, self-opinionated, vain, hard, emotionless, despicable ass) made some alleged cutting reference to him, Hooley whispered something to his companions in the dock which doubled them all up, even though they were on trial.

The case against Fletcher merely amounted to his having been in financial difficulties and having sold his mill to a company which he must have known to be a fraudulent concern.

'And is the net result', said Birkett, 'that you got £22,608 6*s*. 8*d*. for your mill which was worth at least £55,000?'

'Yes.'

'From first to last, had you the slightest intention to deceive anybody in any way at any time?'

'No.'

Sir Richard Muir's cross-examination of this witness was prefaced by the sharpest clash which Birkett ever had with an opponent in Court; and in view of his previously expressed opinion of the Senior Treasury Counsel, this was not surprising.

'Now, Mr Fletcher,' Muir began, 'we will have the truth.'

Birkett immediately jumped up. 'I object, my Lord', he appealed to the Bench. 'That is not a question, and it is charged with the most improper and unwarranted prejudice.'

But the Common Serjeant, who was accustomed to this kind of expression from Muir, who had been prosecuting at the Old Bailey for over thirty years, was not inclined to interfere. He allowed Muir to continue.

'Now, Mr Fletcher, I repeat—we will have the truth!'

Again Birkett was on his feet protesting. During the next few minutes he interrupted Muir seven times. Eventually the Senior Treasury Counsel bellowed at him 'Will you sit down, sir!'

'No, I will not sit down', Birkett retorted with some heat. 'I will not sit down while my learned friend so grossly misconducts himself.' Then, addressing himself to the Bench, he added, 'I insist that a note be made by your Lordship of my protest, and I say here and now that, whatever the outcome of this trial, it is likely to be held as invalid by the Court of Criminal Appeal in consequence of the impropriety of the remarks made by my learned friend.'

Fletcher need not have worried. As Birkett anticipated, the jury found him not guilty.

35

The narrator is Sydney Aylett, Mr Longland's Clerk

I PARTICULARLY remember one case in which Austin Longland was concerned. It was a matter of personal injury. Norman Birkett was leading for the plaintiff, a lady, and Longland was a junior on the other side, representing an insurance company. The brother of the plaintiff was a very rich man, who had been angered by the devious and delaying tactics of the Company.

When he met Birkett he told him that money meant nothing to him, though apparently it meant everything to the insurance company, so he wanted to hit them where it hurt most. 'I don't think they will settle out of Court for more than £15,000' Birkett replied. 'That's not enough, I want £30,000', came the answer. 'It's that or nothing, and if they refuse you'll fight them to the last ditch, and if in the end you get nothing, I shall not blame you.'

Birkett couldn't believe his ears. 'Sir,' he said, 'you are giving me the opportunity of a life time. It's an occasion I've always dreamed of. This is the way I see it. They will begin by believing that I'm bluffing. Then they will think that perhaps I've got something up my sleeve, and finally they will be so certain that I have, they will not dare to go into Court. I must warn you, though, that there is the element of risk. Remember, it now becomes a poker game.'

'You got my instructions, good luck to you' came the firm reply.

It went as Birkett foretold. I was able to hear the other side of the story from Longland. At first counsel and client were scornful, then apprehensive, then, when their 'final offer' of £25,000 was refused they were in turmoil. They didn't know what to advise. Finally it was Birkett's broad smile that decided the matter. The client's nerve went, and with a wailing and gnashing of teeth they paid.

36

In the so-called 'Burning Car Case', Alfred Arthur Rouse, a commercial traveller with a tangled love-life, was accused of giving a lift to an unidentified passenger, killing him, and setting fire to the car, presumably in the hope that people would assume that the body was his. One fact which was established was that the nut on the petrol pipe was loose.

AMONG the witnesses called by the defence was a motor engineer from Cricklewood named Arthur Isaacs, who had voluntarily come forward with an offer to give expert evidence after reading of the case in the newspapers and in particular the controversy concerning the nut on the union joint in the petrol pipe of Rouse's car—whether it was loosened accidentally, or on purpose. He was emphatic, when questioned by Rouse's counsel, that his experience of car fires was that a fire invariably loosened this particular joint.

'Do I understand you to say', the Judge intervened at this point, 'that the nut is invariably found to be loose as long as the fire is intense?'

'Yes, my Lord', the engineer replied. He went on to explain that the loosening was caused by the contraction and distortion of the metal threads cooling down after the fire.

This evidence of technical expertise appeared, at first sight, to demolish a principal part of the structure of the Crown Case.

But Birkett immediately rose to the occasion. His cross-examination of the Cricklewood engineer was brief, but deadly.

Birkett: 'What is the coefficient of expansion of brass?'
Witness: 'The what?'
Birkett: 'The coefficient of expansion of brass.'
Witness: 'I am afraid I cannot answer.'
Birkett: 'Do you know what the question means?'
Witness: 'Well, if you put it that way, I don't.'
Birkett: 'But aren't you an engineer?'
Witness: 'No.'
Birkett: 'But your company deals with the heat treatment of metals. What do you make?'
Witness: 'Springs.'
Birkett: 'Have you any degrees?'
Witness: 'No.'
Birkett: 'And as a fire assessor, did you have any training?'
Witness: 'I think so.'
Birkett: 'Where?'
Witness: 'All over the place. In South Africa and in this country.'
Birkett: 'What is the melting point of brass?'
Witness: (after some hesitation): 'Ah! brass! Oh, about 1,800 degrees fahrenheit.'
Birkett: 'If you took half an inch of brass and heated it to 1,500 degrees fahrenheit, what expansion would you get?'

Witness: 'I would not like to say.'

The question about the coefficient of expansion which effectively demolished the evidence of the defence's witness has been cited as the most devastating in its effect of any question ever put to a witness by Birkett in cross-examination. At the time, however, it was criticized in some quarters as a 'trick' question which should not have been asked. But Birkett considered the question quite justified, as he had seen it in the engineer's diary belonging to Colonel Buckle, the expert witness called by the prosecution, and he assumed that any qualified engineer would be familiar with the answer. Asked, many years later, what he would have done if the witness had given the correct answer (0·0000189), he said that he would have gone on to copper, then to aluminium and other metals, eventually leaving the subject as though it was of no particular importance.

THE BLACK BOOK

37

An exposition of abuses in Church and State.

A SERIOUS evil resulting from the Excise system is the power vested in the Commissioners of Excise or Lords of the Treasury to mitigate penalties or stay proceedings against defenders at their discretion. This enables them to make the most odious distinction between persons supposed to be friendly or hostile to the government. We had a singular instance of this in the case of Mr Abbott, brewer and magistrate, of Canterbury. This man had for a long time been selling, according to Lord Brougham's statement, rank poison in the beverage of the people. It appears he had been selling a liquor resembling beer, manufactured from beer-grounds, distillers' spent wash, quassia, opium, guinea pepper, vitriol, and other deleterious and poisonous ingredients. The officers of Excise having examined this worthy magistrate's premises, found 12 lbs of prepared powder, and 14 lbs of vitriol or copperas; in boxes; which, if full, would have contained 56 lbs. Proceedings were instituted against him by the Board. The penalties he had incurred amounted to £9,000; and the case being notorious and atrocious, the Commissioners appeared determined to levy them with rigour. Mr Abbott, however, was a *loyal man* and an *active magis-*

trate; and he prevailed upon some other loyal men to write on his behalf to the Lords of the Treasury. Among other persons who stepped forward in behalf of this virtuous magistrate, were the very reverend the Dean of Canterbury, Dr Gerard Andrews, Mr Baker, MP, and the late Sir William Curtis. All these were loyal men and true; and, in their letters to the Lords of Treasury, spoke in the highest terms of the public and private virtues of the *good* Mr Abbott. Mr Baker styles him 'my much esteemed and valued friend, Mr Abbott'. Sir William Curtis was still more eloquent and touching; stating that he was a very long acquaintance of fifty years, and a 'most honourable and virtuous old man'. The reverend Dean went on in the same strain; stating that he was a 'good neighbour of his, and an useful magistrate'; and that he should regret were his 'usefulness and respectability diminished by a matter that concerned ONLY ALE-DRINKERS!'

Only think of this! Here is a man, a very reverend dean, who regrets that a *good neighbour of his* should be dragged before the public merely for poisoning *ale-drinkers*. Had Mr Abbott been poisoning *wine-drinkers*, we imagine his crime would have appeared very different in the eyes of the reverend dean. It is related of a right reverend bishop, in the House of Lords, that he once remarked that he did not know what the people had to do with the laws but to obey them. One is at a loss to conceive where these notions have been taken up: they certainly belong to another age, or at least to another country than England. For our part, we can only ascribe this unseemly insolence of the clergy to the undeserved respect which they have been accustomed to receive from the people, and which has begotten in them a feeling of superiority to which, above all men, they have the least claim, either on account of their knowledge or virtues, or any other qualification useful or ornamental. The views of some of them in respect of the people are very little more elevated than those of the nobles of Russia towards their boors. We remember an anecdote of a Russian officer travelling through Germany, who, on account of a trifling delay or provocation, shot his postillion. The circumstance exciting some noise, the officer was given to understand that, though such things might do very well in Russia, they could not pass in Germany with impunity. The officer, considering the interruption impertinent, demanded the *price* of a German postillion, and said he would *pay for him*. This was not much worse than Dr Andrews' notion of the social importance of ale-drinkers.

To return, however, to the *good* Mr Abbott: so many testimonies from such quarters, to his various excellences were not to be neglected. The Treasury, without seeking any more evidence, but merely at the instigation of their political friends, ordered the proceedings to be stayed, and penalties to the amount of £9,000 were softened down to £500.

JAMES BOSWELL (1740–95)

38

Thinks about a legal career.

I WANTED much to be a man of consequence, and I considered that I could only be that in my own country, where my family and connections would procure it. I also considered that the Law was my plain road to preferment. That if I would go to the Scotch bar I would soon be well employed and as this confinement [Boswell had been indisposed for some days] has made me see that I can sit in and labour very well I thought I might be able very well to do business.

By this means I would make money which would enable me to jaunt about wherever I pleased in the vacations. I would have an opportunity of being of much real use, of being of service to my friends by having weight in the country, and would make my father exceedingly happy.

I considered that the Law seemed to be pointed out by fate for me.

That the family of Auchinleck had been raised by it. That I would soon be made Advocate Depute on the circuits and in all probability be made a Baron of Exchequer, and by this means have respect and yet an easy life—*otium cum dignitate*. I considered that my notions of an advocate were false. That I connected with that character low breeding and Presbyterian stiffness, whereas many of them were very genteel people. That I might have the wit and humour of Sir David Dalrymple, the show of Baron Maule, and the elegant taste of Baron Grant. I thought I might write books, like Lord Kames and be a buck like Mr James Erskine. That I might keep a handsome machine. Have a good agreeable wife and fine children, and keep an excellent house. That I might show all the dull, vulgar plodding young lawyers how easily superior parts can outstrip them.*

* Unhappily he attained none of these legal plums. Towards the end of his life he did, of necessity, resume the legal career so interrupted by his great work on Dr Johnson, and recommenced practice on the Home Circuit—but did not get a single brief.

SIR ALEXANDER BOSWELL (1775–1822)

39

ALEXANDER, the son of James Boswell had contributed to a rather disreputable Tory newspaper bitter anonymous attacks on one James Stuart of Dunearn, a lawyer in Edinburgh. These attacks were witty but outrageous. Stuart was treated with contempt for having embraced the lucrative profession of solicitor rather than the gentlemanly one of barrister. Alexander Boswell among other things, called him 'a fat coward' and said he would draw 'wills, bills and petitions' or 'aught but a trigger'. Stuart got hold of the office papers of the newspaper and found from the manuscripts of the articles that Alexander Boswell was the author.

Sir Alexander received a challenge, refused to apologise and met Stuart in a duel.

Sir Alexander, a good shot, fired into the air; Stuart, who had never fired a pistol before, fired without taking aim, and wounded Sir Alexander mortally. The spinal cord was severed just below the neck.

He was carried to the nearby house of his elderly cousin, Lord Balmuto and died next day.

When Stuart was tried for murder, Lord Jeffrey, his chief counsel, read to the court those passages of Boswell's *Life of Johnson* in which Johnson defends duelling as a form of self-defence, and Boswell admits that, if he himself were affronted, he would think it necessary to fight.

The jury acquitted the accused without leaving the room.

BERNARD BOTEIN (1900–74)

American Judge

40

In this case a plaintiff was trying to prove that a doctor had overcharged him.

THE doctor's nurse testified on his behalf. Upon cross-examination the plaintiff's attorney questioned her closely, and viciously, upon the number of visits the doctor had made to the plaintiff's home, and the number of times the plaintiff had visited the doctor's office. He openly questioned the genuineness of her office records and denied her protestations that each entry represented a visit. Then he shifted his questions to the fees paid by the plaintiff.

Sneeringly he asked 'Even if all those visits were made, were they necessary or was the doctor building up his fees?'

The witness gripped both sides of the chair so fiercely that the whites of her knuckles showed. She half raised herself, and then the storm broke.

'You've been poking fun at my doctor', she blazed, ' and you're not fit to wipe his shoes. Have you any idea of how much good he does every day? Do you know that he won't let me send bills to half his patients because they can't afford to pay? My doctor is a poor man. There's many a time, when the first of the month comes round, that I have trouble scraping together the rent for his office and his home. I'm ashamed to tell you how many months I draw only part of my pay because there just isn't enough.'

The lawyer gesticulated and shouted 'I object' and 'Move to strike it all out, Your Honour', but she continued, 'Do you think that he and his family live in luxury? They live right in the same neighbourhood in a walk-up flat. My doctor and his wife and three kids. He's a wonderful doctor and he could make a lot of money if he wanted to. But he's devoting his whole life to helping these poor people.'

After she had *fully* finished I recognised the clamouring, red-faced lawyer for the plaintiff. I then granted his motion to strike her answer from the record and gravely instructed the jurors to disregard it.

From the celerity with which they later returned a verdict for the doctor, I doubt they heeded my admonition.

41

SOMETIMES special circumstances, in addition to special knowledge, impel a judge to intervene. At other times experienced and well-controlled lawyers are fearful of a judge's intervention in a lawsuit.

Serjeant Ballantine, a great English barrister of the nineteenth century, told of the time when a judge interrupted him while he was cross-examining a witness, saying, 'Really, this is a long way from the point.'

'I am aware of that', said Ballantine. 'If I were to begin any nearer the witness would discover my object.'

Another story is told of a judge who took the case out of the hands of the lawyers, and examined and cross-examined witnesses at great length and with great vigor. Finally one of the lawyers could not contain himself any longer, and blurted out: 'Judge, I don't mind you trying the case for me, but for God's sake, don't lose it.'

HORATIO WILLIAM BOTTOMLEY (1860–1933)

42

ONE day I heard Horatio Bottomley being cross-examined by Montagu Lush, KC, in one of the many actions in which fraud was alleged against him. Lush was not imposing, being short, squat, and afflicted with a high treble voice; by contrast, Bottomley was impressive, 'calm, deliberate, speaking in a deep resonant voice . . . frigidly impassive . . . betraying neither anger not trepidation, facing his antagonists like an antlered stag . . . or a well-weathered old lion, disdainful, formidable, aloof, remote' as James Douglas wrote of him in a contemporary press article.

In one of his answers Bottomley had mentioned the flotation of a limited company to operate a canal.

'Oh!', squeaked Lush, 'is that our old friend the Basingstoke Canal?' This was an almost waterless ditch some thirty miles long which was renamed and registered as the London & South Western Canal Ltd: thereafter a brisk business was done in the worthless shares of this concern. Horatio eyed his interrogator almost pityingly, and then: 'I don't know anything about your old friends, Mr Lush!'

A small incident, but the King's Counsel was made to look remarkably foolish, as anyone does whose attempted joke or sneer is turned against himself.

It was shortly after this that the promising young leader John Simon persuaded a jury, for the first time, to return a verdict of fraud against Bottomley.

One of the interchanges between the two is worth repeating. Simon was reading to Bottomley a letter which Bottomley had written to one of his victims postponing an appointment on the grounds that he was very busy with the Budget.

'I didn't know, Mr Bottomley,' said Simon sarcastically, 'that the Government were consulting you on the Budget.'

Everyone in Court laughed.

'I don't suppose you did—you lawyer politicians know so little about what goes on the House—you are so seldom there.'

No doubt about who won that round!

43

THE failure of the Law Trust and Guarantee Society was attributed to loans on the security of flats and hotels. According to the magazine *John Bull*, which Bottomley was then editing, loans on inadequate security were largely due to the incompetence of Mr Ronald, junior, and it accused his father, a senior official in the Society, of gross nepotism in appointing his son to a position for which he had no qualification.

Mr Ronald, junior retaliated by suing *John Bull*, its publishers and its editor, Mr Bottomley, for libel.

Bottomley scorned counsel for his own defence, and when he rose to cross-examine Ronald the plaintiff had already been questioned at considerable length by F. E. Smith and Harold Smith. Bottomley, suave and unemotional, proceeded to demolish him as follows:

'Do you put yourself forward as an expert in the valuation of furniture?'

'Oh, no.'

'So when it became necessary to assess the value of the furniture and equipment of the Waldorf Hotel did you employ an expert in such matters?'

'Yes, I called in Mr —.'

'Is he an expert valuer?'

'The best in London.'

'Then why did you take it upon yourself to add £3,000 to his valuation?'

'I considered that his valuation was too low to that extent.'

'But you are not an expert?'

'No.'

'And he is?'

'Yes.'

'Suppose you had found out there was a discrepancy of, say, £10,000. What would you have done?'

'In that case, undoubtedly, I should have sought the advice of some other eminent valuer.'

'You would?'

'Certainly.'

'Well then, now add up your figures again and see whether you have not made a mistake of exactly that amount.'

'Mr Bottomley, I have been in this box for about three days, and I am not feeling very well.'

'Perhaps you were not feeling very well when you added up those figures, Mr Ronald.'

Mr Ronald had in fact made that mistake. Which Horatio kept in secret storage for his cross-examination. He won his case.

44

Mr Justice Hawkins once said that Bottomley was the ablest advocate he had ever listened to and offered to lend him his wig.

ONE of the occasions when Horace Avory failed to succeed in a case was that in which, with the late Sir Richard Muir as his junior, he appeared at the London Guildhall to prosecute the redoubtable Horatio Bottomley. The case was heard during the winter of 1908–9 and was a very involved one. Bottomley was in his best form throughout and conducted a masterly cross-examination of the most expert witnesses. So successful was it that in more than one instance he succeeded in getting these very clever gentlemen absolutely tied up. The prosecution tried in vain to stem the tide which was flowing strongly in the defendant's favour. Had they succeeded in getting the case sent for trial before judge and jury the result might have been different, but as it was, the magistrate, an Alderman of the City of London, greatly impressed by Bottomley's remarkable address, decided that there was no case in which a jury would be likely to convict the defendant, and discharged him. Bottomley's final speech was so clever and impressive, that it is well worth while to repeat the final phrases of it here:

Now, sir, let me just call your attention to what it is that you are asked to commit me upon. For twenty-seven days the Treasury, with all its resources, with all its legal assistance, with its somewhat unusual feature in a Police Court of a learned King's Counsel, as well as perhaps the most distinguished junior at the Criminal Bar behind them, have been engaged rummaging into the history of this company for the purpose of formulating charges against me . . . .

I am one of those, sir, who believe that in these days magisterial enquiries are meant to be something more than formal steps. It was all very well in olden times, when they were not reported, when nobody suffered much injury; but this has been practically a trial, and this enquiry has been a very real thing indeed. The right of a magistrate—certainly the right of a member of your Bench—to preside over such a trial as this is one of the oldest, and perhaps one of the most honourable privileges of this City. And I say, in conclusion, Radical and Democrat as I call myself, I am one of those who honestly has always revered the traditions, the prestige, and the power of this Corporation, and I do not hesitate today, hunted, hounded and harassed on all sides as I am, to come to you, as not the least respected and one of the senior members of its Aldermanic Bench, to give me sanctuary.

45

BOTTOMLEY, during his sojourn in Wormwood Scrubs had, on occasions, to attend the Bankruptcy Court, where he appeared dressed in civilian clothes. A friend, who saw him at Court, remarked on the creases in Horatio's coat. Bottomley replied, 'Never mind. When I get back, I change for dinner.'

CHARLES SYNGE CHRISTOPHER BOWEN (LORD BOWEN) (1835–94)

46

BOWEN's first appearance at Westminster before the Court in Banc was a somewhat trying ordeal to a junior's nerves. The argument turned on an alleged misdirection by Chief Baron Pollock. The Chief Baron himself presided in the appellate tribunal, and had a clear recollection of what his charge had been. Bowen's remembrance was equally distinct, and he had shorthand notes and other corroborative evidence at his back. The Chief Baron grew more and more positive; positiveness presently kindled into wrath. Bowen, resolved on death or victory, was pertinacious, insistent, unabashed. Prometheus defying the Olympians was scarcely playing a more audacious role than this neophyte in the profession essaying to convince the Chief Baron, against his will, as to the language he had used. The wrath was becoming very Olympian indeed, and the consequences threatened to be serious, when a friendly missive from a member of the Court—Sir George Honeyman, if I remember rightly—warned the young combatant that there are bounds to human temerity, and occasions on which the assault should not be pressed too far, and that the Chief Baron's health would be imperilled by a prolongation of the encounter. I remember, as we walked homeward from Westminster that evening—both of us in great excitement at the events of the afternoon, Bowen certain of his cause, but doubtful as to his prudence and his skill—how we reassured ourselves by the reflection that Chief Barons, after all, were mortals like ourselves, must have once worn the stuff gown and sighed for briefs, and would probably have a latent sympathy for an advocate too zealous to be easily abashed.

47

ON the third or fourth day of the trial, the Solicitor-General being absent, Mr Bowen was in charge of the case for the Crown. Of course, Bowen was only the 'devil'; and possibly the length of the case had somewhat irritated Huddleston. Be this as it may, his lordship, on entering the Court, seemed not to be in a very amiable frame of mind, and at once commenced to find fault with almost everything that had been done by the prosecution. Addressing the 'devil', he said: 'I don't see the Solicitor-General in his place, Mr Bowen; but I wish to take this opportunity of stating that I consider that this case has been conducted (of course, I am not blaming the Solicitor-General) in a most slovenly manner. I took all the documents home with me last night, to see if I could get them into some kind of regular shape and order by the time I come to sum up this most involved and intricate case to the jury. Not a single paper, document, or exhibit is distinguishable—not one of them is either numbered or docketed. It is simply disgraceful!'

'Well, my lord,' said Mr Bowen, in that extremely polite and lady-like manner for which he was famed, 'really, my lord, I can't agree with your lordship, for it was only last night, after consultation, that the Solicitor-General and myself, and those associated with me, were remarking how admirably we were instructed, and how excellently the evidence had been marshalled and arranged.'

'Really, Mr Bowen,' said the Judge, 'I will not be contradicted; it is most unseemly in you. But after all, I have no right to blame you. It is those who instruct you to whom I am alluding, and (pointing to the little Jewish solicitor in the well) I see Mr Abrahams there, whom I know by sight, instructing you. It is to him I refer, and it is with him I am finding fault. I am very glad he is present to hear my observations.'

Upon this the little gentleman alluded to threw up his hands, and in a voice not loud enough to reach the Bench, and with an expression on his face that I will not attempt to describe, observed to his counsel: 'My God! and when he was at the Bar, he used to take his hat off to me.'

48

LORD WESTBURY can hardly have gratified the peer who asked him to explain the decision in the Colenso Case by telling him that it would require more time than he could spend and possibly greater effort than he could employ to render the judgment of the Privy Council intelligible to the noble Lord. In fact, the Judicial Committee had declared that a belief in the doctrine of eternal punishment was not essential to orthodoxy—a finding which Lord Bowen (one of the counsel in the case) summarized by endorsing his brief 'Hell dismissed, with costs.'

49

The narrator is Lord Alverstone

WHEN Mr Justice Bowen, afterwards Lord Bowen, was offered a Judgeship in the Queen's Bench, he sent for me, as I knew him very intimately, and asked me what I thought he ought to do. I said: 'Well, Bowen, if you don't accept the Judgeship, you must take a silk gown and go through the hard work of the profession, and I doubt whether your health would stand it.' 'Well,' he said, 'it is strange you should have said that, when I tell you that during my eighteen years at the Bar I have been away for two whole periods of twelve months from ill-health.' Just at this time gossip said that Mr Bowen was hesitating. Mrs Bowen was anxious that he should accept the Judgeship. Block—that was his clerk's name—said, when asked: 'Our voice is weak, and the sooner we get on the Bench the better.' Strangely enough, it was a true summary of the position.

50

BOWEN's contemporaries recall an occasion on which the draft of an address to Royalty was being considered by the Judges. It contained the expression, 'Conscious as we are of our shortcomings.' Exception was taken to the phrase as pitched in too humble a key. No such consciousness, it was urged, besets the judicial mind. 'Suppose', Bowen demurely suggested, 'that we substitute "Conscious as we are of one another's shortcomings"?'

51

The narrator is Sir Henry Cunningham

OF Bowen's after-dinner stories, the best is probably that which I heard him deliver when Mr Justice Charles was entertained by old and present members of the circuit on his elevation to the Bench. Every post-prandial orator has borrowed it since; but in its original form, and delivered with Bowen's characteristic voice and manner, it was inimitable.

One of the ancient Rabbinical writers—I have forgotten his name, but I have no doubt that it can be easily ascertained—was engaged in compiling a history of the minor prophets; and in due course it became his duty to record the history of the prophet Daniel. In speaking of the most striking incident in that great man's career—I refer to his critical position in the den of lions—he made a remark which has always appeared to me replete with judgment and observation. He said that the prophet, notwithstanding the trying circumstances in which he was placed, had one consolation which has sometimes been forgotten. He had the consolation of knowing, that when the dreadful banquet was over, at any rate it was not he who would be called upon to return thanks!

52

LORD BOWEN, in a speech at Balliol Hall, once described the course of a busy human life as resembling a journey in an express train. You choose the carriage and start with the keenest interest in all you see: as you proceed, you scan the features of your fellow-travellers and watch the panorama from the window; presently the scene loses its freshness as the train gathers speed—mile posts and wayside stations flash past you as laborious terms of work and periods of vacation follow one another in uncounted succession. You have long since settled yourself in your corner and there seems no reason why the journey should be ending. But presently you note that the train is slowing down; signs that you are approaching the terminus multiply. You look up and lo! here is the inexorable official coming along to collect your ticket.

ERNEST BROWN BOWEN-ROWLANDS

(1866–1951)

King's Counsel

53

ONE night during Sessions I was dining with Major Knight, the Governor of Swansea Gaol, and I asked him what had happened to a man named Jeans. This man had married a young woman and, for some extraordinary reason, did not wish her to know that he had been married before and had a child who (after his first wife's death) was boarded out with friends.

One day he went and took away the child and, walking to the pier head at Swansea, threw him into the sea.

He was convicted, and sentenced to death. His conduct when awaiting execution I give in Major Knight's own words:

> Jeans was the strangest man I ever had under me. Until the last night of his life, all the time he was in the condemned cell, he never opened his mouth to speak. He turned away when the Chaplain came in, and if he wanted anything he made a sign. The last night I went, as is my custom, into Jeans's cell and I told him that his time was up in the morning and asked him if he had any request to make. And then he spoke. He said that he had been brought up on a farm, and had a hankering for a new laid egg for his breakfast. I said he should have two eggs of my fowls' laying and he thanked me, and said no more.
>
> The next morning when I was shaving—not half an hour before the time fixed for the execution—the Chief Warder came in and said that Jeans was behaving like a madman, shouting, and carrying on, because his breakfast had been served without eggs. I had forgotten them!
>
> I gave the keys of the cupboard to the Warder and told him to get the eggs, boil them and give them to Jeans.
>
> He went off with the keys, and not long after I went with the hangman to Jeans's cell. He was just finishing the second egg. He stood up, and said with a

smile 'Thank you kindly, Sir. I've enjoyed them, and they brought back the old days.'

Two minutes later he was dead.

GEORGE WILLIAM WILSHERE BRAMWELL (LORD BRAMWELL) (1808–92)

54

A DISTINGUISHED Victorian judge, Baron Bramwell, had an equally distinguished expert witness for a brother, and it is related that once, when the Baron had been listening for a considerable time to expert witnesses whose opinions were diametrically opposed, he classified untruthful witnesses as: 'Liars, damned liars, expert witnesses, and then, of course, there is always brother Edwin.'

55

ALTHOUGH the judges in Court usually speak of another judge as 'my brother so-and-so', it does not seem to follow that there is necessarily any strong brotherly affection between them. Lord Bramwell was fond of describing a conversation which took place between himself and Lord Blackburn, with reference to the dinner given in his honour on his retirement. Lord Bramwell was not only an eminent judge, but he was a popular one in the profession. Lord Blackburn was also an eminent judge, but he was *not* universally popular. Lord Bramwell said that on the day of the dinner, he happened to meet Lord Blackburn. He (Lord Blackburn) said: 'I am not coming to your dinner, Bramwell.'

Lord Bramwell: 'I did not suppose you were.'

Lord Blackburn: 'No, I do not like such things. When I retire I shall do so in vacation.'

Lord Bramwell: 'My dear Blackburn, it will be a very unnecessary precaution!'*

* On the vexed subject of these farewell dinners see the comment of Sir Edward Clarke at p. 70.

56

A MEMBER of the Common Law Bar, Mr A., once told me a characteristic story of Lord Bramwell. Mr A., who did not previously know him, was staying weather-bound at a small hotel on the Continent, at which Lord Bramwell was, from the like cause, detained. As often happens under such circumstances, they became rather intimate, and when the time arrived for their departure on different ways, Lord Bramwell expressed the hope that he should meet Mr A. the next term. Mr A. said unfortunately he had not much Court work, and that Lord Bramwell would have forgotten him. Lord Bramwell ridiculed that suggestion, but at Mr A.'s suggestion a watchword was agreed on, so that Lord Bramwell might, in case of need, be reminded. It was 'Waddy waddy', or some such unmeaning phrase. Mr A. said he had nothing to do in the Court of Exchequer for sometime afterwards, but at length he had to make an unimportant motion in the Court, and found Baron Bramwell presiding. Mr A. said he was rather nervous, and in ordinary course said: 'I have to apply . . .' Before he got further, Baron Bramwell interposed:

'Apply for what, sir?'
Mr A.: 'My lord, I hoped . . .'
Baron Bramwell: 'Hoped what, sir?'
Mr A.: 'Your lordship might remember . . .'
Baron Bramwell: 'Remember what, sir?'
Mr A.: 'Waddy waddy!'
Baron Bramwell (after a momentary pause): 'Mr A., I humbly beg your pardon.'

JAMES BURNETT (LORD MONBODDO)

(1714–99)

57

LORD MONBODDO's annual journeys to London were invariably made on horseback. These equestrian performances continued until he was upwards of eighty years of age. On his last journey he took ill, and it was with great difficulty that a friend, who had overtaken him on the road, persuaded him to enter a carriage, which sorely touched his dignity as well as cast a slur upon the Ancients. But he was ill at ease, and, on the following day, he again mounted Alburac, and arrived in Edinburgh without further mishap.

In May 1785, Monboddo was in the court of the King's Bench when a rumour that the building was falling caused a general stampede. The Scottish judge, however, took the matter very coolly, as the following extract from a contemporary newspaper sufficiently testifies:

In the curious rout of the lawyer's corps, it is singular that the only person who kept his seat was a venerable stranger. Old Lord Monboddo, one of the Scots judges, was in the court of the King's Bench, and being short-sighted and rather dull in his hearing, he sat still during the tumult, and did not move from his place. Afterwards, being questioned why he did not bestir himself to avoid the ruin, he coolly answered 'that he thought it was an annual ceremony with which, as an alien to our laws, he had nothing to do!'

SIR JOHN BARNARD BYLES (1801–84)

58

TOM JONES, notorious for his brusqueness with the Bench, was once moving for a new trial before a full bench of the Common Pleas, Mr Justice Byles being one of four judges. Our friend grew very warm and earnest in urging his client's claims, and at length he said, in emphatic tones:

'No-one, my Lords, who looks at this case with common fairness and honesty can hesitate for a moment in declaring that there ought to be a new trial.'

Byles observed, 'This is rather strong language to use to us Mr Jones. I hope you think that we, at least, are commonly fair and honest.'

'We shall see, my Lord', said Tom. 'We shall see.'

IAN BYRNE (Contemporary)

Australian Barrister

59

A PROMINENT Canberra barrister, Ian Byrne, appeared for an Italian who was seeking workers compensation for an injury which he claimed he received at work.

It was alleged on his behalf that he had difficulty in moving, bending and even walking. He could not lift any heavy article, nor could he indulge in his hobbies of gardening and tennis. Before the injury he performed painting work around his house and did his own brick-laying and concreting.

Prior to the trial the respondent insurance company engaged a loss-assessor to follow the applicant Italian, photograph him when he was unaware, and report with a view to giving evidence at the trial.

In due course the application came on for hearing. Ian Byrne put his client (whom I shall call Bruno) in the witness box. He told his story of pain and suffering. He showed that he had severe limitation of movement, could not bend or carry weights, and was a completely useless member of the community because of his unfortunate injury.

At the end of his examination-in-chief Ian Byrne's opponent, a somewhat inexperienced Counsel, sprang to his feet, enthusiasm gleaming in his eyes, and said 'Your Worship, I have here over 1,000 feet of film which shows this man Bruno bricklaying, lifting weights, concreting, vaulting a fence, working on his own house and even running. I would ask leave of Your Worship to run the film before I begin to cross-examine the applicant.'

The film was then run. It showed the applicant running, making a brick wall, carrying wheelbarrow loads of bricks, picking up slabs of concrete, climbing up and down ladders, digging in the garden and running behind a lawn mower. Further, it depicted the applicant's home and his small truck with his name clearly marked on the door, and also showed him wearing a red cardigan which he was wearing in the witness-box. At the finish of the screening the enthusiastic Counsel for the insurance company commenced his cross-examination.

'You saw that film?'

'Yes', said Bruno.

'There is nothing wrong with your back at all, is there?'

'Yes', said Bruno. 'Everything that I said before isa truea. That was notta me in the picture. Thata was my brudda.'

'But', exploded Counsel. 'That was your house wasn't it?'

'Yeah', said Bruno.

'And the same cardigan you've got on today is the one shown in the film?'

'Yeah', said Bruno, 'I lent it to my brudda. My brudda he is very good to me. He doesa for me, he painta da house, he cementa da paths, he mowa da lawns.'

'But', said learned Counsel, 'His Worship has seen the film and he knows it is you.'

'It is notta me. It's my brudda.'

In due course Ian Byrne called the brother, and when he walked into Court it was obvious to all that he was the identical twin of the applicant; and after a few questions it was obvious that he was the one in the film doing all the physical acts.

The angry Counsel for the defendant had the applicant recalled and said to him, 'You have tried to deceive the Court. You and your brother knew he was being photographed.'

'Yes', said the applicant, 'we thought it verra funny.'

HUGH McCALMONT CAIRNS (LORD CAIRNS) (1819–85)

60

SHORTLY after the General Election of 1880 Lord Cairns, whose three elder sons were educated at Wellington College under a son-in-law of Mr Gladstone, remarked to a friend that the great majority of school masters throughout the kingdom were Liberals.

'What a dark look out', said the friend.

'On the contrary', he replied. 'I see in this great hope for our nation's future. The *boys* are certain to be Conservatives.'

JOHN CAMPBELL (LORD CAMPBELL) (1779–1861)

Lord Chief Justice

61

The narrator is Edward Vaughan Kenealy, QC

I HAVE seen such old rogues in scarlet and ermine as it would be difficult to match even in Norfolk Island.

Campbell, from whom I have myself suffered much injustice, was a man of great talent, but, from the cruelty and bias of his disposition, quite unfitted to be the representative of the majesty of the law, certainly not in any capacity so comprehensive as that of Lord Chief Justice of England. He used from the Bench to display so much ferocity, even malignity, as to render everybody present most unhappy; the infliction of torture appeared to be a luxury to him, a luxury in which he frequently indulged. His acrimony and want of humanity resembled the characteristics of a fox, to which animal he has been likened.

I remember an incident which shows, although only in a slight degree, his natural lack of courtesy and consideration.

A number of ladies crowded into one of the passages at Westminster Hall for the purpose of getting a glimpse of the Lord Chief Justice, who was then a celebrity of some note. As he passed his button caught in a beautiful lace *berthe* worn by one of his fair admirers. After a vain struggle to disengage himself Campbell deliberately took out his penknife—everybody thought for the purpose of cutting off his button and releasing the lady. Not at all. He coolly cut a hole in her handsome lace and passed on with his sweetest smile.

62

NEVERTHELESS [says the imaginary narrator of Robert Graves's book *They Hanged My Saintly Billy*], the Usher of the Central Criminal Court assured us on the first day of the trial, 'Sir. Doctor Palmer will swing, you may be bound.'

Upon our questioning him we were told, 'I know Jack Campbell's hanging face well, and his hanging manner.'

'What is that?', we asked.

'His hanging face, Sir, is bland and benignant, and his hanging manner unctuous. As soon as the prisoner entered the dock and Lord Campbell invited him to be seated I would have offered long odds against his chances of life.'

'But it takes twelve good men and true to hang a criminal', we insisted. 'And there are a couple of other judges on the bench beside the Lord Chief Justice.'

He shook his head sagely. 'Sir Creswell Creswell is a humane and honest man', he pronounced, 'but Alderson would as lief hang Shee as he would Palmer.' [Serjeant Shee was the Counsel appearing for Palmer.]

'Those two legal gentlemen have always been at loggerheads. I can't say why—it may be a political disagreement, it may be a personal one. Moreover Attorney General Cockburn is a beloved compatriot of Jack Campbell's and he's out to destroy Palmer. Even if the pair of them weren't as thick as thieves it would take a mighty firm Lord Chief Justice to handle a determined Attorney General. Cocky, you know, is due for his judgeship any day now, and wishes to make this a memorable farewell to the Bar. A savage's feast day, with fireworks, drums, bloody sacrifices and all. So that's three of them teamed together—Jack Campbell, Alderson and Cocky. They can do what they list, for the Under Sheriffs have a hand-picked jury ready to serve them. Will you dare lay against Palmer's conviction?'

'I'm not a betting man' was our cautious answer.

BENJAMIN NATHAN CARDOZO (1870–1938)

Justice of the Supreme Court

63

The Judge demonstrates his determination.

BEN was esteemed for his wisdom. Yet, if he generally held himself aloof, he joined his classmates in the most dangerous task of undergraduate life. There, with the determination which was as much a part of him as his gentleness, he acquitted himself in characteristic fashion. All of us who are old Columbia graduates, know that not even in the football days, when the 'Flying Wedge' was the battering ram sometimes fatal in its consequences, was anything more dangerous to life and limb than the 'Cane Rush'.

Here the entire Freshman and Sophomore classes would engage in the struggle at whose conclusion hands were counted. A long broomstick theoretically became the cane. If Freshman hands on it exceeded in number those of the Sophomores the entering class would be allowed certain privileges otherwise withheld. The pummeling, the tearing at faces, the gasping for breath under the writhing mass of over a hundred boys were so intense that casualties were ever likely to result.

In the eighties one lad died from his injuries and the Cane Rush was temporarily abolished until, after its resumption in the nineties, a second fatality led to its being permanently placed under ban. But no danger ever prevented Ben Cardozo from using strength of mind and body in seeking to achieve. When hands were counted in the Cane Rush of his Sophomore year, his frail and delicate fingers were wound firmly round the broomstick.

64

THERE were limits to Cardozo's interest in pleasing clients, says Charles H. Tuttle (Republican candidate for the governorship of New York when Franklin D. Roosevelt was his successful opponent). One of the chief attorneys of the Shuberts invited Cardozo, then a consulting lawyer of those theatres managers, to attend a Shubert production where glamorous girls were the main attraction. There was, for Cardozo's taste, too much frankness in the words of the songs and in the exposure of feminine beauty.

He offered no criticism, beyond saying to the Shubert lawyer: 'Very interesting, very interesting indeed.' At the first entr'acte he rose to leave. He explained that he had much work to do before the morning.

65

CARDOZO was amused to find in his mail one morning a letter which read: 'Dear Judge Cardozo, I read in the newspapers that you are a liberal judge. Will you send me ten dollars, as I'm really very hard up.'

EDWARD HENRY CARSON (LORD CARSON) (1854–1935)

66

When one of the rent collectors for the Gas Light and Coke Company was charged with fraud he succeeded in confusing the jury to such an extent that he was acquitted. He was then rash enough to sue the Company for damages. Carson appeared for the Company.

IN the present case Carson had seen at once that the prosecution at the Old Bailey had failed because of the complexity of the evidence. His favourite method was to seize on one point in a case and to hammer that point, and win on it. This method, of course, depended upon his insight into his cases and the powerful personality which enabled him to force his way along. Solicitors who worried, and insisted upon all sorts of points being put were politely put in their places.

Carson concentrated on one item in the collector's accounts.

'In January 1894 you had collected £94.'

'Yes.'

'In March 1894 you had accounted for £24.'

After hesitation, 'Yes.'

Carson leaned forward, stuck out his chin, and shot out the question 'Wha-a-t became of the £70?'

The large florid man hesitated, looked round, shuffled about the witness box, and seemed to deflate before our eyes.

'Did ye put ut in yer pohkut?' demanded Carson.

The large man made feeble protestations, but it was obvious he had no answer.

Carson looked at the judge, drew himself up to his impressive height, and swivelled round to the jury. One glance at them sufficed. They were looking down their noses in a way juries have when they have found out a man's shame and do not care to look at him too long.

Carson sat down. The case was over.

67

The case of Wilde v. Queensberry was, on the face of it, an action for criminal libel by Oscar Wilde against the Marquess of Queensberry for stating that Wilde 'posed as a Somdomite' (sic). In fact it developed in a very different way. The defence was based on 'justification' and 'the public interest'; and this meant, in effect, that Carson (acting for Queensberry), had to prove that Wilde did *indulge in unnatural practices. After two days of general, and not entirely effective questioning on the degeneracy of Wilde's published work, Carson came to the heart of the matter.*

NAME after name was mentioned, Sir Edward Clarke [counsel for Wilde] looked nervously at a letter of one of these people which Carson was handling. Surely it was hardly possible that Carson could be calling these young men to admit terrible charges against themselves. He said really his Lordship had better see a very ordinary, respectful letter which Wilde had himself produced from one of the persons named.

'Never mind that,' said Carson grimly. 'The young man himself will be in the box and the jury will see what he is like.'

A whisper of excitement went round the court. So Carson had the evidence to prove his allegations after all.

Name after name was mentioned: throughout this terrible ordeal Wilde had behaved with quiet dignity and restraint. No matter how wounding had been Carson's suggestions, this arrogant man had never faltered. His evidence of the days before had not been forgotten. The Press had been generous in praising his fine work. There was much that seemed fine about the man himself under this severe cross-examination by his own contemporary at college. If the case was not exactly the butterfly on the wheel, it seemed at any rate to be the man of genius on the rack; would the inexorable lawyer never leave the poet alone?

Wilde had never faltered up till now. Carson mentioned the name of a young servant at Oxford almost casually.

'Did you ever kiss him?' asked Carson with sudden emphasis.

Wilde made a gesture of disgust. 'He was a particularly plain boy. He was unfortunately very ugly. I pitied him for it.'

It was a deadly question and a fatal reply. That one question told the jury more than all the previous two days of questioning. Carson had almost finished his cross-examination, and this question had been a mere bow drawn at a venture. Both witness and counsel knew the truth was out. The former struggled to escape, but Carson would not let him pass from it. He fastened onto Wilde's answer like a hawk.

Why had he given that reason? Why? Why? Wilde strove to explain. Several of his answers began inarticulately: some were broken off unfinished: all were excited and indignant. But Carson was relentless. Why had he mentioned the boy's ugliness? Wilde was almost in tears now, on the point of a breakdown. Finally he pulled himself together and gave the reason 'You stung me by your insolence, sir. You are trying to unnerve me', he cried out pitifully. This was a very different Oscar Wilde from the man of the previous two days.

For he was broken.

68

The narrator of this and the following anecdote is Edward Abinger

ONE morning Carson came to my room at the Metropole (where, as I have already mentioned, a number of well-known lawyers used to stay) and asked me if I would do him a service.

'I had two hundred and fifty pounds in bank-notes', he said, 'which I left on the mantelpiece in my dressing-room to go to my bath. When I came back they had gone. I want you, like a good fellow, to go and stop the numbers (which he gave me) at the Casino, at the Railway Station, and at Smith's the bankers.'

I did so and paid the cabman a louis.

I did not see Carson until lunch-time, when I found him at Ciro's. I was about to ask him whether he had any news of his £250 when Lady Carson held up a warning finger and I desisted. After lunch I asked her her reason for stopping me speaking to her husband on the subject. She said: 'Ned afterwards found them in the pocket of his pyjamas!'

About twenty-five years afterwards I met Carson (he was then living in Thanet) in the train going up to town. He seemed depressed. His usual sparkling conversation was missing, and I asked him what was the matter.

'I am suffering from neurasthenia', he told me. I could not make him laugh, but determined to do so. So I said to him suddenly: 'Carson, you owe me a louis.'

'Do I?' replied Carson. 'What for?'

'Why,' said I, 'don't you remember you sent me rushing all round Monte Carlo stopping the numbers of your bank-notes which you afterwards found in the trousers of your pyjamas? I engaged a fiacre to go round to the various places and paid a louis. I will thank you for it!'

Carson became gravely reflective for a few moments and said: 'May I ask you how long ago this was?'

'Oh, many years ago', I replied.

'How many?' said he.

'Over twenty years.'

'Shure, then,' said Carson, 'I plead the Statute of Limitations.'

69

In due course Carson became Solicitor-General. He told me one day that he thought this was partly due to the fact that he had quite early on his arrival in England been invited to a reception at Lord Londonderry's, where the Prime Minister, then Lord Salisbury, was present. He told me that his noble host's major-domo had come to him and said: 'His lordship has directed me to tell you to go and talk to the Prime Minister.'

He conversed with the Prime Minister for some twenty minutes, no doubt displaying his fascinating native wit, quick powers of repartee, delightful mannerisms and stories. The next day Carson met Lord Londonderry at the Carlton Club. The noble lord asked him what right he had to monopolise the Prime Minister for twenty minutes.

'Shure,' said Carson, 'your own major-domo told me to.'

'I think not,' said Lord Londonderry, 'but I will enquire.'

The following day they met again at the Carlton Club, and the noble lord said to Carson: 'I owe you an apology, because I have now ascertained that although I had requested my major-domo to tell Lord Castlereagh to go and talk to the Prime Minister, he, by mistake, came to you!'

Of such is the Kingdom of Heaven!

JAMES COOLIDGE CARTER (1827–1908)

American Lawyer

70

MR CARTER was one of the Counsel for the United States in the celebrated Bering Sea Arbitration. Throughout the hearings he exhibited little preference for teamwork. He was assigned—or perhaps it would be more proper to say he assigned himself to make the opening argument. He said he would make only a 'reasonably full presentation' of the case; though as a matter of fact his address lasted for eight days during which much of his *ex-cathedra* manner was manifested.

The great barrister Sir Charles Russell, afterwards Lord Chief Justice, made the opening argument for England. His opening words were, 'I have listened with great interest to our friend Mr Carter. He has carried us far into the vague domain of natural law. In reply I can only remind him of the experience of a young barrister who, asserting the relevancy of a certain proposition of law was confronted by the following comment of his Lordship, "Where did you get that from, Sir?" The young man said, "That is a settled principle of the Law taken from the great book of Nature." His Lordship said "What page, and what edition, if you please?" So I say to Mr Carter with reference to his argument of the last eight days, "What page and what edition, if you please?" '

Mr Carter was perceptibly annoyed and after the argument, with flushed face he burst into the conference room where his associates were assembled with 'Did you hear what that —— said about me today?' The reader must himself fill in the space.

SAMUEL CARTER (*fl.* 1847–67)

MP for Tavistock

71

HE had, in truth, the bitterest of tongues, and always seemed to glory in the unconventional violence of his language. Even the judges fought shy of an encounter with so doughty and implacable an opponent. 'Mr

Carter, you are wasting the time of the court!' said Blackburn, J., once to him at Bodmin. 'Time of the court!' retorted the truculent veteran, glaring fiercely at the Bench. 'Your Lordship means—your Lordship's dinner!' The judge threw up his hands in despair—one could almost hear him appealing to Heaven—and Carter continued his harangue. It is really difficult to see what more the judge could have done. To have committed the offender, or to have adjourned the court, would have been only a temporary expedient, and something worse would inevitably have followed on the next day. Besides, it was undeniably true that it was nearly seven o'clock. At any rate, Carter proceeded with his speech in triumph, and finally crowned his iniquities by obtaining for his client a most unrighteous acquittal. The same redoubtable advocate was on another occasion defending a man at the assizes on a charge of obtaining money by false pretences. 'False pretences!' said Carter, with fine scorn. 'Why, we all make them every day! barristers and solicitors and judges—the whole lot of us. Talk of the purity of the judicial ermine!' Here he pointed derisively at the learned judge who sat cowering on the Bench. 'Why, it's only rabbit-skin!' Shouts of laughter greeted this irreverent statement, which indeed I suspect to be literally true.

[*The young John Coleridge, later Lord Chief Justice, said in a letter to his father in 1852, 'Carter adds seriously to the length of proceedings. A larceny of potatoes took very near five hours to try, the other day, from his defending it.'*]

SIR JAMES DALE CASSELS (1877–1972)

72

Cassels had defended Thorne who was charged with the murder of Elsie Cameron. Many lawyers and doctors thought at the time, and still think, that he was wrongly convicted, in over-reliance on the testimony of Sir Bernard Spilsbury.

THE jury found Thorne guilty. He heard their verdict stoically. Indeed, it seemed as if it would be the judge , not Thorne, who would break down, for Mr Justice Finlay's voice began to falter as he pronounced his first death sentence. Thorne was still calm and collected as he waited in the cells below Lewes's small, grey-stone courthouse for the police van that was to convey him to Wandsworth Prison. He asked for pencil and paper and sat down, and wrote to Cassels, thanking him for the fight he had put up for his life.

Thorne's composure was not a façade. He had been perhaps even more calm and collected than Cassels who spent the half hour that the jury was out walking up and down the corridor smoking his pipe. Cassels learned later that a senior prison official had been with Thorne during that half hour.

How had Thorne behaved? the official was asked. 'Extremely well', he replied. 'Thorne was full of life, full of conversation and explained to me the superiority of the Buff Orpington hen over the Plymouth Rock.'

The fight was not yet over, for Thorne appealed, asking that the verdict be set aside because the weight of the evidence was against it and because the judge had misdirected the jury. He also asked for a special medical commissioner to be appointed, under the terms of the 1907 Criminal Appeal Act, to resolve the conflict of expert medical evidence. He was confident that he would be set free and even discussed whether he should go out through the front door to receive an ovation or slip away quickly through a side door.

But the Appeal Judges rejected his plea and refused to appoint a special medical commissioner. The downfall of his hopes smashed Thorne's composure, and as he was taken back down the prisoners' corridor his voice rang out again and again in despair, 'It isn't fair. I didn't do it.'

He faced death, however, with equanimity. He had not said goodbye, he wrote to his father after his last visit, because he knew they would meet again, for 'if there is a hell there is more surely a heaven'. He added , 'It is most wonderful the strength and comfort I am experiencing now as a result of praying and trusting.'

Patrick Mahon may have play-acted on the threshold of eternity in an effort to save his life, but there are few who can doubt that Thorne was sincere when he wrote that last letter.

He was executed on April 22nd, 1925. It would have been Elsie Cameron's twenty-seventh birthday.

73

MOTHERS-IN-LAW were frequently the third person in some marriage problems and Cassels believed that they should know their place—and most often their place was not in the home of their newly married son or daughter. When mothers-in-law were in a home a tiff could easily become a quarrel and 'making-up' so much more difficult.

To thirty-three-year-old Robert Dixon, who set fire to a pile of wood shavings in the centre of his flat in Woodgrange Avenue, Ealing, Cassels said, 'You're old enough to know that the way to get rid of a mother-in-law is to turn her out, not smoke her out.' He bound him over to keep the peace for twelve months.

When a couple stayed in the home of a mother-in-law it was even more likely there would be the trouble. Cambridge schoolmaster Ronald Hook returned from two and a half years' war service in the Middle East to discover that his wife had moved in with her mother and her sister. 'A very formidable female formation', commented Cassels when giving his decision on the wife's petition for divorce on the grounds of her husband's cruelty.

Mr Hook did not insist, as he had a right, Cassels went on, that his wife should leave and come with him. He took the easier course and stayed. Within eight days his wife declared, 'I loathe him.' Within nine days she had consulted a solicitor, and before a month was up the three women had got rid of him by dumping his pyjamas and shaving-kit on the doorstep.

Cassels dismissed the wife's petition. 'It hasn't yet been held that if a husband happens to be rude to his wife's mother that's a cause for dissolving the marriage', he declared.

74

'Ronald' is Cassels' solicitor son.

WHILE Ronald had been a pupil with a famous firm of solicitors he attended the conferences when the progress of the various cases in which they were engaged was reviewed. He returned home one day to tell his father of a discussion during that morning's conference.

'We need a rude man for this one', said the clerk in charge of the common law side of the business while detailing the various things that had been done in regard to one case.

'We've chosen Sir Patrick Hastings', he added.

'Excellent', said the senior partner.

One of the tribulations of a solicitor's life, however, is the barrister who has to return a brief at the last moment because another case has lasted longer than he thought it would, and so the senior partner continued, 'You'll need a second string to your bow. Who have you got in mind?'

'Cassels', replied the common law clerk.

'Excellent', said the senior partner again.

The story amused Cassels tremendously. 'Now you know your father is the second rudest man in the Temple', he told Ronald.

75

AT the annual dinner of a Welsh Society in London, where he was the principal guest, Cassels declared that Judges had to be extremely careful when they were on circuit in Wales. He recalled the case of the judge who was asked by the defendant's counsel if he could say a few words in Welsh to the jury at the end of his closing speech. The judge, anxious that there should be no appearance of even a linguistic bias, agreed. The counsel spoke for only twenty seconds in Welsh, thanked the judge and sat down. The judge summed up and the weight of the evidence was dead against the prisoner but, without leaving the jury box, the jury found him not guilty. Back in his private room the judge puzzled for some minutes, then sent for a court attendant and asked him what the defence counsel had said. It was, 'The prosecutor is English, the prosecution counsel is English, the judge is English. But the prisoner is Welsh, I'm Welsh, and you're Welsh. Do your duty.'

THE HON. SIR EDWARD CHANDOS-LEIGH (1832–1915)

King's Counsel

76

Rough days in Birmingham.

I WAS retained to defend an old man for murder at the Warwick Assizes before Lord Justice Thesiger. The prisoner had been in the employ of Lloyd's Bank. His duty was to collect small debts. Doubtless he was no favourite in the worst parts of Birmingham. When I read my brief I came to the conclusion that my defence was manslaughter and might even go as far as justifiable homicide. The victim was a young girl of a low type, and it seemed that on a Saturday night in one of the worst parts of Birmingham—Heneage Street—the prisoner was hustled by a noisy crowd; thereupon the allegation was that he took out his knife and stabbed the girl in the breast. Her dying deposition was to that effect. The witnesses then asserted that he threw away his knife; but the police searched where the knife was alleged to have been thrown away and never could find it.

At this point my junior received a scrap of paper to this effect. 'I am in terror of my life. The prisoner never stabbed the woman. I was looking out of my window. One of the witnesses for the prosecution made a stab at him and by mistake stabbed the woman instead.'

I thereupon applied that the woman who wrote this note should be brought into court under police protection; she gave this evidence and was not shaken under cross-examination. My next step was to call a very eminent detective-sergeant of police, one Seal, who had been in the Birmingham police force for nearly forty years. I asked him if he knew the old man.

He said, 'Yes, in former days he was in our police force.'

'What is his character?'

'A very inoffensive, harmless creature', replied Seal.

'Now,' I said, 'Seal, would *you* walk down Heneage Street at eleven o'clock at night without the company of another policeman?' His answer was, 'Certainly not.'

'Why do you say that?'

'Because at that time of night it would be infested with Corkery's gang.'

'You have seen the witnesses who have been called today. Do any of them belong to Corkery's gang?'

'A good many do', he replied.

'Then', I said, 'who is Corkery?'

Seal replied, 'Mr Leigh, you ought to know. You defended Corkery for the murder of a policeman in Heneage Street and he was hanged.'

I thereupon sat down and asked the jury if, after this evidence, they cared for me to address them. After some hesitation the jury said they did not—which meant a verdict of not guilty.

I was walking down to Westminster some time afterwards and met Lord Justice Thesiger. He said to me, 'I shall never forget that trial, Chandos. How pale you were!'

I answered, 'Not half so pale as you were!'

SIR ERNEST BRUCE CHARLES (1871–1950)

77

Dr Halliday Sutherland, who tells the story, was being sued for libel on account of comments he made in his book about Dr Marie Stopes and her theories on birth control.

EVERY afternoon when the Court rose our counsel met in conference at the office of Sir Charles Russell, our solicitor, to discuss the evidence from day to day. At these conferences I was present. I had the whole case from A to Z in my mind, and if any of the leaders made the slightest unimportant slip I immediately corrected him. This annoyed Sir Charles Russell, and on the eve of my going into the witness box there was nearly a scene. It was Mr Charles KC who made peace.

'Leave him to me, Russell. If you get him upset tonight there's no saying what will happen tomorrow morning'; and to me: 'Now Doctor Sutherland, I know exactly what the trouble is. You're attempting to carry every detail of this case in your head. You forget that you're not defending yourself, and that I'm here to defend you. Why not leave it to me? Very well. Tomorrow I'll be able to help you in your evidence-in-chief and in re-examination, but I can do nothing when Pat Hastings is cross-examining, and whatever he says, don't lose your temper.'

'Ha!' said Sir Charles, clenching his fists, 'if he dares to lose his temper, he'll never enter this office again.'

'One other thing,' added Mr Charles, 'there was once a young man who wished to be ordained in a Primitive Methodist Church, but failed on many occasions to pass the examination in scripture. At last the examiners took pity on him, and decided to ask him a very simple question. When the young man appeared they said, "Now, Mr Jones. Can you tell us, Who was Saul?"

' "He was a King of Israel."

' "Excellent, Mr Jones. Thank you, that is all."

'At the door of the examination room Mr Jones turned and said, "His other name was Paul."

'Moral, never vouchsafe what you're not asked.'

JOSEPH HODGES CHOATE (1832–1917)

American Lawyer

78

BEFORE Courts he was perfectly independent, never obsequious, and there were times when he could remind judges that they were not above criticism. This independent spirit was illustrated on an occasion when he indulged in a comment before a judge who, becoming incensed, said from the Bench, 'If you say that again I shall commit you for contempt.' Upon which Mr Choate replied 'I have said it once. It is therefore unnecessary to say it again.'

On another occasion a judge allowed his attention to be diverted from an argument that Choate was making. Mr Choate stopped, and the judge looked up in surprise. Mr Choate addressed him: 'Your Honor, I have just forty minutes in which to make my final argument. I shall need not only every second of my time to do it justice, but I shall also need your undivided attention.'

'And you shall have it', the judge courteously replied.

79

AN action was brought by a distinguished architect Richard M. Hunt to recover from Mrs Paran Stevens fees earned in the construction of a hotel.

Mrs Stevens's origin was humble and her husband, in earlier years, had been proprietor of the Fifth Avenue Hotel. In after years, having acquired wealth, she posed as a prominent society leader.

No more cutting remark was ever made in a court-room than Choate's utterance in summing up, as he sketched, in eloquent terms, Mrs Stevens's rise from humble conditions to social prominence, concluding: 'And, at last, the arm of Royalty was bent to receive her gloved hand. And, how, gentlemen of the jury, did she reach this imposing eminence?' (An impressive pause.) 'Upon a mountain of un-paid bills.'

RUFUS CHOATE (1799–1859)

American Lawyer

80

HIS accounts of who owed him and how much, he must have chiefly carried in his head. His office partner could not have known them, and there was not seen there any book of original entries. One of his old students of former years, however, used to come in to us and tell the story of a traditionary set of books which Choate commenced with the intention of keeping them by double entry. So, on the first day he opened them, he had occasion to send out for a gallon of oil—it was before gas days; accordingly he entered in the bulky volume, 'Office debtor one gallon of oil', so much. A few days after, an old client came in and asked for his bill. Choate told him he really was very busy and if he'd call again in a week he'd have it ready for him. In a week he called again and demanded his bill. 'O, yes,' said Choate, 'I really—you must pardon me,—but I've not had time to draw it off; but you may pay whatever you think right.' This did not suit the client, who said he'd call once more; and so he did a fortnight after. This time Choate was in despair. 'Well there,' said he, 'take the Books and just draw off a minute of the account yourself.' The worthy man took the Book, despairing of any other information, opened it, and there at the top of the page, in staring characters of vast size to make them legible, was the entry, 'Office debtor one gallon of oil',—standing as lonely on the page as its author in his life. He never asked for his bill again, but paid what he thought fair, and asked for a receipt in full, which Mr Choate promised to have ready for him, next time he called.

81

The narrator is Edward Parker

IT was a singular paradox that his scale of charges in his mind, his ideal of a professional account, was rather high than low. If he named any charge, he named a pretty fair, though never extravagant one. I think as he grew older, he was somewhat talked into putting a proper estimate on his own services. Sometimes his want of discrimination in this regard operated hardly.

One day, a poor fellow from Charlestown, who had a snug trifle accumulated by daily labor, came in with his Tax Bill, 'to consult Rufus Choate' as to whether it was rightly levied or not. Choate turned him over to me, at the same time vaguely indicating the principle and authority which must be looked up. Occupied in trying a large case, he did not come back to the office for two or three days. Meantime, I had brooded laboriously over this almost the first professional matter ever entrusted to my hands. The 'opinion of Rufus Choate' was elaborately prepared by me, and when at last he did come back to his office, I presented it to him for his scrutiny and signature. He looked it over, and scrawled his autograph at the bottom. 'What shall I tell him is your charge, Mr Choate', was my next inquiry. 'Well,' said he, 'I think we ought to have $25 for that, don't you?' Of course I acquiesced, though it seemed to me then a fabulous sum on so trifling a matter, for the whole Tax Bill was only $10. When the client came, I presented him the 'opinion', and told him the charge. 'Twenty-five dollars!', he exclaimed, 'why I think that's too much! I haven't got but $15 ready money in the world.' Of course he was let off on payment of the $15, but not without much misgiving on my part, lest the master of the office would be displeased. When Mr C. came in, I hastened to tell him that I had given the Charlestown man his opinion; and then I waited anxiously for what, in my ignorance of him, I supposed would be his inevitable question, 'Did you give him the Bill?' But no such question came, or would have come to the day of judgment. So, in a moment, during which the whole subject seemed to pass away from his mind, I ventured timidly to suggest that I couldn't collect the Bill. 'Ah!' was the only reply. 'No,' said I, 'the man said he hadn't got but $15 in the world, and he paid that.' 'Oh,' said Choate, with a rich smile mantling over the lower part of his face, 'you took all he had, did you? Well, I've nothing to say to that—that's strictly professional.'

82

IF he was interrupted in an unimportant point—unless he thought it would distract the jury from attending—he would make much parade of acquiescence. 'I desire to be fair. I believe you are right, sir—quite right. I submit to my Brother's correction', he would say. To be corrected, never troubled him merely because he was proud of being right. He was troubled only because he was afraid of its effect on the jury. He was far, very far above the small vanity so conspicuous in his great rival for American forensic fame, William Pinkney. Pinkney would swell and domineer if he was disputed as to an authority which he quoted in respect merely to its position on the page. He said to the Supreme Court of the United States on such an occasion, 'Send for the book; and now, before I open it, I will tell your Honors not only the exact authority, but the exact place of the authority as it stands on the page, and the page itself with equal exactness.' The book was brought, and it was all even so. But Choate never would have done this. He would have preferred even to appear in the wrong about an unimportant point, if only to save a brother lawyer from mortification. He had hardly any pride of opinion. He cared for victory, not opinion.

But I have seen him, when attention was diverted from the current of his talk to the Jury by an unseemly disturbance of an outsider, very savage and stormy. Once, in a great Patent case, the opposite party to the suit, an elderly man, sat some little distance behind him with his counsel. During all Choate's unusually brilliant argument—for the achievements of great inventors always inspired him—this adverse gentleman kept up a constant but subdued derisive chuckle; and at length, at a grand burst of enthusiasm and spasm of gesture in the advocate, he laughed quite audibly. Choate was just sweeping his doubled fist about his head, his eyes glancing flame, and screaming out, 'I tell you, Gentlemen of the Jury, as the great Italian artist said, glowing with the consciousness of commensurate genius, "We also are painters" '—when he heard the laugh. Hardly finishing his sentence, he turned directly upon the chuckling enemy with both fists clenched and as much fight in his face as was ever seen there; he advanced upon him two or three steps scowling terribly, till he fairly quailed under the broadside of his fierce glance. 'Sir', said he, in slow, measured words, every syllable of which was a volley, 'let him laugh who wins.'

83

FEW, comparatively, of his legal arguments have been preserved. He was extremely reluctant to aid in their preservation. In the great Quaker case, in the fall of 1852, which filled Boston with broad brims and brown coats, one of the Quaker gentlemen was resolved to get Choate's speech and keep it. He employed a phonographist, and when the report was ready, he took it to Mr Choate, and telling him how important the Quaker fraternity considered it, asked him to correct it as he would wish it to stand. Choate took it. When the gentleman called for it he had, *of course accidentally*, mislaid it. The applicant knew his man, and drawing forth another copy, 'Well, then, Mr Choate,' said he, 'I have two more, and if you don't correct it, it shall be published just as it is.' Mr Choate looked up laughingly. 'You have indeed! Why, then, let me have it and I will correct it.' He took it, and when the Quaker called again, he *had not lost it*. Thus it was that that report happens to be now in existence.

84

AT the time of Mr Choate's great speech for Buchanan, in Lowell, there was a sudden settling of the floor of the hall where they were. A Lowell gentleman, well known as a lawyer and politician, volunteered to go out and examine the supports underneath. He did so; and, to his horror, found them in such a state that if there should be the least rush of the audience they would inevitably give way, the roof and floor would go together, and all be involved in a common ruin. With great fortitude he went quietly back; and, to prove *there was no danger*, walked the whole length of the crowded hall up to the platform where the speakers and president were.

As he passed, Mr Choate leaned down and asked him if he found danger. The gentleman, keeping his face perfectly unmoved, so as not to frighten others, whispered into Choate's ear with characteristic abruptness, 'If I can't get this crowd out quietly, we shall all be in h–ll in five minutes.' As might have been expected from so blunt and terrible a communication, Mr Choate's face instantly became ashy pale; but he controlled himself and sat perfectly steady.

The gentleman mounted the stage, assured the people there was no real danger; but to guard against the mere possibility of danger, he advised them to withdraw *quietly*, very quietly, to the open air, where the speech would go on. In five minutes the hall was clear.

Dreadful as had been the moment's shock to his feelings, Mr Choate's humour did not even then desert him; for as he stepped from the hall himself, he said to his friend who had made the announcement to him, 'And did you *really* think, my friend, just now, that I *was bound for the same place with you?*'

85

IT was in the mixture of the grave with the gay thoughts that his humor often glanced the brightest. About the time that Minot's ledge Lighthouse, in Boston harbor, was carried away in a terrific winter storm which lasted a day or two, he happened into the Athenaeum Library; and gazing from its ample windows on the broad open space before him, flanked by Park street church; 'Well, Mr F—,' said he to the librarian, with a smile, 'after all this blast, there stands my old friend, Park street steeple, unshaken, intact, unterrified.' Then his glance fell on the wide intervening graveyard, his smiling eyes dropped, his voice sank into a rich, mellow, mournful tone, and with much emotion, he continued, 'Ah, Mr F—, the dead are safest, midst all this hurly-burly!' The thoughts and the manner in the two clauses of this sentence would have brought inevitably to any one present, first a smile, then a tear.

SIR EDWARD GEORGE CLARKE (1841–1931)

Queen's Counsel, Solicitor-General

86

Three members of the Staunton family, together with a young relative, Alice Rhodes, were accused of killing Harriet—by starving her. The trial was before Mr Justice Hawkins. He sentenced all four to death.

I THOUGHT then [says Sir Edward Clarke], and I think now, writing forty years later, that only a wicked judge would have sent out a jury at nearly ten o'clock at night, exhausted by sitting in one place for nearly eleven hours listening to a single voice, to consider a verdict involving the lives of four human beings, whose cases required separate consideration, and against whom popular feeling had been so strongly excited.

The misconduct of the Judge saved the prisoners' lives. The indignant protests of Charles Reade and Clement Scott might not have availed, but when the *Lancet* made a strong appeal to the medical profession and four hundred doctors, with Sir William Jenner at their head, signed a declaration that the symptoms were not symptoms of starvation but were the usual and characteristic symptoms of certain forms of disease of the brain, it became clear that the death penalty could not be inflicted.

Sir Henry Hawkins continued his career of public disservice. There were other cases, notably the *Hansard Union Case*, the *Portsea Island Building Society Case* and the *Salisbury Baby Case*, in which his worst characteristics were shown. When he retired in 1898 I wrote to Sir Richard Webster, the Attorney-General, to say that if it were proposed to follow, in his case, the mischievous practice which had sprung up of having a public leave-taking at which the Attorney-General made a complimentary speech attributing all sorts of virtue to the retiring judge, I should make a public protest.

The protest did not become necessary, for Sir Henry went one afternoon to the Middle Temple Hall, and there took leave of his friends.

[*It is interesting to compare this with the account of the same episode given by Hawkins in his own autobiography:*

Thereupon, without any needless ceremony of leave-taking, at the close of the year 1898 I took my leave of the Bench with a simple bow. Silently, but with real affection for all I was leaving behind me, I quitted my occupation on the Bench. I considered this to be a far more dignified way of making my exit than greeting face to face the whole of the Court and its practitioners and officers and leaving it to the eloquent and friendly speech of the Attorney-General to flatter me far beyond my deserts in the customary farewell address which he would have offered to me. I thought it better to rely upon the expressions and conduct of those who knew me well, and to feel that they appreciated the discharge of the many and arduous duties which I had been called on to perform.]

87

Sir William Gordon Cumming was accused of cheating at a very select card party at Tranby Croft at which the Prince of Wales was present.

ON the day of the trial the court had a strange appearance. Lord Coleridge had appropriated half of the public gallery, and had given tickets to his friends. The Prince of Wales occupied a chair at the front of the Bench between the Judge and the witness box. Lady Coleridge sat close to her husband's right hand, and had the duty of checking the occasional inclination to sleep which had by this time become noticeable. The rest of the Bench was filled with a group of fashionable ladies, in front of whom, and one might fitly say 'close to the footlights' one of the judge's daughters-in-law sat with a sketch-book on her knee, busily sketching the actors in the drama. Lord Coleridge's angry exclamation, when the crowded court cheered my closing speech, 'Silence, this is not a theatre,' sounded, in the circumstances, rather amusing.

JOHN CLERK (LORD ELDIN) (1757–1832)

88

ELDIN lavished his affection on cats, as his predecessor, Gardenstone, had lavished his on pigs. Instead of a wife to grace his hearth, he preferred half a dozen cats. When a client called, Clerk would generally be found seated in his study with one of his feline companions perched upon his shoulder. But cats are not always the best friends when business has to be done and Eldin's affection for these animals was often sorely strained. One day, when pondering a law paper, a feline disturbance occurred at the back of his house, and so great was the commotion that he threw up the window, and tried *viva voce* to quell the row. This method, however, completely failed, but before resorting to stronger measures, Eldin magnanimously resolved to give the cats the full benefit of law as provided in the case of rebellious human beings. His lordship then slowly and solemnly read the Riot Act. The cats, however, remained obdurate, and it was not until the judge had fired a pistol among them that the animals scampered off.

A. G. CODD (*fl.* 1851–70)

89

THERE was on the South-Eastern Circuit a hard-working barrister by the name of Codd, who had a large family, and was always struggling in his profession. In a Post-Office prosecution tried before Baron Bramwell, I think at Chelmsford Assizes, Codd was defending the prisioner. Among the witnesses was Mr Anthony Trollope, the well-known novelist. He knew nothing about the facts of the particular robbery in question, but having an official position in the Post-Office, he was called to prove the practice in the Post-Office as to the sorting, removing, and otherwise dealing with letters, so that the jury might understand what opportunity the prisioner had had for committing the theft. I need not say that in such cases the witness is as a rule not cross-examined, but makes his statement and leaves the box. Accordingly Mr Anthony Trollope, to whom Bramwell had nodded, was leaving the witness-box, when Codd, who saw an opportunity for making a point, said: 'Stop a moment, Mr Trollope.'

Trollope came back.

'What are you, Mr Trollope?' said Codd.

'I have already told the court that I am a supervisor in the Post-Office.'

'But are you anything else?'

Trollope replied: 'Yes, I am an author.'

'Ah!' said Codd, 'you are an author, are you? What was the last book you wrote?'

Trollope replied: 'Barchester Towers', or whatever it was—the particular book is immaterial.

'Well, then,' said Codd, 'was there a word of truth in that book from beginning to end?'

'I do not understand what you mean,' replied Trollope.

'You can answer a plain question: Was there a word of truth in that book from beginning to end?'

'Well,' said Trollope, 'if you put it in that way, there was not.'

Codd said: 'Thank you, Mr Trollope', and sat down. He called no witnesses, but made a violent speech to the jury, in which he asked them how they could possibly convict the prisoner on the evidence of the principal witness, when the principal witness was a man who was obliged to admit that he had written a book without a word of truth in it. If I remember right, Codd's effort was not successful.

SIR ARTHUR COLEFAX (d. 1936)

90

ON one occasion (when Lord Hanworth, Master of the Rolls, was presiding over the Court of Appeal) a silk who had figured a lot at the Patent Bar in the old days was arguing a case. This was Sir Arthur Colefax—grown very deaf—but still carrying on in spite of his handicap. He had been arguing some very elementary law and Hanworth began to get restive.

'Really, Sir Arthur', he intervened. 'You would think that we know no law at all.'

Sir Arthur, by reason of his infirmity, heard not a word of this; but was determined not to admit it. Drawing himself up, with a bright smile, he looked at the Master of the Rolls and said 'I entirely agree my Lord'. Then, ignoring the gathering frown on Hanworth's face he added, looking round at the silks beside him, 'and my learned friends who are associated with me are of the same opinion'.

This was too much for the long-suffering Master of the Rolls. He dashed down his papers on the Bench in no uncertain manner and Colefax, at last scenting danger, hurried on to another point.

JOHN DUKE COLERIDGE (LORD COLERIDGE) (1820–94)

Lord Chief Justice

91

COLERIDGE must have been one of the most accomplished classicists to have sat on the English Bench. He started early. At the age of eight he asked his father to buy him a new Virgil since his own was so torn he could hardly read it. At ten he could say by heart a thousand lines of Homer.

When Bowen published his translation of the Aeneid he was constantly sent for by Coleridge to hear comments, which were not always favourable. 'He shoots over me every morning as I were a Scotch moor', said Bowen.

92

COLERIDGE once rose to reply to a toast at a Balliol dinner with the immortal words: 'I, my lords and gentlemen, have been asked to respond for Oxford as a whole. And, my lords and gentlemen, what a whole Oxford is.'

SIR ARTHUR JOHN HAMMOND COLLINS (1834–1915)

93

The narrator is J. Alderson Foote

PRISONERS are not always polite. I recollect the case of one man who was tried before the then Recorder of Poole—now Sir Arthur Collins. He was a professional acrobat of great physical strength, who earned part of his living by submitting to be bound with ropes in the street and then bursting his bonds like Samson. For some alleged larceny he was committed to the sessions, and in the meantime he was confined in the local prison at Poole. There was only one elderly man in this establishment to discharge the duties of warder, who was completely terrorized by his formidable guest, and the prisoner eventually came up for trial with two indictments against him for assaulting the gaoler, in addition to the original charge. His main defence was that he had not been properly fed; and he caused to be produced to the court nearly a score of specimens of Irish stew, preserved in large glass jars for the occasion. These he invited the Recorder and myself (as prosecuting counsel) to smell. Collins treated him with the utmost politeness until the jury had convicted him, when he astonished the ruffian by sentencing him to penal servitude for seven years. The prisoner promptly threw a heavy leaden inkstand, which just missed the Recorder's head, and he was then dragged out of the dock by six policemen, declaring in the most frightful language that he would cut out the judicial liver as soon as he was released. Arthur Collins remained on the circuit for six years more, and then applied for and obtained an Indian judgeship—no doubt for the better preservation of the organ indicated. So various are the roads which lead to the judicial Bench.

JOHN SINGLETON COPLEY (LORD LYNDHURST) (1772–1863)

94

JOHN SINGLETON the younger was educated at a large private school at Chiswick kept by the Revd Thomas Horne, father of Sir William Horne who became Attorney General in 1830 and was a good classical scholar but not free from some infirmities of temper. Here he remained until July 1790, when he was entered as a pensioner at Trinity College, Cambridge. Being already destined for the Bar, his father's first choice had fallen on Trinity Hall, which was then the only foundation that professed to instruct students in the Law. But a chance stage-coach acquaintance on the journey from London, Dr Gretton, afterwards Dean of Hereford, persuaded the elder Copley of the transcendent merits of his own college, Trinity, and the die was cast. We are reminded of the budding Freshman who is said to have emerged from Cambridge Station with a query to the nearest cab-driver, 'What is the college the gentlemen usually go to?' To this accident Lord Lyndhurst attributed his whole future career.

95

It was with the acquisition of strictly technical knowledge that Copley was concerned during his sojourn in the chambers of the great practitioner Mr Tidd (immortalised by Uriah Heep). There he acquired the mysterious learning which surrounded the written proceedings in an action at law: the declaration, the plea, the replication, the rejoinder. But he also took a leading part in the famous society which met weekly at Tidd's chambers for the discussion of juridical problems. It consisted of pupils for the time being and any former pupils who chose to attend and the debates were limited to questions of Law. Campbell, later himself a Lord Chancellor, relates that Copley argued most admirably, but that his fault 'which afterwards he corrected', was being too loud and declamatory; and he adds a story of his waxing so long and vehement over the law of libel that the porters and laundresses collected round the window in King's Bench Walk, and finally the Temple fire-engine was sent for. Tidd's pupils do not seem to have suffered from want of the imaginative faculty.

96

Generous to the verge of prodigality, the new chancellor had nothing in common with the illustrious men who have continued habits acquired in poverty and obscurity long after wealth and fame have been reached. And he was one of those who considered that a large official salary entailed corresponding obligations. *Quot homines tot sententiae.* The tenure of the Seals by his predecessor, Lord Eldon, had been marked by a domestic frugality which made the contrast with Lyndhurst's jovial reign all the more conspicuous. 'What would people have said of me', Lord Eldon asked his favourite son, William Henry Scott, 'if I had been seen driving about in a cabriolet?'

'I will tell you what they would have said, dear father', was the answer. 'There goes the greatest lawyer and the worst whip in all England.'

97

Lord Romilly told me today a story of Lord Lyndhurst which he heard from a Registrar of his Court. A counsel addressing Lord Lyndhurst for some time seemed to make little way, and Lyndhurst muttered audibly, 'This man is a fool.' The counsel continued for some time and got into the heart of the matter, upon which Lord Lyndhurst muttered, 'Not so great a fool as I thought.' Toward the close of the address, which was masterly, Lord L. a third time muttered, 'It is I who was the fool.' This was a fine trait in Lyndhurst.

EDWARD WILLIAM COX (1809–79)

Serjeant-at-law

98

MR SERJEANT COX was an amiable, kind hearted, courteous judge but little able to control the turbulent Bar that then practised at Clerkenwell. His court was, at times, a perfect beer-garden. On one occasion, during the trial of a case of larceny of live pigeons, Richard Harris, who defended, purposely opened the hamper and let the birds fly about the Court. After a wild chase, on the part of ushers and police, the pigeons took refuge on the canopy over the judge's seat. Mr Serjeant Cox took it quite as a matter of course, and rather enjoyed the scene. He was very deaf and heard little of the evidence. He summed up from his copy of the depositions and was often interrupted by objections that the witnesses had said something quite different.

In one case, when he came to sum up he was directing the jury that the prisoner, Smallbone, might probably have been at the horse's head when some tea was stolen and must have seen what occurred.

Mr Besley: 'I interfere with you, my Lord and I say you have no right to put the question in that way.'

Mr Serjeant Cox took no notice.

Mr Besley (emphatically): 'I will be heard, my Lord, go on as your Lordship may, you are assuming. . . .'

Mr Serjeant Cox: 'No. I am not. Sit down sir, and understand that I am assuming nothing.'

Mr Besley: 'It is of no use, my Lord. I shall stand here and argue the point, with all respect. It is not competent for your Lordship to assume that which has not been proved in evidence. It has been shown that when the property was stolen, Smallbone was somewhere else, and now you, my Lord, are putting it that he was at the horse's head.'

Mr Serjeant Cox: 'No, no. I am not. I am saying that whoever was at the horse's head must have seen the theft committed.' (To the witness.) 'Now don't you think that anyone standing like Smallbone, at the horse's head would see the theft committed?'

The Witness (carman's boy): 'No, sir. Nobody could see that because there was no one at the horse's head then at all.' (Great laughter.)

The Jury, after some further passages of this kind, acquitted the prisoners.

JOHN D. CRAWFORD (1861–1946)

Judge

99

I CALL to mind a case in which an exhibition of meddling folly occurred. It was a case in which a child had been injured in a street accident; the father or mother—I have forgotten which—brought an action to recover damages for the injury done to the child. In these cases, what are called special damages figure prominently. These are monies which are supposed to have been expended for extra nourishment, or for repairing damaged clothing, or buying new clothes to replace those damaged in the accident. I use the word 'supposed' advisedly.

I had often to criticise these claims severely. They were put in to swell the claim, often with very little justification. In this case I thought the claim in respect of the child's clothing was inflated, and that the parent could have purchased clothing for the child at a less figure—even if new clothes were reasonably necessary.

Somehow or other—I could never understand why—this case was reported in some of the newspapers. Again angry women wrote demanding what I knew of a child's clothing. Some of the inquisitors, I don't remember whether they were connected with the Press or merely one of the meddling fools of whom Solomon has spoken—rang up my house on the telephone. As the telephone instrument is in my wife's room, she answered the call. After stating that I was not at home, the following question was put to her: 'Has Judge Crawford any children of his own?'

Heaven has blessed me with a wife who is wise as well as being beautiful and good. She replied: 'That is a question you must ask Judge Crawford.' It is almost unnecessary to add that the tormentor was silenced.

I had to put up with many letters from indignant females. I am not a cynic, human folly never interested me, still less did the contemplation of it give me pleasure. So I put the letters into the fire or the waste paper basket, whichever happened to be the most convenient receptacle. I wish I had kept them, my readers might then have known something of the minor worries of a County Court Judge.

My comments on girls' clothing, and the money spent on them, seemed to have aroused the attention, if not the indignation, of our fair sisters on the other side of the Atlantic. Someone sent me a page of the *Chicago-American*, which, I gather, is a journal published in Chicago. The following appeared in large type: 'Girls Defend Garb Expenditures.' Below these headlines were photographs of girls exhibiting a considerable amount of stocking. Across each, there were the following insets:

'He's poor Judge.'
'It can't be done.'
'$26? Huh?'

Below each photograph were the girls' opinions of me as a Judge—which, it is needless to say, were not flattering. The *Chicago-American* then continued a paragraph with the striking headlines characteristic of American journalism.

CHEAPER GARB HORRORS!
GIRLS RAP CRITIC

Chicago working girls would like to tell a certain London Judge a few things about shoes and gloves and muskrats and petticoats and things. The Judge is John D. Crawford of the Edmonton County Court.

SIR WILLIAM CHARLES CROCKER (1886–1973)

Solicitor

100

DURING my school holidays father let me spend as long as I liked in his office, which had moved from Borough High Street to the more respectable neighbourhood of Finsbury Pavement, E.C. His Common Law Clerk, Ernest Albert Harris from Walsall, who used double negatives ('No, the Guv'nor's not come back yet') and did his own typing, would at times favour me with some account of the cases on which he was engaged.

On one such vacation visit I attended an interview between Harris and an Italian named Bresci who wished to sue the British Museum for assault and battery. He had been ejected from the Reading Room for spitting in books which preached political views contrary to his own. Harris advised him there was no case. When the Italian muttered that in his own happy country the dispute would have been settled, presto, with the knife, Harris said 'We don't use no knives not here.'

This episode, which made a deep impression upon me (I was then about fifteen) had two sequels.

The first was that, shortly after his abortive call, Bresci sent Harris a news clipping reporting a Grimsby brawl, in which fish-gutting knives had come into play, a note to which the clipping was pinned, read 'Thus parrots talk!!!' The envelope was addressed 'To the Clerk at the writing machine'.

The second sequel was that this unbalanced malcontent went back to Italy and assassinated Umberto I, King of Italy.

101

LAW students in those days came to London from all over England and Wales to the most famous of all Law coaches, Gibson and Weldon. Their services were not open to me. I was not merely an articled clerk, but a solicitor's clerk doing a full-time job. I could not have done it with half my days spent in a Chancery Lane classroom. I had to compromise. There was an elderly and slightly Bohemian crammer, one Montague whose heart-breaking occupation was coaching Gibson and Weldon's 'lame ducks', men who had failed their examinations over and over again. By his own especial magic he would finally drive most of them through. He agreed to give me individual tuition at short notice whenever I could spare an hour to go to him.

Unfortunately I have a freakish memory. It hoards any number of useless facts, but jibs at retaining the uninteresting things that really matter. I could remember neither Montague's mnemonics, of which he had scores, nor their points. The remedy was to invent mnemonics of my own. The toil of doing this left in my mind, long after I had forgotten the mnemonic, the information I wished to have by heart. The only example which survives to me is Dirty Drive, identifying the Highways Act 1835—important then, but now as dead as a fly in amber. I found it impossible to learn by rote *The History of English Law*, narrated so tediously in the preface to the *Commentaries*. Warned by Montague that at least one question would spring from this dry material I tortured *the whole of it* into rhymed couplets.

My brother, Archibald Crocker, Solicitor, knew every line of this pantomime verse and found it most useful. As for me, the labour of turning Stephen's heavy prose into jingling lines, with plausibly musical endings, had done the trick. My odd mind was now stocked (for the necessary few months) with everything the examiners might wish to know on this subject. All that remains to me of the masterpiece itself is the triumphant:

> Hail then the Statute blessed for ever more
> 12 Charles the Second. Chapter 24.

SIR HENRY HONYWOOD CURTIS-BENNETT (1879–1936)

King's Counsel

102

HE became known at the Bar for an audacity which so often proved successful. He regarded no argument as doomed to failure, particularly when he was putting it to a jury or a Bench of magistrates. The manner and the trick became known by an expression that is used today to describe a certain combination of honest bluff, cheek, opportunism and a genius in choosing a phrase and in timing; an action informed with guile yet so ingenuous as to cause a smile. They called it 'Doing a Curtis'. A vague phrase, it is yet perfectly understood by every barrister and solicitor who saw Curtis in action. Curtis used it himself about his own methods, readily admitting that it had 'come off' again. He said it of himself, years later, when he had put on weight, about his cycling days. 'It's difficult to believe, Curtis, that you were ever a champion cyclist', said a friend, surveying his ample girth.

'I'll tell you about that', he said. 'I chose the outside position up on the bank, and when the starter's pistol went off I turned my wheel down the bank and rode across the front of the other competitors, and they never caught me after that. I "did a Curtis" for the first time.'

Originally, the phrase was used to describe his manner when submitting 'No Case' at the end of a prosecution's evidence, with one eye on the jury in the hope that even if the Judge had to hold there was a case in Law, the jury might be so affected by what he said that they would stop the case themselves. But later, 'doing a Curtis' came to mean any typical gesture or move of ingenuous guile.

At the old Bailey, in an important case, the Judge had resumed his seat after the luncheon adjournment before Curtis had returned. A messenger was sent to the Barristers' room to find him. As he came into court, calm and unhurried, he looked at the clock and, instead of the expected humble apology, remarked suavely: 'It is unfortunate, my Lord, that the clocks in this building are not synchronized. If they were, your Lordship would not be kept waiting. . . .'

He readily admitted his own pleasure at the success of 'a Curtis'. Considering a manslaughter case, he shook his head slowly, and when the solicitor expressed surprise, saying he had an excellent case, Curtis explained: 'It's a very good case. But there aren't enough red herrings. You want a lot of red herrings in a manslaughter case. . . .'

And again, in another manslaughter case, when he was replying to several congratulations after an acquittal: 'Yes, I had six hares to start. I started that one first. I saw one juryman fairly leap at it. I knew that one was a safe winner and so I ran it hard the whole way, and didn't start any of the others.'

This was in line with his oft-repeated advice: 'Don't confuse the jury. When you have one good point, run it for all you are worth. Repeat it and din it into them; never let them forget it. You can forget all the other points.'

Sometimes he liked to shock the Court, so that when the jury considered their verdict, they would still be reeling under the surprise of his pleading. Imagine for instance, the feelings of a jury, asked to decide whether a defendant was a knave or a fool, when Curtis stood up and said: 'You may think my client is a fool. I tell you so myself—he *is* a fool! But you can't convict on that, or the Courts would be full!'

He often used to say that his client's case was at its best *before* he went into the witness-box—the tragic Thompson case being the classic example of his client insisting on defying his advice.

But the greatest example of the value of this audacious approach, this courageous, seemingly care-free gesture that was so carefully rehearsed, was during a motor-car accident case which presented a not-unusual complication. A married man and a married woman, both happy in their separate domestic circles, decided to spend a week together. They took every precaution to hide their identity and their escapade from busybodies; alibis were carefully manufactured, telephone calls were arranged to allay suspicion, and they even garaged their cars and hired another vehicle in which to travel to the country hotel. Their plans were perfect in the execution, but on the way back to London they ran into a man and he was killed.

Curtis was briefed by a distracted couple who saw themselves and their families, their married lives and their futures, involved in a terrible scandal as the result of one temporary escapade. More tragic than a verdict of criminal negligence would be the revelation, that would at once follow, that the driver of the car was accompanied by the woman. Their movements would be traced; their escapade would be public property and their two homes would be wrecked. 'I had the devil's own job', said Curtis.

At the inquest, he was able to assure the relatives of the dead man that their claims would be recognised at a figure that was more than generous. He successfully disposed of any suggestion that there should be a prosecution, and he was tying up his brief, sighing with relief, when the police inspector who had charge of the case asked aloud in Court: 'Wasn't there a passenger in the car?'

In another moment success might turn into ruin, if the Coroner or the police suggested that this valuable witness of the accident should give her evidence.

Curtis went on tying up his brief. With an air of supreme unconcern, he said: 'I don't think the passenger can carry the matter any further or assist the Court.'

He had 'done another Curtis'.

103

R. v. Armstrong.

DURING the first week of the trial of Armstrong at Hay, Curtis suggested to Mr Matthews that they should visit the grave of Mrs Armstrong. They went one cold afternoon when the snow was thick on the ground, and Curtis was fortunate in having chosen a moment when he was not pursued by newspaper-men. Mr Matthews stayed in the car while Curtis wandered over to the snow-covered grave; he returned in a few moments white and shaken; and only to a few intimate members of his family did he tell what had happened while he stood in the snow at the graveside.

When he went there, he could see no sign of a living thing. The graveyard was empty and silent. But as he approached and stood near to the grave, he was suddenly confronted by a mongrel dog. The animal stood on the mound of Mrs Armstrong's grave and snarled; Curtis, who knew and loved animals, saw that the animal would prove dangerous if he moved any closer; his hackles were up and he appeared to be really savage; Curtis made a gesture of friendliness, but the mongrel bared his teeth. Curtis knew that he was making much out of an incident, but it struck him as peculiar that he, the defender of the man accused of murdering the woman whose body lay in that grave, should be forcibly kept away. He said nothing to any man at the time; but he asked in the town if the dog had been seen before in the graveyard, and was told that every other visitor had approached the grave without trouble. Nobody knew of such a dog; if Curtis had imagined for a moment, in his over-wrought state of mind, that the animal was the property of Mrs Armstrong, he soon verified that the dead woman had never kept a dog. The mystery remained; he kept the incident to himself until long afterwards.

104

PERHAPS the earliest legal witticism on the subject of fat men, which Sir Henry [Curtis-Bennett] inherited by natural right, was that which concerns the question put by a judge to a barrister (who has taken silk) 'Do you move?' The classic reply from the gargantuan barrister is 'with difficulty, my Lord'. The story had been told as originating from Sir Henry. Probably he would have said it, if it had not been a hoary jest in legal circles since the 20-stone Mr Murphy said it. Curtis, at any rate, never claimed it as his own. He had to find new stories of fat men and give utterances to them as they occurred.

Shortly after Bottomley's release from prison, Curtis was lunching at Romano's in the Strand, when he saw Horatio at another table. When he finished lunch he went over and greeted him. Saying how well he looked Horatio looked him up and down solemnly for a moment or two: 'Yes—it saved my life', he said. 'And it looks as if three years wouldn't do you much harm. . . . '

105

R. v. Mahon.

MAHON and Emily Kaye Low engaged in a violent struggle—again according to Mahon; the strong and well-built girl forced him on to the ground and knocked him unconscious while she herself fell and split her head open against the coal-scuttle. Recovering consciousness, Mahon had found that she was dead. He had rushed out of the bungalow and becoming calmer had realised that he was in a terrible predicament. He had already invited Ethel down to live with him three days later. He might stand accused of murdering Emily at any moment. In a frenzy he dragged the body into a bedroom and locked the door. Nothing must interfere with his plans. Next day he went to London, met Ethel and brought her back to the bungalow. She noticed that there were a number of women's clothes about the room, but Mahon explained this by saying his wife had recently visited him there. He saw the danger of the secret in that room for which he now bought a new Yale lock. Therefore, he sent a telegram to himself and told Ethel that they must return to London as soon as possible. Weighing on his mind was the thought of that body in the bedroom and he went back to the bungalow with a new plan.

Looking around he saw nearby the instruments which would serve him well. With the carving knife and saw he cut the body of Emily Kaye in pieces limb by limb, and thrust the limbs—some into the stove and some into a cauldron of boiling water. There was the head with its long flowing blonde hair. He thrust it into the stove, and as the hair caught alight he watched the features of the face contract into an almost living expression of agony: and at that moment, as he covered his eyes in horror, the heavens opened and over the Crumbles swept a terrifying storm that was preceded by one detonating clap of thunder. Mahon packed the various remaining members of the body into a trunk, into a biscuit tin, and into a hat box and stowed them in the bedroom. The next day he went to London to meet Ethel and escort her back to his bungalow.

On April 28, he packed the knife and several pieces of Emily's blood-stained clothing into a bag, sprinkled them with Sanitas, and left it at Waterloo Station. There was no plan in his mind save to keep away from that house where he would ever be reminded of that last grim scene when the features of his mistress contracted before him. He knew, however, that it would be unsafe to leave the bag in the left-luggage office. On May 2 he returned to Waterloo and produced the cloakroom ticket. As he turned, there was a hand on his shoulder. The police had been too quick for him. The bag was opened in his presence and he was arrested for murder.

They asked him at Scotland Yard how he could account for the grim contents of the bag. 'I am fond of dogs', he said. 'I suppose I have carried some meat for the dogs in it.' But late that night he made a long statement which left little to be discovered. He told his story of those sordid days and nights in the Crumbles bungalow, and left nothing to the imagination. He gave every detail in picturesque language: how he had cut up the body and devoted great attention to the storm which had shaken his courage when he had watched the eyes of Emily Kaye open as the flames devoured her hair.

His solicitors briefed Mr J. D. Cassels, KC, for his defence. Yet it almost happened that Curtis-Bennett was briefed. A young magazine writer had offered to pay for the whole of Mahon's defence, and expressed a desire that it should be in Sir Henry's hands. This proposition, however, came to nothing.

Curtis was briefed for the Crown, and seldom encountered a prisoner for whom he had greater dislike. He could hardly restrain the instinct to show his disgust of this calm, good-looking man who appeared so eager to inspect every gruesome exhibit in the case.

It was noticed when the trial began on July 15, at the Lewes Assizes, that Mahon was looking considerably more healthy than at the police court proceedings shortly before. He seemed sunburnt and fat, although there was a striking contrast in the colour of his hands, which were pale and delicate. As a matter of fact, Mahon had expressed a wish to obtain some chemical tan while in gaol and had actually attempted to give his face an artificial tan with tobacco juice. He had bought a new 9-guinea suit especially for the trial, and his clear-cut handsome features radiated confidence. The trial excited national interest, although few legal niceties were to be debated, and the attention of the public—and of an American Judge who sat beside Mr Justice Avory—was concentrated upon the shocking details of this most callous killing.

Before him, Sir Henry Curtis-Bennett had the knife and saw, together with the keys of the bedroom, and the little coal-scuttle which, according to the prisoner, had caused the death of Emily Kaye. He had also a perfect model of the bungalow, built to scale, the bedroom furnished and the wall-paper identical with that in the house of death. Sir Henry's opening speech was no more than a narrative of the known facts, with the conclusion: 'If these facts are proved it will be my duty to ask you for a verdict that Patrick Mahon is "Guilty" of the murder of Miss Kaye.' As in the Field and Gray trial at the same Court, before the same Judge, with Curtis and Cassels opposed to each other, the illness of a juryman meant five hours' delay, while Curtis restated his case, but by the end of the second day the prosecution was concluded and Sir Bernard Spilsbury had given his opinion that it was impossible for the girl to have died through falling on the coal-scuttle.

On that third day Mr Cassels put his client into the box. He had a pleasant level voice, although his imagination was apt to run away with his tongue, for Mr Justice Avory was frequently obliged to pull him up with the words: 'You are asked what you did, not all this imagination.'

He told his version of the struggle and continued: 'I went into the garden crazy with fear. It dawned on me what a horrible thing it was that she was lying there and dead. The thought that she was dead flooded my mind.' And now, answering Mr Cassel's questions, he came to the details of how he had cut up the body and boiled certain portions, while others he put in the stove. His counsel was perhaps remembering that interview he had had with Mahon in Brixton Prison when Mahon had described his terror at the sudden crash of the storm as Emily Kaye's hair flared up in flames.

'And then you burnt the head', suggested Mr Cassels. Mahon began to reply: 'Yes,' he said, 'I put the head in the stove and when . . .'

Suddenly a clap of thunder shook that Court-room. It had been a sultry day, but the unexpectedness of that terrifying peal was enough to startle every hearer. Mahon realised that the heavens had provided an amazing coincidence, he gripped the edge of the witness-box with white hands and fear blazed from his eyes. Alone in the Court he and Mr Cassels realised the strange and eerie coincidence. It was as if the elements had provided another reminder of that dreadful moment when he had looked into the eyes of his dead victim. It was fortunate that the incident came at the end of the day. Patrick Mahon saw the hand of God in that moment. It was as much as he could do to answer the last formal question of his counsel: 'Did you desire the death of Miss Kaye?'

'Never at any time', came from the trembling lips of a limp and moaning prisoner.

106

MORE than once Curtis was opposed by his son Derek in licensing cases. He usually had a word to say for the opposition that he knew was coming from his 'young and learned friend whose name I seem to recognize'. And in reply to his occasional sarcasm, his son would say: 'My learned friend ought to have known what I was going to say, for I learnt at his knees all that there was to learn for and against licensing. Do not be lured by the art and attractiveness by which out of his sage experience he can present such applications. The way he submits his argument puts you in a sort of anaesthesia for a time—when you come out of it—and I hope you are emerging now—you realize that there is absolutely nothing in it at all.'

107

Advice from Counsel.

IF you are ever stopped by the police don't, for goodness sake, touch the car in any way, or you will be said to be leaning on it for support. Don't sway at all when you are walking, or you will be said to be staggering under the influence of drink. Spring smartly to attention. Stand upright outside the car, and say, 'I am not guilty of whatever you are about to charge me with doing.'

WILLIAM OTTO ADOLPH JULIUS DANCKWERTS (1853–1914)

108

The narrator is J. D. Casswell

WHEN I came down from Oxford, I went straight into a solicitor's office in Essex Street, Strand, where for six months I learned quite a deal of the solicitor's side of the profession and gained some useful insight into the drafting of briefs and instructions to counsel. It was here that I first learnt the value to a barrister of a clear, logical mind going immediately to the kernel of a problem and ignoring all extraneous matters. I had drafted long, detailed instructions for an opinion by William Otto Danckwerts KC on an intricate local government law case and I waited anxiously to receive the document which stated his considered views. I was somewhat disconcerted on the return of the papers to find that his opinion was as follows:

'(1) No
(2) No
D'

109

The narrator is Sir Henry Dickens

THERE is another man who in my time played a great part in the legal world. I allude to Mr Danckwerts, KC. He was generally considered to be one of the best lawyers in the profession whether on or off the Bench. Unfortunately both for himself and the profession, he had a violent and uncontrollable temper, which quite unfitted him for the position of a judge. He and I were on quite good terms and he always called me 'Copperfield'. He could be very outspoken at times. On one occasion he was arguing before Lord Alverstone and two puisne* judges, one of whom was not in Danckwerts' good books; their names I omit for obvious reasons. Lord Alverstone, in the course of the argument, announced that the arrangements for the Courts would make it

* A junior judge. The expression is now obsolete.

impossible for the Court as then constituted to continue the case. 'Unless, therefore, counsel agree to continue the case with two of them, there must be a long adjournment.' To which Danckwerts replied, with marked emphasis, '*Which Two?*'

110

DANCKWERTS was a rotund man, of considerable girth, with a red face, pleasant enough in repose, but liable to assume a truculent expression if he found any obstinate contention, or foolish contumacy towards his expressed opinion. He had no suavity of manner, his voice was aggressive, and his sense of humour limited.

Soon after Lord Alverstone was made Lord Chief Justice, a case was being arranged about Crown Office practice, in which branch of the Law Danckwerts was a zealous expert, and a question arose which sort of writ ought to be issued: *mandamus, quo warranto* or *prohibition*. Lord Alverstone expressed the opinion that something should be done quickly in the matter, as 'all these remedies were much the same thing', and adjourned the matter for the right one to be applied.

Above the din and bustle of the Court, Danckwerts was heard solemnly soliloquizing, in the back row, in slow and measured tones: '*Mandamus*, a writ in the King's name commanding a specified act to be done. *Quo warranto*, a writ against a person or corporation that usurps a franchise. *Prohibition*, a writ to forbid any Court to proceed. And the Lord Chief Justice of England thinks that all these remedies are much the same thing. Oh Lord!'

There were cries of 'Order' by the usher, counsel started a new case hurriedly, and Lord Alverstone gazed at the ceiling.

111

The narrator is Sir Edward Parry

MY master in law, the great Danckwerts, was abominably rude to judges, and many of them feared him. Mr Justice Mathew was not one of these. Once when Danckwerts, who was of huge size, shaped like a tub, and generally reported to be of Boer extraction, was arguing an Admiralty case about a collision in the Ship Canal between a Dutch boat and an English steamer, Mathew with a charming smile, looking curiously at Danckwert's figure, said: 'What is troubling my learned brother and myself, Mr Danckwerts, is that you have not given us the measurement of *your* beam.'

CHARLES JOHN DARLING (LORD DARLING) (1849–1936)

112

CHARLES DARLING was not obsessed with his profession, and was even able to see that there was something humorous about the Law. Many lawyers are keenly aware of the funny things that happen in Court, but very few—and still fewer successful ones—can see anything actually funny about the Law. But Darling did; for he was not only a raconteur, but a humorist.

He had his first brief when devilling for Baron Huddleston. He looked absurdly young, as he conducted his case in the glory of wig and gown for the first time. Frank Lockwood, who was in Court, was so struck with this that he drew a cartoon of Darling as a baby in the arms of Huddleston who was dressed in nurse's costume. He entitled it 'Huddleston's Darling', and circulated it round a delighted Court. Such was Darling's first entry to the practice of Law.

113

KING'S BENCH 4 presented an unusual spectacle when Darling sat to hear the case of *Huntington v. Lewis & Simmons*. There were distinguished counsel such as Sir John Simon, Mr Hemmerde and Mr Douglas Hogg, who were for the plaintiff, and Mr Leslie Scott, who was for the defendant; there was one young counsel whose fame was to lie in another sphere, Mr Philip Guedalla, who held a watching brief for Duveen Brothers. But distinguished counsel were a commonplace of King's Bench 4, as was the tightly wedged throng of spectators. What made the occasion unusual was the large assemblage of Royal Academicians and other distinguished painters and art dealers, who had come to swear either that the picture was or was not by Romney, according to their revelation. Most peculiar of all was the presence of the picture itself decorating the sombre court. It did not decorate it alone for long, for at the luncheon adjournment on the first day Sir John Simon asked Darling's permission to hang four undoubted Romneys, the loan of which the plaintiff's solicitors had procured, adjacent to the disputed picture. Permission was granted—Darling saying, 'You can leave them here permanently, if you like'—and the four Romneys were duly hung framed, surrounding the unframed picture; to anybody with a knowledge of art the result was considerably to overshadow the disputed picture, and it was not without its effect on Darling. From time to time he indicated points under discussion on the canvas. On one occasion, wishing to draw attention to something at the top of the painting he stood on his chair, and pointed with his umbrella. Suddenly the chair gave a lurch in the direction of the picture and for one long moment of suspense it seemed as if Judge and umbrella might be precipitated through the canvas. This would have raised the interesting question: What is the position at law when the subject matter of the action is destroyed by Judicial incidence? The chair righted itself, however; Darling regained his balance; the picture remained unscathed, and the question unanswered.

114

In the year 1904, Mr Justice Darling had a vivid experience in the Courts, though not in connection with a case which he was himself trying. In that year Whitaker Wright, the famous North Country financier—whose rise and fall is perhaps the most dramatic of all that long series of dramas centring round the fallen favourites of fortune who have worn the tinsel crown of unsound financial greatness—was tried on charge of falsifying balance sheets. On the final day of the trial, when the Jury returned, Darling, whose list finished early that day, unrobed, and accompanied Mr Justice Bigham, later Lord Mersey, who was trying the case, to the bench. The Jury found Whitaker Wright guilty, and (as Darling said later) 'I looked at Whitaker Wright as sentence was passed upon him, and saw his hand go in the direction of his pocket. I was horrified. "Good heavens!", I thought, "he has got a gun, and is going to have a shot at Bigham." These people are always too strung-up to aim straight, and he is bound to miss Bigham and hit me. What a way to end my judicial career—shot, and not even in my own Court.'

[*In fact Whitaker Wright was getting out of his pocket the tiny tablet of cyanide of potassium with which he committed suicide a few minutes later.*]

115

WHAT I noticed particularly about Mr Justice Darling was his scrupulous care in avoiding exercising his wit at the expense of a prisoner. There must have been many occasions when he was tempted to take advantage of some maladroit observation by the accused, but fully aware that a retort might add to the difficulties of a man already gravely hampered by his position, he refrained, but if a witness or counsel gave him an opening he took full advantage of it, and took it so skilfully that it could never be said with truth that he lowered the dignity of the Bench.

This may account for the disappointment of a veteran frequenter of penal establishments who, in the course of a career full of vicissitudes, had made the acquaintance of at least a dozen judges, but who somehow managed to avoid or miss Mr Justice Darling. When, therefore, he was informed that in consequence of his latest failure to outwit the police he would have to occupy the dock at the Old Bailey about the time that famous judge was expected to preside in the principal court the old lag was not displeased. On the contrary, he expressed his delight at the opportunity of playing the leading part in a trial which would be rendered memorable by the witty sallies of his Lordship and to which the papers would give considerable space. For your habitual criminal loves his Press notices, and his vanity at times can reach the Himalayan heights of a young actor playing his first speaking part. 'Can I do anything for you, Jim?' a pale-faced woman huskily asked her husband after he had been sentenced to seven years' penal servitude. 'Yes,' he answered promptly, not at all perturbed by his punishment, 'keep the newspaper reports until I come out.'

Our friend the burglar was duly ushered into the dock and with a grin already sketched out on his face he waited for the cascade of wit, but all he got from his Lordship was a cold stare, two admonitions to hold his tongue and a curt dismissal to penal servitude. There was no wit and no approach to it either—only an economy of time and speech which was chilling in its effect. The experience undoubtedly added to the bitterness of conviction, and the judge lost one adherent, if not admirer, when he failed to make humour out of an exceedingly commonplace trial.

That unlucky adventurer in search of mirth would have envied a brother of the same craft who was also tried by Mr Justice Darling. The magistrate who had committed the prisoner for trial had done so because he was of opinion that the accused was an habitual criminal and deserved a greater sentence than he could give him. At the Old Bailey, therefore, it was the special endeavour of counsel for the defence to prove that the prisoner had lapsed into crime by a combination of chance and misfortune, while, on the other hand, counsel for the prosecution laboured to convince the jury that the anaemic little cockney in the dock resembled one of those quaintly unlifelike characters of that special brand of fiction labelled 'thriller', in that he was for all his physical disadvantages an exceptionally dangerous character with a perverted brain. The result of the forensic debate was a matter of momentous consequence to the prisoner, for if the prosecution won all its points it meant penal servitude instead of hard labour, and when the jury with significant rapidity returned a verdict of guilty it seemed that all was lost. However, the prisoner made one last effort to save himself.

'I don't see why they call me a professional crook', he protested, keeping back his tears with difficulty. 'I've only done two jobs, and each time I've been nabbed.'

'It has never been suggested', said Mr Justice Darling, in his suavest tone, 'that you have been successful in your profession.'

116

Mr Pemberton Billing was being tried for criminal libel in connection with a statement he had made about a 'Black Book' alleged to be in the possession of the Germans and to contain the names of 47,000 *prominent Englishmen and women of unnatural sexual tendencies being used by the Germans to influence such persons in the conduct of war. A Mrs Villiers Stuart was called to give evidence.*

MRS VILLIERS STUART gave evidence that she had been shown the book by two politicians, since killed in action. This vivacious lady had not been long in the box before a brisk squall arose. Mr Pemberton Billing asked if her life had ever been threatened in connection with the case. On her replying that it had, Mr Hume-Williams asked what that had to do with the case?

'Nothing at all', said Darling. 'You know, Mr Billing, I have allowed you a good deal of latitude but you are putting questions which I should not allow any counsel to come near putting. If you undertake to conduct your own case, you ought to know you must conduct it according to the ordinary rules of evidence.'

'I know nothing about evidence,' replied the unabashed Accused, 'and I know nothing about Law.'

'You cannot come into this Court and say that because you do not know the Law you may put any questions you like. I only tell you that any questions which are not such as can be put according to the rules of evidence I am bound to reject and I ask you to try and put only such questions.'

Here the Accused made a dramatic interruption.

'Is Mr Justice Darling's name in that book?' he shouted to the witness.

Above the gasp of astonishment which followed this question Mrs Villiers Stuart was heard to reply: 'It is, and that book can be produced.'

Darling remained unmoved. 'It can be produced?' he asked simply.

'It can be produced,' shrieked the witness in reply, 'it will have to be produced from Germany, it can be and it shall be. Mr Justice Darling, we have got to win this war, and while you sit there we will never win it. My men are fighting, other people's men are fighting.'

Mr Pemberton Billing recalled the excited lady to the matter in hand. 'Is Mrs Asquith's name in the book?'

'It is in the book.'

'Is Mr Asquith's name in the book?'

'It is.'

'Is Lord Haldane's name in the book?'

'It is in the book.'

Here Darling intervened. 'Leave the box', he said sternly.

'You daren't hear me', screamed the witness.

Darling turned to Mr Pemberton Billing. 'Have you finished asking questions of that kind?'

'I have not.'

'Then if you are going on asking questions of that character I tell you to sit down because they cannot be asked. I have not the least objection to your having asked the one regarding myself, but I am determined to protect other people who are absent. Now will you resume your examination please and remember what I have said.'

[*The rebuke did not deter Mr Billing who went on to win an acquittal.*]

117

A favourable view.

THE present generation can remember Lord Darling only as a great judge, but those of us who are in their sixties still have some recollections of the dapper little barrister whose appointment to the Bench in 1897 infuriated a small coterie of noisy nonentities into a ridiculous demonstration of disapproval. When the name of the new judge was announced these malcontents lashed themselves into a jealous fury which made them a derision for the amused contemplation of the level-headed.

The agitation, so obviously absurd and uncalled-for, became a joke, and the joke turned to sheer farce when the profession learned that the *fons et origo* of the agitation was Charles Gill. He did his best to incite not only the profession but the public against the elevation of Charles Darling to the Bench, but anticipating defeat, and naturally desirous of avoiding its consequences, he kept well in the background. But it was from Gill that the newspaper paragraphs emanated which stated that there would be a great meeting of barristers to protest against the latest judicial appointment.

Of course, this was sheer bluff. To begin with, no barrister of any standing or decency would have thought of publicly challenging the right of the Lord Chancellor to exercise his own discretion in filling vacancies among the judges, and even if he had a poorer opinion of the chosen one's merits than the occupant of the Woolsack had, he would not be such a fool as to think of airing those views in public. Gill and his friends, conscious of their own insignificance and lack of influence, tried to persuade a couple of Queen's Counsel to join in a written protest to the Chancellor, but the attempt failed, and the agitators, frightened by their own impotence, subsided into an inarticulate obscurity.

As so often happens the agitation did Mr Justice Darling a good turn in the long run for it brought to his Court a crowd of capable critics, chiefly members of the Bar who wished to see for themselves if the confident prediction of Gill and Co. that he would prove a ghastly failure would be justified. When, therefore, they saw how he handled his first case they admitted that he possessed in the very highest degree the judicial manner, for they discovered in the course of an afternoon a fact which the public took a little longer to appreciate, that Lord Halsbury had made no mistake. And for nearly thirty years afterwards Mr Justice Darling continued to prove that the great Tory Chancellor had backed the right horse.

118

An alternative view.

ANOTHER real shocker was Mr Justice Darling. He would lie back in his chair staring at the ceiling with the back of his head cupped in his hands paying scant attention to any argument but waiting until some footling little joke occurred to his mind. When this happened he would make the joke, the court would echo for about thirty seconds with sycophantic laughter, and then the process would start all over again.

During the hearing before the Judicial Committee of *Hoystead v. Commissioner of Taxation* Lord Darling (as he had by then become) interrupted the closely-woven argument of Clauson KC, which he did not appear to have been following, with a quotation from *The Compleat Angler*. Lord Sumner was so cross that he threw the book he was looking at onto the floor.

CLARENCE SEWARD DARROW (1857–1938)

American Lawyer

119

Darrow cross-examining William Jennings Bryan in the Scopes (Evolution) case.

Darrow: 'Do you think the earth was made in six days?'

'Not six days of twenty-four hours.'

'Doesn't the Bible say so?'

'No, sir.'

'Mr Bryan, do you believe that the first woman was Eve?'

'Yes.'

'Do you believe she was literally made out of Adam's rib?'

'I do.'

'Did you ever discover where Cain got his wife?'

'No, sir; I leave the agnostics to hunt for her.'

'Do you think the sun was made on the fourth day?'

'Yes.'

'And they had evening and morning without the sun?'

'I am simply saying it is a period.'

'The creation might have been going on for a long time?'

'It might have continued for millions of years.'

'Yes. All right.' Darrow waited a long moment to allow this admission to sink in. 'Do you believe the story of the temptation of Eve by the serpent?', he continued.

'I will believe just what the Bible says. Read the Bible and I will answer.'

'All right, I will do that. "And I will put enmity between thee and the woman and between thy seed and her seed; it shall bruise thy head and thou shalt bruise his heel. Unto the woman he said, 'I will greatly multiply thy sorrow and thy conception; in sorrow thou shalt bring forth children; and thy desire shall be to thy husband, and he shall rule over thee.' " That is right, is it?'

'I accept it as it is.'

' "And God said to the serpent, 'Because thou hast done this, thou art cursed above all cattle and above every beast of the field; upon thy belly shalt thou go and dust shalt thou eat all the days of thy life.' " Do you think that is why the serpent is compelled to crawl upon its belly?'

'I believe that.'

'Have you any idea how the snake went before that time?'

'No, sir.'

'Do you know whether he walked on his tail or not?'

'No, sir, I have no way to know.'

This answer brought a laugh, one with more derision than humour in it, the kind Bryan did not like. He flushed, turned to the judge, 'Your honour, I think I can shorten this testimony. The only purpose Mr Darrow has is to slur at the Bible, but I will answer his questions, I shall answer them at once. I want the world to know that this man, who does not believe in a God, is trying to use a court in Tennessee . . . '

'I object to your statement', exploded Darrow. 'I am examining you on your fool ideas that no intelligent Christian on earth believes.'

120

AFTER he had been indicted in Los Angeles he was greatly depressed by a report that the District Attorney was going to introduce into evidence a photograph purported to have been taken of him as he left the house of a beautiful Pasadena widow at dawn. One of his friends consoled him by saying, 'Don't be downcast, Clarence; your enemies will believe the worst of you, even without photographs, and your friends will know it is a fake. They will know that if you spent the night in the home of a beautiful widow you wouldn't leave at dawn. You would stay for breakfast.'

121

The narrator is Irving Stone

HE always gave me the impression of being slow and deliberate in his movements, relaxed and loose jointed. In this respect and in others, he was as Lincoln had been represented. I do not recall ever having seen him hurry. In conversation especially he was slow of speech and he chuckled with a rapid shrug of the shoulders when something struck him funny. His eyes were bluish grey, kindly and deep-set under a large and very full brow, and I noticed that his ears joined the skin under the jawbones, without the usual lobes. His hands were long, and the fingers were long and tapered. His skin was pale and frequently sallow and muddy. I heard him say in connection with dental work, which he found had to be done, 'Hell, nature never did know how to make teeth.' He had Lincoln's simplicity of statement and argument, his directness and sincerity, and he did not hesitate to present ideas that were unpopular.

He was like Lincoln, too, in that he told simple jokes about serious matters in an attempt to lessen the emotional intensity and bring people to a friendly, even fraternal, basis. His devoted secretary, Ethel Maclaskey, whom he hired because he first met her at a free thinkers' meeting and said, 'We free thinkers and liberals should patronize each other', observes of him, 'I believe he went on the assumption we were all like children, and jokes made a common meeting ground.' In the case of Mrs Simpson, who had shot and killed her husband while he was on the witness-stand attempting to secure a surreptitious divorce, the judge who had been sitting in the divorce proceedings was subpoenaed to come into court and testify against the woman. The state's attorney insisted upon calling the testifying judge 'Your Honour', to which Darrow objected, saying that no man should be called Your Honour except when he was on the bench.

'Why, Clarence,' exclaimed the Dutch judge presiding over the murder hearings, 'I took you to lunch once, and you called me "Your Honour." '

'Sure,' replied Darrow, 'but that was because you paid the bill.'

122

GEORGE LEISURE, a young lawyer whom Darrow took with him to Honolulu on this case, gives a picture of Darrow's superb technique and power under the glare of the international spotlight. 'I was interested in learning how a great lawyer put the steelwork together for making a moving address to a jury', says Leisure. 'I had made the opening argument to the jury on behalf of the defence and Mr Darrow was to follow the next day with the closing argument for the defence. Up to the night before he was to argue the case I had observed that he had not made a single mark on a paper in preparation for his summation. Consequently, when some of the navy men wanted to call on us that night, I was about to tell them on the telephone that Mr Darrow would be busy. He interrupted me, however, and told me to tell them to come on over. We sat and talked until ten o'clock that evening, when Mr Darrow went to bed.

'The court convenes in Honolulu at eight-thirty, so as soon as we had breakfast we went directly to the courtroom. Mr Darrow had made no visible preparation up to that time. During the five minutes we were in the courtroom before the judge called the court to order, Mr Darrow made four or five little half-line notes on a yellow pad, which he proceeded to throw down and leave behind him on the desk when the court said, "Very well, you may proceed now, Mr Darrow."

'He walked out in front of the jury and delivered his address until the noon hour. At lunch-time, as soon as we had taken lunch, I walked out of his room, assuming that he would want to jot down a few thoughts for the remainder of his summation. When I called for him again in ten minutes I found him asleep. We proceeded immediately to the courtroom, where he continued his summation all afternoon without reference to any notes and without the help of any memoranda of any kind.

'In only one recorded instance did he lose patience with a judge. Darrow was concentrating on his defence when the judge rather suddenly interrupted the proceedings to ask how long he had practised law in Chicago.

' "Twenty-one years, Your Honour", replied Darrow. "How long have you practised?"

' "Twenty-eight years, Mr Darrow", replied the judge.

'After a lapse of a minute or two Darrow turned to the court: "Now that we have both acquired additional knowledge, may we proceed with the case?" '

123

DARROW evolved a formula for jury picking that has served succeeding generations of lawyers. 'Never take a German; they are bullheaded. Rarely take a Swede; they are stubborn. Always take an Irishman or a Jew; they are the easiest to move to emotional sympathy. Old men are generally more charitable and kindly disposed than young men; they have seen more of the world and understand it.'

[*Compare this with Samuel Leibowitz's discussion of the same problem.*]

HORACE DAVEY (LORD DAVEY) (1833–1907)

124

SIR HORACE DAVEY (later Lord Davey) did not trouble the House of Commons much, for he experienced great difficulty in securing a seat. He wooed constituency after constituency in vain. As an orator he was uninspiring. 'You should try a bit of repartee sometimes Sir 'Orace', said one of his many election agents after a stormy public meeting. The poor candidate agreed. 'Tell me,' he added sadly, 'what ought I to say if somebody calls out, "Speak up, you old toad?" '

WILLIAM DAVY (d. 1780)

Serjeant-at-Law

125

SERJEANT DAVY, many of my readers may remember as a limb of the law famous for brow-beating witnesses. He had been originally a druggist at Exeter, where he failed, and the perplexed state of his affairs requiring some legal knowledge, by his own personal investigation and study he attained such dexterity, and discovered so much relish for the law and its mysteries, that he was soon after called to the Bar.

At an assize in the West of England many years after he had occasion to examine an old woman, in a cause where her memory and faculties of recollection were highly serviceable to her friend, but very much against the Serjeant's client. The cause was going against him and he was nettled.

'I can remember . . . ', said the old woman. 'Remember!', interrupted Davy, 'why I suppose you remember everything for and nothing against a friend who pays you so generously.'

'I have no reason to complain of my memory', she said. 'for I can remember, though it is, God help me, two and twenty years ago, that you yourself were a broken druggist at Exeter.'

The Serjeant sat down.

SIR GEORGE DENMAN (1819–96)

126

The narrator is Charles Mathews

IN Mr Russell's young days in silk, when the late Mr Justice Denman was going the Northern Circuit, just before the rising of the Court, on a warm summer afternoon, some very high words were flung from the Bar to the Bench in a tone and with a vehemence which caused the learned judge to say that he would not trust himself to reprove them in his then condition of sorrow and resentment, but would take the night to consider what he ought to do, and when they met again the next morning he would announce his determination. In considerable commotion the Court broke up, and on the following day it was crowded in anticipation of 'a scene', an anticipation somewhat encouraged by Mr Justice Denman's entry into Court with if possible more than ordinary solemnity, and on taking his seat, commencing the business of the day by saying: 'Mr Russell, since the Court adjourned last evening I have had the advantage of considering with my brother judge the painful incident . . . ' Upon which Russell quickly broke in with, 'My Lord, I beg you will not say a word more upon the subject; for I can honestly assure you that I have entirely and for ever dismissed it from my memory'—a turning of the tables which provoked a roar of laughter in the Court that even the learned judge himself could not but join in it.

ALFRED THOMPSON DENNING (LORD DENNING) (1899–)

Master of the Rolls

127

I WAS instructed by the Attorney General to defend a young sailor who was charged with murder. I went to see him the night before in the cells at Winchester. There he was, dirty and unkempt. I asked him what his defence was. He said the girl had slapped his face. He put his hands round her throat, and she died. Was there any defence? Not much of a defence of provocation so as to reduce it from murder to manslaughter.

But I thought I would put it to the Jury. I told the young man to clean himself up before the next day. There he was, as smart and nice a young sailor as you ever did see. The Judge was Mr Justice Charles. He ran dead against my client. I put him into the box and asked him: 'Did you have your ship torpedoed under you three times?' The Judge boomed out: 'Many a sailor has had his ship torpedoed under him and he doesn't go and strangle a woman.' Next, when I was going to put my defence of provocation to the Jury, the Judge said he wasn't going to put it. There was not sufficient provocation here to reduce it to manslaughter. Was I, as Counsel, to put it? I did. It is the duty of Counsel to put every legitimate defence. The Judge did as he said he would. He told the Jury that there was no defence of provocation here. That was virtually a direction to find him guilty of murder.

Well, it was a Hampshire Jury, and I am a Hampshire man. The Jury found him guilty of 'manslaughter only'. The Judge turned to the Jury and said 'Get out of the box. You've been false to your oaths. You're not fit to be here.' He was not the first judge to find out that if he goes too far one way the jury will go the other way.

128

I LUNCHED daily in the Middle Temple Hall. Often at the same table as Theobald Mathew, the best of raconteurs. He could make lightning sketches. He wrote the humorous classic *Forensic Fables*. In one of them he portrayed—with some exaggeration—a contest in which I was opposed to Martin O'Connor, who had a big running-down practice. Mathew entitled it 'The Double First and the Old Hand'. (I was the Double First and Martin O'Connor was the Old Hand.)

A Double First, whose epigrams were Quoted in Every Common-Room of the University, became Weary of Tuition and went to the Bar. His Friends were Satisfied that he was Bound to become, in the Near Future either Prime Minister or Lord Chancellor. They Doubted, however, whether Either of these Jobs Afforded Sufficient Scope for his Splendid Abilities. Shortly after his Call, a Near Relative provided him with a Brief. He was to Appear for a Public Authority which Owned a Tram-Car. The Plaintiff was a Young Lady who had Sustained Injuries while being carried Thereon from her Place of Residence to her Place of Business. Her Story was that the Conductor, without Any or Alternatively Sufficient Warning, had Rung the Bell whilst she was Stepping off the Vehicle, and that by Reason of his Said Negligence she had Fallen Heavily in the Road, Abraded her Shinbone and Suffered from Shock and Other Discomforts. Her Claim (including Extra Nourishment and Various Items of Special Damage) Totalled £583 4*s*. 9*d*.

The Double First had Little Doubt that the Claim was Grossly Exaggerated if not Actually Dishonest. He was Confident of Victory. When he got into Court the Double First found himself opposed by an Old Hand of Unrivalled Experience in that Class of Action. He Looked Harmless Enough and the Double First Felt no Alarm. But Strange Things Soon Happened. The Old Hand conducted the Case for the Plaintiff in a Manner which Shocked the Double First Exceedingly. After the Jury had been Sworn he informed his Solicitor in a Whisper which could be heard in the Central Hall that he would not Settle for less than Five Hundred and he Asked the Double First in Stentorian Tones with Reference to the Plan whether he would Agree (i) The

Exact Spot where the Pool of Blood was found and (ii) the Precise Locality where the Conductor had Admitted to the Policeman that he had Done the Same Thing on Another Occasion. When the Double First Cross-Examined the Plaintiff, the Old Hand asked the Judge to Protect his Client from Insult; and when he Addressed the Jury the Old Hand repeatedly Begged that he would not Deliberately Misrepresent the Evidence. The Double First struggled against these Tactics in Vain. In his Final Speech, the Old Hand Reminded the Jury of the Possibility that Tetanus or Paralysis might Hereafter Supervene and the Certainty that a Disfigured Tibia would seriously Impair the Plaintiff's Matrimonial Prospects. Apart from his Successful Application for a Stay of execution on the Ground that the Damages (£1,000) were Excessive, the Double First had a Disastrous Day.

Moral: Despise not your Enemy

129

DR ALAN BARTHOLOMEW recounts an appeal he heard before Lord Justice Denning at the Assize Court in England. Denning was hearing a plea on behalf of a man charged with an act of bestiality with a duck. For the Defence was called a guttural-voiced Viennese psychiatrist whose evidence went, as all psychiatrists' evidence goes, something like this:

'I have known the prisoner, My Lord, for a long time and for many years he has been a patient of mine, but now he is responding to treatment, and is showing a marked improvement.'

His Lordship said, 'By "showing a marked improvement", Doctor, are you suggesting that he is about to graduate up through the animal and bird kingdom until he gets to little boys and girls.'

'Oh no, my Lord,' said the psychiatrist, 'he'll always stick to ducks.'

SIR HENRY FIELDING DICKENS (1849–1933)

130

The narrator is Lord Simon

I WAS once a guest on a yacht with others years ago. Henry Dickens was also a guest, and I slept in a bunk in the same cabin that he had.

Although there was no greater lover than myself of Charles Dickens, I never could sum up courage to refer to his father at all.

The yacht en route went to Dieppe, and we all sent cards to a distinguished Count and Countess. In due course we received an invitation to dinner at the château there. We tossed up whether we should go in blue or in evening dress. The toss decided we should go in blue. When we arrived at the château we were greeted by the Count, who was in evening clothes. He asked us to excuse him for a moment and reappeared in complete blue yachting suit!

We were introduced to the Countess, and Dickens, being the most distinguished guest, was given the place next to her. We were waited upon by men-servants who wore white kid gloves, and were treated to a most sumptuous repast, during the course of which the Countess, to my intense surprise, said: 'Mon cher Monsieur Dickens, dîtes moi quelque chose de l'infortune Oscar?'

I looked at Dickens—his face betrayed such an extraordinary air of consternation and surprise, becoming quite scarlet, that I nearly exploded with laughter. He made no reply.

Later, the Countess said to me in French: 'What was the matter with Monsieur Dickens? Why was he so surprised? Why did he not answer my question?'

'Madame la Comtesse,' I said, 'the question you put to him is not a topic of conversation discussed in England in the presence of ladies.'

'Bah!', replied the Countess. 'You English, you are dreadful hypocrites. You are all courtesy and politeness in the presence of the ladies, but when, according to your customs, the ladies retire and the gentlemen remain to drink port wine, I have been told the conversation est effrayant!'

When we took our leave the Countess said to Dickens: 'Mon cher Monsieur Dickens, when you come to Paris with Madame Dickens I hope you will do me the honour of coming to see me at my hotel in the Champs-Elysées.'

Dickens turned to me a moment or two afterwards and said: 'God forbid! What a dreadful woman!'

131

AT one time, when I was leader of the circuit, a question of great nicety arose, upon which there was found to be a very great difference of opinion: the question being one as to the eligibility of a 'coloured' man for election to the mess—or rather, I should say, as to the 'desirability' of electing such persons as members of the mess. There was an Indian who offered himself as a candidate for the election which was to take place at Lewes Assizes. He was a Parsee, a type of Indian who has always showed loyalty to the British Crown; he was of good parentage; a perfect gentleman both in look and manner, and one against whom nothing detrimental could, by any possibility, be said except that he was 'coloured'. Hearing that there was to be a strong opposition to his election on this ground I, with a few others like Mr English, Harrison, Fred Low (afterwards Mr Justice Low) went down to Lewes specially to vote in his favour. In a private club I can understand that such a feeling of opposition might arise, but the result of his not being a member of the mess was a matter which directly interfered with his prospects of work, for the reason that in the Hall of the Bar Circuit Inn there was always to be found a printed list of the Bar who were on the circuit prepared to take briefs. But in this man's case, if he was not a member of the mess, his name would be absent from this list, and his presence absolutely ignored.

The election came on in due course, when in spite of the efforts of myself and those who thought with me, he was black-balled. It struck me, however, that this was far too large a question to be decided on a ballot of a few members of the Bar who happened to be at Lewes at the time, so I exercised the right that I had as Leader, to call a meeting of the whole circuit in London to consider the question. We had a large gathering present at the meeting, when the pros and cons were discussed; but I was startled and, may I add, somewhat disgusted, to hear one member of the Bar give as his reasons for objecting to the candidate's admission that 'we had won India by the sword and it should be made clear that we intended to keep it by the sword!' However, even in the face of such an inconsequent and dangerous form of argument as this, the Parsee was rejected by five votes. Thus the matter ended so far as the circuit was concerned. But the question arose in a far more direct and convincing form, when the same gentleman was black-balled for the Bar mess at the Central Criminal Court. In this case there was a direct injury done to the candidate. At the CCC the members of the Bar attending the Sessions at the Old Bailey were entitled in rotation to what is called 'soup', that is small briefs for the prosecution in cases which had not been taken up by the Treasury. In practice, these briefs had always been distributed among members of the Bar mess only, as distinguished from the members of the Barristers who practised at these courts. In this particular case therefore his omission from the Bar mess had in effect deprived him of his undoubted right to 'soup' as a member of the Bar. This, I thought, was a real injustice, so I took up the cudgels in his favour and put the matter before the Attorney-General (F. E. Smith, as he then was). After considering the matter, he appointed Mr Rigby Smith, KC (now the Judge), to look into the question. Upon the enquiry which followed, I attended on behalf of the Parsee, as a friend, of course, and, in consequence of a report made by Mr Swift, the Attorney-General advised the proper officials at the Central Criminal Court that they were not justified in withholding these briefs from him so long as he remained a member of that Bar.

132

IT was at Westminster that I had a little brush with Chief Baron Kelly. He was somewhat stilted in his formal way of speaking. He went by the name of Apple-Pip Kelly, a nickname which came to him in consequence of a defence of his in a poisoning case. He was well on in years and became very sleepy after lunch.

I was arguing a case of what we lawyers call 'estoppel', which, broadly speaking, means that a man is debarred from setting up a case which is totally opposed to his own words and actions, with a view to get some advantage to himself. The defendant, it appeared, had written a letter in which a certain state of facts was set out as being the truth but which turned out to be false, and had handed it to a third person to show to another that he might act on it, which the other person did to his detriment. In the course of the case I put my argument this way: 'My lords, if a man chooses to put a weapon of this kind into another man's hands . . . ' 'Stop, Mr Dickens; stop a minute. I have heard of no weapon in this case.' 'It was a metaphor, my Lord.' 'Mr Dickens,' said Kelly very slowly and solemnly, 'a celebrated member of your family was very skilful in metaphor; but I do not think it will assist us in a court of law.'

There is another case in which my parentage was alluded to by that very great and lovable old judge, Baron Bramwell. When addressing counsel Bramwell had a peculiar habit of pointing his forefinger at him to emphasise what he was saying. In course of time I got used to that forefinger and began to think something must be wrong if I did not see it wagging at me in the usual way. On the occasion to which I am referring, much later in time, I was arguing a case in the Old Chancery Court of Appeal before James, LJ, Bramwell, LJ and Bagallay, LJ, a weighty tribunal in more senses than one, for they were all three big and heavy men. The question I was arguing was a point of great practical importance at the time, namely, as to whether a man who has lost his money through a crime of another could sue him at common law before putting the criminal law in motion against him. My leader, Mr De Gex, an old bankruptcy lawyer, had left the case for me to argue. My wife had come into court to hear the argument, and, being somewhat alarmed at the manner in which the Court fired questions at me, she had told the children when she got home how the judges had been 'sitting upon their papa'—a heavy physical load for me to bear! This opened up a new sort of game in which the children sat upon one of their number, the game being called 'The judges sitting on papa.'

JACOB McGAVOCK DICKINSON (1851–1928)

American Lawyer: afterwards Secretary of War

133

Dickinson opens the case for the United States in the Alaska Arbitration Case. He was himself a veteran of the Civil War.

I WOULD not have anyone suppose that I would rashly choose to enter upon such an undertaking. It is a responsibility which has been forced upon me by the necessities of the occasion. So far from feeling any sense of confidence, I am in a position to sympathize very deeply with the feelings of the Confederate soldier who, when the battle line was sweeping forward in the last fearful charge at Chickamauga, and a rabbit jumped up and ran through to the rear cried out 'Run, cotton-tail, run. If I did not have any more character at stake than you, I would have run, too'

DONAHUE (Contemporary)

American Judge

134

The narrator is Samuel P. Sears of the Boston Bar

WE have a judge in Boston who is indeed brilliant, but a character. A jury case was being tried before him, a personal injury case, and the jury sent a note to him with a question asking if, even if there was not any liability, they could still give the plaintiff some money.

Donahue sent for the jury. He said to them, 'I have your written question, and I assume from the question that you have found there is no liability.'

The foreman said, 'That is so, Your Honour.' He said, 'All right, sign this slip then.'

After they had signed the slip, which directed a verdict for the defendant, he said, 'I will now answer your question. You may retire to the jury room and pass round the hat.'

HERBERT DU PARCQ (LORD DU PARCQ) (1880–1949)

135

MR JUSTICE SWIFT was invited to the Bar mess at Exeter when he was on circuit. Du Parcq, as senior silk that night, presided and had the duty of saying the two-word grace: 'Benedictus benedicat', before dinner. 'Benedicto benedicatur', after.

'My dear Parcq,' said the judge, 'do you think the Almighty will be very angry with me if I don't stand up while you say grace?'

'Oh, no, Judge, I don't think so', was the reply, 'he'll just think you don't understand Latin.'

SIR PETER HENRY EDLIN (1819–1903)

136

The narrator is Bowen-Rowlands

NOW leaving the Old Bailey, the Sessions House at Clerkenwell gloomily invites us, with Sir Peter Edlin in one court and Mr Loveland-Loveland (q.v.) in the other. Sir Peter was an extraordinary figure of a man and he was also particular in his ways. He interrupted Counsel continually: the regular practitioners in his court understood that he meant to be Counsel for the Crown, Counsel for the Defence and Judge as well; others who knew him less well did not understand this. I remember defending a man before him in his inconvenient court. The Counsel's benches were perched up aloft and the Judge's Bench was even higher up fronting them. It was a court hard to hear in and hard to speak in. I could make no headway at all. At last I said that, as I was not permitted to speak without Sir Peter's interruptions, and his parrot-like cry of 'Am I master in my own court or not?', I would sit down.

To my surprise instead of asking me to go on, he said 'very well' and began his charge to the jury. If I remember rightly he got my man off.

137

Hicks' Hall. The Court opens.

THE daily opening of the court lost a display that used irreverently to be called the 'Punch and Judy show'. Before Mr Edlin appeared on the Bench door the gaunt usher, officially styled the Beadle, but popularly known as 'the bus-horse', wearing a panelled velvet gown thrust into the doorway the silver-crowned Mace—a weapon some six feet long—and his own remarkable head, adorned with big cocked hat worn with the points sideways, and cried 'Silence!' As he withdrew there appeared the bent, diminutive figure and shrivelled face of the Assistant judge.

138

The narrator is Sir Travers Humphreys

Hicks' Hall. The Court in action.

WHEN I first saw Sir Peter at work, he seemed to be rather a figure of fun. He was short and fat, with the oldest and dirtiest wig I should think ever seen on the Judicial Bench. He had the habit of putting out his hand and uttering the one word 'Pray', which was very disconcerting, and a positively alarming method of clearing his throat which may have been due to a desire to expectorate but which appeared in most cases to be a mere indication of his disagreement with the proposition last put before him. Upon any application for the fixture or postponement of a case, or upon the mere mention that there was any case other than the one being tried, or upon occasion even without such an excuse, he would interrupt the business of the Court in order to air his grievances upon the subject of the vast amount of work which he had to get through. The beginning was always the same: 'We sit here *de die in diem*. Up to the present we have not been called upon to sit on Sundays, but it will come. We work early and late, but it is impossible to cope with the amount of work put upon us', and so on with the result and, as many thought, with the object of wasting as much time as possible. If no applications were made and those present in Court did not include anyone who in the opinion of the learned Judge would be likely to champion his cause in the County Council, then the peculiarities of the building would afford an excuse for a little grumbling.

The London Sessions sat in two buildings. Cases arising in any part of London north of the Thames were tried in the old Building formerly occupied by the Middlesex Quarter Sessions, just off the Farringdon Road on an island site. The building was originally known as Hicks' Hall, and the curious may still be able to observe that the milestones on the Great North Road are marked with the distance in miles to Hicks' Hall. The cases arising on the south side of the Thames were tried at the building in Newington Causeway, formerly devoted to the Surrey Sessions. They were small in number in comparison with those tried at the North London Sessions, as they came to be called.

Hicks' Hall was a nearly circular building, and the first Court, presided over by the Chairman, was semi-circular in shape and was provided with a number of doors opening on to the Bench from a corridor. Those doors were a perpetual source of irritation to Sir Peter, whose seat was in the centre of the semi-circle. In addition there were two doors opening on to the Hall through which the public entered the Court, a door at one end of the Bench leading to the Barristers' robing room, and of course a door leading to the cells from the dock. The Magistrates came and went through their doors into the corridor—the barristers naturally were always moving up and down the staircase from their door to the well of the Court, the public, the police and the witnesses again were on the move to and from the Hall, and I suppose the resultant noise and draughts were apt to be trying to an irritable old gentleman. To poor Sir Peter they were maddening, or appeared so. He used to declare, 'There are eleven doors opening into this Court, and they are opening and shutting all day long—it is impossible to hear anything—Pray, Pray, Mr Besley, I cannot continue with this noise, I shall adjourn—it is not fair upon the Jury (he pronounced the word 'Jeeury')—I must protect the Jury' (who as a rule were not in the least discomposed) and off he would go.

As may well be imagined, the learned Chairman was by no means popular with the Bar. He had his friends and supporters in or out of the London County Council, but for the most part those who appeared before him were profoundly indifferent to his demands for an increase of salary, an increase which I am satisfied would have been granted almost as a matter of course if Sir Peter had not been so unwise as to show, as he did, his dislike of the new type of elected County Councillor who had usurped, as he considered, the place of the old Justice of the Peace who with all his faults was generally a gentleman and a man of breeding and education. His own sense of grievance made him, so it appeared, regardless of the feelings or interest of others. It has always been said that one of the advantages of our system of appointing Judges of all sorts from the ranks of the Bar is that the Bench and the Bar will work together with mutual respect, each performing his allotted task but giving such assistance as may be possible to the other. It is the belief of all judges and barristers that the system works well, but it cannot be said to have functioned harmoniously at the North London Sessions, '*consule* Edlin'.

The Bar and solicitors could get no assistance in fixing their cases, and when the case had been called on the proceedings were liable to constant interruptions from the Bench. At the same time I doubt if we juniors took the matter very seriously, but looking back, as I was able to after a few years, with the added experience of how a Court of Justice should be conducted, derived from attendance at the Central Criminal

Court, I realized how shocked some of the more educated spectators may well have been. Some members of the Bar showed an almost complete lack of respect for the Bench. An actual example occurs to me which may illustrate the state of affairs which existed, though I appreciate that it is impossible to convey by the mere written word the pandemonium which prevailed during the scene I have attempted to describe; a scene which was repeated at least two or three times at every Session, that is roughly every fortnight.

Some of the stations on the Metropolitan Railway in the days of steam trains were filled with sulphurous fumes, badly lighted and very crowded. This applied particularly to Baker Street, Portland Road and Gower Street stations. The carriage doors were so constructed that if left open by the occupants, as they generally were, they could be shut from outside by being swung to. The trains made a very brief stop at the station, and the practice was for two persons to be stationed on the platform, one close to the engine, the other generally the guard, half-way down the train, to shut the doors as the train steamed away into the tunnel. There was, of course, no time to turn the handle; the passing door was given a shove and would shut with a bang. The noise of twenty or thirty such bangs, with an ever decreasing interval of time between each as the train gained momentum, is easier to imagine than describe.

These stations were the happy hunting ground of the railway station pickpocket, and the learned Counsel almost invariably chosen to represent the members of the gang who had the misfortune to be arrested, was one Thorne Cole. Thorne Cole looked rather like a beer barrel with limbs, and was the possessor of a particularly loud and raucous voice. Between him and Edlin there was no love lost. Thorne Cole's defence was naturally based upon the difficulty of identifying with accuracy any individual in the conditions prevailing. He would remind the Jury, standing within three feet of the corner of the Jury-box, of the general confusion while the train was at the platform by stamping on the ground, knocking a book or two off the desk and imitating the waving of the green flag and the blowing of the whistle by the guard. He would then give what a music-hall programme would describe as his 'inimitable representation' of the scene of the exit of the train. With a large book held in both hands he would bang repeatedly on the desk in front of him with, at first, intervals of a second or so, rapidly lessening as the train was supposed to be gathering speed, until any books or papers belonging to other Counsel would be jumping about. Meanwhile poor Edlin would be protesting loudly with his 'Pray, Pray, Mr Thorne Cole, Mr Thorne Cole, spare us, spare us.' Thorne Cole would be shouting, the Bar and the Jury and frequently the spectators would be roaring with laughter until with a final whistle Thorne Cole would subside, leaving Edlin to sum up while he retired to the robing room, at the door of which he could occasionally be seen watching the summing-up with a pint pot of stout in his hand.

GEORGE ELLIOT (1860–1916)

King's Counsel

139

The narrator is Travers Humphreys

I HAVE also mentioned, that George Elliot often had defence briefs at the CCC both before and after he took silk. He was a most delightful man. He would certainly have been known as Tubby if he had not already become Georgie Porgie to his friends. He was the essence of rotundity and gentleness, friendly with every one alike, high and low, rich and poor. Juries loved him; so did Justices of the Peace. He never omitted to mention all the titles of any person to whom he was referring, and the number of persons in Court who were his 'learned' friends took no account of the rule that only a member of the Bar is entitled to be spoken of as 'learned'. To George Elliot all the Justices of the Bench were learned magistrates; the youth from the office who assisted or deputised for the Clerk of the Justices was 'your learned and most experienced legal adviser' until one would not have been surprised at hearing that the learned usher had sworn the learned policeman. Incidentally, all police constables were to him Inspectors, a perfectly safe gambit to play, since a correction could and was invariably met with a low bow, an apology and 'I feel sure that I am only slightly premature in my congratulations.'

There can be no doubt that Elliot was a most successful defender of prisoners. His pudgy little hands, almost covered by cuffs always too long, either clasped as if in prayer or gently waving to and fro like pieces of seaweed in a pool, seemed part of the soothing syrup which his carefully modulated voice was administering. How he did it is beyond me, but that he could hypnotize a jury sometimes into returning a verdict directly contrary to the evidence is attested by the statement of that hard-headed matter-of-fact and shrewd observer, Charles Gill, KC, which follows.

On the occasion in question, Charles Gill came into the Bar room. 'I simply cannot understand George Elliot—He is defending *A* and I appear for *B* who are charged with an offence (he told us the facts). Obviously they are both guilty or both innocent. My man appreciated from the first that there was no defence and pleaded guilty; the other, to everyone's surprise, pleaded Not Guilty, and George Elliot is fighting the case—at least I suppose so—though he has not challenged a single witness and his only cross-examination has been of the surveyor who proved the plan of the Turkish bath (where the men had been arrested). He got the admission that the room where the men were is approached by a swing door, and you cannot see through a swing door. No one has ever suggested that they *did* see anything through the swing door, but that doesn't matter to George. He is now addressing the jury on the assumption that the issue in the case centres round that swing door. He is waving his hands and swaying his body to and fro, *and some of the jury are beginning to do the same*. When I left it was because I felt that in a few minutes I should find myself swinging from side to side. When Atherley-Jones (the presiding Judge) begins to imitate the trunk of a Zoo elephant the end will come and I shall for the first time believe in mesmerism.'

In a few minutes Gill's clerk came in and spoke to him. 'He's done it—the jury have stopped the case,' announced Gill, 'and now I have to face my client who is going to be sentenced for an offence he could not have committed.'

FREDERICK ELWYN-JONES (LORD ELWYN-JONES) (1909–)

Lord Chancellor

140

ONE of my earliest post-war cases was at Chester Assize before Lord Chief Justice Goddard. The Director of Public Prosecutions instructed me to prosecute a motorist aged 80 who had been committed by a coroner's court on a charge of motor manslaughter. I formed the view that there was no prospect whatever of the prosecution succeeding. The Director agreed and I went off to the Assizes to offer no evidence against the defendant. The defendant's Counsel, however, asked for a formal verdict of not guilty from the jury, to which he was entitled. The Lord Chief Justice ordered: 'Very well, let a jury be sworn.' Unfortunately there were not enough jurors present to form a jury of twelve.

The Lord Chief then said to me, 'I take it you pray a tales.'

I had not the least idea what a 'tales' was. I felt like one of the stout countrymen of his day of whom Defoe said they would fight to the death against Popery without knowing whether Popery was a man or a horse.

I whispered anxiously to the row of counsel sitting on either side of me, 'What is he talking about?' No one could help me.

'My Lord,' I said, 'I am afraid I am not with your Lordship.'

'Not with me. Are you against me?'

'No, my Lord, but I regret I am not clear what is in your Lordship's mind.'

'Have you not read your *Pickwick Papers*?'

'Yes, my Lord', I replied weakly, finding the clue totally unhelpful.

'Well,' said the Lord Chief, 'you don't seem to have made yourself familiar with the career of Sergeant Buzfuz.'

I had entirely forgotten that when Mr Pickwick was tried at the Guildhall for breach of promise Sergeant Buzfuz too had to 'pray a tales'. I made a leap in the dark and said obediently, 'My Lord, I pray a tales', still without knowing what the consequences would be. Everyone in court was enjoying this except me.

The moment Lord Goddard explained that, by ancient custom, if there were not enough jurors, *tales de circumstantibus*—'such persons as are standing about'—may be sworn in to complete the jury, it all came back to me.

A jury was formed and the defendant found not guilty.

HERBERT VERE EVATT (1894–1965)

Australian Barrister

141

'BERT' EVATT had resigned as Associate to Sir William Cullen (Chief Justice of New South Wales) and now had only his bar practice and what he could make from journalism. It is a legal convention that a barrister is not paid directly by the solicitor who briefs him. The barrister's clerk collects the fee and places it in the barrister's bank account. Sometimes there was not much in the Evatt account.

Mas (his wife Mary Alice) and Bert divided what Bert earned into two. On her half she ran the flat and bought what she pleased, if there was anything over. Her own account was with a private bank, one of which, she did not realise for years, it was the aim of her husband's party to abolish. Bert paid the rent for his chambers in Phillip Street, his clerk's salary, and, later, a typist's salary. Mas found that part of her work was secretarial. Her husband dropped letters into his pocket—he never answered letters—and she collected them at the end of the week and replied to them.

Evatt worked late into the night. Of course you get drowsy, he told Mas, but if you just kept on working it wears off. He was surprised how inconveniently most people went to bed. In the early hours of the morning, when he wanted to talk to someone, they were all asleep. At first Mas, studying to be the perfect wife, took out some sewing.

'For God's sake, what are you doing?', Bert cried. 'I can't bear to see a woman sew. Do something useful, get a book. Here's something. Have you read all the Everyman's Library?'

'No.' Mas repressed a shudder.

'Well then, there you are! You can read it right through.'

For two years Mary Alice read the Everyman's Library. At that time it contained 828 volumes.

JOHN EVELYN (1620–1706)

142

Lawyers' Tricks.

[November] 26 [1686] I din'ed at my L. Chancelors, where being 3 other Serjants at Law, after dinner being cherefull and free, they told their severall stories, how long they had detained their clients in tedious processes, by their tricks, as if so many highway thieves should have met and discovered the severall purses they had taken: This they made but a jeast of: but God is not mocked:

WILLIAM ARTHUR FEARNLEY-WHITTINGSTALL (1903–59)

Queen's Counsel

143

Mr Justice Croom-Johnson: 'I cannot see you, Mr Fearnley-Whittingstall.'

Mr Fearnley-Whittingstall: 'My lord, I am before you wigged and gowned.'

Mr Justice Croom-Johnson: 'I still cannot see you, Mr Fearnley-Whittingstall.'

Mr Fearnley-Whittingstall: 'My lord, is it my yellow waistcoat that you cannot see?'

Mr Justice Croom-Johnson: 'Yes, it is.'

Mr Fearnley-Whittingstall: 'Well, my lord, you *can* see me.'

Mr Justice Croom-Johnson: 'Oh, very well, let's get on with the case.'

GEORGE FERGUSSON (LORD HERMAND) (1743–1827)

144

Two young men, after spending many hours over the punch-bowl, had a quarrel, which resulted in one stabbing the other to death. The survivor was convicted of culpable homicide, but received only a lenient sentence, much, however, against Lord Hermand's will. He felt that an injury had been done the cause of drinking, and was strongly in favour of transportation. 'We are told', he said, 'that there was no malice, and that the prisoner must have been in liquor. In liquor! Why, he was drunk! And yet he murdered the very man who had been drinking with him! They had been carousing the whole night, and yet he stabbed him after drinking a whole bottle of rum with him! Good God, my Laards, if he will do this when he's drunk what will he not do when he's sober?'

JOHN ALDERSON FOOTE (1848–1922)

King's Counsel

145

There stands in the market-place of one of our Wessex towns a memorial cross—not, indeed, ancient, and scarcely beautiful, but bearing an inscription which is still read at assize time with wonder and rustic awe. It tells how one Ruth Pierce, of Potterne, did in the year 1753 combine with three others to buy a sack of wheat, each contributing her share of the price. When the money was collected a deficiency appeared, and each woman protested that she had paid her full share, Ruth, in particular, declaring that if she spoke untruly she wished that God might strike her dead. Thereupon it is recorded that she instantly fell lifeless to the ground, and the money was found hidden in her right hand. The inscription adds that this signal judgement of the Almighty was commemorated by the direction of the Mayor and Aldermen for the instruction of posterity.

It is probable, if not certain, that the event thus recorded actually happened; nor do I presume to doubt that it happened in accordance with that Divine omniscience and omnipotence, without which we are taught that not even a sparrow falls. Yet when we reflect how many liars have used the same blasphemous invocation with what seems to us impunity, and, at any rate, without the same immediate and awful retribution, it is difficult to resist a suspicion that some light upon the death of this poor Wiltshire cheat might have been derived from a post-mortem examination. We are reminded vaguely of those eighteen upon whom the tower in Siloam fell. The ancient sceptic, who was shown the votive tablets of grateful mariners hanging in the temple at Cythera, asked significantly in what shrine were preserved the offerings of the drowned. So have I, when passing from the market cross of Devizes to the Assize Courts hard by, reflected how much more easily justice would be administered if all perjury were cut as short as that of ill-fated Ruth.

146

THERE was once a man put into the dock on a charge of indecent assault, who answered to the not uncommon name of John Smith, as did another man in the calendar. When called upon to plead to the indictment, he earnestly protested that a mistake had been made. He was told that he would have an opportunity of addressing the jury later on, and in the meantime he must only say 'Not guilty'—which he did. After he had made several futile attempts to interrupt counsel in the narration of his supposed iniquities, the prosecutrix was put into the witness-box and asked to identify him, which she somewhat indignantly refused to do. Persuasion and encourgement proved unavailing, and the judge was ultimately compelled to direct a verdict of acquittal. 'All I wanted to say, my lord,' observed the prisoner meekly before leaving the dock, 'was that what I am really charged with is stealing an umbrella!'

FELIX FRANKFURTER (1882–1965)

Justice of the Supreme Court

147

I REMEMBER very vividly Harriman, a powerful fellow, who couldn't understand all this restrictive legislation of the Roosevelt administration; made no bones about it. When he was asked whether he wasn't interested in acquiring one railroad system after another, and would there be any limits to it, he was frank to say that if he were allowed, if he had a free hand, he would if he could acquire all the railroads in the United States, and he could run them pretty well. I have no doubt he could run them pretty well. He was a very masterful fellow. You couldn't listen to him without feeling that here you had a powerful mentality and a still more powerful will.

He had a retinue of lawyers. He was handling the matter himself. He knew more about his business than his lawyers did. There were the lawyers, some of the greatest of the day—John G. Milburn, Robert S. Lovett, and several others, half a dozen or so lawyers. From time to time as this duel, this intellectual duel between himself and Chairman Lane, was going on he would turn to his lawyers and ask them a question or two. The way Mr Harriman spoke to his lawyers, and the bootlicking deference they paid to him! My observation of this interplay between the great man, the really powerful dominating tycoon, Harriman, and his servitors the lawyers, led me to say to myself, 'If it means that you should be that kind of a subservient creature to have the most desirable clients, the biggest clients in the country, if that's what it means to be a leader of the Bar, I never want to be a leader of the Bar. The price of admission is too high.'

148

The narrator is Felix Frankfurter

The House of Truth.

THIS was the original group that lived in the House of Truth—Valentine, Winfred Denison, Eustace Percy, Loving Christie, and myself. We were all young, in our late twenties or early thirties, and all desirable, available young men for dinner parties, where we met young women. So a gay time was had. I forget who dubbed it the House of Truth but the name stuck; namely something about the fact that it was a place where truth was sought, and everybody knew it couldn't be found, but even trying to seek the truth conscientiously is a rare occupation in this world.

We'd have all sorts of people come there for dinner. We'd take turns at the various duties. On one occasion it was my job to shake cocktails. In those days we shook cocktails in a shaker. During one month that was my task. In connection with that I remember how heart-searing—how a compliment can have, what shall I say, unwarming ambiguity. I was shaking my cocktails one night when our guest was Mr Justice Lortin, he said to me, 'I hope you mix drinks as well as you argue cases.'

Well, to be praised by a Justice of the Supreme Court, for a kid like me, that was something. Wasn't I proud and happy? He sipped his cocktail and said, 'You mix drinks even better than you argue cases.'

If ever one compliment displaced the pleasure of another, that was it.

149

I REMEMBER a Boston man, a Yankee, the son of a rather important Boston Lawyer, whose intellectual endowments made it reasonably certain that if he went into one of the Boston offices, in no time he would gain recognition there and eventually obtain a partnership with a sufficiently lucrative practice; but there was the lure of New York. I remember talking with him and suggesting that he would be happy in Boston, staying in his habitat; but there was the lure of the *ignis fatuus*. He thought that he'd go to New York and canvass the offices, and I said, 'All right. I'm sorry you, too, fall for this lure.'

He went down to New York, spent two or three days, came back, and said he'd decided to accept the offer he'd had from a Boston firm. I asked him, 'What made you so clear, as you now say you are clear, that that's where you want to practise?'

He said, 'I had an experience that sort of took all the savor and flavor of New York out of my mind and made me feel that isn't the kind of life I want to lead.'

'What was it?'

He said it was a leading lawyer in the big firm of Cravath and Henderson. He'd had a note to this lawyer, whom I knew. He spoke of the opportunities in New York, that they excelled the opportunities in any other place. 'A man with real guts, real fire, ought to go where the biggest opportunities are, and New York affords the biggest opportunity. I was the son of a poor minister, no money at all, brought up on a farm, came to the Harvard Law School with no money at all. I then came to New York and this firm, and now I have an apartment which has eight bathrooms'—'That finished me,' said my young friend, 'that he should talk of life's success in terms of eight bathrooms!'

GERALD AUSTIN GARDINER (LORD GARDINER) (1900–)

150

A future Lord Chancellor displays a lack of tact.

TALKING to Gerald when he was still a schoolboy at Harrow, his father shot a query at him with arrow-like swiftness. 'Tell me, my boy, who d'you think is the greatest living Englishman?'

Gerald, utterly taken aback and struck dumb with shyness under the intent gaze levelled at him, gulped; and after some hesitation he blurted out: 'Winston Churchill, I suppose.'

His father exploded. 'Churchill? That —, my God!' Angrily striding away, he left Gerald sorely baffled. Winston at that time was out of favour with the Conservative party, having joined the Liberals, but the boy was unaware of this.

His mother, finding him alone and miserable, inquired the reason, and on learning it, laughed.

'Why, darling,' she said, 'when he asked who you thought was the greatest living Englishman, you should have answered, "You, father!" and everything would have been all right.'

This was the first and last time Gerald remembered his mother showing a touch of humour.

151

'A humble member of the Bar.'

DURING the 'phoney war' period of 1939–40 Gerald Gardiner became involved in a legal contretemps concerning imprisonment under Regulation 18B on the direction of the Home Secretary, Sir John Anderson, of a man called Liversidge.

There had been much criticism of this regulation in the House of Commons. In 1941 Liversidge appealed against his detention in Brixton prison and his case went to a second appeal in the House of Lords. Lord Atkin, who believed that Liversidge should be released, dissented from four of his fellow judges in the interpretation of the Regulation saying that he had listened 'to arguments which might have been addressed to the Court of King's Bench in the time of Charles I'.

These were strong words. They roused the editor of *The Times* to indite a 1000-word leader expressing *his* views of the case.

Two days later this elicited a reply from Lord Maugham, the Lord Chancellor, who took the somewhat unprecedented step of commenting on his distinguished colleague, Lord Atkin. He explained that, in accordance with the tradition at the Bar, Counsel for the Home Office could not reply to Lord Atkin's dissentient speech. He added, 'I think it only fair to say that I presided at the hearing and listened to every word of their arguments and that I did not hear from them, or anyone else, anything that could justify such a remark.'

Gerald, who had followed the proceedings, and discussed them with the Inner Temple fraternity, felt impelled to compose a letter in defence of Lord Atkin's judgement, which he asked a sympathetic barrister to countersign with him. His colleague, however, excused himself on the grounds that he hoped to be appointed a judge. So, on November 7th, the letter went to *The Times* signed solely by Gerald.

He concluded—'It may be presumptuous for an ordinary lawyer to express a view upon the decision of the House of Lords, but as so distinguished a lawyer as Lord Maugham has thought your columns an appropriate place in which to comment upon part of a speech of another member of the Tribunal, it may be permissible for a humble member of the Bar to follow his example and to say that, in places where lawyers meet, the view being yesterday expressed by lawyers of all shades of opinion was one of admiration for and gratitude to Lord

Atkin for his dissenting speech, the contents of which appear to some lawyers to be unanswerable.'

The letter landed him in hot water with the Benchers of the Inner Temple, many of whom were profoundly shocked by the presumption of a Junior Counsel in daring to criticize the judgements of the eminent Lords of Appeal. However, after it had been argued over at some length among them, the storm in a teacup blew over, the majority of the Benchers coming to the conclusion that if Lord Maugham wrote a silly letter to *The Times*, then he must expect a silly answer.

DAVID EARL LLOYD GEORGE (1863–1945)

152

The Rector of Llanfrothen had refused the dying request of Robert Roberts, a Methodist quarryman, to be buried in a plot, now belonging to the Church, where his daughter had been buried. The quarryman's son appealed to the local solicitor.

'CARRY the burial right through at once,' said the solicitor, 'and I will defend you.'

The name of the young man was David Lloyd George.

He took notes of all that had happened, studied the case of the original unconditional gift of the land and of its subsequent so-called 'conveyance' to the Rector and advised the family to break open the barred gate and bury their dead where they willed in God's acre.

So it was done. The Rector went at once to Court. He sued the quarryman's son and seven others for damages for 'wrongfully entering the plaintiff's land, digging a grave therein, burying a corpse, and conducting a burial service'.

Mr D. Lloyd George appeared for the defence. He immediately applied for a trial by jury.

He handled his case in masterly style, confining his eager argument to the single issue—did the ground belong to the Parish (as a result of the original gift) or did it belong to the Rector under the terms of the 'conveyance'. But he also made a passionate protest against the conduct of this Christian clergyman who had told the old quarryman's family that he could be buried 'not in the last resting ground he had asked, beside his daughter, but in a place, bleak and sinister, in which were buried the bodies of the unknown drowned, or of suicides, or of the few Jews that died in the district'.

The jury found for the defendants. Fortunately, the foreman made a note of their precise finding.

The County Court judge reserved judgement. There were, he said, questions of law still to be decided.

Two months later he gave his decision. He paid tribute to the 'ingenuity' of Mr Lloyd George, but entered a verdict for the Rector for five guineas and costs.

At once Lloyd George sought leave to appeal, which was granted. He also asked the judge to amend his note of the findings of the jury. This was refused.

When Lloyd George urged that the shorthand of the court reporter would show that His Honour's note was in error the judge retorted that he did not care if there were fifty shorthand records. It was then that the audacious young attorney reminded him that the jury, at any rate, had taken the unusual precaution of putting their own verdict in writing 'and the sequel shows that they were right in doing so'.

So to the High Court of Justice went the case of the quarryman of Llanfrothen. When it was heard the Lord Chief Justice, Coleridge, gave judgement for the quarryman. He also gave a severe admonition to the County Court judge for his refusal to amend his notes, despite all the evidence to the contrary. After a few pertinent observations on the legal habit of County Court judges His Lordship added: 'As for this paper and these shorthand notes, I shall simply send them to the Lord Chancellor without comment, and if he does not take some steps I shall be surprised.'

HARDINGE STANLEY GIFFARD (EARL OF HALSBURY) (1823–1921)

153

The narrator is F. W. Ashley, his clerk

THE great man did not care for his clients to become aware of his distaste for reading briefs, and to this end he rarely had a consultation until he had gained, generally from a 'devil', some knowledge of the case. I remember seeing him stride in one day when his room was full of persons attending a consultation in a very important case. I knew he had not disturbed the tape around his brief and neither had he troubled to acquire orally any information about it.

I expected him to pass us and go straight into his room where the crowd was, but to my surprise he turned into the clerk's room and ordered one of them to bring his brief from his desk. This was done, and Sir Hardinge, seating himself at the clerk's desk, read the pleadings and turned over a few sheets of the brief.

'Take it back to my room', he said, and a few minutes later he followed it in.

'Ah, Giffard,' said his junior, 'we're just talking about that twenty thousand pounds.'

'You mean nineteen thousand eight hundred and seventy four pounds two shillings and sevenpence', said Sir Hardinge, 'please be accurate.' The client was delighted at this proof of his counsel's knowledge of his case down to the smallest detail.

154

COUNTLESS examples of Lord Halsbury's remarkable memory could be quoted. His son joined the Chester Circuit in 1906 and was shown an old brief of his father's. It was a very large brief, dated 1855. There was not a mark on it, except on the last page. Here the times of three trains to London were jotted down. He asked his father about the case. Lord Halsbury not only remembered it, but also recalled every witness, what each had said, which broke down, and which had been believed. Moreover he told his son of the two important letters which had won the case, the name of the judge and numerous minor details. Yet fifty-one years had passed.

Sir Harry Poland remembered an occasion when Giffard had attended a political Debating Society called The Belvedere. The leader of the Radicals was a Mr Southwell who made a brilliant speech which brought down the house. He had not allowed for Giffard's memory. Not only did he 'remember' the speech, but the name of its real author, and where it was printed. The book was produced. That seems to have been the end of Mr Southwell.

155

GIFFARD was always marvellous in reply, and made more use than anyone I have heard of the advantage of the 'last word'. I remember one example, where he apeared for the plaintiff in an action for slander, against some members of a charitable association. The defendants' counsel had quoted the passage from the New Testament which defines true religion as being 'to visit the widows and the fatherless in their affliction, and to keep oneself unspotted from the world'. 'My friend has forgotten the text which follows', said Giffard. 'If any man amongst you seemeth to be religious, and bridleth not his own tongue, that man's religion is vain.' Nobody in court knew whether this followed the quotation or not, but in fact it immediately precedes it.

156

AS is well known Queen Victoria was very particular that all appointments should be submitted to her before they were made public. In 1882 Lord Halsbury had been anxious to appoint a man to be judge who happened to be in Ireland at the moment. This was very awkward, in view of the fact that there never was an Irish post-office that did not pass on information, and if he were to telegraph to the man, the news would be broadcast, and in all probability the Queen would refuse her consent. It was awkward, but Lord Halsbury was not easily baffled. He sent a telegram the like of which, it is reasonable to suppose, no Irish post-office had ever received before:

Judex rude donatus petit quietem volo veniam Reginae petere te nominare sedi vacanti opportet respondere quia mensibus proximis novus judex munere fugatur. Cancellarius.

The Lawyer received it and was extremely perplexed. Unfortunately he had not brought his Latin dictionary on holiday with him. Luckily, however, he was accompanied by his son who, having just left Harrow, might reasonably be supposed to have remembered a few words of Latin. The boy was called in, and after much trouble they managed to make out the meaning of this unusual message. They did more: they concocted a reply in the same language, though it was couched in such remarkable terms as to cause the Lord Chancellor to laugh so much that the tears rolled down his cheeks.

SIR CHARLES FREDERICK GILL (1851–1923)

King's Counsel

157

AFTER his retirement Gill built himself a beautiful house in the country. The Vicar asked him why he never attended Church. This annoyed Gill, whose answer was, 'For two very good reasons, Sir. The first is that, as Recorder of Chichester, I am prayed for in the Cathedral every Sunday morning; and the second, that I have defended more clergymen at the Old Bailey than any living barrister.'

AUBREY SINCLAIR GILLESPIE-JONES

(Contemporary)

Australian Barrister

158

The narrator is Gillespie-Jones

The solicitor as vocalist.

A SOLICITOR friend of mine became Mayor of the City of Ballarat and it was his duty to open the South Street Competitions for the best musician in Australia in the various age groups. In opening the competition he mentioned that he had been a competitor himself some forty years ago.

He said, 'I had been entered in the under-twelve singers section by my proud parents. In fact, there were only two entrants, myself and another eleven-year-old. I had to sing first, and I wandered out onto this stage, which now appears small, but then appeared to be roughly the size of the Melbourne Cricket Ground, with a sea of faces stretching away into the distance. At a nod from the Adjudicator I commenced to sing, and after a while I happened to glance at the Adjudicator who was frowning and had his head between his hands. This did not deter me, and I continued singing until the end of the song. There were a few desultory claps—I imagine they were my parents—and then my rival came out onto the stage.

'He stood there for a while, waiting for the Adjudicator to raise his head. At last he summoned up courage, and said to the Adjudicator, "Sir, shall I start now?", and the Adjudicator said, "No, don't. You've won." '

RAYNER GODDARD (LORD GODDARD) (1877–1971)

Lord Chief Justice

159

Lord Goddard's clerk, Arthur Smith, observes that even tragic accident cases can produce moments at which the self-control of the Court is severely tested.

I REMEMBER a well-known Queen's Counsel who was appearing (before Lord Goddard) for a housewife who had fallen off an omnibus. He alleged that the conductor had rung the bell to start the bus before she had got off, with the result that she was thrown off her balance and had struck her face and jaw very heavily on the metal rail of the platform. The case was a jury action and the Silk was making a pathetic appeal (which he would have been very much more diffident in making before Lord Goddard sitting alone) for the sympathy of the jurors for his poor client, a hard-working housewife of humble circumstances and the mother of three dear children.

'Through this most unfortunate accident, caused by the gross negligence of the servant of the Defendant Company, my unfortunate client suffered this most grievous injury to her jaw with the dire result that she could not, for quite a long time afterwards, bite her bottom with her top teeth.'

160

The narrator is Arthur Smith

THE junior barrister on circuit holds an unpaid administrative post entailing the collection of circuit dues, the organising of circuit dinners, liaison with Bar hotels and so on. There are also certain benefits which are attached to holding it, and the most important of those is a first claim to any Poor Persons Defences granted by the Court. The circuit junior that year was Waller (now a distinguished Queen's Counsel). He made full use of this privilege and appeared before us in almost every town.

Shortly before Christmas we arrived in Leeds. On the first day of the Assizes the circuit junior and the judge's marshal met in the robing room.

'You've got a tough judge haven't you', said Waller, 'I've appeared before him five times round this circuit and have been given thirty five years all told. Average, seven years per appearance.'

The marshal grinned, and reported the conversation to the judge. The next day a prisoner was brought into court on a charge of rape. Now it is a strict rule of practice that the judge should warn a jury in the strongest possible terms of the danger of convicting a man of this crime on the uncorroborated evidence of the woman who makes the accusation. Experience has shown that complaints of this kind are often untrue. When the prisoner asked for legal aid the Clerk of Assize turned to the judge to tell him the names of persons available to take Poor Persons defence.

Goddard leaned forward. 'Mr Waller.'

'My Lord.'

'Will you take this case?' Then, as Waller came forward, in a whisper which was plainly audible to everyone, 'This should bring your average down. There's no corroboration.'

161

ON December 2nd 1938 Lord Goddard and Lord Clauson were to hear the case of a Mr Frank Harrison, over some property left to him by an uncle. Mr Harrison was waiting outside the Court of Appeal that morning before the doors were unlocked. Once inside, he listened to the dismissal of his request for a new trial of the original County Court action. When he heard the Court's decision, Mr Harrison jumped to his feet and shouted 'I want justice.'

The noble Lords of Appeal were already leaving the Court rooms. Mr Harrison fumbled in his jacket pocket and pulled out a tomato. A second later it burst against the wall near the judge's head. Several more tomatoes followed, none of them landing quite so near the target as the first.

Mr Harrison was sent to prison for six weeks for contempt of court. After three weeks in Brixton he sent a written apology to the Court, and a day or two later he was freed. He denied that he had gone to Court with the intention of hurling tomatoes at the judges. 'I bought them for my lunch', he said.

NATHAN GOFF (1843–1920)

American Lawyer and Secretary of the Navy

162

GOFF was captured in the action at Moorfield during the Civil War and incarcerated in the notorious Libby Prison. He and three others—one being Emil Frey, afterwards President of the Swiss Republic—were held for capital offences because the death penalty might be exacted of a citizen of a seceding state or a foreign country who had joined the Union Army. Those likely to be executed were confined in a cellar where the waters of the James River seeped into their quarters.

Into their quarters some law books, including Blackstone's *Commentaries*, were smuggled out of which, a few hours every day, Frey and Goff after a fashion managed to read. Their quarters were over-run by rats and the prisoners began their extermination by arranging an old fashioned dead fall trap, the weight used being one of the *Commentaries*.

After an unsuccessful attempt to escape Goff was liberated on an exchange of prisoners and proceeded under orders to Washington. On arrival he was directed to be at one of President Lincoln's receptions where he stood in line so long in his emaciated condition that his fear was he might not survive the ordeal.

As he approached the President, Lincoln, looking down at his shoulder straps, said 'Well Major, what can I do for you?' Goff replied that he had been ordered to be present. Lincoln, saying, 'My God, then you are Major Goff', told him to go into an adjoining room and lie down on a sofa and sent in some milk and sandwiches to him. Later Lincoln, sitting by his side, asked him to tell the story of his incarceration in the Libby Prison.

The President listened without interruption and then said, 'Are you able to tell this story again to Secretary Stanton and me?' On Secretary Stanton's arrival Major Goff repeated the story. Thereupon Lincoln, rising up to that benevolent height which so often seemed like the foreword of a benediction said, 'Stanton, I've told you that those stories of the Libby Prison—now confirmed by the twice told tale of Major Goff—were true. Those boys shall come home.'

After Stanton had retired, Lincoln sat down and said, 'Well, in as much as you have been reading Blackstone under such unique conditions perhaps you have determined to be admitted to the Bar.' Goff replied that he had made up his mind to study Law.

Towards the end of this historic interview Lincoln asked Major Goff 'Can I do anything further for you?' Goff gave him the names of persons who ought to be released forthwith. The President noted them down and added, 'The plight of your friends shall be attended to as you wish. *And you can now have the satisfaction of knowing that even before admission to the Bar you have won your first case.*'

SIR HAMILTON GRANT (1872–1937)

Knight Commander Indian Empire

163

The narrator is Lord Simon

HAMILTON GRANT was a most precocious youth, with powers both of humour and of satire decidedly disconcerting to the less endowed. He got into some scrapes with the college authorities, for he was not a model of industry. But he had notepaper prepared, bearing in the top left-hand corner the pretended telegraphic address, 'Work: Oxford.'

Dr Jowett, the Master of Balliol, required members of the College on the foundation to bring him an essay once a week. On one occasion, Grant had neglected to write his essay, but he had put down in his notebook an opening formula and, after leaving a gap, had also written out a peroration.

'Read me your essay', said Jowett, in his mild, high-pitched voice.

Grant, seated at a little distance from the Master, started off with the first sentence he had prepared and then improvised an elaborate and connected argument, turning over the blank pages at suitable intervals, until he finally worked himself into the concluding passage. Then he shut the book, thankful that the performance had passed off so smoothly, and awaited the Master's comment.

Jowett stared into the fire and said nothing at all for a couple of minutes. Then 'Read it again, Mr Grant.'

SIR WILLIAM GRANTHAM (1835–1911)

164

HE was honest, simple, outspoken, cocksure, keen to do right and English to the backbone [was the verdict of Sir Edward Parry, who as a barrister, often appeared before Sir William Grantham]. There was no policy or finesse in anything that he did, and he was out for work and business. That is why he was so welcome and beloved on the Northern Circuit. But his slackness in finesse often cost him tricks in the Court of Appeal. Here is an example.

I appeared in the last case of the list at a Summer Assize for a small carpenter whose shop had been injured by the pulling down of adjoining buildings to clear the site for a new infirmary. The defendants were the Trustees of the Institution. The claim was for £175 11*s.* 2*d.* and I got a verdict for every pound, shilling and penny.

Grantham started his summing up as follows—I quote, of course, from memory:

'Gentlemen of the jury, if you are as heartily glad as I am that this is the last case at the Manchester Assizes, and that, after this, we shall be able to get away into pleasanter surroundings, you will not be long in doing substantial justice to the plaintiff.'

I shall never forget how strange the words sounded in the cold grey light of the Court of Appeal. Smyly, QC led me, and Esher, in one of his wild humours, romped round the court with playful savagery. One gem of Grantham's was in reference to the defence: 'Then, gentlemen of the jury, Mr Parry is told he should have sued the contractors instead of the trustees, and the contractors would have said "sue the foreman". And the foreman would have said "sue the hodman", and so it would have been like the house that Jack built.'

'Which house is that, Mr Smyly?', said Lord Esher.

'Really, my Lord . . .'

'Is it on either of the plans you have put in?', continued the Master of the Rolls, waving them about impatiently.

'I am not certain', said Smyly cautiously, 'that the house in question is in any way connected with this case.'

'It must be,' said Lord Esher, 'or why did Mr Justice Grantham tell the jury about it.'

I was tugging away at Smyly's gown, and he turned round and asked what on earth the house that Jack built was all about.

'A nursery rhyme. Don't you know it? "This is the house that Jack built. This is the wall . . ." '

'Oh, of course,' interrupted Smyly, turning round to the Court with great seriousness. 'I have consulted my learned junior, and he agrees with me that the house that Jack built is not set out on the plans, and that the house referred to by the learned Judge is in the nature of a literary allusion.'

The appeal was lost.

SIR JOHN GURNEY (1802–62)

165

BARON GURNEY was considered very snappish to counsel and very severe to criminals. It was commonly said amongst us, though I do not mean to vouch for the truth of the report, that he was never seen to shed a tear but once, and that was when on a visit to the theatre to witness the performance of the *Beggar's Opera*, it was announced on the stage that Macheath had been reprieved.

SIR CHARLES HALL (1814–83)

Queen's Counsel and Vice-Chancellor

166

CHARLES HALL, who was a great favourite in Royal circles, often permitted the fact to leak out. Hence an incident which gave satisfaction to the Bar. On the last day of the summer sittings, being about to join the Prince of Wales at Cowes, he arrived at the Guildhall to arrange that a case in which he had been briefed should be adjourned. As he was in yachting costume he was 'invisible' to the Court, and an unemployed junior was requested to make the necessary application. The junior saw his chance and seized it. 'My Lord,' he said, 'at this moment we are all anxious to be off to Margate. Will your Lordship release my learned friend, Mr Hall.'

SIR EDWARD MARSHALL HALL (1858–1927)

King's Counsel

167

SIR JAMES CHARLES MATHEW was a Lawyer of the first-rank, a witty Irishman with a gift of dry and sarcastic humour which penetrated the chinks in Marshall Hall's armour and wounded him deeply. Marshall once told a distinguished colleague at the Bar of a certain Assize when he held no less than twelve briefs before Mathew and lost them all. Finally he became very truculent and was told by the learned judge to sit down; he did not obey, but slowly turned round and carefully surveyed the public, sitting at the back of the Court and in the gallery.

'Sit-down', repeated the Judge, but Marshall only repeated what he had said before. Finally, thoroughly infuriated, the Judge thundered out, 'Sit down, Mr Hall.'

'Oh, your Lordship is addressing *me*,' replied Marshall. 'I thought you were addressing a lady at the back of the Court. Certainly, my Lord, if your Lordship would prefer me to address you sitting down. I will do so.'

But Mr Justice Mathew rarely lost his temper, and Marshall did not always come off so well with him. The Judge's cold and hostile manner had a way of withering Marshall's expansive and exuberant nature. He was an exceedingly sensitive man and after some years he grew tired of the chilling atmosphere of Mathew's Court and wanted to make friends. Sir Frank Lockwood undertook to put matters right and the two of them tracked the Judge to his club one evening. It was arranged that Lockwood should go in for a minute or two, to explain what

Marshall wanted, while he should wait outside till Lockwood came to call him in to the Judge.

'I had only to wait two minutes,' said Marshall in the aggrieved and naïve tone which he used to adopt when telling a story against himself, 'in less than that time Lockwood came tripping down the club steps, calling out to me, long before he reached me: "It's no use, Marshall. The Judge says he hates you." '

168

In 1907, in one of his most famous cases, the Camden Town Murder, Marshall Hall secured the acquittal, against a hostile judge, of Robert Wood. The case had an unusual sequel.

YEARS afterwards Marshall left a provincial Assize Court and was accosted by a smart, happy looking little man. 'You don't know me, I see, Sir Edward', he said. 'No', said Marshall, taking his hand, 'you must forgive me. I've got a terrible memory for faces.' Then he noticed the man's very deep-set eyes. 'Why,' he said, 'isn't your name Wood?' 'No', replied the other gravely, 'it's not, but I'd like you to know I'm doing very well, and I owe it all to you.' If this was indeed Wood it was a very moving incident and one which was rare in Marshall's experience. The acquitted man shows a perhaps natural desire to avoid every memory of his trial.

Marshall once defended a financier and obtained an unexpected acquittal. Advocate and client met again some time afterwards, placed next to each other in the stalls of a theatre. As soon as the client caught sight of Marshall Hall he excused himself to his hostess and went out.

But, now and then, clients are grateful and gratitude can take strange forms. While Marshall was once buying a railway ticket a clever thief ran away with his precious dressing bag. This contained many of his treasures and a wad of notes. Marshall, always very excitable, nearly went mad and immediately advertised its loss. A few days later the bag, with all its contents, was deposited at his house with an anonymous note to the effect that one good turn deserves another, and that if the thief had recognised Marshall Hall the trouble would never have arisen. Not one note was missing.

Thieves, however, do not always turn out to be grateful clients. On another journey he lost a suitcase. The thief was discovered, but too late for restitution. Nevertheless, Marshall interviewed him for the purpose of tracing his possessions, and, incidentally, upbraiding him for his wickedness. 'Well you see, Sir,' was the disarming explanation, 'me and the missus got married on that there bag.'

169

The narrator is John Mortimer

MY father remembered Marshall Hall and it was not his classic profile that he described to me, nor his flamboyant oratory. ('Look at her', Sir Edward once said to a jury, pointing to his trembling client in the dock, a young prostitute accused of murder, 'God never gave her a chance, will you?') It was Marshall's dramatic entry into a courtroom that impressed my father. His head clerk would come in, carrying the brief and a pile of white linen handkerchiefs, then came a second clerk with the water carafe and an air cushion (lawyers and pilots, as a result of sitting for long hours, are martyrs to piles). Sir Edward himself would then burst through the swing-doors, to be installed in his place by a flurry of solicitors and learned juniors. He would subside on to the inflated rubber circle, and listen to the case for the prosecution. If the evidence against Marshall Hall's client looked black he would, so my father assured me, slowly unfold the top handkerchief and blow a clarion call to battle. When the situation became really desperate he would remove the air-cushion and re-inflate it, a process which always commanded the Jury's undivided attention.

SIR WILLIAM HANSELL (1856–1937)

170

The narrator is E. C. Bentley

HANSELL was a vigorous man, with a dry humour, and an unsparing judgement of his fellow-creatures—'We have to bear in mind', I remember him saying 'that the Judge in this case is a silly old man.' His speech and manner were a virile combination of Oxford and the Bar. As a practical instructor in the work of the Bar he was admirable. For instance, once he was asked for Counsel's opinion in a certain case, and I, with much labour, prepared a draft for him. He began by striking out the latter half, or thereabouts, of this. 'I advise only on the points that are put to me', he observed. 'When solicitors end, as they do here, "and to advise generally on the case", they are asking *me* to raise points for *them*, and that is not my business. When they do that I always conclude my opinion with five short words which you would do well to commit to memory: "I—have—nothing—to—add".'

I have heard his style as an advocate described as truculent; but he had more often an ironical suavity that was much appreciated by those who were not the subjects of it. He was a member of the English Church Union, and wore a little golden cross on his watch-chain, but there was nothing ecclesiastical about his conversation. I do not mean that he was of the same school as a very successful King's Counsel whom a friend of mine once heard say, in a mild and fatherly tone to the boy who brought him in his cup of tea, 'God damn and blast your —— soul to hell, my boy, how many times have I told you *not* to knock on the door.' But Hansell was the first person—though not the last by many—from whom I heard the limerick about the young lady of Joppa. Once, for some reason, I turned up at his chambers in a frock-coat, a garment almost universally worn in those days for occasions of ceremony. After surveying me in silent admiration for some embarrassing moments, Hansell told me that he had never had but one frock-coat in his life, and its one fault was that the tails did not meet at the back when it was buttoned up. He had kept it, therefore, for private theatricals (for which he had a taste), because whenever the play seemed not to be going well, he had only to turn his back to the audience to create a burst of enthusiasm.

SIR GEORGE HARDINGE (1744–1816)

171

THE thing that I found most interesting in Presteign was a grave in the churchyard. The head-stone reads thus:

> To the memory of Mary Morgan who young and beautiful, endowed with a good understanding and disposition, but unenlightened by the Sacred truths of Christianity, became the victim of sin and shame and was condemned to an ignominious death, on the 11th April 1805, for the murder of her bastard Child.

Rous'd to a first sense of guilt and remorse by the eloquent and humane exertions of her benevolent Judge Mr Justice Hardinge, she underwent the Sentence of the Law on the following Thursday with unfeigned repentance and a fervent hope of forgiveness through the merits of a redeeming Intercessor.

This Stone is erected not merely to perpetuate the remembrance of a departed penitent, but to remind the living of the frailty of human nature when unsupported by Religion.

Thomas Brudenell Bruce, Earl of AILESBURY

And on a small stone at the foot is this inscription, which I fancy was *not* written by the unctuous pen of the noble Earl.

To the memory of
MARY MORGAN
who suffered April 18th 1805
Aged 17 years.

He that is without sin among you,
let him first cast a stone at her.

The 8th Chapter of John, part of ye 7th verse.

The story told by these stones is tragic enough; but the additions of local tradition make it more tragic still. For they tell you that the man who seduced the poor girl was upon the Grand Jury that found a true bill for murder against her. And that the junior of the circuit, who defended her, rode off to London with desperate haste to try to get a reprieve before the day fixed by the 'benevolent Judge' (as was then the practice) for her execution. He had only a week. He got the reprieve, and rode feverishly back to Presteign. He arrived on the fatal day, but an hour too late. She had suffered the ignominious death—at the age of 17.

The 'benevolent Judge' of Mary Morgan was George Hardinge (1744–1816), called to the bar at the Middle Temple, 1769, Senior Justice of Brecon, Glamorgan, and Radnor, 1787–1816. When he was in the House of Commons, during the dispute with the American colonies, he produced with all solemnity the fatuous argument that they were not being taxed without representation. 'For all the grants of land in America were to be held of the Manor of Greenwich in the County of Kent, and therefore the Knights of the Shire for the County of Kent represented all the Americans.' Clearly he was an ass: and equally clearly he was not a benevolent judge. For he had the power himself to reprieve her, and recommend her to the Royal Mercy. He has the full responsibility of having 'left her for execution' a week after her conviction.

ST JOHN BERNARD VYVYAN HARMSWORTH
(1912–)

172

HARMSWORTH, a cousin of Lord Rothermere, had been a stipendiary Magistrate at Marlborough Street since 1961 and soon made his mark in a busy court as a competent, courteous magistrate before whom it was always pleasant to appear. Off the bench, viewed from behind he had a curious gait which, with his thickset figure, made him look rather like a walking Toby Jug. As with so many of the better magistrates, he had a puckish sense of humour. Thus when (as sometimes happens) a prisoner in the cells was shouting and screaming at the top of his lungs, to the consternation of all in Harmsworth's court, he looked across to the police officer who was examining his book before shepherding the next accused into the dock and said, 'Gaoler, is that someone assisting the police with their enquiries?'

SIR RUPERT CHARLES HART-DAVIS
(1907–)

173

WHENEVER I have a free morning in London I haunt the Queen's Bench. Why? Because at least four times in six there is good entertainment, as Max Beerbohm found.* What is the theatre or county cricket in comparison? A good cross-exam or even more a summing up gives me intense pleasure. But I hear less well than I did, or else the judges

* See p. 24.

mumble more than they did, and I am often tempted to call out 'speak up', thereby emulating the bravest man I ever heard of who, as Lord Russell of Killowen began his summing up, said to him 'make it snappy, old cock', and evoked a tornado of wrath which would have flattened a forest.

I never, now, go to the criminal court, though I have in my time seen three murderers at close quarters, one being Brides-in-the-Bath Smith, a very unattractive looking man, who from time to time, hurled coarse and abusive words at counsel and witnesses. But as a man on trial for his life cannot, obviously, be committed for contempt, the judge merely reminded him mildly that he wasn't doing his case any good, and reduced him to mutterings, which being close by, I understood were directed mainly to casting doubt on the legitimacy of the judge's birth, which even a layman like myself could see were irrelevant.

CYRIL PEARCE HARVEY (1900–68)

Queen's Counsel

174

If you know the form of your judge from previous experience, well and good. If you do not, you should leave no stone unturned to find out by asking the advice of those who do or, better still, by finding the time to listen to the judge in action. This sort of information is particularly important in those cases, not uncommon nowadays, where a doctor or hospital is sued for damages as a result of some surgical operation which has turned out badly. So many of us have undergone surgical operations in our time, and with such varying results, that we are all apt to regard ourselves as knowledgeable on the subject, whereas in fact we are only prejudiced.

It is almost an even chance that any particular judge will approach a case of this sort with some kind of subconscious bias based upon his own experience in hospital or nursing home. In one such case not long ago purposeful (though unavailing) efforts were made by the plaintiff's counsel to discover by underground channels whether the judge was still in possession of his own appendix.

There is much to be said for such cases being tried by juries.

SIR PATRICK GARDINER HASTINGS
(1880–1952)

King's Counsel, Attorney-General

175

On his way home from service as a Trooper in the South African War.

THE journey home was very different from the outward voyage. There was none of the excitement of a new life, and none of the enthusiastic longing for a new continent: I was going back to a country of which my early recollections were not entirely pleasant, and where my prospects were anything but bright. I was twenty-one, and all those years had not brought me one step nearer to the selection of a profession. There were so many things I wanted. First of all, I wanted to earn money; I had already known enough experience of having none. But that was not all: I had tried many things, and hated them, but I could not change my mind indefinitely. I fully realised that my next choice must be the last. There was no-one with whom I could have discussed my problem, even if I had wished, certainly no-one to whom I could have looked for any help, so I spent most of my time in the bows of the ship watching the flying fish, who were equally uninterested in my future prospects.

However, it was necessary that a decision should be made, and I reached it just at the moment when we entered the port of Tenerife. It was a somewhat inauspicious moment. I had just been arrested by the sergeant-major for my final military offence. A large portion of the duties of this estimable but somewhat florid warrior had consisted in marching me under an appropriate guard into the presence of the appropriate tribunal, where he endeavoured, somewhat incoherently, to describe my various crimes.

Upon this occasion, being pardonably and indeed justifiably annoyed by one of my more eloquent defences he revenged himself on leaving the court by remarking, ' 'Astings, you ought to be a bloody lawyer.' I was overcome with gratitude.

'You are quite right, Sergeant-Major,' I said, 'I shall.'

176

I MYSELF had a very curious and remarkable experience of the working of the Peace Treaty. At that time the French were in military occupation of the greater part of the Ruhr, and it was no doubt anticipated that military law would be enforced. It was one of the terms of the Treaty that any German subject brought before a French Military Court should have the right of being defended by an advocate of whatever nationality he might select, which provision was no doubt intended for the protection of prisoners against any undue severity, and may well have been thought to have been an unnecessary provision. I am bound to say that that was not my experience. I do not tell this story without fully realising the position of a victorious nation who have themselves suffered intolerably and have only achieved their triumph after a long and bitter struggle; and moreover, I have no doubt that if the positions had been reversed the action of our enemies would have been infinitely more severe. I can only hope that never again will scenes such as those I witnessed be possible in any part of Europe.

[*It is clear from Sir Patrick's account that the French were prepared to make every effort to prevent his attending the Court, which was in a district commanded by General de Goutte. The fact that he managed, eventually and by a roundabout route, to get there was due to the efforts of Percival Phillips, the influential foreign correspondent of the* Daily Mail.]

The military Court sat in a small village about five miles from Essen, and it strangely enough bore the name of Verdun. Phillips came with me and additional security was provided by the beflagged *Daily Mail* car. It was the strangest tribunal which I have ever attended, and it had been sitting continuously for years; it seems incredible that its performances had not been brought into the public knowledge. The desire for reticence may well have been the main cause of the unpopularity of my visit. The court room was a small hall with a raised dais at one end, and it was supposed to be a public court but between the space allotted to the public and the Court itself stood a double row of soldiers with fixed bayonets. While the trial was proceeding the soldiers faced the Court, but when sentence was to be pronounced the soldiers faced the other way and presented their bayonets at the shivering audience. It was no doubt thought undesirable that there should be any public protest at anything that might take place.

Immediately the Court assembled the first case was called. I find it difficult to speak with restraint about the trials I witnessed. It seemed impossible to realise that peace had returned to a civilised world. I heard a boy of sixteen tried for espionage. The only evidence that I could hear against him consisted in the allegation that he had looked over a railway bridge and watched French soldiers unloading coal. He received a sentence of three years in a military fortress. I saw a boy of ten charged with a breach of one of the regulations made by General de Goutte. A stranger had given him a brown paper parcel to be delivered at some address in Essen, and for his trouble had handed him a German mark. The parcel was said to contain some subversive literature. It had not been opened, and it must have been extremely doubtful if the child would have been capable of reading its contents, but upon that evidence he received a sentence of twelve months' imprisonment. Neither of the prisoners had been defended and no one said a word on their behalf, and I began to understand why it had occurred to someone that a new form of procedure might be adopted in the interests of common decency.

After these two trials I had heard enough. I rose in my place to make my application. It was quite simple; I merely asked that the trial might be adjourned to whatever date might suit the Court, and that notice should be given to me both of the date of the hearing and of the nature of the alleged offence. The five officers constituting the Court rose to their feet in silence. Then the President addressed the prosecuting officer. He stated that the Court had decided not to hear any application nor to give any decision upon it. I hoped that I succeeded in concealing any personal feeling of my own, but I am bound to say that it was the first time that I had ever had an experience of such abominable rudeness. As the Court remained standing I merely stated that I would renew my application after any adjournment that the Court might make and again upon the morning of any future day upon which the Court might sit. Without a word the entire Tribunal turned and left the hall. Phillips looked depressed. He could see this enterprise lasting a good deal longer than he had hoped, and we left the Court to consider our next step. While we were so doing the prosecuting officer joined us and asked if he could talk to me in private. He was polite but extremely stiff; he told me that he had received instructions to enquire what was my real object in visiting the Ruhr and how long I proposed to stay. I told him that my object was a simple one. I was there to do two things; first, to discover the nature of the charges against my client, and then to defend him, and that I proposed to stay as long as was necessary to ensure both results. His attitude became distinctly menacing. He asked if I was not satisfied that justice would be done in a French Court without the intervention of an English advocate? I told him that I had listened to two trials and I was not prepared to answer. He then burst into a tirade. He said it was incredible that an Englishman should think it right to interest himself in criticism of his own Allies and in support of our mutual enemies, and that I must not be surprised if I found myself greeted with intense dislike and every possible obstacle placed in my way.

Then occurred one of those odd happenings that we call coincidence. In the course of his lengthy outburst he told me of his own suffering from the Germans. He had been in a prison camp and had suffered cruelly, and he spoke of an English officer who had shared his hardships, a man, he said, whose personal courage had been the admiration of French and English alike in his many and daring attempts to escape; and he, too, was an English advocate. He would never have demeaned himself by defending Germans; Gilbert Beyfus at least never criticised the French. I told him that Gilbert was a very great friend of mine and that I had been lunching with him only three days before. I asked him what his view would be if upon my next appearance Gilbert came with me?

From that moment his whole demeanour changed. I could not help feeling that his previous outburst had been more the result of official instruction than his own personal conviction, and as he spoke English far better than I spoke French, thereafter we both spoke in English. He was obviously anxious to find some way out of the difficulty, but he told me he was afraid the Court would persist in refusing to hear my application, and that I would be powerless to change their decision. I told him frankly that I had been shocked by what I had already heard, and that unless something were done I should go directly to Paris and there renew my application to the Cour de Cassation, and if necessary I was determined to take some steps in London. It was quite obvious from his attitude that this was anything but what would be acceptable to his superiors, and he asked me to wait in order to see if he could persuade the tribunal to take some different course. After half an hour I was invited to return to the Court, and I there found the tribunal had returned. I was treated with equal coldness and completely ignored, but the President addressed the prosecuting officer in a manner which he no doubt intended to be chilly, and stated that the English advocate's application would be granted and that the clients would receive full notice of the charge and at least seven days' notice of any future hearing.

As no observation had been addressed personally to me I considered the more dignified course was to remain in my seat without reply. This seemed to cause the President some perturbation. Again addressing the prosecution officer he said that the Court would be glad to know that the English advocate was satisfied with that assurance. This seemed to call for some reply. I, in my turn, addressed the prosecuting officer and told him that I could see no alternative except to be satisfied with the assurance given, but I stated that I had already informed him of the course which I had proposed to adopt, and that if anything should occur which might seem inconsistent with the assurance given my determination would remain precisely the same. Upon that cheerful note of mutual goodwill the Court dispersed and nobody spoke to me again.

Phillips came back with me to Essen. He was delighted that there was no further reason for my continued presence in the Ruhr, and he insisted upon driving me out of the the country immediately. He suggested the road to Cologne as he seemed anxious that I should see for myself the difference between the occupation by French and English troops. For about half the distance the French military were in occupation, many of them native soldiers. We drove through many villages in which they were in control; and there were no signs of life in any of them; except for the presence of armed sentries the whole countryside seemed dead. The line of demarcation between the French and British zones was defined as sharply as though it had been the frontier of a different country. The first English sentry that I saw was sitting on a cottage doorstep having coffee with the villagers; and children were playing with his rifle and his helmet. The village life appeared absolutely normal, and as far as I could see the occupation was the source of annoyance to nobody; the same state of affairs existed throughout the remainder of the journey to Cologne. If the English had been the only army in occupation of German territory, I sometimes wonder whether another war might not have been avoided.

177

The art of cross examination.

IN 1934 Hastings appeared for Princess Youssoupoff in her action for libel against the Metro Goldwyn Mayer Corporation of America. The plaintiff claimed damages because, although a character in the film had been renamed Princess Natasha, it was clear from the context that it referred to her, and the scenario depicted her as having been seduced by the wicked and notorious Rasputin. Sir William Jowitt, on behalf of the defendants, and for some reason best known to himself, had called a Welsh domestic servant to say that she had seen the film and that she at least, did not think it referred to Princess Youssoupoff. It was odd that Jowitt should have called her as a witness at all, since she established nothing, and the fact that she—never having heard before of the princess and not being likely to have done so—did not believe the film referred to her, did not begin to establish what someone *knowing* the Princess and her life would have believed.

Sir Patrick Hastings rose slowly to his feet to cross-examine and there was a hushed expectancy in Court.

'I see your name is Gwyneth Jones.'

'Yes, sir.'

'You have come from Llanelli?'

'Yes, sir.'

'I imagine you like Llanelli and are happy there?'

'Yes, sir.'

'It's a very long way from Llanelli to here, is it not?'

'Yes sir, it is.'

'And I imagine you are very anxious to get back there, are you not?'

'Yes sir, I am.'

Sir Patrick slowly resumed his place and, with a wave of his hand towards the witness box said, 'Well, you run along then.'

178

An acute American observer at the same trial, Felix Frankfurter, Judge of the American Supreme Court, observed certain differences between English and American procedure.

PRINCE YUSUPOV (*sic*) was examined by Counsel for his wife. His English was perfect, his answers were clipped and short, clear and courteous. When Sir William Jowitt got up to cross-examine him Prince Yusupov wouldn't be seen, if he could avoid it, in the same room. Just as in the old days American employers wouldn't be seen with labor leaders because in their eyes, that would involve 'recognition'. And so the Prince just wouldn't look at Jowitt. He turned away and answered out of his mouth, but not giving Jowitt his face. There were several questions without interruption. Patrick Hastings sat there, nonchalantly. Jowitt asked a series of questions and didn't get very far. Prince Yusupov held his own extremely well. Jowitt went on, and asked the same question over and over again. Actually he told the story of what they did to Rasputin in great detail and how they threw him into the icy river to make sure he wouldn't survive. Patrick Hastings got up and instead of doing the conventional American thing, 'your honor, I object, immaterial, irrelevant, impertinent, calling for a conclusion and opinion', and all the other stuff, he just got up. Before he said anything Jowitt said, 'My Lord, it's the last question I'm putting to the witness.'

Hastings didn't even put his objections, saying 'My Lord, my learned brother has asked this witness the same question twelve times.' He didn't even open his mouth. Jowitt saw, and knew what objection he was going to make, and he bent before the storm.

179

I ONCE fought a case against Marshall Hall which related to pearls. Lady Mond had sent a valuable pearl necklace to a firm of jewellers to be cleaned and alleged that owing to some neglect the pearls had been injured by excessive heat. Marshall was for the defence and he was, of course, an expert on pearls. He came into the Court surrounded by pearls; big pearls, little pearls, and all the appliances required for testing their value. There were test-tubes, microscopes and scales, in fact the only thing that appeared to be missing was a complete outfit of oysters to explain their early life.

Marshall's defence was that pearls could not possibly be affected by heat and he was prepared to give, and in fact gave, a great deal of personal evidence upon the subject. We were in great danger of being swamped by his enthusiasm when a Jewish gentleman, who was supposed to be helping me, came to the rescue. He handed me two magnificent pearls in a handsome velvet case.

'This 'ere Marshall seems to know all about pearls', he said. 'Show 'im those two and ask 'im which of 'em has been burnt, and 'ow much of its value 'as gone.'

Marshall was in his element. He took the pearls and examined them through his microscopes; he bit them and smelt them and applied the appropriate tests, while the whole Court awaited his decision with breathless interest. Finally he gave us his expert opinion.

'My Lord,' he said, holding up the larger of the two, 'this pearl has undoubtedly been affected by excessive heat.'

'Never mind about that,' shouted the little Jew, 'how much of the value has been lost?'

Marshall pondered deeply. 'Without further examination it is difficult to express a decided opinion, but I should estimate the damage at about five hundred pounds.'

The Jewish gentlemen leaped to his feet; for a moment I thought he was going to kiss me. 'Tell 'im they're duds', he said, in a voice that all could hear. 'He can have 'em both for a bob.'

Poor Marshall! There was, of course, another scene in Court. The microscopes were swept away and Marshall swept out after them. He had been wounded in his tenderest spot and it was at least a week before we were friends again.

HENRY HAWKINS (LORD BRAMPTON) (1817–1907)

180

Hawkins started his legal career as an articled clerk in the office of his father, John Hawkins, solicitor of Hitchin, Herts.

HAWKINS was turned out of the firm for perpetrating practical jokes at the expense of the clients, and sent up to London 'to sink or swim'.

He forged a letter to the *Herts Mercury*, in his father's well-known writing, announcing the sudden and lamentable death of John Curling, Chairman of the Hitchin Bench; to the astonishment and rage of the editor who heard, four days later, after printing a suitable obituary notice, that Curling was presiding as usual at Petty Sessions.

It did not stop there, however, for Hawkins as soon as the hunt had died down, procured two other insertions announcing the premature deaths of Miss Beaumont and Miss Christina Times. He felt that all these people *should* be dead and that the flutter of even a false alarm might possibly shorten their days.

181

In the famous Tichborne Claimant case the point at issue was the identity of the Claimant. He asserted that he was the rightful heir to the Tichborne baronetcy. The family were convinced that he was the son of a butcher from Wapping. Much turned on the question of tattoo marks. The Claimant was demonstrably untattooed. Bogle (Sir Roger Tichborne's black servant) had sworn that Roger had no tattoo marks either. Hawkins cross-examines.*

'How do you *know* Roger had no tattoo marks?'
'I saw his arms on three occasions.'
'The sleeves, how were they?'
'Loose.'
'How came you to see his naked arms?'
'He was rubbing one of them—like this.'
'What did he rub for?'
'I thought he'd got a flea.'
'Did you see it?'
'No, of course not.'
'Where was it?'
'Just there.'
'What time was this?'
'Ten minutes past eleven.'
'That's the first occasion. Come to the second.'
'Just the same.'
'Same time?'
'Yes.'
'Did he always put his hand inside his sleeve to rub?'
'I don't know.'
'But I want to know what you saw.'
'The same as before.'
'A flea?'
'I suppose.'

* See also Kenealy, p. 190.

'But did you see him, Bogle?'

'I told you, Mr Hawkins, I did not.'

'Excuse me. That was on the first occasion.'

'Well, this was the same.'

'Same flea?'

'I suppose.'

'Same time? Ten minutes past eleven?'

'Yes.'

'Then all I can say is he must have been a very punctual old flea.'

182

The narrator is Serjeant Robinson

Judges in undress.

I WAS pulling up the river at Guildford, after mess, with my old friend, Richard Corner (afterwards Chief Justice of the Gold Coast, and subsequently transferred to Honduras in the same capacity). We had rowed for a mile or two along the narrow stream, without meeting with a single human being, for on the one side there are trees bordering parks and fields attached to distant residences; and on the other an unfrequented foot-path. But, on approaching a lock, we could perceive, standing erect on the middle of the lock-gates, two strange forms that somewhat startled us. We did not recognise them at first, but, on getting nearer, we found that the figures represented our two learned friends Henry Hawkins and Edwin James. The only clothing we could detect about them was a hat on the head of one and a pair of boots in the hand of the other. As for James, fat and pursy as he was, he looked the colour of a recently boiled lobster, while Hawkins, thin and spare, gave one the idea that he had been painted blue. There they stood trembling with fear, while Corner and I were puzzled to guess what it all meant; for we had kept our heads turned to the right while nearing the lock, but, on a hint from the boots which pointed to the left, we turned round and the mystery was at once cleared up.

On the pathway was a raging bull, digging his horns into the habiliments of our friends, tossing them in the air, and evidently annoyed that he could not treat the owners in the same fashion. It seems he had come rushing towards them as they were preparing to take a bathe, and they had only just time to seize the first article of raiment that came to hand, and run upon the lock with all speed, to save themselves from the animal's fury.

We were of course prepared to render the prisoners the help they beseechingly implored. Having the coign of vantage—for the banks shelved gradually, and the bull could not reach us in mid-stream—we managed after a time by shouts and by brandishing our oars to drive the beast away. When the reprieved captives saw that he was at a respectful distance, they came ashore, dressed themselves as well as they could in their tattered garments, and thanked us warmly for the service we had rendered them; and well they might, for had it not been for our providential appearance, and if the bull had been of a determined and obstinate frame of mind, they might have remained upon their perch, nude and upright, until the next morning.

183

IN January, 1881, England was well nigh submerged in snow, as the result of the extraordinary blizzard which occurred towards the middle of that month. London streets became impassable, the snow extending right up the sides of the houses. The Assizes at Maidstone were about to be held, and at four o'clock one afternoon a train left Victoria for that town, among the passengers in which were the Circuit Judges, Mr Justice Hawkins and Mr Justice Denman and several members of the Bar, including myself. We started at the height of the storm; but we had not gone very far on our journey when it became clear that there was a serious danger of our being snowed up, so we had to hasten to retrace our steps to London, where we arrived very late at night. It was quite impossible to get home; my dressing-bags had been taken to Maidstone by my clerk earlier in the day, so I and two more of us had to take refuge for the night, minus our luggage, at the Grosvenor Hotel. We learned next day that the train immediately preceding ours had been forced to return even before we had started, which naturally made Mr Justice Hawkins extremely angry; and I have little doubt that he showed his displeasure with some degree of acrimony. In order to appease him the manager of the station arranged to have a special train for Judges and Bar as soon as circumstances would allow of our making a start; and he made provision for Her Majesty's Judges accommodation by supplying them with a lunch on the train, in which champagne was not forgotten. The Bar were left to find luncheons for themselves; and I suppose nothing else could well have been expected in this not unimportant respect.

Well, we started and arrived at our destination early in the afternoon. There was a large crowd awaiting us at the station, and on the platform were the High Sheriff, the Under Sheriff, the Chaplain, all in full canonicals, awaiting the advent of the Judges. I happened to be in the carriage next to that of the Judges and saw distinctly what followed. There was a great deal of bowing and scraping, the carriage door was opened with a flourish in the sight of the officials and some of the waiting crowd, hats were removed and, lo and behold! out rolled an empty champagne bottle, followed by Mr Justice Hawkins, with all the dignity of which the circumstances would allow.

184

The narrator is Edmund Purcell

MR JUSTICE HAWKINS took a malign pleasure in inconveniencing Counsel. I once had to defend, at Hertford, a shooting burglar caught in Lord Salisbury's grounds. At the London station I met the judge, and he invited me into his reserved compartment. During the hour's journey he was continually telling me stories of his judicial experience to prove his anxiety that prisoners should get justice if innocent, or leniency if guilty. Whenever I could I interposed expressions of agreement and admiration. The bill against my prisoner was returned very early, and on the strength of what had passed in the train I ventured to ask the learned judge if he would dispose of the case as it was only a plea of guilty. With the familiar merciless smile which Roman emperors must have worn when in the gladiatorial fights they turned their thumbs down, his reply was simply 'no, not today'. I think I travelled down three or four days and it was only on the last day of the Assize that he dealt with my case. There was no public object whatever in the delay.

185

Judge after Judge had complained bitterly of the lodgings made available to them in a certain Assize Town. All to no avail. However . . .

IT happened that at an autumn assize Sir Henry Hawkins was the judge on circuit and a sheep stealing case came before him. The stealing had taken place in August just after the summer assizes; the sheep had to be killed, but their skins were preserved in a box to be produced at the trial for the purpose of identification.

Sir Henry, in the hottest days, never allowed a window or door to be kept open. The air therefore, in a densely crowded court, was none of the purest, but when the skins were unpacked the odour was almost insufferable and many persons were ill.

After identification of the skins counsel for the prosecution asked the judge if they might be taken away.

Perfectly indifferent to any smell he said: 'Yes, oh, yes. You may take them away if you wish.'

The policeman in charge of the skins asked where he should take them to.

'You had better', said Sir Henry, 'take them to the drawing-room of the Judges Lodgings. The smell will not be noticed there.'

Everybody laughed, who was well enough to do so, except the Judge who looked in front of his desk without a smile.

The next day the local press teemed with the story, with such effect that before the next Assizes the lodgings had been rendered fit for human habitation.

The power of ridicule sometimes removes mountains.

186

The narrator is Sir Travers Humphreys

HAWKINS' last nine years on the Bench were my first nine years at the Bar and my opportunities of watching the Judge and to some extent judging the man were those of a comparative outsider, the class of person who is popularly supposed to see most of the game. What I saw was an elderly but vigorous man, very sure of himself, very certain of the law, willing to hear argument, but once his view had been stated, allowing no further discussion upon the matter; what I heard was a beautiful voice with a slight purr in it which seemed to resemble the sound made by a pleased cat; when there was an interruption or a sound of any kind displeasing to the speaker, which is the same thing as saying any sound but that of his own voice, the resemblance to a domestic cat vanished. There was no raising of the voice, still less anything resembling a feline spitting of rage, but the voice would be heard murmuring that the slightest interruption from any quarter would be followed by a clearing of the Court, and if necessary a further step which would have the effect of making the interrupter very sorry for himself. And it sufficed. I have never known a Court so still as Hawkins' or, be it said, so stuffy. He had a horror of draughts, and often had the available windows not only closed but pasted over with brown paper so as to exclude any suspicion of fresh air. And yet Hawkins was fond of good air and cold air, for he attended every race-meeting on Newmarket Heath which he could get to, and it was said that he was pretty unscrupulous in disposing of his list on the morning of a big day. No man who is in the habit of attending meetings in the spring or autumn at Newmarket can be accused of harbouring a dislike of fresh air.

Hawkins always seemed to me to try his cases beautifully. The impression on my youthful mind was that of a man who knew more about the subject than anyone else in Court and was therefore right. I do not think that his worst enemies would deny that he was a master of the criminal law and one whose opinion on any legal question was entitled to the greatest respect. What I observed, therefore, at the CCC, where he was a frequent visitor, and at the Law Courts, where Hawkins when sitting at *nisi prius* was always to be found in Court V, which indeed came to be known as Hawkins' Court, was a somewhat old gentleman of whom everyone appeared to be afraid.

It was on Circuit that I heard of, and on one occasion at least witnessed the Judge's extraordinary behaviour towards the Bar. If the stories current were to be believed, Hawkins took a fiendish delight in making things as difficult as possible for those who had business before him. He steadily refused to fix cases in advance to oblige anybody. He was invariably polite and courteous in manner. He would so much like to oblige Mr Blank, but unfortunately the state of the business did not permit him to say in advance when he could take the case mentioned, though as Mr Blank was aware he was always anxious to study the convenience of the Bar. The result was that Counsel, solicitors and witnesses were kept hanging about for days. It was our Clerk of Assize on the South Eastern Circuit who first suggested to me a possible explanation of Hawkins' behaviour. His suggestion was that the Judge was anxious to keep up the old Circuit traditions, and with that object to encourage barristers to stay at the various Assize towns, whereas he found there was a tendency to come down by an early train in the morning and get back home to sleep. There may be something in that suggestion so far as the towns near London were concerned, but at distant towns such as Norwich and Ipswich, those in the first case in the morning were always bound to stay at the Bar hotel and dine in mess. The view of the Bar was that Hawkins was simply indulging in a practice which pleased him because it annoyed others, and they held that it was for the same reason that he refused to state at what hour he would rise. Sittings on Circuit in those days were often very late. Hawkins, so I was told, was quite equal to keeping the parties in the case following the one he was trying at the Assize town until the last train had gone and then 'for the convenience of the Bar and the witnesses' announcing that he would 'try to take the case some time tomorrow'. I witnessed one such incident which is perhaps worth repeating if only because for once the learned Judge met his match.

There was on our Circuit a barrister named Ogle, a capable and very popular member of the Mess. For some reason Hawkins was even more disobliging to him than to the remainder of the Bar. The incident occurred at Chelmsford, where the last train to London which would enable the traveller to reach the Metropolis for dinner left at 5 p.m. Hawkins was quite aware of that fact, and regularly refused to release any case until after five. Ogle had one case left, and particularly wanted to get to town, where he had a brief the next morning. He accordingly asked the Judge at about 4.30 whether he would adjourn the case until the next afternoon, telling him how he was placed.

'How long will the case take, Mr Ogle?'

'About two hours, my Lord, too long I think for your Lordship to try it tonight after the present case, which I understand will last until 6.30 at the earliest.'

'Oh, no, Mr Ogle, we often have to sit as late as that. I may be able to take it tonight.'

Ogle retired. At 4.50 Ogle came into Court, having ascertained from the Judge's butler that His Lordship was entertaining friends to dinner at eight and would certainly not sit beyond 7.30. Ogle was disrobed but had his robe-bag in his hand, nodded good-night to his friends and was seen by the Judge to leave, obviously going to catch the 5 o'clock train.

At 6.30 the case in hand was finished. Hawkins, with his most seraphic smile, announced, 'Now we can oblige Mr Ogle. Call his case on.'

Ogle's case was called on, when to Hawkins' disgust there appeared Ogle, robed, with his brief, who proceeded to express his profound thanks to the Judge for his great kindness in taking the case that evening! There was nothing to be done but try the case, and Ogle took good care that the case should last the full two hours, to the intense and evident annoyance of the learned Judge who had to keep his guests waiting.

187

A CHAPLAIN who had preached the Assize sermon failed to obtain, by indirect methods, any compliments from the Judge. At last he asked his Lordship point-blank what he thought of the discourse.

'It was a divine sermon', said Hawkins. 'For it was like the peace of God—which passeth all understanding. And like his mercy, it seemed to endure for ever.'

ARTHUR GARFIELD HAYS (1881–1954)

American Lawyer

188

At the time of industrial strife in a coal town in Pennsylvania Mr Hays had been set upon by the coal and iron police. He swore out warrants for the arrest of his assailants.

IN an effort to serve these warrants I started for the coal-company office, where the police were taking refuge, whereupon an officer jumped on me, dragged me along the street, and threw me into the hoose-gow. I am told there was great consternation when, an hour or two later, my captors discovered that they had locked up a New York lawyer.

My trial then took place.

The justice of the peace was an employee of the coal company.

Said he: 'This is a very serious matter, Mr Hays.'

'I am ready for trial, your honor.'

'All right. I find you guilty and fine you five dollars.'

'I want a trial.'

'I was near enough. I know what happened.'

'You don't understand me. I said I was ready for trial. People all over the United States are interested in what happens in these closed towns.'

'Well, you don't have to pay the five dollars if you get out of town.'

'I don't intend to pay the five dollars and I don't intend to get out of town.'

'Well, it's all over.'

'I won't let a verdict of guilty stand against me.'

'All right, then, you're not guilty.'

MAURICE HEALY (1887–1943)

King's Counsel

189

Irish Juries.

IT must be admitted that there were some very bad juries in Ireland, and I have seen some very bad ones in this country as well. But the Irish juries, even when bad, had sometimes the mitigating grace that they added to the gaiety of the Court. There was the very rural jury in Listowel that once was assisting Judge Shaw to try a case of rape; the jurisdiction of Quarter Sessions was wider in Ireland than over here.

The prosecutrix gave her evidence with a complete absence of embarrassment, and with such readinesss to go into detail, that the Judge turned in disgust to the Jury and said: 'Ah, gentlemen, you daren't hang a dog upon evidence like that.'

The Jury collogued; then the foreman said, 'Your Honour, we're unanimously of the opinion that the boy didn't do it: but should your Honour be wishful to hear any more evidence, we wouldn't be stopping you.'

190

Irish Witnesses.

THE Englishman goes into a Court of Law unwillingly, fearfully, and particularly apprehensive of cross-examination. No doubt there are occasional witnesses of that kind in Ireland, too, but the vast majority give their evidence as a cricketer walks to the wicket. Each is confident he will not be bowled until he has knocked up a good score; each is very disappointed if the bowler limits his efforts to preventing the score from rising, and does not attack the wicket.

To see a Kerryman climb onto the table and take the oath would inevitably recall Macaulay's lines:

> But hark! the cry is Astur
> And lo! the ranks divide,
> And the great Lord of Luna
> Comes with his stately stride

The witness would settle himself in the chair with which every Irish witness is accommodated, and would turn upon the enemy 'a glance serene and high', which he would renew from time to time during his examination, especially when he thought he had scored a hit. He would answer his own counsel condescendingly, much as the gardener might explain to you about his roses; and every now and then he would turn to the Judge in a friendly way and explain the effect of his last answer, so as to make it easy for him.

As the opposing advocate stood up to cross-examine him he would stiffen; every faculty brought under strict control, he would listen to the first question to see if he could not get in something really contemptuous in his reply. Sometimes he would merely turn to the Judge with a pitying smile, as much as to say 'Will you listen to what this poor omadhaun is asking me!' At other times his eye would sweep around the galleries. Much as Mr Gladstone might have emphasised a point by turning a flashing glance towards his supporters. To attempt to overthrow the testimony of such a highly-skilled partisan by the usual 'I-suggest-you-are-wrong' kind of cross-examination would be to court disaster. An apparent preparation for a frontal attack, very quietly made, would be followed by a thundering charge upon an unsuspecting flank: and then, in the confusion of this surprise, some vigorous cut and thrust might well take place. Carson was not good at this. In the late Edward Marjoribank's *Life of Carson* he cites a number of instances of English witnesses being bowled out by a cross-examination, deadly in England but which would not have knocked a feather off a Kerryman.

Instead of the awkward silence chronicled in the biography, there would have been an indignant repetition of the question, followed by a turn towards the Judge, who would be swamped in a deluge of irrelevant matter, as though it were a complete explanation of the problem under examination; and by the time the witness would be brought back to the point he would have thought of a plausible answer to the actual question he had been asked.

The difference of atmosphere between the two countries was exemplified in a case of my father's which came to be tried in London before Mr Justice Darling. The point at issue was the identity of a valuable picture, and hosts of witnesses, many of them humble Irish folk, were examined on either side. One of these Irishmen who had tuned his harp to the romantic air of his own County Court was a shock to a judge of pedestrian imagination. Darling at last turned to him sternly and said 'Tell me, in your country, what happens to a witness who does not tell the truth?' 'Begor, me Lord,' replied the Irishman, with a candour that disarmed all criticism, 'I think his side usually wins.'

NEVILLE GEORGE CLEVELY HEATH (1917–46)

191

It is probably unnecessary, even nearly forty years after his execution, to remind readers that Heath was convicted, on the clearest evidence, of the beating, mutilation, and murder of two women. J. D. Casswell QC, who defended him, reports the postscript.

JUST a few days before his execution on October 26th at Pentonville Prison, he wrote to C. A. Joyce, the Governor of the Borstal Institution to which he had been sent eight years previously.

> You and your dear wife and, perhaps more so, your ideals which we all worked so hard for once, occupy a very special corner of my long list of pleasant memories. I shall always remember 8.30 p.m. and the 'Brotherhood of this House' (the time and name given to their prayers). In that, if I may say so, you have something that will never fail. I will be with you nightly at 8.30 for as long as you care to remember me.

And just before he was led out to the execution chamber he is reported to have asked the Prison Governor for a whisky. While this was being brought he corrected himself and said: 'You might make that a double.' No playwright could have written a better last line.

FARRER HERSCHELL (LORD HERSCHELL) (1837–99)

Lord Chancellor

192

LORD HERSCHELL, then Mr Herschell, had a clerk who was a great character. In the year in which Mr Justice Willes died, Herschell came back at the end of the Long Vacation and asked his clerk what was going on. The clerk said: 'Nothing particular.' 'Well,' said Herschell, 'but haven't they been asking you anything?' 'Oh yes!' he said, 'they have asked me whether we're going to take a puisne Judgeship.' 'What did you reply?', said Herschell. 'I said, "Thank God, we haven't fallen as low as that!" '

GORDON HEWART (LORD HEWART) (1870–1943)

Lord Chief Justice

193

THE Counsel for the appellant has taken seventeen objections to his conviction. He has argued each one. We have listened to him and we find that each one comes to nothing. Nothing multiplied by seventeen is still nothing. The appeal is dismissed.

WILLIAM JOYNSON HICKS (LORD BRENTFORD) (1865–1932)

Solicitor and Home Secretary

194

IN 1887, at the age of twenty-two, William Hicks's training ended, and he was admitted as a solicitor. His first step was to beard the senior partner of the firm to which he had been articled, and to demand a partnership. He was incontinently refused. So the next year he rented an office in Old Jewry Chambers, set up a brass plate, engaged an office boy . . . and waited hopeful to the end of the day.

With hope renewed he arrived each morning at 9.45.

'Any letters this morning?', he would enquire of the office boy.

'None, sir.'

That meant there was no work. Nevertheless, William Hicks, Solicitor, sat at his desk until six o'clock, reading. Sometimes he read law books; sometimes classical works. Sometimes as a punishment to the office boy for sucking oranges in business hours he would give the boy one of the few deeds in the office to copy.

In spite of all, at the end of his first year of practice his account book showed that, after paying all expenses, he had earned a personal income of £100.

His professional correspondence must have shocked some of the old-fashioned solicitors of his day. If he had to threaten drastic action, he would warn the debtor to 'look out for squalls', rather than use the sinister phraseology which the solicitor usually employs to strike terror into the hearts of defaulters. And he assured a man in Lincolnshire, which county had been suffering from violent storms, that his past experiences would be as nothing compared with the tornado which would break over his head if he did not pay what he owed.

Towards his own clients he adopted quite a different tone. If a bill of costs had been outstanding for too long, he would employ irony, enquiring gently whether the client would care to pay his bill, or did he prefer that it should be written off as a bad debt? In those days, it seems, people chose to respond rather than to incur such discredit.

William Hicks was an excellent judge of character. This attribute, which was of immense use to him in after life, never stood him in better stead than one day, early in his career, when a woman came to his office and told him she would not, and could not, pay the debt which she owed his client. William Hicks was certain the woman was lying.

'Very well', he said. 'I must proceed to the full extremity of the law.'

'But you can't,' said the woman, 'the disgrace would kill me.'

'I don't mind that at all', said the hard-hearted solicitor.

Hysteria supervened. 'If you don't let me off I shall come up here to your office and commit suicide in your room—I can't bear it.'

'Madam,' replied William Hicks in the suavest of tones, 'there is only one personal favour I ask: if you must do this, please do it on a Wednesday—the night when the office cleaner comes.'

195

SIR WILLIAM, as he was at the time, was acting for a lady who had refused to pay rent because, as she contended, the house which she had agreed to take was uninhabitable, owing to the presence of mice which 'stank vilely'. Joynson-Hicks was now a Member of Parliament; so also was his friend Mr Rigby Swift, KC, who was counsel for the opponents. Joynson-Hicks was giving evidence as to the virulence and all-pervading nature of the smell, when Mr Swift put a very clever question to him in cross-examination: 'Tell me, Sir William, did you visit this house in your capacity as the solicitor for the defendant, or as her friend?' The witness saw that he was in danger. If he replied, 'as a friend', the value of his evidence would be discounted because it was not impartial. If he said 'as a solicitor', his ability to give expert evidence upon the smells of mice would be ridiculed. Immediately he wriggled out of the trap by replying, 'I visited the house in my capacity as a human being.' He won that round of the fight, but counsel, as an able barrister always should, had the last word. 'Really, Sir William, I have had the pleasure of meeting you in many capacities, and I am delighted to meet you in a new one.'

SIR GEORGE MALCOLM HILBERY (1883–1965)

196

The narrator is George Lyttelton

TALKING of Judges I spent this morning in the Court of Mr Justice Hilbery. Not very interesting. A lot of talk about how far a stiff ankle reduces the agility of a foreman-plumber. Hilbery pooh-poohed a good many points of both counsel, which I suppose shewed his impartiality: he is one of the rather grumpy mumbling judges, but I believe not a bad one. I heard him once holding forth to great purpose in dismissing a claim for compensation to a man who had fallen off a perfectly sound ladder. 'Nowadays, if a man chokes over a biscuit he sues the confectioner; it's all rubbish.'

GEORGE HILL (1716–1808)

Serjeant-at-Law

197

MR SERJEANT HILL was not only the most learned but one of the most eccentric Lawyers of his time. His colleagues called him Serjeant Labyrinth. He had the habit of becoming so absorbed in his profession that it rendered him perfectly insensible to all objects around him. He was engaged to an heiress, and on the morning appointed for the wedding went down to his chambers as usual; but, becoming immersed in business, forgot entirely the engagement that he had for that morning. The bride waited for him so long that a messenger had to be despatched to his chambers. He obeyed the summons; and having been married returned to work. At about dinner time his clerk, suspecting that the Serjeant had forgotten the proceedings of the morning, ventured to recall them to his recollections; and sent him home to dinner.

REGINALD LESLIE HINE (1883–1949)

Solicitor

198

The narrator is Reginald Hine, Solicitor and local historian, of Hitchin

HOW often do I turn aside from our bleak and precedent-prepared modern testaments, and dip into my glorious collection of Hitchin wills in medieval, Stuart, and Georgian days when beds and coffers and tables, 'silver spongs', 'platterys and pewter dyshes', saucers and candlesticks and even warming pans were handed down to children and even grandchildren with tender care, as though each prize possession were an heirloom.

So likewise—and even to a later period—was it with the doublets, gowns, kirtles and cloaks with which our forefathers arranged themselves when they were 'in the body!' Elizabeth Joyce enriches her sister-in-law with 'my best beaver hatt, my damaske gowne and damaske petticoat of a sea-green colour'. Mary Corrie passes on to brother George 'a bible and a pair of sheets'. Mary Swain, spinster, has no-one to love and very little to leave: 'To my niece Mary Swain my best stays and my worst. To May Doggett my second best stays, my red cloake and a frying pan.'

Years ago, at the end of a lecture that I had delivered on medieval England to a village audience, a fine old country couple came up to me and said 'Muster 'Ine, we proper fancied what you said about them 'deeval wills and, if you don't moind, the missus and me 'ud like to 'ave ouren done after the same fashion.'

For a moment I was taken aback. It rather looked as though I had been touting for business. So I hurried my new clients out of the hall, and then the three of us, linking arms for safety in the dark, jogged down the lane to their cottage so that I could make an inspection of their treasures. They had been quite right in their feelings; along with the tawdry trinkets, the oleographs, the hand-stitched scriptural texts, and the terrible photographs, there were some admirable pieces: a Dutch dower-chest, a Welsh dresser, a red-lacquer corner-cupboard, a copy of the Breeches Bible, and a portrait of John Bunyan that looked like an original.

Having taken instructions on how to share these among the sons and daughters, I enquired about grandchildren, and learned that there was but one. 'What can we do for Hannah?', I asked. The old man scratched his head, but the woman looked suddenly bright.

'I have it', she declared. 'I have it. You mentioned bells, sir, in your talk.'

'Yes, indeed, I did', I replied. 'I told you about Edward Pryor, barber-surgeon, who died wondering what he could do to amuse his little girl when he was dead and gone, and how he slipped into his will: "I give my daughter Mary bells for a child to play with." ' 'That's it. That's the very thing.'

And with that she flew to the corner-cupboard and fetched out a miniature set of hand-bells, made at Biggleswade of all unmusical places. We tried playing *The Bailiff's Daughter of Islington* upon them with very poor results.

'But Hannah will do better,' I declared. And then, muddling up my modern and medieval notes and drinking to their long life in nauseous cowslip wine, likely to shorten my own, I took my leave.

HENRY HOME (LORD KAMES) (1696–1782)

199

AN example of Kames' judicial manner is furnished by Lord Cockburn. In 1780 at Ayr Kames tried Mathew Hay (with whom he used to play chess) on a charge of murder. On learning that a verdict of guilty had been returned his Lordship exclaimed 'That's checkmate to you, Matthew.'*

ERNEST TERAH HOOLEY† (*fl.* 1922–3)

A company promoter, convicted of fraud

200

The narrator is A. E. Bowker, Birkett's clerk

In the course of twenty months Hooley floated no less than twenty-six companies with a capital of £18,000,000, *and gained the name of 'The Modern Midas'.*

EVENTUALLY justice caught up with him, and he came to grief over the 'Jubilee Cotton Mills' case and there arose out of it a rather complicated conspiracy charge in which there were six defendants, including Thomas Fletcher, a former Mayor of Derby for whom Norman Birkett appeared.

Of course Hooley was the real culprit, and the others had simply been caught up in the toils of his specious projects.

A great character, this man, extremely likeable, friendly and generous to a fault. I saw a lot of him with our client poor old Tom Fletcher. We would meet in the big upstairs hall of the Old Bailey before the day's hearing, all being on continuous bail.

Our man was in his late sixties, and felt his position terribly. The very thought of appearing in the dock was, to him, a dreadful ordeal

* This is inaccurately recorded in Lockhart's *Life of Scott* (First Edition) at Chapter 34, in which he gets the name of the Judge, the locale of the trial, *and* the nature of the crime all wrong.

† See also Birkett v. Muir, p. 28.

and we did our best to reassure him that he was certain to be acquitted: as, indeed, we felt sure he would be on the evidence.

Not so Hooley. His perverse sense of humour would not let our client glean the least grain of comfort from our assurances. He would say to him, 'now, don't you worry about anything, Tom. You just leave it to me. Once we get inside I know the ropes and I'll see what I can do about getting you a job in the prison library.'

And Tom would writhe with anguish at the bare thought.

And morning after morning, as the group of defendants would be waiting in the great upper hall during the twenty-three days of the trial, Hooley would turn to dear old Tom and remark casually: 'Well Tom, only another few days of liberty and then it's us for the big jump. Now, don't forget what I've told you. If there isn't a job going in the library, you just ask the prison MO if he will recommend you for the laundry or the kitchen. You can always fiddle a bit more grub in the kitchen, you know, and you're not strong enough to sew mailbags. That's heavy work for the hardened old lags.'

And poor Tom's eyes would goggle with apprehension.

There is no getting away from it that Hooley was the life and soul of the party, and although he knew the heavy gates of prison were liable to close behind him for a few years he never once lost his sense of humour. A likeable fellow, as I have found so many of the scamps who have passed through our hands.

Tom Fletcher aged daily through that trial; but I am glad to say we succeeded in proving him innocent of any conspiracy with either Hooley or any of the other defendants, and the jury returned the verdict of Not Guilty.

SIR THOMAS GARDNER HORRIDGE (1857–1938)

201

The narrator is Henry Cecil

MR JUSTICE HORRIDGE was quite a good judge, though a little on the stern side. Young advocates found him rather intimidating. Some witnesses found him difficult, though at first they were disarmed by what appeared to be the kindly smile with which he looked at them. Sometimes a rather bumptious witness, encouraged by his smile, would try to crack a joke. The judge jumped on him immediately, and the poor fellow couldn't think what he had done to change the benevolent and encouraging looking judge into what appeared to him to be a judicial monster. The solution was quite simple. Half of Mr Justice Horridge's face was paralysed, and made him look as though he were smiling. It was rather bad luck on the witness.

'How do you make your living?', asked Horridge.

'The same as you do, my Lord. My job depends on the stupidity of the public, so we're in the same boat, eh my Lord?'

'Behave yourself', said Horridge. 'Stand up. Take your hands out of your pockets, and don't try to be funny.'

WILLIAM FREDERICK HOWE (1829–1902) and ABRAHAM HENRY HUMMEL (1850–1926)

American Lawyers

202

THE firm of Howe and Hummel had almost a monopoly of the criminal business in New York in their day. They were the attorneys for all the major brothel owners. When seventy-four madams were rounded up during a purity drive in 1884 every one of them named Howe and Hummel as counsel. Mother Mandlebaum, the leading fence of the age, paid Howe and Hummel a retainer of five thousand dollars a year to defend her and her army of thieves. The firm had the legal business of General Abe Greenthal's Sheeny mob, a nationwide syndicate of pickpockets, of Chester McLaughlin's Valentine gang of forgers; and of the Whyos, an organisation of thugs and killers that was perhaps the toughest of all the nineteenth-century gangs.

They found loopholes large enough for convicted murderers to walk through standing up. Once, in 1888, Howe produced a state of terror in the city by invoking a technicality which, if it had been allowed by the higher courts, would have set free not only the murderer he was defending, but every other first-degree murderer then awaiting execution and every defendant then awaiting trial.

On another occasion Hummel almost depopulated the city prison on Blackwell's Island by discovering a technical error in the procedure by which two hundred and forty petty criminals had been committed. After collecting a small fee from each man, they obtained the release of the entire group. Only sixty-some-odd prisoners were left on the island.

203

It seems to have been fairly common practice for prisoners who escaped from the Tombs to head straight for the offices of Howe and Hummel where a skeleton force was on hand all night, and to proceed from there to the next hideaway. Danny Driscoll, the leader of the Whyos, once came running into the office brandishing a knife and oozing blood from several bullet wounds. He was caught later on, and it was subsequently charged, though never proven, that the knife with which he had hacked his way out of prison, cutting up several guards as he moved along, had been supplied him by an employee of Howe and Hummel who had visited his cell ostensibly to discuss his defence.

William J. Sharkey, who made the most notable of all escapes from the Tombs, stopped off at Howe and Hummel to discard the black wool dress, green veil and alpine hat in which he made his getaway. Sharkey, an ex-pickpocket and a Tammany district leader at the time he killed a gambling companion, was never caught. He finally got to Ireland and lived the rest of his life there.

There was excitement of sorts in the office even when escaped prisoners were not supplying it. The place was a nest of practical jokers. According to a still active attorney who started as an office boy with Howe and Hummel, their establishment was one in which buckets of water could be expected to tip from any transom and chairs were being constantly yanked out from under anyone who tried to sit on them. ‘Every morning when I went to my desk,’ this man recalls, ‘I had to look underneath to see there wasn’t any glue there—someone was always gluing my shoes to the floor so when Mr Howe called me I couldn’t move. You couldn’t say it was a dull place to work.’

WILLIAM FREDERICK HOWE (1828–1902)

American Lawyer

204

IF by chance a particular defendant did not have a pretty wife, fond children or a snowy-haired mother Howe would supply them from the firm's large stable of professional spectators. Repulsive and ape-like killers often turned up in court with lamb-like children and wives of fragile beauty. There are several cases on record in which the Bench felt called upon to rebuke Howe for insinuating that the incarceration or execution of a defendant who, to the best of the court's knowledge, was single and childless when he was arrested, would bring tragedy into the lives of so many people seated about the courtroom; and there is one instance of a stern reprimand from the Judge who felt that a jury was somehow being imposed upon when, just as Howe reached the family motif in his summation, a young lady on the front bench found it the appropriate moment to bare her breast to the infant in her arms and look tenderly at the prisoner at the bar.

205

OWEN REILLY, one of a number of young men who supported themselves by setting fire to buildings for people who felt that the insurance on their properties was more to be desired than the uncertain revenues they might bring them in the future, had ignited a row of the stores on the Lower East side. He was arrested, and he retained Howe to defend him.

Howe, or some other legal eagle in the office, read up on the statutes covering arson, and found that by pleading Reilly guilty to attempted arson, rather than let him stand trial for having committed arson, they could save the firm the bother of a trial and save Reilly the possible inconvenience of going to prison for the rest of his life. The District Attorney and the judge agreed to accept the lesser plea.

When Reilly came up for sentence Howe rose and stated that the law provided no penalty for the crime of attempted arson. The court begged enlightenment. 'The sentence for attemped arson,' Howe said, 'like the sentence for any crime attempted but not actually committed, was half the maximum imposed by the law for the actual commission of the crime. The penalty for arson was life imprisonment, no less. Hence, if the court were to determine a sentence for Reilly, it would have to determine half a life. Scripture tells us that we know not the day nor the hour of our departure. Can this court sentence the prisoner to half of his natural life? Will it then sentence him to half a minute, or half the days of Methuselah?'

The court agreed that the problem was beyond its earth-bound wisdom. Reilly walked out, presumably to arm himself with a new supply of matches and tinder, and the legislature revised the arson statutes soon thereafter.

SIR JOHN WALTER HUDDLESTON (1815–90)

206

MRS BROADWOOD (late Miss Tree) is said to have been the author of this hoax on Huddy. A few days ago Mr Huddleston arrived in Baden-Baden and duly inscribed his name and his 'QC' and 'MP' in the hotel book of visitors. But to this inscription somebody subsequently added the words 'Tuft-hunter and Toady', in handwriting so similar that the whole read as one continuous and genuine announcement. In this light the authorities seem to have viewed it. They copied the words *literatim*, honestly believing them to convey some social distinction, and next morning, greatly to the amusement of the social coterie, 'Huddy's' name appeared in the official list of visitors with the queer additions of 'Tuft-hunter and Toady' tacked on to his titles.

ABRAHAM HENRY HUMMEL (1850–1926)

American Lawyer

207

Hummel's speciality was the affidavits which he obtained from ladies who reported that men, who were sometimes well-known and wealthy, had made too free with them. The victim, or his lawyer, was served with the affidavit and told how much it would cost him to suppress it. He usually paid up. Half the proceeds went to the girl, half to Hummel. He was curiously scrupulous in his conduct of this business.

IT was a matter of both principle and good business with Hummel to see to it that a man who had once been successfully blackmailed was never again troubled by the same girl. As far as he was concerned it was a matter of a single bill for a single seduction.

Naturally it sometimes occurred to the brighter young women that it would be sound economy to make an old investment pay off a second time if that were possible. They would start proceedings through another lawyer. As soon as Hummel heard that one of his victims was being troubled again, he straightened things out for the victim in short order. Hummel once explained to a group of friends how he managed this.

'Before I hand over her share,' Hummel said, 'the girl and I have a little talk. She listens to me dictate an affidavit saying that she has deceived me, as her attorney and that, in fact, nothing at all between the man involved ever took place; that she was thoroughly repentant over her conduct in the case, and that, but for the fact that the money had already been spent, she would wish to return it. She signs this and I give her the money. Whenever they start up something a second time I just call them in and read them the affidavit. That does the trick.'

SIR RICHARD SOMERS TRAVERS HUMPHREYS (1867–1956)

208

First time up.

THE Judge always attended for the first time on the Wednesday of each Session, and there used to be a great gathering of the briefless when the proceedings commenced. That was the time when any stray small briefs might be picked up, a dock brief might be secured by anyone whose appearance was calculated to inspire confidence, and if the learned Judge, who had read the depositions, considered that any of the prisoners ought to have free legal aid he would ask some member of the Bar to 'assist the Court' by looking after that prisoner's interests. Very early in my career Mr Justice Denman happened to be the Judge and asked me to 'assist the Court' in that manner. I wish I could record that my massive brow or the sparkling intelligence in my bright blue eye had attracted the attention of that most able, courteous, and altogether delightful Judge. Candour, however, compels me to repeat what 'from information received' I have reason to believe is the truth of the matter. Denman asked Avory, the Clerk of the Court—'Who is that white-faced boy at the end of the third row?' The answer was, 'Young Humphreys, son of C. O. Humphreys the solicitor.'

'Ah, I thought I knew his face; his father is an old friend of mine', and the request to 'assist the Court' followed, together with the Judge's copy of the depositions.

Forthwith my friends and acquaintances were called to my aid, and never had a case with three witnesses such a galaxy of talent enlisted in the endeavour to find a defence. Lockyer, Besley's clerk, consulted with James, Geoghegan's clerk, without success. I asked Bodkin, I asked Besley himself, Tickell looked at the indictment, a friendly detective looked at the Jury in the hope of finding someone who could be challenged, but all without avail; the unanimous verdict was, 'He must plead Guilty.' I went to the cells to interview my client, who was at first inclined to resent my interference as tending to delay the commencement of the sentence which he knew was awaiting him, but when I unloosed upon him the information that it would make no difference as all sentences date from the first day of the Session (it was about all the law I knew) he unbent and gave me the rather grubby writing he had intended to hand in with the object of softening the heart of the Judge. On the subject of fighting the case he was much amused; he had never intended to do anything else but plead Guilty.

In the afternoon the dread moment arrived. My client confessed to stealing three books from Sotheby, the well-known seller of rare and valuable books, and a detective went into the witness-box. I heard nothing of what he said, or if I did I failed to take it in, being engaged in strenuous and fortunately successful effort to avoid being sick. The prisoner at the bar was duly 'called upon'. That was my cue and I arose. What I said I probably did not know at the time, and I certainly do not know now, but I wound up with a passionately eloquent appeal (at least that was what I meant it to be) on the subject of my client's wife and chidren, which drew from the learned Judge the polite rejoinder (he was far too great a gentleman to laugh), 'You may not have heard what the detective said, Mr Humphreys, he did not speak very clearly, but I understood from him that your client deserted his wife and children some years ago and that the lady with whom he is now—er—er—cohabiting is not his wife.'

My client got twelve months; he had expected eighteen, and was perfectly satisfied, and my friends assured me that I should do better next time. The faithful Lockyer indeed informed me in an alcoholic whisper that he had been told by that good judge of a counsel, the clerk of the late Mr Ribton, that I 'reminded 'im of 'Awkins'.

THOMAS WALKER HOBART INSKIP (LORD CALDECOTE) (1876–1947)

Lord Chief Justice

209

An argument as to the liability of a Sporting Club to tax.

AFTER a consultation at which the probable cost of an appeal, the amount at stake and the chances of success were canvassed at some length, it was decided that an appeal was a good sporting proposition.

Before the Court of Appeal, consisting of the Master of the Rolls, Lord Pollock, and Lords Justices Greer and Russell, the same arguments were put forward on each side. It became apparent that the court was divided. The Master of the Rolls, an ex-law officer, inclined to the view of the Crown, but the two Lords Justices strongly disagreed.

The last scene of the drama took place in the House of Lords, on February 15, 1929, before Lords Buckmaster, Sumner, Dunedin, Blanesburgh and Warrington. The Attorney-General, Sir Thomas Inskip KC, opened for the Crown and, being quite unversed in everything connected with betting and the Turf, he soon found himself in deep water. Their Lordships had difficulty in following the facts, and groped for clarification.

Lord Dunedin: 'I am not certain that I am following you, Mr Attorney.

Let me take an analogy. Take the game of roulette—we all know how that is played.'

The Attorney-General (hastily): 'Oh, My Lord, I am afraid I know very little about roulette. All I know is that it is played with cards.'

An astonished silence.

Lord Buckmaster: 'Did you say "cards", Mr Attorney? Your childlike simplicity is most refreshing!'

RUFUS DANIEL ISAACS (LORD READING) (1860–1935)

Lord Chief Justice

210

The narrator is Gervais Rentoul

RUFUS ISAACS' strength lay in his knowledge of business routine, and his ability to elucidate figures and make them clear to a jury, as well as his suavity of manner and keen logical brain.

He never made the grave mistake of quarrelling with the judge, no matter how much in the right he might be. I well remember admiring his self-control in a case before a judge, who shall be nameless, but who had acquired his position more through family influence than by reason of any judicial or professional qualifications. Suddenly his Lordship barked out, 'Mr Isaacs, you have been wasting the time of the Court for the last half-hour.' As a matter of fact he had been conducting, with immense skill, a most difficult cross-examination, in which he had nothing much to go on, but by gently probing here and there had been endeavouring to extract some admission which might be of assistance to his client.

Instead of displaying any annoyance at this interruption, Isaacs never turned a hair, but replied, 'I trust your Lordship will bear with me a short time longer when it will be seen, I hope, that my questions have a definite relevance to the issues in dispute. Nothing is further from my mind than to take up unnecessarily your Lordship's most valuable time.'

He then proceeded, unruffled, with his cross-examination.

211

IN one of his rare after-dinner speeches Rufus Isaacs laid down the maxim that 'the Bar is never a bed of roses. It is either all bed and no roses or all roses and no bed.' From an early stage it was his own destiny to forego bed in favour of roses and he was fortunate in being physically able to make the sacrifice without undue strain. He was perfectly refreshed by five hours sleep and even these hours were not wasted.

Some subconscious faculty was at work while he slept and he would awake to find a complete set of facts, the proper arrangement of which had given him much thought on the previous night, neatly sorted and pigeon-holed in his mind on the following morning.

Nor was it only during the night that he could sleep, but at almost any moment of the day, in any place, and for any given time. When he was at the height of his practice it was his habit on returning to chambers after the rising of the court in the afternoon to have a hurried cup of tea and then settle himself in an arm-chair to sleep for a quarter of an hour. At the end of that time he would wake automatically and embark upon a series of consultations alert and refreshed.

Probably this capacity for sleep saved him. It certainly illustrates the power of control that he was able to exercise over his brain. Few men, with their minds charged with the facts of several cases, and their nerves taut after the daily excitement of the courts, could thus at will have dropped a curtain over all their preoccupations for a specified length of time.

It may be that here his sailor days were a godsend to him (at the age of sixteen Rufus had sailed as a deckhand to South America and India) for he was not only able to sleep in a bed or in an armchair but in a train or a car or indeed in almost any place or position, however uncomfortable, that presented itself.

In the course of one of his most voluminous and complicated cases, *Wyler v. Lewis*, when Friday night came and the hearing was adjourned until the following Monday, he suggested to his friend and 'devil' Branson who was associated with him in the action, that they were both so exhausted that, although they had to work over the weekend, it would do them good to go down to Brighton and study their briefs in a different atmosphere.

They duly arrived at the hotel, took a sitting room, and ordered lunch to be served in it. At the end of lunch they got out their papers and prepared to work for the afternoon as soon as the waiter had cleared away. Before that moment came Rufus had dropped off to sleep. Almost immediately Branson followed his example: awaking with a guilty start, to find, to his vast relief that not only was his leader still sleeping but that the waiter was still in the room, so he could only have dozed off for a few minutes.

But suddenly something struck him as strange. He observed that the waiter was no longer clearing away lunch, but laying dinner. They had slept in the chairs without moving for five hours.

212

R. v. Seddon.

THE Attorney-General rose to question the prisoner. Throughout the long cross-examination, which lasted for most of two days, Rufus Isaacs never once raised his voice, putting his questions with studied courtesy and always addressing the witness as 'Mr Seddon'. The deadly tone was set by the first two questions, which were phrased with the utmost skill.

'Miss Barrow lived with you from 26th July 1910 till the morning of 14th September 1911?'

'Yes.'

'Did you like her?'

'Did I like her?', the prisoner repeated.

'Yes. That is the question.'

No wonder Seddon hesitated before replying for the question placed him in a dilemma. If he said 'yes' then he would expose himself as a hypocrite, in view of his arranging for the cheapest possible funeral. On the other hand, if he said 'no' he could immediately prejudice himself in the eyes of the jury. He gave the best answer he could:

'She was not a woman you could be in love with, but I deeply sympathised with her.'

213

The narrator is 'Khaki' Roberts who among other accomplishments had played rugby football for England.

IN August 1920 Scranton was summoned to appear at Bow Street on charges of fraudulent conversion of jewellery entrusted to him on the understanding that he would sell it to his stage friends. Most members of the Bar were away from London enjoying the Long Vacation, so I was instructed to represent this sporting and dramatic character, a squat little figure, to whom I was introduced outside the court. Eyeing me closely up and down he said:

'You don't look like a lawyer. You look like a prizefighter!'

And feeling my biceps in a most unprofessional approach he added:

'If I had you for six months I could make you heavyweight champion of the world!' (Little did he know that this reference to 'six months' was somewhat prophetic.)

When Scranton was duly committed to the Old Bailey, Sir Richard Muir led me for the defence; the prosecution, instigated by the jewellery trade, was in the hands of Sir Ernest Wild, KC, a strange reversal of the normal roles of these two eminent Counsel. Evidently Scranton was fortunate in having some good friends, since the fees paid to his defenders bore no relation to the microscopic figure of his assets.

Muir, on the penultimate day of the trial, before the Common Serjeant (Sir Henry Dickens), retired to bed with a chill. This left me to examine Scranton and our witnesses, and to make the final speech for the defence. I welcomed the opportunity gratefully, though the effect of this defection upon our client was painful to behold.

The case against him was not overwhelming. Of the jewellery valued at around £19,000 received by him, he had failed to account for only some £3,000 worth. But the prejudice created by his colossal insolvency was hard to surmount.

Sir Ernest, when pompously cross-examining Scranton about his dealings with one Moey Tarsh, put various questions.

Sir Ernest: 'Who was Moey Tarsh?'
Scranton: 'A moneylender.'
Sir Ernest: 'A Jew, I suppose?'
Scranton: 'Yes, I think he is a Hebrew . . .'

Scranton emerged from the ordeal his usual perky self. Dickens, who had come round in favour of the defence, summed up strongly for an acquittal, but the jury listened with faces of stone. In a very short time they returned a verdict of 'Guilty'.

The judge then indicated his sympathies by passing the most lenient sentence possible in the circumstances, namely six months in the (now obsolete) second division, and by taking the exceptional course of himself giving leave to appeal.

So, a few weeks later, the stage was set for the final act of the drama in the Court of Criminal Appeal. Reading, the Lord Chief Justice, presided, his brethren being Darling and Sankey JJ.

The case for Scranton was put most attractively by Sir Richard. Then Sir Ernest, trying to establish that the verdict was justified by Scranton's own evidence, read copious extracts from the shorthand notes of the trial. Coming to the 'Moey Tarsh' passage, he shied away from it and asked their Lordships to turn over a couple of pages.

Too late!

'Not so fast', said the LCJ—the former Rufus Isaacs. 'Turn back to page 96. What did you mean by the question: "A Jew, I suppose?" What inference were you going to ask the jury to draw from that fact, if it was established?'

Imagine the scene! The Lord Chief Justice of England, a Jew by race, of which he was intensely proud, superb in his robes, aquiline, dignified, stern but courteous, was asking Counsel to justify or to explain an observation apparently which could have had no purpose other than to appeal to racial prejudice.

The court was packed. Every eye was on Sir Ernest, hoist wretchedly with his own petard. Every ear strained to hear his answer, and answer came there none. He grew red. He went white. His mouth opened and closed without the production of any sound. His eyes went up in mute appeal to the roof of the court, as though imploring providence to open the floor so that he might sink from the scene.

The Lord Chief Justice was insistent. 'I ask because it seems to me that the only meaning is that some unfavourable inference is to be drawn from the fact that the man was a Jew. It might be thought that I was prejudiced, and so I have consulted my brethren, who agree with me.'

By this time Sir Ernest was nearly 'out' in boxing parlance. He mumbled something scarcely intelligible about: 'It is well known, My Lord, that there are some Jewish money lenders who are dishonest, but of course there are many Christian ones who are no better.'

Mr Justice Darling tried to come to the rescue with a little judicious levity about a witness being asked whether he was a Scotsman or not. The LCJ brushed it aside.

Eventually poor Sir Ernest was allowed to continue his argument, which he did in a chastened and subdued condition.

The issues on each side of Scranton's case were very nicely balanced. The judges were clearly undecided up to the very end of the arguments. The shadows lengthened and the court grew dark. In the dock, clutching the rails with both hands, was the white-faced appellant. Before being released on bail he had been in gaol and he, most emphatically, had not enjoyed it. He was desperately anxious not to have to repeat the experience. The LCJ began to give judgement in his clear, beautiful voice. He reviewed the facts; he dealt with the law. He gave no indication of the conclusion at which he was going to arrive. Scranton, in all his chequered racing career, never saw a closer finish, or one in which he was more agonizingly concerned. At last, in his closing sentences, the LCJ announced that the court thought the evidence so finely balanced that it was not satisfactory to support a conviction. Therefore 'the conviction is quashed and the appellant is discharged'.

214

SIR RUFUS had for years past been the recipient of what would be called nowadays a fan mail. These letters emanated from people who appeared to spend their lives listening to his cases in court. Certain of them, although they knew him only by sight, would address to him letters not only of appreciation but also of criticism, designed to be helpful, and pointing out how, if the writer had been cross-examining a certain witness, he would have framed a particular question, in preference to the form in which it had actually been put.

There were also the usual lunatics, two being especially methodical and persistent in their correspondence.

One was under the impression that he was the rightful King of England and when Sir Rufus became, in succession, Solicitor and Attorney-General, he addressed to him letters, couched in grandiloquent language, which constituted his patent of appointment to these offices.

The other was a lady who wrote several times a week for many years from a private asylum. She conducted the correspondence on the basis that they were engaged to be married, and much of her letters was taken up in warning him against 'that Alice Cohen' (to whom Rufus had been married for many years) whom she looked upon as seeking to alienate his affections from herself. She also gave, in great detail, her ideas for the decoration of their future home, though unfortunately her taste ran chiefly to green plush.

SIR GEORGE JEFFREYS (1644–89)

Lord Chancellor

215

Judge Jeffreys did not spend the whole of his time condemning prisoners to death. Occasionally he combined clemency with somewhat gruesome wit.

THE two prisoners were brothers, Thomas and John Johnson, found guilty of stealing lead from the roof of Stepney Church. They were lucky to have been caught before they had taken off five shillings worth, for in that case they would have been hanged.

Said Jeffreys, 'You are brethren in iniquity, Simeon and Levi. I find you are not Churchmen the right way. But you are mightily beholden to the Constable. If he had given you but half an hour longer you had been in a fair way to be hanged. Your zeal for religion is so great as to carry you to the top of the Church. If this be your way of going to Church, it is fit you should be taken notice of.'

The brothers were fined £20 each and bound over.

WILLIAM TRAVERS JEROME (1859–1934)

District Attorney, New York City

216

His first term. The Dictionary of American Biography *says: 'To prove that the Tammany administration was protecting gamblers Jerome went with a squad of aides into precincts whose police captains had reported them free of gaming, broke into the reserves and set up his own magistrates' court on the spot.'*

WITH an axe in one hand and a Bible in his hip pocket, accompanied by a pick-up force of bailiffs and friends, he would sally forth from the Criminal Courts Buildings to raid gambling places on the Lower East Side. He would 'rush' the gambling joint hoping to smash through its 'icebox' doors before the inmates could take alarm and hide the evidence. Once inside the citadel with captured gamblers, shattered gambling equipment and exploding flash bulbs all around him Jerome would haul out his Bible, post himself behind a crap table and declare court in session. Witnesses were sworn in, testimony taken and culprits arraigned on the spot.

One of his more sensational exploits was descending on an exceptionally prosperous gambling house at 20 Dey Street. He had asked the police to raid it, but they had kept stalling him claiming they were 'having a hard time nailing down evidence'. When Jerome and his cohorts broke in they found eight police officers in mufti who maintained they were 'working under cover', had been staked out there for thirty-five days, and found no signs of gambling. Jerome smashed through another door and discovered a hundred men busy at the roulette wheels, the faro bank and the crap tables.

After the usual scuffling and shouting died down one well-dressed and distinguished looking man detached himself from the low-life herd and came up to Jerome, whispering, 'Mr Jerome, I can't afford to be found here, you must help me to get out.'

'Court's in session', Jerome snapped. 'Hold up your hand and be sworn.'

When the man refused to give his name Jerome remanded him to the House of Detention for contempt of court. The man then revealed his identity. He was the Honorable Maurice Holahan, President of the Board of Public Works.

Holahan protested to the newspapers that he had come to the gambling house in search of his 'wayward son', an alibi which caused the town to shake with irreverent laughter. His paternal concern was ill-rewarded. Holahan's son so resented being used as an alibi that he spilled out the story of his father's crooked dealings with contractors doing business with his department.

217

His second term.

ON taking office Jerome found himself in a morass of work left undone, inefficiency, incompetence and demoralisation; nothing, certainly, had changed for the better since he had left the office a dozen years before. Eight hundred and sixty-one indictments had piled up in a bureaucratic logjam, awaiting a top level decision on how to proceed. He had inherited a crumbling bureaucracy staffed for several years mostly by dimwits and political appointees. It was like walking into a

Roman house after it had been buried under volcanic ash and expecting the plumbing to work.

To keep his promise to the people of the Lower East Side that their daughters would be protected from the pimps and procurers he opened a combination 'branch office' and dormitory at 8 Rutgers Street. The place was to be kept open night and day so that complaints could be heard and investigated without delay.

Every night from ten to forty people visited the 'branch office' slowly becoming convinced that Jerome meant it when he said that 'Justice would be dispensed at every level of society.'

One complainant was a serving woman who earned fifty cents a day. She wanted her fifteen-year-old daughter rescued from a house of prostitutes. Jerome himself happened to be on 'ghetto duty'—as his irreverent assistants called it—that night and heard her plea. She tried to give Jerome ten dollars, all she had, because experience had taught her that no politician would keep his promise without an emolument. When Jerome insisted on returning the money, she burst into tears and fled, convinced that his refusal meant he wouldn't do anything about returning her daughter. Before the night was out, however, his detectives had located and returned the daughter to her mother.

THOMAS JERVIS (*fl.* 1820–30)

King's Counsel

218

The narrator is Lord Campbell

THE only other silk gown on the circuit was Jervis, a very gentlemanly man in his manners and very honourably inclined, but famous for drawing a long bow. The stories he told were, and probably still are, by tradition a source of amusement to the Oxford circuit. As a specimen he said he 'kept up a flock of above 1,000 turkeys at his place in Kent which he fattened on grasshoppers', and that 'one morning he saw twenty jays sitting on a tree and was going to fire at them when one of them said "good morning to you, Mr Jervis, good morning Tom Jervis" and allowed them to fly away unhurt.'

I once mentioned to him that I had been reading the Iliad, and that, with the help of an occasional peep at the translation, I could construe it pretty well. He said, 'I make it a rule to read through the whole of Homer's work once a year.' He had never been to University and did not know a word of Greek. We proposed that his epitaph should be, 'Here ceaseth to lie Thomas Jervis.'

F. TENNYSON JESSE (1892–1958)

Barristress and Author

219

Samuel Herbert Dougal, who was tried at Chelmsford for the murder of a Miss Holland, was also the seducer of a large number of girls in the neighbourhood, most of whom bore him children. He was a compulsive letter writer to the end.

F. TENNYSON JESSE writes in the introduction to the case in *Notable British Trials*:

The cream of all Dougal's letters is to be found in one written to one of the newly-made mothers. 'I dare say the girls have received their notices to attend next Monday at Chelmsford; have they not? There will be several from about there, and it would be a good idea to club together and hire a trap and drive all the way. It is a delightful drive, through undulating country and at this time of year it would be a veritable treat for them all.' When one considers who 'all the girls from about there' were, and in what relation they had stood to Dougal, his thought for them makes of this a truly novel sort of mothers' meeting.

SIR WILLIAM MOORE JOHNSON (*fl.* 1885–1908)

220

The narrator is Serjeant Sullivan

JOHNSON was a monument of kindness and stupidity. He was universally know as Wooden-headed Billy. One morning he came into the Divisional Court with his hand bandaged. 'My dear Johnson,' exclaimed the Chief Baron, 'what has happened to you? Nothing serious I trust.'

'Oh no, thank you,' replied the Judge, 'merely a splinter under my finger nail.'

'He's been scratching his head', audibly observed Johnny Moriarty.

I was once propounding a will in solemn form before Johnson and a jury with Johnny opposing me. The opposition contended that the testator could not have been of sound mind, memory and understanding because, when roused on the arrival of his solicitor who was an old friend, he had indignantly enquired, 'Who are you, sir? Who are you sir?'

In summing up the wooden-headed judge was extremely severe upon counsel who addressed such arguments to an unsuspecting jury. 'When roused from slumber', said His Lordship modestly, 'the most brilliant and erudite intellects may be momentarily confused. I myself remember on one occasion being suddenly awakened and turning to the good lady beside me I exclaimed, ' "Who are you, madam? Who are you?" '

'You did?' said Johnny, 'and who was she?'

WILLIAM ALLEN JOWITT (LORD JOWITT) (1885–1957)

Lord Chancellor

221

Sydney Fox was being tried for suffocating his mother and setting fire to her bedroom to conceal the evidence of his crime.

CASSELS commented at one point during the trial, 'There's no safer answer in the world than "I don't know".' It was advice that Fox should have listened to even though it was unpalatable, because up to then Fox had lived by always having an answer for everything. But 'I don't know' was too sincere and genuine a reply for a confidence trickster. His failure to give that answer to a question from the Attorney-General sealed his fate. Fox, according to his own account, had opened the communicating door between his mother's bedroom and his, and had immediately been driven back by the dense black smoke. He shut the door, ran out of his room, shut his own bedroom door and ran downstairs to summon help, passing on the way the closed door of his mother's bedroom.

'Did you realise,' asked Jowitt, 'when you opened the communicating door, that the atmosphere of the room was such as would probably suffocate anybody inside?'

'If I'd stayed in three or four minutes I should have been suffocated', Fox replied.

'So that you must have been greatly apprehensive for your mother?'

'I was.'

'Fox,' said the Attorney-General in a voice of deadly insistence that stilled the court, 'you closed that door.'

'It's quite possible that I did', Fox answered quite calmly.

'Can you explain to me,' demanded the Attorney-General, 'why it was that you closed the door instead of flinging it wide open?'

Fox barely hesitated before replying, 'My explanation of that now is that the smoke should not spread into the hotel.' In the silent courtroom a gasp went up.

The probable truth is, of course, that Fox decided to take no chances. He could not be certain that there was still not a spark of life in his mother; the longer she lay in that choking atmosphere the more certain it would be that she would never tell what really happened in that hour before midnight.

The jury no longer had any doubt.

222

The narrator is A. E. Bowker, Sir Norman Birkett's clerk

IN 1930 a ship owned by a Greek Company foundered in the far-off Pacific. It carried a valuable cargo, and a writ was issued against Lloyd's underwriters claiming the value of the ship and cargo. A very substantial claim indeed.

Messrs Lloyd's contested the claim on the grounds that the ship, having been heavily insured, had been deliberately scuttled. A serious charge, but Lloyd's, with a reputation of centuries for fair dealing behind them, do not place defences of this sort on the record without good grounds.

The case came on before Mr Justice Branson and a City of London special jury. We appeared for the plaintiffs and Sir William Jowitt KC for the defendants. Mr Birkett put up a very fine fight, but the cards were certainly stacked against him, as you will appreciate from the following.

We called the American captain of the ship, the most cheery sea-dog it is possible to imagine who, for two whole days, stood in the witness-box, chewing gum, and lied and lied and lied. He was without exception the finest and most plausible liar I have ever seen in the witness box, and I've seen a few.

Sir William, splendidly instructed, riddled him from start to finish, and we got quite used to hearing, 'well now, Captain, in view of that fact, your evidence upon that point is a lie?'

And with a cheery smile and unblushing candour back would come the reply: 'Guess that's right, sir.'

This went on all day, the jury thoroughly enjoying it. We did ourselves, although the admissions of this witness were scuttling our case, as surely as the ship had foundered.

But the finale fairly brought the house down.

Sir William had completed his shattering cross-examination and remarked 'well—that is all captain. I don't think there is any other question I want to ask you;' and then, as an apparent afterthought, 'Did you come from America to give this evidence?'

'Yes, that's so.'

'Would you tell the jury what ship you came over on?'

'Sure, sir. It was the *George Washington*.'

SIR JOHN BURGESS KARSLAKE (1821–81)

Queen's Counsel, Attorney-General

223

A CERTAIN member of the Common Law Bar, who enjoyed neither a large practice nor the esteem of his comrades on the Western Circuit, where he had originally been in business as an attorney, applied for the desirable appointment of a County Court Judgeship. He was commended to the Lord Chancellor only by the regularity of his appearance at religious meetings and the fervour of his responses so Lord Cairns asked his secretary to make some enquiries.

It happened that the next day the secretary found himself at the same breakfast table with Sir John Karslake, who was then stone blind, but otherwise in full possession of his faculties.

'Do you happen to know anything, Sir John', said the secretary, as they were leaving the room, 'of a man on your old circuit called "X"?'

'Know anything of him?', was the rejoinder, 'I should just think I did. He's the cleverest fellow I ever knew.'

This was enough for the secretary who fled without waiting for particulars of X's ability, and in the course of the next twenty-four hours X received a satisfactory answer to his application. Meanwhile Sir John, unaware that his interlocutor had departed, went on to complete the sentence with a chuckle—'The cleverest fellow I ever knew. He's the only man who ever did my clerk out of his fees.'

224

The narrator is Lord Alverstone

SIR JOHN KARSLAKE, when asked what were the three things necessary for success at the Bar said the first was tact, the second tact, and the third tact. He was not far wrong. I have seen many errors made, cases lost and clients affronted by want of ordinary tact on the part of the barrister. (When Sir Edward Clarke was asked the same question he said, 'To be very poor, very ambitious and very much in love.' No doubt these qualifications may also have much to do with a man's success.)

EDWARD VAUGHAN HYDE KENEALY (1819–80)

Queen's Counsel

225

The Tichborne Claimant. Kenealy represented the Claimant at his trial for perjury so intemperately that he wrecked his own career at the Bar.

ON the last day of his Trial, when the Jury returned to the Court, the Defendant was perfectly self-possessed. He knew his fate now. What Peel had said at the beginning of the Trial was doubtless in his thoughts—but he flinched not in the least. The hour was come which was to try his soul. I saw Palmer sentenced, and he was pale as death;

every muscle was rigid under the strain. But the Defendant was as cool as though he had been about to raise his much-loved rifle and to fire at a mark for a friend's wager or for his own pleasure.

Mr Justice Mellor fumbled at his desk and took out a manuscript, consisting of several sheets of foolscap paper. He said something to Frayling, the Chief Justice's Clerk, who sat right under him; and Frayling rather harshly said to the Defendant, 'Stand up.' The Defendant did so. I expected him to turn round to me and to ask me for advice. But he did not do so. His manner was full of quiet dignity. I have been told by those who sat in front of him that there was no quiver of the lip, no drooping of the eye, no change of colour, no tremor of any description. The four detectives from Scotland Yard fixed their horrid eyes upon him, as though they expected him to produce a revolver and to use it on himself, or upon the Judges. But there was no spite or malice in this man. Whatsoever bad qualities he may have possessed, malice was not one of them. He listened, as Socrates might have listened, to his sentence. The Defendant was no Greek philosopher, but greater coolness, I had almost said majesty, in the hour of tribulation, no man ever showed.

Mellor read the sentence—that wretched sentence which had been prepared hours, perhaps days before, with full knowledge of what the verdict was to be—with a diabolical exultation in his voice, and coarse features, which grated terribly on the few friends of Tichborne who were allowed to be present, but which was, no doubt, music to his assembled foes.

When the sentence was pronounced and finished the Defendant asked calmly, 'May I say a few words, my Lord?' The Chief Justice leaned forward. 'No!', he said, and the denial sounded like the clash of chains. The natural melody of Cockburn's voice had changed almost to a roar, as indeed, almost from first to last, during the Trial, his whole nature seemed to have changed to that of a hyena, growling, glaring, fierce. The Defendant bowed. He turned round to me, and in the true spirit of a gentleman would not leave without bidding me 'Farewell!' He put out his hand. Every eye was riveted on me. How could I have refused it? I shook it and said, 'Goodbye, Sir Roger, I am sorry for you.' A groan of horror broke from some barristers behind me. One of them exclaimed (I think it was Moriarty), 'He shakes hands with him!', as though I had been committing murder or some other crime. I did press his hand, and I shall never regret it. I should have scorned myself if I had driven a dagger into his heart, by repelling him at that moment. The Tipstaff beckoned and he went out, and as he left the Court he bowed to the Bench.

There was no recognition of the salute, but the highest gentleman in the land could not have behaved with greater courtesy, dignity or decorum.

They led him through a maze of corridors, by private staircases and dark passages, and searched him for pistol or poison. When an officer was about to handcuff him he smiled quietly but sadly, and said, 'That is not necessary, gentlemen; I know how to behave myself.'

And there was that about the man which moved them to desist.

LLOYD KENYON (LORD KENYON) (1732–1802)

Master of the Rolls

226

The narrator is Sir Frank McKinnon

THE following anecdote I have heard related of Lord Kenyon by and before very decent people, and it ought not to be lost, as it illustrates his character and the manners of the age in which he flourished. In those days retiring rooms for the use of the Judges were unknown, and a porcelain vase, with a handle to it, was placed in a corner of the Court at the extremity of the Bench. In the King's Bench at Guildhall the students' box was very near this corner. One day a student, who was taking notes, finding the ink in his little ink bottle very thick, used the freedom secretly to discharge the whole of it into my Lord's porcelain vase. His Lordship soon after having occasion to come to this corner, he was observed in a few moments to become much disconcerted and distressed. In truth discovering the liquid with which he was filling the vase to be of a jet black colour, he thought the secretion indicated the sudden attack of some mortal disorder. In great confusion and anguish of mind he returned to his seat, and attempted to resume the trial of the cause, but finding his hand to shake so much that he could not write, he said that on account of indisposition he was obliged to adjourn the Court. As he was led to his carriage by his servants, the luckless student came up to him and said, 'My Lord, I hope your

Lordship will excuse me, as I suspect that I am unfortunately the cause of your Lordship's apprehension.' He then described what he had done, expressing deep contrition for his thoughtlessness and impertinence, and saying that he thought it his duty to relieve his Lordship's mind by this confession.

Lord Kenyon: 'Sir, you are a man of sense and a gentleman—dine with me on Sunday.'

SIR ROBERT MALCOLM KERR (1821–1902)

227

IT is difficult to describe this remarkable man. Only those who knew him and practised before him can adequately appreciate his unique characteristics. Possessed of very great ability and shrewdness, he could, if he chose, try a case with strength and dignity, but he preferred with sardonic humour to treat criminal trials as a grim joke. The grimness of the joke appeared, when there was a conviction, in the terrible sentences he was in the habit of passing. If he took any part whatever in the trial, it was to the detriment of the prosecution. He constantly disallowed the expenses of witnesses; he never spared a prosecutor who wore a gold watch-chain to tempt thieves, or a shopkeeper who exposed his wares outside his shop. He never interfered with the defence, and counsel enjoyed the utmost possible latitude; if he kept reasonably near the facts, his inferences and comments passed unchallenged and uncorrected. But of prolixity he was absolutely intolerant. His own summing-up was usually in strong Scotch: 'Gentlemen of the jury, you've hard the counsel for the prosecution, and you've hard the counsel for the defence. Consider your vardict.' If counsel talked too long he would wriggle restlessly in the dark alcove in which he crouched. Then he would loudly rattle his keys on the desk. He would cut short counsel's opening speech by bidding the usher call the first witness. At a time when elaborate note-taking by the judge was the rule, he rarely took a single note. He never had such a thing as a notebook; a scrap of paper was all he ever used. One day, in the barely furnished little room that then served as robing-room for the three City judges, he came across the notebook of the Common Serjeant, Sir

William Charley. The Commissioner studied his learned colleague's book. Sir William's writing was a wild scribble, and he took a note of everything. When the Commissioner came into his court he was full of a new freak. He would take notes like the Common Serjeant. Accordingly he filled sheets and sheets of paper with verbatim notes of the evidence, omitting nothing whatever, however trifling. The court officials were aghast. Instead of trying, or to speak more accurately, disposing of some twenty or twenty-five cases in the one day he was required by his appointment to sit, he with difficulty finished two. This freak lasted several Sessions, but at length it got too irksome a joke for himself, and to every one's relief he relapsed into his customary speedy methods. His court was constructed after his own design. It was a small room with two doors nearly opposite two windows; in a dark recess in the wall between these windows was the Bench, usually illuminated by a single candle. If there were too many bystanders, he would have both doors and windows opened to drive them away by the draughts, in spite of the shivers of the jury, who sat close to one window. There were no seats except for counsel and solicitors. The front bench was for solicitors, the back one for the Bar, but as counsel used to get over from one bench to the other, exhibiting their legs, as he said, like ballet dancers, he had the front bench lowered and turned so that its occupants could not face the court. Then, as too many barristers squeezed into their bench and stopped there too long, he had the seat made narrower and farther from the desk to prevent lolling, and had arms put in too far apart for one man's use and not far enough to admit two. The dock was behind the Bar bench, but so high up that prisoners' heads were not far from the ceiling. This singular court, not inappropriately called a kennel, had one advantage. Defending counsel was so close to the jury that by leaning forward he could touch the whole twelve. I used to enjoy the facility of seeing from their eyes how my arguments were working.

The learned Commissioner delighted in smashing up long and complicated cases. He was never more alert and adroit than when searching for a pretext to do so. He did not always succeed. Once J. P. Grain had opened and begun a heavy case in the absence of his leader. The Commissioner had made considerable progress in his destructive tactics when in walked the absent leader, Sir Hardinge Giffard. He deliberately untied his voluminous brief and planted himself squarely before the Judge. The contest did not last long. *That* case was tried out.

228

The narrator is F. W. Ashley

MR COMMISSIONER KERR disliked juries and prolix summings-up, and while it was impossible to avoid the former, he was never guilty of the latter.

One of his summings up remains in my memory.

'Gentlemen of the jury, the prosecutor swore he was crossing Westminster Bridge when the prisoner struck him in the face, snatched his watch and chain and ran away. The constable said he saw the prisoner strike the prosecutor, and, running after him, caught him with the watch and chain in his hand. If after that evidence you think the prisoner is not guilty you will say so.'

This they promptly did; returning a verdict of not guilty.

The judge, unperturbed, addressed the prisoner in grave and measured language:

'John Jones, the jury says you are not guilty, and so you can go. But be very careful in future or the next time you may not be tried by such a highly intelligent jury.'

SIR JOHN LATHAM (1877–1964)

Chief Justice of the Australian High Court

229

LATHAM was driving in St Kelda's Road, Melbourne when he offended against a traffic law. A young Irish constable stopped him and said, 'What would be your name?'

Sir John said 'John Latham'.

The constable said, 'You wouldn't be after being that same John Latham who is a barrister, now would you?'

Sir John said 'Yes. I am that same man.'

'And you wouldn't be after being that same John Latham who is the Commonwealth Attorney General?'

Sir John, whose hopes had begun to rise, said 'Yes, I am he.'

The constable said, 'Well you won't be able to plead ignorance of the law, now will you?'

SIR JOHN COMPTON LAWRANCE (1832–1912)

230

The narrator is Bowen-Rowlands

MR JUSTICE JOHN LAWRANCE was a good judge and in crime one of the best Judges I have practised before. He was not unduly inclined to literature. I remember soon after my call his coming on to our Circuit. I was then doing a great deal of writing for reviews and newspapers. He asked me why I hadn't tried my hand at a novel.

With becoming humility I pointed out that a 'shocker' (published in 1891 by Gale and Polden—price one shilling) had brought me a modicum of fame and money. It was based on a case I had found in a book on medical jurisprudence and afterwards, in ten days, the book became a fact.

Its title was *The White-Eyed Woman*.

He asked me to let him have a copy. I had one. I presented it to him, duly autographed.

The day following, on coming into court, he signed to me to speak to him. It was in the Cardiff Assizes (Crown) Court. I climbed up on the Associates' Bench and stood ready to listen to words of praise, the reward of my literary labours.

Instead he told me that *The White-Eyed Woman* was a horrible book, and had kept him awake all night; adding that he had handed it to his Marshal in the hope that it would keep him awake—in the daytime.

I never saw that volume again, and now, if I wish to renew acquaintance with that effort of my immaturity, I have to go to the British Museum where a copy is preserved.

SIR WILLIAM LEE (1688–1754)

231

IN 1752 the Lord Chief Justice Lee presided over a trial from which he emerged covered with ridicule. The Attorney-General, Sir Dudley Ryder, had filed a criminal information for libel against William Owen, a bookseller, who had published a bold pamphlet censuring the House of Commons.

Lee instructed the jury to bring in a verdict of guilty.

They withdrew, to troop back into the Guildhall two hours later.

Clerk of the Court: 'Gentlemen of the Jury, are you agreed on your verdict?'

Foreman: 'Guilty.'

Some members of the Jury: 'No! No! my Lord, it is all a mistake. We say, "Not Guilty".'

Foreman: 'Yes, my Lord. It was a mistake. I meant to say "Not Guilty".'

Bystanders: 'Huzza! Huzza! Huzza!!!'

Attorney-General: 'My Lord, this must not be. I insist on the Jury being called back and asked their opinion upon the only question submitted to them.'

Lord Chief Justice: 'Gentlemen of the Jury, do you think the evidence laid before you of Owen's publishing the book by selling it is not sufficient to convince you that the said Owen did sell this book.'

Foreman: 'Not guilty, my Lord! Not guilty!'

Juryman: 'Yes my Lord. That is our verdict and so we say all.'

Rest of Jury: 'So we say all. So we say all.'

There were bonfires in the City that night. Ryder was forced, on his way home, to drink a health to the jury and hear a ballad addressed to himself that proclaimed:

> Mr Attorney's grim wig
> Though awfully big
> No more shall frighten the nation.

The wretched Lee went into a decline and shortly afterwards died of apoplexy . . . The Attorney-General, with a sigh of relief, stepped into his shoes.

SAMUEL S. LEIBOWITZ (1893–1978)

American Lawyer

232

Sam's first client.

SAM, coat removed and shirt-sleeves rolled up, was lolling in his chair, his back to the desk and his feet on the sill of the office's one window.

A voice aroused him. A stranger with a furtive eye and an ugly mug was addressing him from the doorway.

'Are you Leibowitz the mouthpiece?'

'Yes', replied Sam.

'I just got a rap but it wasn't a right fall.'

(He had been arrested but the evidence against him was not legitimate.)

'I was standing outside the freak sideshow in Dreamland at Coney Island Sunday afternoon when a sucker squawked he felt my mit in his kick. Can you beat it? And me a cannon (pickpocket) for twenty years. You've gotta spring me, see. I gotta hit the air. June, July, August and September are our heavy months and if you spring me, we'll keep you plenty busy.'

Sam didn't know at that time, that the underworld scouts courtrooms as the major leagues scout the minors, for promising talent.

'What's your fee?' asked the cannon, and Sam, screwing up his courage, blurted out, 'One hundred dollars.'

The client peeled off five twenty-dollar bills from a fat roll and tossed them on the desk. Sam put them in the right hand lower pocket of his vest.

'You'll sure be at the Coney Island Magistrates' Court tomorrow morning.'

'Yes,' said Sam, 'and we will do the best we can.'

The stenographer came in as the cannon left.

'Look,' shouted Sam, 'the ice is broken. Look!'

He reached into the vest pocket. His face went blank. The $100 was gone. He searched his other pockets and ransacked the drawers of the desk. He was on his hands and knees going over the rug when the cannon returned.

'Say, young fellow,' he said earnestly, 'I just want you to understand. I've been twenty years in the racket and no sucker ever felt my hand in his pocket. See? Here's your $100.'

233

How to select a jury.

'SEE that bird,' indicating a thick-set man in his late fifties, with a dimpled chin and firmly compressed lips, 'he'd be a washout as a juror. He's a born hanger.'

Next a tall, bespectacled man with a long narrow face: 'Couldn't take that fellow; a churchman, bigoted.'

A youngish man, round-faced, blue-eyed, passed: 'Ah, there's a natural; sympathetic; he's a let-liver. Men who travel much—commercial salesman, say—make fine jurors. I like them young, too. They're still interested in people, and they have a sense of brotherhood because of their fraternity ties. They're not set in their ways. They're tolerant. They're good listeners. . . . I like to look at a man and figure out what he was in his infancy. Was he a cry-baby? Or was he smiling and friendly and no worry to his mother? Most cry-babies grow up to be reformers. I can spot them a mile away. I want no reformers on my jury.

'Self-made men of the assertive type are to be shunned. Their attitude is always one of contempt for the defendant. They compare their status with his. They have no sympathy for him. He is a victim of his own weakness. The self-made man will send your client to the gallows or the chair without compunction.

'Then there are those men of conscious rectitude; self-righteous and impatient of the peccadilloes to which all of us are prone. They dot their i's and cross their t's in the moral sense. They would cheerfully send culprits to the pillory or to the stake if our laws permitted.

'Some big business men make acceptable jurors; some, especially those with close-set eyes, tight lips and square jaws, don't. They have a pompous disdain for the underdog. They are your true snobs.'

Also included on Leibowitz's blacklist are 'sea-lawyers' who, he says, deadlock juries; writers, because they invariably construct their own case, based upon dramatic values, and ignore the Law and the facts; professors and those who live cloistered lives generally, because they are too easily shocked by the raw facts of life; former policemen and private watchmen, because the chances are at one time or another they have been outwitted by criminals, and have an obsession that all persons accused of a crime are guilty.

All the world's a stage, peopled with potential jurors for showman Leibowitz. Their turn will come some day.

HENRY CECIL LEON (1902–76)

Judge

234

Robert Fortune was the barrister who took Leon as a pupil.

I SOON learned that appearing in Court with Fortune could be a terrifying experience. He was an extremely busy man and often had cases in more than one court at the same time. The result was that he would leave a case in the middle and, if he had no leader or official junior, one of the pupils would be deputed to hold the fort while he was away.

'Just tell the judge the tale, my dear fellow, just tell the judge the tale', he would say as he disappeared.

The butterflies in the tummy which athletes and jockeys experience before a race are nothing to what a pupil used to experience when his master ran away and left him before a High Court judge, like the ghost in Hamlet, 'unhouselled, disappointed, unaneled'. If he had known anything about the case which he was left to conduct he would still have been wholly unable to conduct it.

I remember on one occasion Fortune was led by Sir John Simon, while Sir Douglas Hogg, the present Lord Hailsham's father, was leading the other side with a junior. Sir Douglas Hogg and his junior were in the court the whole time. Sir John Simon was there for half an hour out of the two days. Part of the half hour was taken up in conducting a whispered conversation with his clerk which ended with 'get me a taxi. One that will go quick.' He spent most of the time for which he was paid to be in court in the House of Commons.

For two hours out of those two days I was the only representative of our side, the case was about docks and harbours, and although I had read the brief I hardly understood any of it.

I can still remember my absolute terror. I am not exaggerating when I say that the sense of fear which I then experienced was comparable to that which I felt when I first came under enemy shellfire in the war. The judge, while at first he treated me as though I were in the case and asked me a question or two, as soon as he realised that it was a pure waste of time to invite me to deal with any aspect of it, disregarded me entirely.

The relief which I felt when Fortune returned was very like the relief which I felt when my battalion came out of the line and moved beyond the reach of enemy fire.

ABRAHAM LINCOLN (1809–65)

235

A SUCCESSFUL jury lawyer must needs be something of an actor at times, and during his apprentice years Lincoln displayed no little histrionic ability in his passionate appeals to the juries. Indeed, his notes in the Wright case show that he occasionally reverted to first principles even after he had reached the age of discretion. This case was brought on behalf of the widow of a Revolutionary War soldier whose pension had been cut in two by a rapacious agent, who appropriated half of the sum collected for his alleged services. The facts aroused Lincoln's indignation, and his memorandum for summing up to the jury ran as follows: 'No contract. Not professional services. Unreasonable charge. Money retained by defendant—not given to plaintiff. Revolutionary War. Describe Valley Forge privations. Ice. Soldier's bleeding feet. Plaintiff's husband. Soldier leaving home for army. Skin Defendant. Close.'

Mr Herndon, who quotes this memorandum, testifies that the soldiers' bleeding feet and other pathetic properties were handled very effectively, and that the defendant was skinned to the entire satisfaction of the jury.

Stories are more interesting than logic and far more effective with the average audience, and Lincoln's juries usually heard something from him in the way of an apt comparison or illustration which impressed his point upon their minds.

On one occasion when he was defending a case of assault and battery it was proved that the plaintiff had been the aggressor, but the opposing counsel argued that the defendant might have protected himself without inflicting injuries on his assailant.

'That reminds me of the man who was attacked by a farmer's dog, which he killed with a pitchfork', commented Lincoln.

'What made you kill my dog?', demanded the farmer.

'What made him try to bite me?', retorted the offender.

'But why didn't you go at him with the other end of your pitchfork?' persisted the farmer.

'Well, why didn't he come at me with his other end?', was the retort.

236

'GENTLEMEN,' began Lincoln, 'you must be careful and not permit yourselves to be overborne by the eloquence of the counsel for the defense. Judge Logan, I know, is an effective lawyer. I have met him too often to doubt that; but shrewd and careful though he be, still, he is sometimes wrong. Since this trial began I have discovered that, with all his caution and fastidiousness, he hasn't knowledge enough to put his shirt on right.'

Logan turned crimson with embarrassment, and the jurors burst into a roar of laughter as they discovered that the discomfited advocate was wearing the garment in question with the plaited bosom behind, and for the rest of that trial Logan was not effective against his former partner.

237

WIT and ridicule were Lincoln's weapons of offense and defense, and he probably laughed more jury cases out of court than any other man who practised at the bar.

'I once heard Mr Lincoln defend a man in Bloomington against a charge of passing counterfeit money', Vice-President Stevenson told the writer. 'There was a pretty clear case against the accused, but when the chief witness for the people took the stand, he stated that his name was J. Parker Green, and Lincoln reverted to this the moment he rose to cross-examine. Why J. Parker Green? . . . What did the J. stand for? . . . John? . . . Well, why didn't the witness call himself John P. Green? . . . That was his name, wasn't it? . . . Well, what was the reason he did not wish to be known by his right name? . . . Did J. Parker Green have anything to conceal; and if not, why did J. Parker Green put his name in that way? And so on. Of course the whole examination was farcical,' Mr Stevenson continued, 'but there was something irresistibly funny in the varying tones and inflections of Mr

Lincoln's voice as he rang the changes upon the man's name; and at the recess the very boys in the street took it up as a slogan and shouted 'J. Parker Green!' all over the town. Moreover, there *was* something in Lincoln's way of intoning his questions which made me suspicious of the witness, and to this day I have never been able to rid my mind of the absurd impression that there was something not quite right about J. Parker Green. It was all nonsense, of course; but the jury must have been affected as I was, for Green was discredited and the defendant went free.'

238

HE declined time and again to undertake doubtful causes, discouraged litigation, and discountenanced sharp practices.

'Yes,' Mr Herndon reports him as advising a client, 'we can doubtless gain your case for you; we can set a whole neighborhood at loggerheads; we can distress a widowed mother and her six fatherless children, and thereby get for you six hundred dollars to which you seem to have a legal claim, but which rightfully belongs, it appears to me, as much to the woman and her children as it does to you. You must remember, however, that some things legally right are not morally right. We shall not take your case, but we will give you a little advice for which we will charge you nothing. You seem to be a sprightly, energetic man. We would advise you to try your hand at making six hundred dollars in some other way.'

SIR FRANK LOCKWOOD (1847–97)

Queen's Counsel, Solicitor-General

239

IT was on a petition to the Master of the Rolls for payment out of Court of a sum of money; and Lockwood appeared for an official liquidator of a company whose consent had to be obtained before the Court would part with the fund. Lockwood was instructed to consent, and his reward was to be three guineas on the brief and one guinea for consultation. The petition came on in due course before Lord Romilly, and was made plain to him by counsel for the petitioner, and still a little plainer by counsel for the principal respondent.

Then up rose Lockwood, an imposing figure, and indicated his appearance in the case.

'What brings you here?', said Lord Romilly, meaning, I presume, 'why need I listen to you?'

Lockwood, looking puzzled, Lord Romilly added a little testily, 'What do you come here for?'

The answer was immediate, unexpected, and accompanied as it was by a dramatic glance at the outside of his brief, as if to refresh his memory, triumphant, 'Three and one, my Lord!'

There was Homeric laughter in the old Court of Chancery, and it was fitting there should be, for this was not only Lockwood's first brief and first forensic joke, but it was, I verily believe, the last joke ever made in the High Court of Chancery.

240

I REMEMBER on one occasion defending an innocent man—it has not often fallen to my lot to defend so innocent a man. When I asked the solicitor who instructed me about the case to tell me what the defence was, he said: 'It is an alibi.' Said I: 'No better defence can be proffered to any judge; tell it to me.' He said: 'It was on the 15th of March, as you are aware, that this innocent man is charged with this offence at York.' York is my own constituency, and I defend my constituents on reasonable terms. He said: 'On the 15th of March our client, so far from being in York, was in Manchester attending a race meeting.' I said: 'I don't like it. It may offend the Nonconformist conscience.' 'Well,' says he, 'let that pass. He was at Blackpool.' 'Where?', I said. 'Drinking at the bar of a public-house, and I have got the barmaid to prove it.' This I rejected on the ground that the public-house might be a stumbling block to some. Well, what do you think of this?', says he. 'Wolverhampton, in a second-hand furniture dealer's shop, buying a coffin for his mother-in-law, and I have got the book to prove it.' I said: 'That is the alibi for our innocent man.' Well, we tried that man and he was convicted, and on the conclusion of the trial I had the opportunity of conversing with the learned judge who tried the case. Said he: 'That was a goodish alibi.' Said I: 'It ought to be, my lord, it was the best of three.'

241

The narrator is Edward Abinger

I HEARD a story of Lockwood playing in a cricket match with J. O. Murphy, KC. Murphy was a great advocate, and in my young days appeared in many *causes célèbres*, including the Parnell Commission. He was a man of immense stature, and weighed, I should think, well over 20 stone.

'We must make some fresh rules applicable to Murphy before starting the match,' Lockwood said, 'if any part of his front be struck by the ball, it must be "leg before wicket", but if the ball strikes his stern, it must be scored a wide.'

242

The narrator is Lord Simon

WHEN he died, at the age of only fifty-one, Rosebery said of Lockwood's personality that 'his entrance into a room seemed to change the whole complexion of the company, and I often fancied that he could dispel a London fog by his presence'.

I had the good luck to sit next to this fascinating man. He asked me what I meant to do when I left Oxford. I said that if I could only manage the finance of it I would like to try my chances at the Bar. He looked at me shrewdly. At that time, as C. B. Fry says in his memoirs, I was a 'fresh-faced and curly-haired youth' with a very boyish air. 'Make your hair grow white', Lockwood said. 'No solicitor will ever dare to brief you if you don't look older than you do.' The only other advice he gave me about the practice of the Law that evening (and I religiously observed it in after years both as Junior and as Silk) was that you should never refuse a brief because it required a specialist to handle it. If a man can do one sort of case well at the Bar, he ought to be able, when properly instructed, to do a different kind of case also.

'Look at me', said Her Majesty's Solicitor-General cheerfully.

'Tomorrow I'm going to appear in the Admiralty Court, and all I know about navigation is' (raising his glass) 'that "Port is red".'

RICHARD LOVELAND-LOVELAND (1841–1923)

243

THE second Court* at the Middlesex Sessions was presided over by Warry, QC, who had a very heavy hand; so indeed had Loveland-Loveland, who succeeded Warry; but I do not remember Loveland-Loveland ever passing what could be described as a savage sentence. He also acted as Deputy to Sir Peter Edlin at London Sessions. He was a gentleman of considerable means who was fond of picking up *objets d'art* for the adornment of his very nice house. On one occasion he was trying a man charged with receiving some very pretty and rather valuable stolen Japanese figures a few inches high. They were of carved ivory, and when produced in Court were handed round to Counsel, the Jury and the Judge, who examined them with interest. The prisoner was convicted and an application was made and granted for an order of restitution in favour of the person from whom they had been stolen—an old Jew antique-dealer who throughout the trial had displayed considerable reluctance to parting with them even to the Court. Almost directly after the Court had risen there arose a hubbub, the old Jew shouting that the two most valuable figures had not been returned to him. The Jury had dispersed, but Counsel in the robing room were appealed to and diligently examined their brief bags and even robes in search of the missing articles. They could not be found, and the Jew departed, breathing vengeance against the police, the jury, the barristers, solicitors and Court officials, against all or any of whom he declared his intention of 'having the law'. The next morning the loss was duly reported to the learned Deputy-Chairman, who blandly announced that he had put the figures in question into his pocket with the intention of calling at the shop of the owner on his way to Court on the following day to pay that person the value which he had put upon them in the witness-box! The Jew was sent for, was obliged to accept the price he had himself put upon the articles, being much less than he would have charged to a person of Loveland-Loveland's distinguished

* For an account of Court No. 1, see under EDLIN.

appearance, and finally the learned Judge left the Court with the figures and, as the newspapers are fond of expressing it, 'without a stain upon his character'.

THOMAS BABINGTON MACAULAY (LORD MACAULAY) (1800–59)

244

MACAULAY was called to the bar in 1826, and joined the Northern Circuit at Leeds. On the evening that he first appeared at mess, when the company were retiring for the night, he was observed to be carefully picking out the longest candle. An old King's Counsel, who noticed that he had a volume under his arm, remonstrated with him on the danger of reading in bed, upon which he rejoined, with immense rapidity of utterance: 'I always read in bed at home, and if I am not afraid of committing parricide and matricide and fratricide I can hardly be expected to pay any special regard to the lives of the bagmen of Leeds.' And so saying, he left his hearers staring at one another, and marched off to his room.

SIR HENRY ALFRED McCARDIE (1869–1933)

245

Sir Gervais Rentoul discusses the cases of three well-known lawyers, all friends of his, all of whom committed suicide. The first two were J. B. Matthews, KC and Edward Marjoribanks. Marjoribanks will be remembered as author of the well-known biographies of Sir Edward Marshall Hall and Lord Carson. The third was McCardie.

THE suicide of Mr Justice McCardie was perhaps the most inexplicable of all three, for his was a brain logical and well-balanced. Possibly his own tireless energy, the intolerable strain he put upon himself by persistent over-work, wore him out.

A story has been told that during his travels in the East he dabbled in mysticism and drew upon himself the curse of one of the priests of

Tibet. Of this I know nothing, but I do know that during the last year of his life he had a curious premonition regarding the manner of his death. It was the outcome of a sensational libel action which came before him in 1932, in which spiritualism played a prominent part, for the plaintiff was a noted medium and the defendants the proprietors of a leading newspaper. During the hearing of this case, which lasted several days, Mr Justice McCardie received a number of anonymous letters from spiritualists and opponents of spiritualism. There was nothing unusual in this; it is inevitable in any lawsuit which arouses public interest, and such communications are always disregarded.

However, one letter, which was not sent to the Law Courts, but put into the letter-box at the judge's house, made a deep impression upon him. It purported to be a message from the spirit world, dictated to a medium, and it revealed a most accurate and minute knowledge of the judge's past life. It also contained, among others, the prophecy that he would die by his own hand.

The month and year of his death was given and, I believe, even the actual day.

It is more than probable that the contents of this letter acted on his subconscious brain until it became almost a case of auto-suggestion. His health was suffering under the strain of his work, and he began to experience a depression that was completely foreign to him. The belief that he was destined to put an end to his life took root in his mind. He no doubt fought it at first but the conviction was ever present, and as the specified date drew nearer it became stronger. And so, after a severe attack of influenza had lowered his vitality, he gave way to an impulse that had become irresistible.

SIR FRANK DOUGLAS MACKINNON (1871–1946)

246

The Dictionary of National Biography *records that Sir Frank MacKinnon was 'a great pedestrian'. Successive marshals who attended him (on circuit) testify to the enormous distances they were expected to cover. In 1931—his sixtieth year—he climbed Snowdon on two consecutive icy days in January. What follows is his account of a much shorter walk.*

ON the Sunday my marshall and I were to lunch with my friend the Sheriff of a year ago. His place was near enough to Derby for us to walk there. The first part of the way, out by the race-course, was dismal enough. As we entered a depressing looking street of small houses, and of considerable length, I said: 'Let us attempt a diversion. If you will give me a penny for every house in which there is an aspidistra in the parlour window, I will give you half a crown for every house in which there is none.' The marshal agreed, and we tried it. Though I may not be believed—I won! The vogue of that deplorable vegetable was more than thirty to one.

247

MacKinnon on Divorce.

As for the evidence from hotels—the chambermaid of superhuman powers of observation and memory, who recalls that a man and woman spent a night in a bedroom a year or two ago, that she took morning tea to them in bed, that a blurred snapshot produced to her is a portrait of the man, and that the Petitioner-wife who has just left the box was not the woman—it was obviously incredible. But its production was part of the absurd ritual. I once shocked a regular Divorce Court practitioner very much by saying: 'I am not sure if I can give you a decree. You have called the chambermaid to say her usual piece. She has said she saw them in bed. *But she has not said she took them early morning tea.* I thought that was a necessary incident in the depravity of adultery.'

MICHAEL MACNAMARA (*fl.* 1890–1910)

248

On one occasion the Counsellor (MacNamara was known far and wide as 'Counsellor Mack') was engaged for a Plaintiff in the County Court, and had a great dread that the defendant would swear himself out of the debt by bare-faced perjury. When the defendant came to take the oath the Counsellor addressed him in Irish:

'Listen carefully, now, to the terms of the oath and repeat after me—"If I do not tell the truth in this case—" '

'If I do not tell the truth in this case—'

'May a murrain seize my cattle—'

'What's that, Counsellor? Sure, that's not the oath.'

'Go on and repeat your oath. "May a murrain seize my cattle—" '

'Oh, Glory be to God! "May a murrain seize my cattle" '

'May all my sheep be clifted' (i.e. fall over a cliff)

'Yerra, Counsellor, what oath is that you're trying to get me to take? Sure, I never heard an oath like that before.'

'Go on, sir, don't argue with me. Repeat your oath, "may all my sheep be clifted—" '

'Oh, God help us. "May all my sheep—" yerra Counsellor, are you sure that's in the oath?'

'Go on, sir.'

'Oh, God. "May all my sheep be clifted!" '

'May all my children get the falling sickness—'

'Arrah, Counsellor, tell his Honour that I admit the debt, and I only want a little time to pay.'

ROBERT MACQUEEN (LORD BRAXFIELD) (1722–99)

249

BRAXFIELD was indeed a 'terror of the law'. Lockhart, in his Life of Scott, reports him as having said to an eloquent culprit at the bar: 'Ye're a vera clever chiel, man, but ye wad be nane the waur o' a hangin'.' When Muir, the political reformer, was being tried, Braxfield, parting with the last vestige of judicial honour, whispered to the father of Francis Horner (one of the Edinburgh Reviewers), as he entered the jury-box, 'Come awa, Maister Horner, come awa, and help us to hang ane o' thae d—d scoondrels.' At a time when the procedure in criminal cases was more a mystery than it is now, and the line to be taken often seemed doubtful, Braxfield at all events was ready for any emergency. 'Hoot! jist gie me Josie Norrie (a clerk of court well up in forms and precedents) and a gude jury, an' I'll do for the fallow'—a typical example of his lordship's best judicial manner.

In ribaldry and coarseness, Braxfield would have offended the Lord Chesterfield of that day, a man by no means squeamish, if we are to judge by those flagitious letters he wrote to his son. Even the most sacred things were not immune from his ridicule. In one of the sedition trials, the prisoner, Gerrald, ventured to remark that all great men had been reformers, 'even our Saviour Himself'. 'Muckle He made o' that; He was hangit' was the profane reply of the man who prided himself upon being a 'sincere Christian'. On another occasion two young advocates, looking considerably the worse for a protracted orgy, were about to plead before his lordship when they were admonished in the following fashion: 'Gentlemen, ye maun jist pack up yer papers and gang hame, for the ane o'ye's riftin' punch, and the ither's belching claret, and there'll be nae gude got oot o'ye the day.'

250

OF all the political prisoners brought before Braxfield, Maurice Margarot gave, perhaps, the most trouble. During his trial (1794) a scene occurred to which it would be difficult to find a parallel in legal history. Margarot was no poltroon. Quite early in the trial he proved himself more than a match for the formidable Braxfield. Learning that the court was being filled with people who had paid the doorkeepers for admission, he demanded that the court should be open to all comers. 'That you have no business with', was Braxfield's answer. Margarot said no more, but on entering upon his defence, he again threw down the gauntlet. The scene which then took place was so extraordinary that the passage-at-arms between the prisoner and the Lord Justice-Clerk may well be reproduced in full.

Margarot: 'Now, my lord, comes a very delicate matter indeed. I mean to call upon my Lord Justice-Clerk; and I hope that the questions and the answers will be given in the most solemn manner. I have received a piece of information which I shall lay before the Court in the course of my questions. First, my lord, are you on oath?'

Braxfield: 'State your questions, and I will tell you whether I will answer them or not. If they are proper questions I will answer them.'

Margarot: 'Did you dine at Mr Rochead's at Inverleith in the course of last week?'

Braxfield: 'And what have you to do with that, sir?'

Margarot: 'Did any conversation take place with regard to my trial?'

Braxfield: 'Go on, sir?

Margarot: 'Did you use these words: "What should you think of giving him (Margarot) a hundred lashes together with Botany Bay", or words to that effect?'

Braxfield: 'Go on. Put your questions if you have any more.'

Margarot: 'Did any person—did a lady say to you that the mob would not allow you to whip me? And, my lord, did you not say that the mob would be the better for losing a little blood? These are the questions, my lord, that I wish to put to you at present in the presence of the Court. Deny them, or acknowledge them.'

The consternation which this encounter—surely one of the most extraordinary that ever took place between a judge of the High Court and a prisoner—produced, may be more easily imagined than described. Braxfield appealed to his colleagues as to whether he should answer the questions; but, amazing to relate, all replied that they were irrelevant, and ought not to be answered. A more despicable piece of sophistry can hardly be conceived. Braxfield, at all events, knew that Margarot's questions were not only relevant, but that the story which gave rise to them was true. In a rash moment he had uttered the sentiments mentioned by Margarot at Mr Rochead's house, and a lady had indiscreetly repeated them. In point of fact, his lordship never sought to deny the story. Moreover, at the subsequent trial of Joseph Gerrald, an offer was made to establish its truth by evidence independent of Braxfield, but the Court refused to allow the matter to be gone into—'a proceeding which', as Cockburn remarks, 'it is difficult to reconcile with any hypothesis except one'.

DUDLEY FIELD MALONE (1882–1950)

American Lawyer

251

The narrator is New York lawyer A. G. Hays

The Scopes case, one of the most celebrated in all American legal history, concerned the right of a schoolteacher to cast doubt on the biblical theory that the world was created in 4004 BC *on the twenty-third day of October at nine o' clock in the morning, Eastern Standard time.*

ONE of my outstanding memories of the Scopes case was the time when Dudley Malone made an extemporaneous address appealing for freedom of education.

He told the story of the burning of the famous Library at Alexandria by the Mohammedans. It was said that one of the defending generals had asked his adversary not to 'destroy this great Library because it contains all the truth that has been gathered'. To which the Mohammedan general replied that the Koran contained all the truth; that if the library held the same truth, the library was useless. If it contained anything else it did not contain the truth.

Bryan had said that the trial was a 'duel to the death'. 'Does the opposition', thundered Dudley, 'mean by a duel that our witnesses shall be strapped to the board, and that the opposition alone shall carry the sword? There is never a duel with the truth. The truth always wins, and we are not afraid of it. The truth is no coward. The truth does not need the law. The truth does not need the forces of government. The truth does not need Mr Bryan. The truth is imperishable, eternal and immortal and needs no human agency to support it. We are ready. We feel we stand with progress. We feel we stand with Science. We feel we stand with intelligence. We feel we stand with fundamental freedom in America. We are not afraid. What is the fear? We defy it.'

The courtroom rang with acclaim. The burly bailiff was pounding his desk. 'I'm not rapping to keep order', he explained. 'I'm pounding the desk for applause.'

H. L. Mencken strode up the aisle. While we gathered round Malone with our congratulations it was clear to us that the approval of Mencken would be particularly gratifying to the orator.

'Dudley,' said Mencken, clapping him on the back, 'that was the loudest speech I ever heard.'

EDWARD MALTBY (*fl.* late nineteenth century?)

Solicitor

252

ONLY an elderly reader will be able to recollect the great will suit which occupied the courts for a fortnight in the early eighties. I was for the defendant and all the trouble was caused by the only son of the testator contesting the will on the ground that his father had made it while not of sound mind.

The contested will would not have covered more than a sheet of notepaper. It disregarded the claims of the son and bequeathed everything, except the family Bible, to the grandson.

There was a large sum at stake and consequently the Court had to be most careful in considering the alleged grievances of the plaintiff, otherwise I am sure the trial would not have lasted a day, but there was never really any doubt as to the result, and when judgment was delivered it was not only in favour of the grandson, but it contained a scathing denunciation of the plaintiff.

I had not informed the Court that the plaintiff had not only robbed his mother of her jewellery but had forged his father's name to cheques. I knew that my late client would not have liked the dirty linen of the family exhibited to the public gaze and therefore my instructions to our counsel—we had four, led by Dick Webster (subsequently Lord Alverstone and Lord Chief Justice) were to rely on direct evidence of the testator's sanity. But the plaintiff's cross-examination revealed him for what he really was, hence the censure by his Lordship, which would have finished any man sensitive about his character and reputation.

When it was all over I wrote to the Plaintiff requesting him either to send for his legacy, the Family Bible, or else intimate his willingness to accept it at the hands of one of my clerks.

He was then staying at a private hotel in Albemarle Street, and when I received no reply I sent the clerk round with the parcel. According to the will the seal on the parcel was not to be broken by anyone except his own son, and broken it was by that young scapegrace, for when the clerk mentioned his errand the defeated litigant threw the parcel at him and ordered him to clear off if he did not wish to have any of his bones broken. The clerk brought the parcel back and I placed it in my strongroom.

There it remained for more than twenty years while its legal owner led a restless, adventurous and unsavoury life, enduring the direst poverty and eventually dying in a common lodging house near Euston Station. I might never have known of it had I not seen a small paragraph in an evening paper recording the event and it then dawned on me that the old Bible might have a sentimental interest for the grandson, and I wrote and asked if he would care to have it.

The following afternoon a young man called, and in his presence the ancient parcel was opened and the pages reverently gazed at which recorded the births, deaths and marriages of his ancestors for over two hundred years.

Suddenly he stopped and uttered an exclamation of surprise, but I was staring too by now for I was staring at the banknote, crisp and new as it had been printed that morning, lying conspicuously on the open page. Altogether we found five, each to the value of £1,000.

There may be a moral to this story, but if there is I will not make it the text of a lay sermon. My duty as a lawyer was to ensure that the disinherited son had left neither wife nor child. And when I had done this, formally hand over the Bible and notes to the young man; who had already more money than he could ever hope to spend.

SIR HENRY MANISTY (1808–90)

253

The narrator is Sir Henry Dickens

MR JUSTICE MANISTY had a lot of fine old 1834 port, a vintage quite unknown to the present generation. I drank much of it because I know Manisty and his son-in-law intimately. Well, the old man got seedy and the doctor ordered him off his port. Weeks went by, and he began to droop, until the doctor told him he had better take up his port again. 'Aye, doctor', said Manisty, 'but how about the arrears?.'

SIR JAMES MANSFIELD (1733–1821)

254

MANSFIELD paid little attention to religious holidays. He would sit on Ash Wednesday, to the scandal of some members of the Bar, whose protests made no impression upon him. At the end of Lent he suggested that the Court might sit on Good Friday.

The members of the Bar were horrified.

Serjeant Davy, who was in the case, bowed in acceptance of the proposition. 'If your Lordship pleases', he said. 'But your Lordship will be the first judge who has done so since Pontius Pilate.'

The Court adjourned until Saturday.

JEREMIAH MASON (1768–1848)

American Senator and Lawyer

255

AN interesting account is given in *The Green Bag* of one of Jeremiah Mason's cross-examinations. The witness had testified to having heard Mason's client make a certain statement and it was upon the evidence of that statement that the adversary's case was based. Mason led the witness round to his statement and again it was repeated verbatim. Then, without warning, he walked to the stand, and pointing straight at the witness said, in his high impassioned voice, 'Let's see that paper you've got in your waistcoat pocket.'

Taken completely by surprise the witness mechanically drew a paper from the pocket indicated and handed it to Mason. The lawyer slowly read the exact words of the witness in regard to the statement. *They were in the handwriting of the lawyer on the other side.*

'Mr Mason, how under the sun did you know that paper was there?', asked a brother lawyer.

'Well,' replied Mason, 'I thought he gave that part of his testimony just as if he'd learned it, and I noticed every time he repeated it he put his hand to his waistcoat pocket and let it fall again when he got through.'

SIR JAMES CHARLES MATHEW (1830–1908)

256

J. C. MATHEW was walking in Hyde Park one day when a man tried the 'painted bird' fraud on him, in which the homely sparrow, by a little skilful manipulation, assumes the beauties of a tropical bird. Approaching Mathew, the man assuming an air of curiosity, said, 'I beg your pardon sir, but I have just found this bird. Can you tell me what kind of bird it is?' Mathew eyeing this man without any change of countenance, replied, 'If there is any truth in the old adage that birds of a feather flock together, I should say it was a jail bird.'

THEOBALD MATHEW (1866–1939)

257

The narrator is his clerk, Sydney Aylett

THEO was fond of films. Claudette Colbert was his favourite star, and Maurice Chevalier was his favourite performer. He had a superstition which linked work with the movies. If ever he looked as though he was going through a slack period, he would leave his room at about two, and without stopping to say where he was going, would shout, 'I'm off!'

The moment he left, either the phone would start ringing, a solicitor's clerk would be asking for him urgently, or a messenger would arrive with a brief, demanding an immediate opinion. When he returned home some three or four hours later, either Wooton (the senior clerk) or I would say 'Where on earth have you been, Sir? Everyone's been trying to get hold of you.' Then he would throw his arms into the air and cry, 'It's worked once again. It's worked! I leave the office for only a few solitary hours at the cinema, and everyone realises how much they need me.'

258

The narrator is Sydney Aylett

I'VE mentioned Theo's gifts as an after-dinner speaker. Unfortunately I was never a witness to it, though I was given many subsequent reports. Sometimes I would stay behind in Chambers and help him change, fasten his tie or give him a final brush. I hoped in exchange he would give me some pearl of a story he was going to use, but he never did. I think perhaps he wasn't sure of what he was going to say. One evening, I recall, there was pandemonium. He was speaking at a dinner where King George V was to be the guest of honour. It was, he considered, his wife's or one of his daughter's duties to pack his clothes into a case. To his horror he found that on this occasion the studs of his starched front had been omitted. It allowed him the opportunity to express his fury of, and contempt for, the female sex. When his diatribe was over he panicked slightly.

'What on earth am I going to do, Sydney? I can't present His Majesty with a gaping front.'

Frankly I was at a loss what to advise. The shops were closed, and though there might have been men in the Temple with a set of studs in their chambers, they would have gone home.

Suddenly Theo brightened. 'Have we any paper fasteners, Sydney?' We had, and I sorted a few out. 'Polish the tops with something', he demanded, and then fitted them into his shirt. They not only filled the bill, they looked almost opulent.

The following day I asked him how he had got on. 'They passed muster,' he replied, 'but it wasn't entirely a bloodless victory. I have several scratches to show for my loyalty.'

SIR CHARLES WILLIE MATHEWS (1850–1920)

Director of Public Prosecutions

259

IT was at Winchester assizes; and Mathews was addressing a common jury in a torrent of burning eloquence, probably incomprehensible to most of them, but not the less impressive, while he pointed the finger of scorn at the unhappy prosecuting counsel, who sat cowering at his side. 'Go to it, little un', roared an excited and sympathetic farmer from the body of the court, in the midst of his longest and most incoherent sentence. 'Turn that man out of court!', said Mr Justice Stephen sternly; and operations were suspended for some minutes while this direction was being carried into effect. When order was at length restored, and the audience had settled down into terrified attention, the judge addressed the advocate in dignified and encouraging tones. 'Go on, Mr Mathews, if you please—*exactly where you left off*!'

260

The narrator is Lord Simon

NO advocate I have ever met conveyed so overpowering a sense of the drama of life. I was Mathews' junior in Winchester in the Crown Court in a terrible trial for murder years ago. It was known as the Aldershot Murder. Ernest Charles, I remember, made a fine speech for the defence. We were for the prosecution.

Two soldiers and a civilian were charged with murdering a woman of the town at a little distance outside Aldershot. Never shall I forget how Mathews started his opening in that case to the stolid, serious-faced Hampshire jury. There were none of the conventional sentences about the seriousness of the charge. In the silence which followed the formal recital of the indictment to the jury which ended—'it is your charge to inquire whether he be guilty or not guilty and to hearken to the evidence'—the little figure rose and began in his rather high-pitched vibrating tones: 'At 10 o'clock on the morning of Midsummer Day, the driver of a four-wheeled cab was returning to the town when he observed, near the side of the road, under some bushes, in a little wood, something lying. He got down to look. What was it?' (Almost in a whisper.) 'The body of a woman—dead—barely cold. What was there which attracted the special attention of the cabman as he examined this poor creature? On her feet there were no sho-o-o-es.' This last word was a long-drawn-out croon. There followed a pause while a cold shiver ran down one's spine. And then, in a brisk, matter-of-fact voice Mathews resumed. 'At five o'clock that morning Private X and Private Y who are in the dock behind me' (with a jerk of his thumb over his shoulder) 'entered Malplaquet Barracks after a night's leave. One of them was carrying something. What was he carrying?

'A pair of woman's sho-o-o-es.' The echo was exact.

There was not much good arguing, after that, that circumstantial evidence did not amount to proof.

FREDERIC HERBERT MAUGHAM (LORD MAUGHAM) (1866–1958)

Lord Chancellor

261

My introduction to the Bar was not without a somewhat ominous passage. Robert Romer was kind enough to sign for me the necessary guarantee of respectability. Another signature was, however, necessary and a solicitor offered to introduce me to a barrister who would, no doubt, be kind enough to join with Romer in the guarantee. One morning he took me up a small circular staircase to some chambers on the second floor of the ancient building in the corner of Old Square.

We were admitted by a clerk who told us that the occupant of the Chambers was in Court but was expected back very soon.

It was the first time I had ever been in a barrister's chambers, and I naturally looked round the room with great interest. There was a table with two or three bundles of paper tied with red tape; there were a few plain mahogany chairs; and the walls were covered with rows and rows of books in decaying calf bindings.

The room, as I now know, dated from the reign of Henry the Seventh. It looked to me extraordinarily dirty, and but for my unwillingness to libel generations of laundresses I should say that it had never undergone a thorough cleaning since the building was erected. This added to the romantic feeling that I was going to live my life in just such a room, and perhaps to achieve success and fortune.

The door opened and a middle-aged man in wig and gown entered. He threw these professional adornments angrily, as I thought, on to a chair and greeted the solicitor. On my being introduced he shook hands with me, amiably enough, and after a brief conversation said he would be glad to sign the necessary guarantee. This he did, and as we prepared to leave he looked me up and down in a critical way. He saw, no doubt, a simple lad just down from the University, without a line on his rather pink face, and looking remarkably strong and healthy. He then remarked with much emphasis, 'I may tell you, young man, if I had a son I would sooner he were dead than going to the Bar.'

There was nothing to be said in answer to this observation and we made our way out.

SIR WILLIAM HENRY MAULE (1788–1858)

262

THERE was a very important and intricate case coming on in the House of Lords, and the peers had summoned the judges to attend them to hear the subject-matter argued by counsel and to give their opinions upon it. Follett was retained as counsel on one side and Maule on the other. Shortly before the case came on, Follett strolled into the kitchen of the House of Commons (to which the Bar had always access in the day-time) and called for a biscuit and a glass of sherry. To his surprise, he saw Maule sitting at a table with a rumpsteak and a huge flagon of stout before him, to the consumption of both of which he was applying himself with the most exemplary assiduity. Follett could not help expressing to his opponent his astonishment at seeing him indulging in so solid and carnal a diet by way of preparation for the task he was about to enter upon, and for which a clear unclouded brain was so essential.

'As to clearness of brain,' said Maule, 'I find that mine is too clear already. The truth is, I am striving to bring my intellect down to a level with the capacity of those idiotic judges.'

263

SOCIETY owes, I think, a deep debt of gratitude to Mr Justice Maule, when at the Bar, for accidentally burning down a large portion of its old ricketty tenements, and thus affording scope for the great improvements that have taken place since. It is said that, returning to his chambers late at night or early in the morning, he in a fit of abstraction put the lighted candle under his bed instead of on the dressing-table. I believe he never divulged what was the subject that engrossed him so deeply on that occasion.

264

MAULE was once trying a man charged with an assault upon a female. The defence set up was consent on the part of the prosecutrix, and Maule soon made up his mind that there was abundant ground for it; but it was a question for the jury, although in summing-up he pretty clearly indicated to them his opinion as to the course they ought to take. But, as often happens when an interesting young specimen of the other sex is concerned, juries are apt to wink at little foibles, which they would not tolerate in their own. In this instance they seemed for a long time very reluctant to adopt the judge's view; but he generally got his own way, and, having interposed with two or three sarcastic remarks during their deliberations, they at length acquitted the prisoner; whom Maule addressed in these words:

'Let me, my man, give you a bit of advice. The next time you indulge in these unseemly familiarities, I recommend you to insist on your accomplice giving her consent in writing, and take care that she puts her signature to the document, otherwise, it seems to me, you may get before a jury who will be satisfied with nothing else.'

265

The narrator is Henry Hawkins

ON one occasion before Maule, I had to defend a man for murder. It was a terribly difficult case, because there was no defence except the usual one of insanity.

The Court adjourned for lunch and Woollet, who was my junior, and I went into consultation. I was oppressed with the difficulty of my task, and asked Woollet what he thought I could do.

'Call the clergyman', said Woollet. 'He'll help us all he can.'

With that resolution we returned to court. I made my speech for the defence, and really blazed away. We then called the clergyman of the village where the prisoner lived. He said he had been Vicar for 34 years and that up to very recently, a few days before the murder, the prisoner had been a regular attendant at his church. He was a married man with a wife and two little children, one seven and the other nine.

'Suddenly,' continued the vicar, 'without any apparent cause, the man became *a Sabbath breaker* and absented himself from church.'

This evidence rather puzzled me, for I could not understand its purport. Maule, in the meantime, was watching it with the keenest intensity.

'Have you finished with your witness, Mr Woollet?', his Lordship enquired.

'Yes, my Lord.'

Maule then took him in hand.

'You say, sir, that you have been vicar of this parish for *four and thirty years?*'

'Yes, my Lord.'

'And during this time I dare say you have regularly performed the services of the Church?'

'Yes, my Lord.'

'Did you have weekday services as well?'

'Every Tuesday, my Lord.'

'And was this poor man a regular attendant at all your services? Never missed the sermon, Sunday or weekday?'

'That is so, my Lord.'

'Did you write your own sermons?'

'Oh yes, my Lord.'

Maule carefully wrote down all that our witness said, and I began to think the defence of insanity stood on very fair grounds, especially when I perceived that Maule was making some arithmetical calculations. . . .

'The result of your indefatigable exertions, so far as this unhappy man is concerned, comes to this—'

His Lordship then turned and addressed his observations on the result to me.

'This gentleman, Mr Hawkins, has written with his own pen, and preached or read with his own voice one hundred and four sermons every year.'

There was an irresistible sense of the ludicrous as Maule uttered, or rather growled these words in a slow enunciation and an asthmatical tone. He paused, as if wondering at the magnitude of his calculations, and then commenced again, more slowly and solemnly than before.

'These,' said he, 'added to the weekday services, make exactly *one hundred and fifty six sermons for the year.* These, again, being continued over thirty four years give us a grand total of *five thousand three hundred and four sermons, discourses or homilies* during this unhappy man's life.'

Maule's eyes were now rivetted on the clergyman as though he were an accessory to the murder.

'I was going to ask you, sir, did the idea ever strike you, when you talked of this unhappy being suddenly leaving your Ministrations and turning Sabbath-breaker, that, after thirty four years, he might want a little change? Would it not be reasonable to suppose that the man might think he had had enough of it?'

'It might, my Lord.'

'And would not that, in your judgement, instead of showing that he was insane prove that he was *a very sensible man*?'

The vicar did not quite assent to this, and as he would not dissent from the learned judge, he said nothing.

'And,' continued Maule, 'that he was perfectly sane, although he murdered his wife?'

I resolved to take the other view of the Vicar's sermons, and I did so. I worked Maule's quarry I think with some little effect, for after all his most strenuous exertions to secure a conviction the jury believed, probably, that no man's mind could stand the ordeal. And, further, that any doubt they might have, after seeing the two children of the prisoner in court dressed in little black frocks, and sobbing bitterly while I was addressing them, would be given in the prisoner's favour; which it was.

On the same evening I was dining at the country house of a Mr Hardcastle, and near me sat an old inhabitant of the village where the tragedy had occurred.

'You made a touching speech, Mr Hawkins', said the old inhabitant.

'Well,' I answered, 'it was the best I could do under the circumstances.'

'Yes,' he said, 'but I don't think you would have painted the little home in such glowing colours if you had seen what I saw last week when I was driving past the cottage. No. No. I think you'd have toned it down a bit.'

'What was it?', I asked.

'Why,' said the old inhabitant, 'the little children who sobbed so violently in court this morning were playing on an ash-heap near their cottage; and they had a poor cat with a string round its neck, swinging backwards and forwards, and as they did so they sang:

> This is the way poor daddy will go!
> This is the way poor daddy will go!

266

An action was brought by an attorney against a defendant for calling him a thief, a rogue, and a fiend; and, as the plaintiff had no proof of any pecuniary special damage, he had to rely on the injury that must necessarily be inflicted on him in his professional capacity by such imputations.

In summing up, Maule said,

'As to the word thief, it is a very ambiguous one, and does not necessarily impute what the law considers an indictable offence. For instance, to steal a man's wife, to steal away the affections of another, to steal a march upon anyone, would be no crime in law. Wives, human affections, and such things as marches are not at present the subject of larceny. Rogue is different; it might certainly affect the plaintiff professionally, because a rogue ought not to be allowed to practise as an attorney. But the same principle does not apply to the term fiend; it may not be a complimentary expression, but I do not think to be a fiend disqualifies a man from being an attorney. If the learned counsel will point out to me any case where the court has refused an application to place a fiend upon the rolls, I shall be happy to consider it.'

267

MR JUSTICE MAULE once tried an action in which damages were claimed for a slander which consisted of a statement that the plaintiff was a b—— i.e. a person addicted to unnatural habits. He charged the jury as follows:

'The word is horrible and is said to impute that the plaintiff habitually committed a detestable crime which is not fit to be mentioned among Christians. The defendant says that the word was mere vulgar abuse and did not convey a charge of a crime, and if that is proved, the defendant is entitled to the verdict. Vulgar abuse is not actionable at Law. Now, gentlemen, you must say whether the word imputed a crime to the defendant or not. It is for you to say. And in considering your verdict you will remember that it has been proved before you that on the same occasion the defendant used the same word about a clothes-horse, a black beetle, and a piece of toasted cheese.'

Verdict for the defendant.

SIR ROBERT GORDON MENZIES (1894–1978)

268

I WAS briefed to appear in the County Court at Kerang, in a farming area in the north-west of the State of Victoria. The action was for damages for breach of warranty on a sale of sheep.

It was common ground that the vendor of a number of ewes had said that the rams and the ewes had been 'joined' at such and such a time. The vital question, to be solved by expert evidence, was whether this expression meant merely that the rams and ewes had been given their opportunity, and that no particular result had been guaranteed: or whether it meant that the ewes were in lamb.

It was a fascinating case. George Dethridge was on the Bench, watered ribbon, whimsy and all. Most of the members of the jury were farmers who gave 'expert' evidence of a conflicting kind. My opponent and I made, no doubt, powerful speeches (at least I like to think they were) and the judge summed up. No one enjoyed the case more than Dethridge. I can see him now, looking at the jury for form's sake, and up to heaven for inspiration, swinging his glasses on their ribbon, saying 'Gentlemen, this is eminently a case for you. It turns on the meaning of a simple English word, *joined*. Like all simple English words it is capable of quite a few meanings. Thus, I might, in all innocence, say that I had joined my wife at the railway station. *Wouldn't mean what any of your sheep men think it means.*'

MIDLAND CIRCUIT RECORDS (1784)

269

MR ISTED presents Mr Willis for saying to Mr Barker, an Attorney, in the Court at Warwick, 'My dear Sir.' Paid 2/6.

Mr Clarke presents Mr (illegible) for dancing with an Attorney's daughter at Derby.

Mr Moody presented for giving a Supper to 3 Sisters of an Attorney (being his Sisters-in-law)—not guilty. [Under the old usage this may have meant his step-sisters. Cf. Sam Weller's use of 'Mother-in-Law' for Stepmother.]

Mr Onslow presented by Mr Willis for bringing an Attorney in his chaise to Warwick—2/6.

SIR EDWARD MITCHELL (1858–1941)

King's Counsel

270

The narrator is Sir Robert Menzies

IT should be understood that in our High Court, unlike the Supreme Court of the United States, where the full arguments are submitted in writing, the whole argument is submitted orally, and there are no time limits.

Great cases tended to be legal marathons. One story was told at the

Bar of a case in which the late Sir Edward Mitchell KC was engaged. He had commenced his argument on a Tuesday morning, had mapped out his course, and was following it slowly and ponderously.

On Tuesday afternoon one of the judges invited Mitchell's attention to a point, and asked what he had to say about it. Mitchell's reply was: 'I propose to deal with that matter on Thursday afternoon.'

WALTER TURNER MONCKTON (LORD MONCKTON) (1891–1965)

271

IN answer to a letter sent to a number of judges asking for details of their cricketing prowess Lord Evershed wrote:

> The name of the present Lord Monckton naturally springs to mind. He was a first-class wicket keeper and also is the only cricketer of my acquaintance who succeeded (when playing in a match with me) in scoring two leg-byes off the side of his head off the first ball of the match.

SIR RICHARD MUIR (1857–1926)

272

ONE of the most efficient and cold blooded of Treasury Counsel was Richard Muir. Nothing seemed to disturb him or put him out of his stride. As he grew older his asperity and lack of geniality became more marked. His cases were prepared with the utmost care, and he was usually armed with the most elaborate notes in red and blue pencil: blue for the more important statements of his own witnesses, and red for those which told against him. Although scrupulously fair in his presentation of a case—and perhaps because of it—very few guilty persons escaped when Muir appeared for the prosecution. If occasionally he failed to prove the guilt of the accused, no one was more surprised, and indeed annoyed, than Muir himself.

On one sultry hot day he was overcome by the heat and had to be assisted out of Court. There was a good deal of commotion, and everybody wanted to know what had happened.

'Oh, it's only that Muir has fainted', said a colleague, 'because one of his prisoners has been acquitted.'

CLAUD MULLINS (1887–1968)

Metropolitan Magistrate

273

AN old man once pleaded guilty before me for a somewhat mean theft. He was about sixty and had served eleven terms of imprisonment in twenty years. During a week's adjournment, the Probation Officer grew almost fond of the old man, and on his reappearance in court appealed to me to place him on probation. Such a step should never be taken without the full consent of a Probation Officer, for it is he who has to do the work. I made a probation order and warned the old man that if he did commit more crimes, my action would be a warning to his next court that kindness was useless, so that he would probably receive a severe sentence. Later in the day I asked the gaoler how the old man had taken my decision. I took down what he told me. 'He nearly fainted on me,' said the gaoler; 'and when I calmed him down he said: "It's the first time I've had a knock like this. I could have taken five years without turning a hair." '

274

I HAD found a young man guilty of stealing a pair of skating boots from an ice-rink. His defence had been that somebody on his previous visit had stolen *his* boots. He was rather a dull lad, and with such it is useless to use other than the simplest words and examples. I wanted to convince him of the rightness of my decision and to show him when exchanges of property were right and when they were wrong. So I said something like this to him: 'The other evening someone in the train took my umbrella by mistake and left his own, so I had to take his home as it was raining. I told the stationmaster, but I still have that man's umbrella, as he had not claimed it. That, you see, is an innocent exchange. But yours was not innocent. You deliberately took someone else's boots.' Soon after I reached home that evening there was a knock on the door of my house. When I was called, I saw two men on the doorstep. One of them had a camera and said: 'May we take your photograph under that umbrella?' I hope I rose to the occasion. Anyhow, those two men travelled in their car another seventeen miles back to Fleet Street without achieving their ridiculous object.

275

ON the subject of 'drunks', I recall one who was the cause of some fun. One afternoon at the Savile Club a friend came up to me with a smile and said: 'What a lot of good you could have done if you had died.' A little bewildered, I asked for further details. I was handed the *Evening Standard* for the day. A prominent headline read: 'SAVED UP TO BUY WREATH FOR MR MULLINS.'

I was used to strange headlines, but this one seemed more fantastic than usual, so I read on. A knife-grinder, sixty-five years old, had appeared before my colleague that morning for his one hundred and twenty-second conviction for drunkenness. My colleague had noticed that there had recently been a gap of about a year in these convictions, so he had asked him the reason. The man replied: 'Mr Mullins was bad, and I was saving up enough money to buy him a wreath. But he recovered, and I took to drink again.' When I got back to court, I asked the gaoler if this had really happened as described. He said that the report was quite correct, so apparently my methods for dealing with these people had roused a little affection in one of them.

WILLIAM MURRAY (LORD MANSFIELD)
(1705–93)

Lord Chief Justice

276

ALEXANDER POPE introduced Murray to Sarah, Duchess of Marlborough, no easy client. On one occasion he came back late to his chambers to find the entrance blocked by her carriage and the Duchess sitting in his chair. Instead of making any apology she said 'young man, if you mean to rise in the world, you must not sup out'. On another occasion she waited in vain until after midnight for his return and left without seeing him. His clerk, reporting next day, said 'I could not make out, Sir, who she was, for she would not give me her name; but she swore so dreadfully that she must be a lady of quality.'

MICHAEL ANGELO MUSMANNO (1897–1968)

American Judge

277

Miss Marian Ludlow, daughter of the President of the United Mineworkers, had been arrested by Coal and Iron policeman Randall Thompson when, in resisting his attempts at flirtation, she called him 'a conceited prig'. He charged her with disorderly conduct. Musmanno, defending her, concluded his summation.

'I RESPECT and admire the policeman's uniform when it is occupied by someone who does honour to it. You cannot drape a uniform round a skunk, and say that that will make the skunk a policeman. A skunk will smell through the drapings of a dozen uniforms. You cannot put a uniform on a criminal and expect that the uniform will make the criminal a respecting and respected upholder of the law. Thompson, standing here, is a disgrace to his uniform. He sullies, dishonours, debases and corrupts. He stains it with his criminality.'

The Court shrunk as if it had been hit by an exploding bomb.

'Judge,' the Coal Company's attorney sang out indignantly, 'I must strenuously object to the language employed by Attorney Musmanno. He may not, because he is a lawyer, slander my client. By what right does he refer to my client as a criminal?'

'Because he is', I replied.

'What proof have you?'

I extracted certified copies of court records showing that Thompson had twice been convicted of aggravated assault and battery. I handed them to my opponent who glanced at them, gulped in embarrassment, and handed them back. He dropped his current objection and took up another one.

'Why did you call him a skunk?'

'Do you want to defend him on that ground?'

'Well—ah—' He appeared at loss for words fearing, I suppose, that

I could produce some document which would prove that Thompson was a full-fledged, full-pedigreed *mephitis mephitis*.

'I did not say that your client was a skunk, but I would be pleased to have you tell me *what* he is after you read the details of what he has done. You will find that he spurred his horse into a crowd of women and children, inflicting injury on many. I would like to have you inform me what part of the animal kingdom would take him if you learned that he struck a woman with a babe in her arms. I infer from your protest that he does not belong to the skunk family. I do not think he does so either—the skunk has *some* pride.'

The Court rocked with cheers and laughter as the miners back-slapped each other. This is the type of 'castergation' they had been waiting for. It was particularly sweet that a man of the law was administering it.

Justice of the Peace Rogan decided against my client, as I had anticipated, but we appealed to the Allegheny County Court where we obtained an easy reversal.

PETER O'BRIEN
(BARON O'BRIEN OF KILFENORA) (1842–1914)

Lord Chief Justice (Ireland)

278

THE Lord Chief Justice was Sir Peter O'Brien. He didn't like the title that introduced his christian name. Everyone called him 'Pether'. He later acquired a peerage and became 'Baron O'Brien of Kilfenora' in the County of Clare. It was no use. Everybody continued to call him 'Pether' and so he lived and died. As a pupil of Palles he learned the principles of the Common Law, and he had ability, if he chose to use it. He rarely did. He assumed the attitude that his office was much beneath his merits and that the discharge of its duties would be demeaning to him.

A feature of 'Pether's' judicial career was the extraordinary effect that he allowed to be produced upon him by a pretty girl. His conduct was often ludicrous. He treated a pretty girl as conclusive, or nearly conclusive, evidence in favour of the party whose witness she might be, and on one occasion, when he was compelled to decide in favour of a client of mine against whom two charming but irrelevant beauties had been paraded, he actually suggested that money that had been lodged in court by my clients should be divided between these young ladies; and he was very indignant when I objected.

In the County of Limerick there used to practise a native genius who, had he come earlier to the bar, would have made a lasting name. 'Pether' loved him, and he played up to 'Pether' with consummate ability. In a hopeless case at one assizes he put into the witness box, as his last reserve, a supremely pretty girl. 'Pether' beamed upon her, but, catching the eye of a cynical bystander, his Lordship somewhat quailed.

'Mr Kelly,' he said, 'Mr Kelly, this will not do. This will not do, Mr Kelly. I don't mind admitting that there may have been occasions when testimony of this kind might have affected me, but that is a long time ago, Mr Kelly. I am an extinct volcano.'

This was extremely disconcerting to Paddy Kelly, who found no reply to make but he noticed that Pether, notwithstanding the protest, had commenced to ogle the girl, and the more she blushed, the more ardent Pether showed himself.

'I dinnaw, me Lord,' said Paddy in his broad brogue, 'but there might be a few rumbles in the old crater yit.'

Pether was delighted, and judged accordingly.

279

Amende Honorable. At the Cork Assizes in 1877 a man called Humphreys was accused of conspiracy to defraud. The issue of the case depended on the jury understanding what constituted conspiracy. The Revd Mr Pearson describes the scene.

LATE in the day Judge Keogh, a man of somewhat arbitrary temper, was charging the jury. The Court was crowded with all the leading citizens of Cork. The judge was giving the jury a definition of the Law of Conspiracy when O'Brien, who was defending Humphreys stood up and said, 'Respectfully, my Lord, I would ask your Lordship to put it in this way to the jury' (mentioning another legal definition). Judge Keogh said 'Mr O'Brien, resume your seat. If you stand up again I shall have you removed from Court.' O'Brien resumed his seat and waited until the judge had finished his charge and the jury had retired.

He then said, 'My Lord, when your Lordship was defining the law of conspiracy, I rose to suggest an alternative definition. I did so most respectfully. Doubtless I was a little irregular in not waiting until the jury had retired, but your Lordship said, if I did not resume my seat, you would have me removed from Court.'

Judge Keogh: 'Yes, certainly.'

Mr O'Brien: 'Well, my Lord, on behalf of the Munster Bar I strongly protest against any such language being addressed to any member. If such language can be used by the Bench, we may say farewell to the freedom of the Bar.'

The hour being then about 7.00 p.m. the Judge said he would go to dinner and return at 9 o'clock to take the verdict of the jury.

When nine o'clock came, the court was so crowded that we felt sure Judge Keogh would be in a towering rage and have us all removed.

There seemed to be no check on the crowd coming in and filling up every passage. 9.30 came, and 10 o'clock, and still no judge.

It was fully 10.30 when he came on the Bench, and the Sheriff started to call out the jury.

'Wait a moment', said Judge Keogh. Then, turning to O'Brien, he said, 'Mr O'Brien. I said something to you this evening which I regret, and you resented, very properly. I fully withdraw it. That statement was made in the presence of a crowded court, so I sent word that the doors of the court should be kept open *so that as many might be present when I withdraw those words as were here when I uttered them.*'

SIR TERENCE JAMES O'CONNOR (1891–1940)

Solicitor-General

280

The narrator is Sir Gervais Rentoul

TERENCE O'CONNOR (who later became Solicitor General in the National Government), when I went to speak for him at Luton, offered to motor me down in the huge, open, somewhat old fashioned Rolls which he drove himself, but often, I am afraid, with entire disregard of the speed limit or of other traffic that might be on the road. I confess that my heart was in my mouth as he took me by an alleged short cut along narrow country lanes, full of innumerable twists and turns, relying as it seemed to me entirely on his brakes and headlights.

In the course of the journey I happened to mention that I was engaged in a murder trial at the Old Bailey. Terence listened for a while, and then suddenly remarked: 'I do not know why people make such a fuss about murder. I myself have murdered two men and never lost a wink of sleep in consequence.'

This somewhat startling disclosure naturally intrigued me, and I invited him to relate the facts. During World War No. 1, he was temporarily in charge of a lonely post in Tanganyika which had recently been captured from the enemy, and in addition to occupying the German Commander's quarters he had kept on the same native servants. Gradually he found himself becoming very ill and could not make out the reason until his own 'boy' revealed that the cook was mixing quantities of powdered glass with his food. Terence kept careful watch, and satisfied himself that this was the case. The question then arose, what was the best thing to do. They were surrounded by hostile tribes, and a formal Court Martial, apart from the difficulty of obtaining satisfactory evidence, might have led to considerable trouble. He therefore solved the matter in his own characteristic way. He decided to go on a short safari and ordered the cook to accompany him as a bearer. In the course of it he took him up a steep mountain path on the side of a precipice, turned round, caught the cook round the waist and hurled him into the abyss a thousand feet below. He then returned to camp and reported that there had been a melancholy accident.

The other incident, of which I forget the details, was somewhat similar, and was typical of a man who never hesitated to deal with an emergency in the most drastic and startling manner if he felt it necesary to do so.

SIR JAMES ALAN PARK (1763–1838)

281

PARK's face was the exact counterpart of that of George the Third as shown on the coins of that King. This remarkable likeness led many to say he was a natural son of that monarch.

It so happened that on the trial of a cause before that Judge at Warwick something turned upon likenesses. Serjeant Goulbourn was addressing the jury, and while attempting a logical deduction from likenesses as pertinent to the matter in hand, was interrupted by Park who, standing up with his hands in his pockets and gently swaying himself backwards and forwards, exclaimed, 'Brother Goulbourn, brother Goulbourn, don't dwell too long upon that. It has been said I am the son of his late Majesty George the Third, because of my likeness to him. All I can say upon that subject is this: George the Third was never in Scotland, and my mother was never out of it; so if you can make me out to be his son, do. Go on.'

282

HE was called 'St James's Park', to distinguish him from the judge of the same name who was called 'Green Park'. . . . In his later days he had acquired a habit of thinking aloud.

While trying an old woman upon a charge of stealing faggots he unconsciously ejaculated, 'Why, one faggot is as like another faggot as one egg is like another egg.' The counsel defending the case heard the observation and repeated it to the jury. 'Stop', said Sir James. 'Stop. It is an intervention of Providence. *This was the very thought that passed through my mind.* Gentlemen. Acquit the prisoner.'

THOMAS PARKER (EARL OF MACCLESFIELD)

(1666–1732)

Lord Chancellor

283

The cost of becoming a Master in Chancery.

ONE Peter Cottingham, it seemed, was the gentleman who acted as broker for the Lord Chancellor in the matter of the sale of Masterships, and the offerings made by candidates, which varied in amount, were handed sometimes to his Lordship and sometimes to the partner of his joys. Master Bennet, who had succeeded in this candidature, was a principal witness.

'I applied to Master Cottingham', said Master Bennet, 'and desired him to let me know my Lord Chancellor's thoughts.' Soon afterwards, 'my Lord expressed himself with a great deal of respect for my father and was glad of an opportunity to do me a kindness'. He added, 'that he had no objection in the world to me, but that there was a present expected and that he did not doubt but I knew it'. Master Bennet replied that he was willing to do what was usual, and inquired what would be expected. To this Mr Cottingham rejoined that 'he could name no sum'. Master Bennet therefore went off to consult his brother, returned to Mr Cottingham, and offered £1,000, adding that 'he would not stand for guineas'. Mr Cottingham 'shook his head' and observed, 'That won't do, Mr Bennet; you must be better advised. A great deal more has been given.' Master Bennet said he was sure his brother did not give so much, but Mr Cottingham was firm, and (condescending to particulars) said that Mr Kynaston had given 1,500 guineas. 'Then I began to consider', said Mr Bennet, 'and was loath to lose the office, and I told him I would give £1,500. He said, Mr Kynaston had given guineas.' Then Mr Bennet asked if it must be in gold. 'In what way you will,' replied the prudent Mr Cottingham, 'so it be guineas.'

On June 1, proceeded Mr Bennet, he went to be sworn in by the Lord Chancellor. He was received by Mr Cottingham, who asked at once if he had brought the money. Mr Bennet explained that he had got two bank bills—one for £1,000 and one for £575. These having been absorbed by Mr Cottingham, Mr Bennet went upstairs to be sworn in.

It was Master Elde who availed himself of the clothes-basket as a convenient receptable for his gift. Anxious to be appointed, Mr Elde saw the Lord Chancellor himself, who was even more delicate than Mr Cottingham. Lord Macclesfield said he thought Mr Elde would make a good officer, and asked Mr Elde to consider of it. Mr Elde considered of it accordingly for two days, and then returned to say that 'if his Lordship would admit him he would make him a present of £5,000'. To this Lord Macclesfield virtuously replied, 'You and I must not make bargains.' A few days later Mr Elde met Cottingham. Cottingham, when told of his offer of £5,000 to Lord Macclesfield, significantly rejoined 'Guineas are handsomer.' Determined to secure the office, Mr Elde repaired to his chambers, found a clothes-basket, placed in it 5,000 guineas in cash and notes, handed it to Mr Cottingham at the Lord Chancellor's house, saw Mr Cottingham carry it upstairs, was invited to dine by the Lord Chancellor, and was sworn in after dinner. Some months later his basket was returned to him but, added Master Elde, with no money in it.

CHARLES HENRY PARKHURST (1842–1933)

American Clergyman and Reformer

284

The jury takes a hand.

NEAR the beginning of the year 1892 the Grand Jury considered the matter of indicting one McGlory, the keeper of a notorious resort on 14th Street. There was no legal evidence at hand that would be sufficient to convict and the District Attorney was asked by Charles Parkhurst to secure some. An innocent imagination would have supposed that he would jump at the opportunity. The request was repeated by the Grand Jury, apparently without effect.

Our guileless District Attorney, with the down of innocence upon his blushing cheek, failed to respond to the demands for evidence made upon him by the Grand Jury. The jurors themselves therefore assumed experimentally the character of detectives, and the proprietor of the place was, of course, soon caught. An indictment was then found. It remained to secure witnesses that would be willing to testify. For while the jurors had been willing to visit the place they experienced a natural delicacy in having their names publicly associated with such a resort. Accordingly instructions were given to the captain of the precinct to procure the necessary evidence.

This was followed by another touching exhibition of modesty and blushing hesitancy. The captain declared reiteratively that evidence against McGlory was something he could not obtain. Finally the Grand Jury threatened to indict the captain himself, whereupon the evidence was at once produced and McGlory convicted upon it.

SIR EDWARD ABBOTT PARRY (1863–1943)

285

Sir Edward Parry, then Judge in the Manchester County Court, explains that one of his routine tasks was to examine complaints against 'certificated' Bailiffs who were employed to carry out distraints for rent and similar jobs for the Court.

THERE was one firm consisting of father and son, against whom several complaints were made. The senior partner was charged with wrong-doing, and just before the summer holidays in 1898 I held a long inquiry into the evidence against him. As it was seven in the evening before it was finished I said I would give Judgement in the morning. I talked it over with the registrar and came to the conclusion that if the older man's certificate was withdrawn, and the son allowed to continue, it would meet the justice of the case without ruining the business.

The next day I delivered a short judgement in the bailiff's certificate matter and, as I finished, a barrister to my right in the court rose to make an application. I turned my head to ask him to wait a moment. This movement probably saved my life. For a terrific explosion took place near the left of my face and my head fell with a bump on the table. I was under the impression that it was a dynamite bomb. Then there was a second explosion which caused me intense pain. I knew then that someone was firing at me. The first bullet, which would have smashed my face had I not turned my head, only ran along the side of my jaw, tearing the muscles; the second entered at the back of my ear and lives with me still. But the third, which seemed to give me even greater pain, never hit me at all.

By that time Henry Thomason, one of our clerks, had bravely tackled my assailant who was the man I had deprived of his certificate, and as they fell together the man fired again and the bullet went into the plaster of the opposite wall and then out into the Court. Thomason was fortunately uninjured and the man was secured.

I do not think I ever lost consciousness altogether, though, of course, I was not capable of knowing what had happened except that someone had tried to destroy me. Montgomery, a friend of mine and a very able young surgeon, who happened to be in Court, climbed onto the bench, lifted my head up as though it was an exhibit in an action, opened my mouth forcibly and explored it with his forefinger. I was disgusted and indignant, but could not protest at what seemed to me a cold-blooded contempt of Court. Then I heard Montgomery say to someone near him in a cheerful tone, 'There is no perforation you know.' I had no idea what it meant, but it sounded comforting.

They carried me into my room and laid me on my hearthrug, making me as comfortable as might be. George Wright, the surgeon, came, and another friend, Dr Judson Bury, and I gave them to understand that the movement of boots, walking round my head was driving me crazy. I shall never forget those boots walking round my head by themselves. They were horribly insulting and exasperating.

In quite a short time the ambulance arrived and I was taken to a nursing home in Nelson Street. I had a lot of doctor friends to look after me, and though I was in great pain and not very sensible of what was happening for some days, I soon began to make a wonderful recovery. When I got a little better I found I was stone deaf in my left ear. Wright said that probably my eardrum was blown askew by the concussion caused by the explosion of the revolver shots, and later on we would get Larmuth, the eminent aural surgeon, to have a look at it. 'Don't worry about it, Judge,' he said, 'it's only the left ear, and in the Manchester Court that's the defendant's side and you never listen to him, you know.'

286

THE precise legal difference between real and personal property is very confusing; and in an Irish case where the question was whether a dung-heap was real property a lawyer made an admirable argument to show that it was. Then the farmer was called upon to reply and said, 'I'm puzzled indeed by all these strange words. But the lawyer says—fair play to him—that cows is personal property and the hay they eat is personal property, and I ask your Honour, as one man to another, how, baiting miracles, *personal* property can go on eating *personal* property and evacuating—he used a homelier word—*real* property. Well, your Honour, it's beyond my understanding.'

JOHN HUMPREYS PARRY (1816–80)

Serjeant-at-Law

287

The narrator is Alderson Foote

I HAVE seen prodigious damages given as the result of an unsuccessful attack upon the lady's character; and the advocate's best chance is to make her appear ridiculous. The greatest adept at this resource that I remember was Serjeant Parry. There was a case tried at Westminster, some thirty or forty years ago, in which the plaintiff had made the acquaintance of the defendant at the top of Regent Street, and had been promised marriage the same day in a private hotel somewhere near the Strand. The introduction had been effected, according to the lady, by the gentleman offering to protect her against a vicious terrier; and Parry, who appeared for the defendant, had a little misunderstood the story. 'You say you were alarmed at two dogs fighting, madam?', he asked her. 'No, no,' answered the fair plaintiff, 'it was a single dog.' 'What you mean, madam,' said Parry, 'is that there was only one dog; but *whether it was a single dog or a married dog you are not in a position to say*!' Nor was she, after this correction, in a position to say much more.

SAMUEL SHELDEN PARTRIDGE (*fl.* 1860–1935)

American Lawyer

288

Maribel Weldon was an attractive woman and a persistent litigant. Most of her cases were disputes about the tenancy of her farm. In this case she wished to get rid of a tenant called Edward Horton who had displeased her, maintaining that his lease was only verbal. The narrator is Samuel Partridge's son and biographer.

THE situation must have been very much to Maribel's liking. The hall was packed to suffocation, and it was packed with men. She could not help but realise that all these men had come to watch and admire her, for she was the only woman in the room. She was the center of attraction and whenever she raised her eyes she saw men—nothing but men—and the men saw nothing but Maribel. Thus far it was one of the most successful lawsuits she had ever put on.

'Mrs Weldon, I show you a letter dated February 15th of last year.' This was my father speaking, 'Is this letter in your handwriting?'

Her attorney, a pompous old fellow from Geneva named Lyman S. Barkin was quickly on his feet. 'One moment', he rumbled. 'Let me see that letter.'

The letter was handed to him. He and Mrs Weldon ran through it. She was not a very legible writer. But the letter was harmless and Barkin conceded that it was in her handwriting. My father had it marked and received in evidence but he did not read it out. He laid it on the table and held out another letter for Mrs Weldon to identify. Barkin skimmed through it, and again conceded her handwriting. Whereupon my father put up the letter in evidence and produced another.

Barkin barely glanced at the third letter, 'We concede that the plaintiff wrote it', he said, 'but I don't see the purpose of putting all this junk in evidence.'

'I'll try to explain a little later', said my father and produced another letter.

Barkin did not even glance at this one. He held it up for Mrs Weldon to see. 'Did you write that?'

'Yes. That's my handwriting.'

My father kept the letters in his own hands where nobody would be looking at them and did not refer to them again until he was making his summation to the jury. Then he declared that they constituted a complete refutation of the plaintiff's claim that the lease was verbal. He took up the letters and read them aloud to the jury. He read the harmless ones first, but soon came to one that had meat in it. In this letter the plaintiff agreed to furnish feed for the stock until new pastorage was available: a promise which she had denied on the witness stand. This was one of the letters Barkin had not read. He squirmed over it and demanded to see it. As he sat reading it my father took up another letter.

This was written shortly after Horton's return to his home after the first inspection of the Weldon farm. It began by discussing some of the questions under consideration, but once these were out of the way Maribel went into personal matters in one of her most kittenish moods. Her detachable flat iron handle had not been seen since the day

Horton was there. My father read this part out clearly and distinctly, not only to the jury, but to the entire courtroom.

'Ed Horton, I want to know what you did with my flat iron handle the day you were here. If you swallowed it I hope it don't stick out in some funny place and make your wife think she's got a freak on her hands . . .'

He could read no further for some minutes so great was the tumult and laughter in the courtroom. Indeed, the room was never again completely in order during the rest of the trial. Barkin tried his best to repair the damage, but he was unable to get control of the crowd long enough to put in a serious argument to the jury.

The plaintiff's case collapsed and Maribel Weldon—who could face anything but ridicule—held no more of her levées in court.

289

Kate's revenge.

KATE was a pariah. She lived alone in a little house on a back street. She had no occupation, no pension, no visible means of support, but she lived well and always paid her bills. Everybody in town knew what she was, though of course some men knew better than the others.

Dan Richman, when he became Village President, proposed to clean up the town. He said that Kate must go. (All his strenuous efforts to get rid of her were unavailing. She lived in the village until she died, and was awarded a splendid funeral.)

My father did not produce her will until after the funeral, and then he handed it to the Town Clerk who had been named as executor. It appeared that Kate had left her entire estate in trust for the comfort, care, benefit and burial of her brindle bitch, also called Kate. After the death of her aforementioned namesake the residue was bequeathed 'to one who has long been a valued friend, Dan Richman'.

Dan indignantly declined the bequest. He said that he had never spoken to the woman in his life, and that under no circumstances did he care to become the residuary legatee of a dog. The orphan asylum named as alternate legatee had no such scruples.

SIR GILBERT JAMES PAULL (1896–)

290

Mr Randolph Churchill had made a number of speeches criticizing certain organs of the Press for publishing pornography. In retaliation, The People *accused Mr Churchill (among other matters) of being a 'paid hack'. Mr Churchill sued them for libel, and the following is an extract from his lengthy duel with Mr Gilbert Paull QC. Mr Churchill was in the box for nearly two days. He was awarded damages of £5,000 and costs.*

Q: 'LET us go on. It was in those circumstances, was it not, that you then made an attack upon Mr Ainsworth and Odhams Press?'

A: 'How do you mean "in those circumstances"?'

Q: 'Having made the first speech and not having had that published, having then attacked Sir William Haley, you then went on to attack Mr Ainsworth, did you not?'

A: 'It is not true that the speech was not published anywhere. Large parts of it were published in many newspapers, but as *The Times* suppressed it and did not print one line I, naturally, in the next speech drew attention to this.'

Q: 'Then in those circumstances you proceeded to say the words about my clients. Let us just see what you really did say about six lines from the bottom of page 13: "The four nastiest and most caddish stories were all published in the same paper, one that goes by the name of *The People*. I fear I have no time to deal with these stories in detail, but I think we ought to put upon the record the name of the editor Mr H. Ainsworth, and the Company which owns it, Odhams, who also publish *Horse and Hound*, the *Hairdressers Journal*, the *Daily Herald* and *Debrett*." Odhams publish a good many other papers as well, do they not?'

A: 'I picked out the four I thought would appear funniest in juxtaposition.'

Q: 'It is a little dig at them, is it not? "Here is the publisher, Odhams; they also publish *Horse and Hound*." '

A: 'I was talking to a group of journalists and advertisers in Manchester who enjoy talks about newspapers. I am sorry you do not think it funny, but the people at the luncheon thought it quite funny and I got a little laugh which helped to ease the thing along.'

Q: 'You thought it was what you ought to publish afterwards in that book?'

A: 'Certainly. I would not have wanted to tamper with my own speech. If I am going to publish my own speech I will publish it accurately.'

Q: 'It was a little malicious to put them in that order?'

A: 'No, except to the smallest degree. Obviously they publish 23 papers and I could not have given a list of all of them, so I picked out the ones I thought would be of most general interest and most amusement to my audience.'

Q: 'They publish papers like the *Daily Herald* and *Illustrated*?'

A: 'I mentioned the *Daily Herald*.'

Q: 'I know; in third place.'

A: 'I mentioned *Debrett*.'

Q: 'I suggest you chose this order because you thought "it will tickle them up"?'

A: 'I thought it would get a smile at least, and it is hard work to get even a smile.'

Q: 'Then having done that you go on in the second paragraph on page 14 in effect to call them the "lowest mongrel cur in Fleet Street". That is your language, is it not?'

A: 'That arose inevitably out of Dog Don't Eat Dog. If you are taking a metaphor from the canine world, you naturally use other metaphors drawn from the same world; otherwise you complicate the issue and do not carry your audience with you.'

Q: 'Do let us get it clear and not become lost in a load of irrelevance. Did you call them the "lowest mongrel cur in Fleet Street"?'

A: 'Certainly I did, and make no bones about it. It was not a slip of the tongue, I said it on purpose. I meant it then, and I mean it now. I suppose if Mr Ainsworth disagreed about it, he could have published something in his paper saying he disagreed, or he could have written to me and said it was unfair, and if he had convinced me I would have withdrawn it. But I have never heard one word about it.'

Q: 'I suggest we are now getting to the truth of it, that you are a man who simply makes attacks on everybody and anybody?'

A: 'I cannot stop you suggesting anything, but it is not true. You keep saying "everybody". I have denied that I attack everybody, but it does not prevent you coming back to the same words.'

Q: 'Then we will go on a bit further and see what the position is. Did you think that it was a bit malicious to call my clients the lowest curs in Fleet Street?'

A: 'I had never met Mr Ainsworth: I had only recently heard anything about him. I only saw him today for the first time, as far as I know.'

Q: 'Are you really surprised that, when you used that sort of language, in their turn they turned round and attacked you?'

A: 'I am surprised if anyone tells lies merely because they have been criticized. That is what surprised me. I would have thought if he disliked what I said he would have written to me, published an article in his own paper, written to *The Recorder*. He could have written me a personal letter or put his lawyers on me and brought an action for libel. None of these remedies did he use. He waited until he became a director of the paper and had more authority, and he then authorized someone else to tell lies about me, and that is what the case is about.'

Q: 'Let us go a step further so that we can see your mentality in this. Had the editor of the *Sunday Express* been an unctuous humbug?'

A: 'Which editor?'

Q: 'John Gordon.'

A: 'He is not editor, he is called editor-in-chief; but he has very little function.'

Q: 'Call him editor-in-chief. You call him an unctuous humbug?'

A: 'I would not be surprised. Yes. Have you ever read his articles? Of course he is. I think the words are carefully chosen. They were not said by accident, they were said on purpose. That is what words are for.'

Q: 'That is one more to add to it. Tell me this: you rather enjoy a spot of malice, do you not?'

A: 'No, I would not put it like that. A spot of mischief perhaps, but I do not think I am a malicious person.'

Q: 'Have you ever said this when you were talking about *The Times Literary Supplement*: "In any case I would rather have a dash of malice from an anonymous author than the sort of self-protective phrase so many of them are apt to give the public when they criticize books in their own name." '

A: 'I am talking about literary criticism, not politics, or public life. I certainly have always thought it is a mistake to have one author review another's books. They all tend to scratch each other's backs and write nicely in the hope of getting favourable reviews themselves. I have always defended *The Times Literary Supplement* for giving anonymous reviews. I do think you get a more independent and manly review from an anonymous writer in *The Times* than you do elsewhere.'

Q: 'I dare say, but is it the fact that you prefer, as you call it, a dash of malice?'

A: 'In literary criticisms, yes, I do.'

Q: 'But not when it comes to criticism of you. Is that right?'

A: 'I object to lies when I am being criticized, and I object to them even more if in fact I believe them to be malicious.'

Q: 'You see, there is no doubt about it is there, that since the opening of this campaign, as you call it . . .'

A: 'I think it was your word, not mine.'

Q: ' . . . you have gone on using that sort of thing, have you not?'

A: 'What sort of thing?'

Q: 'The sort of thing I have read about. You have gone on using that sort of thing in reference to the Defendants in this case.'

A: 'I have not made any more speeches. Actually I only made three speeches on this topic.'

Q: 'And in each of them did you use very much the same sort of phraseology?'

A: 'No, I tried to be different. I do not like to make the same speech over and over again, it is such a bore for the audience. I try to say something new.'

Q: 'Attacking the Defendants as strongly as you possibly could?'

A: 'Drawing attention in plain, clear and simple words to the disgusting publications for which they were responsible, and I certainly intend to do so until they reform their wicked ways.'

SIR WILLIAM FREDERICK POLLOCK (1815–88)

291

CHIEF JUSTICE ABBOTT, afterwards Lord Tenterden, was presiding at the Yorkshire Assizes, which were then held at York only, and Pollock had to open the case for the plaintiff in a very heavy dispute about a colliery contract. He was called at five o'clock in the morning in order to read his brief, but happened to take up 'The Heart of Midlothian', and was so interested in it that he never touched the papers until breakfast-time. The Court in those days sat at nine, and there was therefore no chance whatever of his mastering the case so as to present it in a proper form to the jury; he found, too, that some two or three hundred letters had passed between the parties. Accordingly, with the greatest coolness, he said to the jury: 'I could not better present the facts of the case to you, gentlemen, than by using the language of the parties themselves, and I shall therefore read to you the correspondence which has passed in chronological order.' This he proceeded to do, and had continued reading for nearly an hour, when Chief Justice Abbott, who was very much afraid of Pollock, thought it was time to intervene: 'Mr Pollock, is it absolutely necessary for you to read all this correspondence? Cannot you condense it a little?' To which Pollock replied: 'Absolutely necessary, my Lord, for I never read it before.' Of course, in the face of such sublime impertinence there was nothing more to be said, and the case proceeded.

SAMUEL POPE (1826–1901)

King's Counsel

292

POPE was big in both ways. He had a broad, equitable common sense and never did anything mean or little. He made speeches it was impossible not to listen to, and I believe that if he had remained at the Common Law Bar and on the Northern Circuit, where he was holding his own against Charles Russell, and if he had got into the House instead of being tempted by the 'fleshpots' in the corridor, he would have gone further and fared better. He was wanting in the assiduity which marked several of his contemporaries, but he did remarkably well without the painstaking which is said to be genius, but is a very poor substitute for that inspiration.

He used to measure his oratorical displays—for he was really something of an orator, and his speeches were exhausting—by the number of collars which they reduced to wet rags. A one-collar speech or a two-collar speech—and he sometimes sent more to the laundry, notwithstanding a fan with which he armed himself. And in his moments of triumph he used to speak of getting a great speech, not off his conscience, but off that part of him which was more conspicuous than his conscience—although his conscience was there all the same.

At one time he was honorary secretary to the 'Alliance', a kind of teetotal league. But from his practice it would have been difficult to determine its tenets, for, although a moderate drinker, he could put away a whisky-and-soda as a bath sponge will greedily take up a pint of water.

In a Barry Bill one of the directors of the company gave evidence in chief in a bombastic way, and tried to make himself peculiarly offensive to the Taff Vale Railway Company, for which Mr Pope was appearing. The gentleman had overshot the mark. When Mr Pope rose to cross-examine he said:

'What has the Taff Vale Railway Company done to you that you should come here and snarl at it?'

The witness took a little time to reply, and Mr Pope said to the Committee, 'he doesn't know the value of moderation', and sat down.

SIR ANDREW PORTER (1837–1919)

Master of the Rolls

293

SIR ANDREW PORTER, the Master of the Rolls, was a fine lawyer of noble presence and of true dignity. Disturbance of the decorum of his court caused him extreme annoyance, and an interruption of a judgement meant severe chastisement for the offender. There arose before him in a dispute about some property, a controversy as to the meaning of a somewhat complicated will. When the arguments closed, the Rolls gathered before him the necessary books and papers and commenced to deliver his Judgement.

He read the will, and recounted the events that had caused the present complication. 'Now I am perfectly certain', he continued, 'that under these circumstances the testator intended his farm to go to his nephew, James.'

'Indeed he did not, me Lord', said a voice at the back of the Court.

'Bring that man forward', commanded Porter, and the delinquent was escorted to the table by the attendant policeman.

'Who are you, sir?', asked Porter.

'Please, me Lord, I'm the testator, and never intended James to have the farm', explained the culprit.

His statement proved to be true. He had gone away years previously to Australia and had never written home. Under these circumstances he had been presumed to be dead, and his relatives had commenced to litigate about his property.

EDMUND DELANGES PURCELL (1815–1916)

294

The value of wife and child.

THERE is a form of crime peculiarly dangerous to its perpetrators and perhaps for that reason uncommon. It is inveigling jewellers into a trap and then with deliberate violence rendering them unconscious and robbing them of their property. I only know of three cases. The earliest was the Torpey case. Michael Torpey and his wife, Martha Torpey, induced the assistant of a Bond Street jeweller to visit lodgings in the West End, taken for the purpose of the crime, with £5,000 worth of jewellery to show them. While the husband was examining the jewellery the wife came behind the assistant and held to his face a handkerchief saturated with chloroform; the husband at once seized, gagged, and bound him, the interesting pair when he was unconscious decamping with his jewellery. The husband escaped abroad, but I think was afterwards caught; the wife was arrested in this country. She was defended by Montague Williams before Mr Russell Gurney the Recorder, and was acquitted by the jury on the ground that she acted under the coercion of her husband. It was before my time, but I was told that the most potent argument in the case was her innocent, guileless appearance seated in the dock with her fair hair hanging down her back and her infant in her arms. I have myself had experience of the potency with juries of such arguments. A husband and wife, shopkeepers, were tried at Sessions for receiving stolen property. The man's position was singular, for he had been summoned as a juror to the very Session to which he had been committed for trial; and I contemplated transferring him from the jury-box to the dock, but the device was defeated by the police informing the officer of the court, who did not impanel him. There was no evidence against him, and the case was stopped by the judge. My defence for the wife was that she had really acted under his coercion; it failed, but she was carrying in her arms and moaning over it a baby that yet seemed to me too bulky for its mother's arms and this pathetic pose won a recommendation to mercy that saved her from prison. The next I heard of her was that she was committed to the Central Criminal Court for attempting to murder her child, but the Grand Jury ignored the bill against her.

DAVID RAE (LORD ESKGROVE) (1724–1804)

295

ESKGROVE's judicial manner and speech, as well as his jokes, provided sport for the Philistines. His peculiarities were almost inexhaustible. Witnesses and juries never knew what indignity they might suffer at the hands of this eccentric judge. In the trial of Glengarry for murder, a lady of great beauty was called as a witness. She came into court wearing a veil, a circumstance which seemed to ruffle his lordship, who, before administering the oath, addressed the lady as follows: 'Young woman! you will now consider yourself as in the presence of Almighty God, and of this High Court. Lift up your veil, throw off all modesty, and look me in the face.'

His behaviour towards juries was often insufferable. Sometimes he would 'charge' for hours, brevity not being one of his judicial virtues. A lackadaisical person is never in a hurry, and Eskgrove's moralisings were frequently so protracted that a juryman unable to stand any longer (he insisted upon the jury standing during his address) would resume his seat. But woe betide the unfortunate juror who was caught in the act, for his lordship would sternly remind him that 'these were not the times in which there should be shown any disrespect of this High Court, or even of the law'.

As an instance of some of the hardships inflicted on juries and prisoners by his lordship's verbosity and irrelevancy, it is recorded that in a case in which three men were charged with having broken into Luss House, assaulted Sir James Colquhoun and others, and robbed them of a large sum of money, Eskgrove not only inflicted on the court an elaborate and learned disquisition on the nature of assault and robbery, but enlightened it as to the etymology of 'hamesucken'. Then he proceeded to remind the prisoners that they attacked the house and the persons in it, and robbed them. 'All this you did,' continued his lordship, 'and God preserve us! joost when they were sitten doon to their denner!'

JAMES ALEXANDER RENTOUL (d. 1919)

Member of Parliament

296

Rentoul was a judge of the City of London Court as well as being the member for the Ulster constituency of East Down from 1890 *to* 1902. *His son, Sir Gervais Rentoul KC, himself a Recorder and a member of Parliament, is here discussing his father.*

ONLY on one occasion during those years did my father's constituents betray any burning interest in what was happening at Westminster and that was when a proposal was brought forward to erect, within the precincts of the House, a statue to Oliver Cromwell. It so happened that John Redmond, the famous leader of the Irish nationalists, who was a great friend of my father, although a strong political opponent, approached him one day in the Members' Lobby and said, 'Rentoul, have you heard about the idea of putting up a statue to Oliver Cromwell?'

My father replied that it was news to him.

'Well, at all events,' said Redmond, 'you know enough of Ireland to realise that it will be regarded as a deliberate insult by thousands of our fellow countrymen. Is it worthwhile to stir up this absurd bitterness in order to erect a statue to a man who has been dead and gone a couple of hundred years?'

Needless to say, when put like that my father agreed with him.

Redmond then added, 'In that case I wish you, as an Ulster man, would vote against the scheme.'

This my father promised to do and was, of course, as good as his word. His action, however, aroused so much resentment among some of the more fanatical of his protestant supporters that a deputation was sent from Ireland to voice their protest. My father received them with due solemnity, and courteously enquired the reason for their mission.

'We want to know', said their spokesman, a typical Ulster farmer, 'why you voted against the statue to Oliver Cromwell?'

My father appeared to ruminate for a moment and then remarked, quite innocently, 'Did I really? I quite forget. But who was Oliver Cromwell anyway?'

As this momentarily nonplussed the Deputation he went on 'Oliver Cromwell—the name seems familiar. Wasn't he the man who said that all Catholics should be sent to Hell or Connaught?'

'That's him', said the Deputation enthusiastically. 'He was a grand man.'

'Exactly', said my father. 'And that's why I voted against his statue. *I wouldn't have given them a choice.*'

This sally evoked so much merriment that all further protest was abandoned, and the Deputation retired in great good humour.

I am afraid, however, it is only Irishmen who could be handled in so light-hearted a manner. The Lord Protector ultimately got his statue, but a compromise was effected by putting it outside instead of inside the house and no-one seems a penny the worse.

SIR GERVAIS RENTOUL (1884–1946)

King's Counsel and Metropolitan Magistrate

297

WHEN two or more women and their families share the same house and have to use in common certain domestic amenities, the causes of friction are apt to be numerous.

But sometimes other difficulties arise.

I remember one case in which two women arrived at my Court in a high state of indignation, each charging the other with assault. The trouble in this case was all about a piano, which belonged to one of the complainants, whom I will call 'Mary'. Having left the door of her room unlocked the other woman (Matilda) *had entered her flat and played on the piano without permission*. Mary was furiously aggrieved.

When she began to tell me about the desecration of her beloved instrument I visualised it as a proud and upright form, a piano carved and aged in dignity. It was apparently a favourite piece of furniture, and she spoke of it with awe.

'We live, that woman and me,' said Mary, 'in the same house. I had lived there eight years, and she had lived there but two, and all the time there has been trouble. It started with arguments about her cat and went on with arguments about my dog. To crown it all, I comes home the other day to find what—her and her friend—sitting in my flat, smoking cigarettes *and thumping away on my piano*.'

Up jumped Matilda, very angry and highly injured.

'Why, you haven't got a piano', she shouted across the Court.

'I haven't now,' said Mary, 'but I can prove that I had one. If you, sir, will come round to my place, you will still see the top of the piano in my room.'

'The top?', I exclaimed.

'Well. I was so furious at her playing it that I took the piano to bits.'

'What?' I said incredulously. 'Take a piano to bits because someone else has played on it?'

'Yes, I did. I took out the notes, and gave some to the lady next door, and some to the woman across the street. They used them as firewood.'

When it comes to tearing a precious piano to bits to prevent someone else using it, a magistrate may be pardoned for finding himself non-plussed.

'Well,' I said, 'it cannot have been very much of a piano.'

'No, sir,' admitted Mary, 'I got it second hand. But I paid five shillings for it.'

GEOFFREY DORLING ROBERTS (1886–1967)

Queen's Counsel

298

He was known throughout the legal profession as 'Khaki' Roberts.

MY years of pupilage over, I had the honour on May 1, 1912, of being called to the Bar at the Inner Temple. In July of that year, in my new gown, and wig of whiter-than-whiteness, I rose for the prosecution in the case of attempted suicide at the Quarter Sessions in Exeter Guildhall.

All that was required of me was a few words outlining the details of the wretched business and to then call the police officer. Failure seemed impossible. But the importance of the occasion, and the presence of my father, seated beneath the Deputy Recorder, as Clerk of the Peace, and my mother, sister and hosts of friends in the gallery, having come to 'hear Geoffrey doing his first case', all conspired to bring on an attack of nerves which deprived me of the power of speech!

I was completely tongue-tied and could only produce animal noises making not a grain of sense. Finally the judge put an end to the painful scene by calling the police officer and doing my job for me.

My shame and mortification may be better imagined than described—reminiscent of Mr Winkle, who, after giving evidence at another Guildhall in the leading case of *Bardell v. Pickwick*, was found some hours later at his hotel 'groaning in a hollow and dismal manner, with his head buried beneath the sofa cushions'.

On the whole, the youth of the 1960s are much more self-possessed than members of my own generation were at their age, but one Counsel making his maiden speech, namely an address in mitigation for some criminal who had pleaded guilty, could get no further than: 'May it please Your Lordship, my unfortunate client . . . (long pause) . . . my unfortunate client . . . my . . . '

Mute with fright and embarrassment, he could not get any further, whereupon the judge kindly observed: 'Pray proceed, Mr ——. So far, the court is with you!'

299

THE period between the wars was the time when another technique of swindling reached its peak: the delicate art of 'long-firming'. I received my initiation into this, and other types of fraud, in the chambers of Roland Oliver and his fellow-Treasury Counsel, Muir and Humphreys.

The long-firmer built up a business which, after years of regular trading, established a reputation for honesty and reliability. Then suddenly overnight it became a fraudulent concern, obtaining as much merchandise as possible on credit. None of these goods was paid for; they were promptly sold for cash, and when the money had been stowed safely away the proprietor filed his bankruptcy petition. He hoped, not always vainly, that in the tortuous, labyrinthine procedure of the Bankruptcy Court the criminal proceedings he had so richly deserved would be indefinitely postponed.

At first sight it is strange that so many men, having carefully created honest businesses, should have been ready to throw all away and risk imprisonment as well, but the lure of easy money, the attraction of the vast profits to be derived from fraud, proved too strong a temptation. The legal profession owes quite a debt to these gentry, who not only provided Treasury Counsel and their devils with briefs and luscious refreshers, but also caused fashionable silks to visit the Old Bailey in vain endeavours to defend their fraudulent clients. Marshall Hall, Henry Curtis-Bennett and Henry Maddocks were three of the most frequent and the most welcome of such silks in the early days after the First War.

The story for the Crown never varied from the one I have outlined. But many and strange were the defences put forward. In one case an unfortunate trader travelled by train from London to Manchester carrying, so he said, a valise containing many thousands of pounds in notes, with which he intended to pay his creditors, who were textile merchants. But alas! he left the compartment for a moment, and found on his return the valise had been stolen.

The defence, led by the worthy and wordy J. B. Matthews, KC, suggested that when the train stopped at Leicester a man carrying a valise was seen to hurry towards the ticket barrier. The ticket collector, giving evidence for the accused, was asked by Matthews:

'Did he look like an ordinary first-class passenger?'

At this, Henry Dickens, the Common Serjeant, a son of Charles Dickens, in whose court most of these trials took place, interjected:

'What does an "ordinary first-class passenger" look like?'

'An ordinary first-class passenger on my line,' said Matthews, with painful memories of his daily trips to and from his Kentish suburb, 'is one who, when asked for his ticket, produces a third-class one!'

300

FORTUNATELY there are not many instances of disappointed litigants, or their sympathisers, giving physical vent to feelings when actually in Court . . . The only instance I can personally recall occurred in a Chancery Court when a tomato was hurled at the presiding judge. It missed its mark.

In criminal courts it is not possible for an indignant prisoner to register an emphatic protest like that, because he is searched before entering the dock and would certainly not be allowed to have a tomato in his possession. At the West Kent quarter sessions at Maidstone in 1959 a convicted prisoner tried to register disapproval by hurling one of the chairs in the dock at the Chairman, my very old and valued comrade, the late Tristram de la Poer Beresford ('Chimp' as he was known to his innumerable friends). The range was too long, and the missile got no further than Counsels' seats, where it nearly brained the defending barrister, who had, indeed put up a valiant fight for the incensed prisoner.

'Chimp' was in no way perturbed by this surprise attack. 'Bad shot', he murmured calmly before passing sentence.

301

I VIVIDLY recall another outburst from the dock, this time at Bristol. It came at the very end of the Midsummer Sessions in July 1955, from one Kenneth Royston Pearce, a man with a long criminal record on whom I had just passed a sentence of four years' imprisonment, the jury having convicted him of office-breaking. On hearing his fate he screamed out something which to me was unintelligible, but having listened to his Counsel's speech in mitigation I merely ordered him to be taken away, and down he went. Then I perceived signs of ill-concealed mirth among the warders and police officers, of both sexes, clustered in and around the dock. I whispered to my Deputy Clerk of the Peace, seated beneath me:

'Did you hear what he said?'

That official, blushing with embarrassment, whispered back:

'I'm sorry to say that he called Your Lordship a "—nt".'

So I entered up the Official Register with the verdict and sentence concluding: 'After being sentenced K. R. Pearce called the Recorder a "—nt", and on this note of romance the Quarter Sessions ended.

Pearce appealed to the CCA, but it availed him nothing; the evidence was overwhelming. Nevertheless the shorthand note of my summing-up to the jury and the subsequent sentencing had to be transcribed for the use of the judges. When one of the latter remarked to me at lunch: 'What horrible names they call you at Bristol, Khaki!' I asked for a copy of the transcript from the Master of the Crown Office, my friend Highmore King. He sent it along—with a note saying that apparently Pearce must have mistaken me for 'Roberta'; a subtle allusion, the significance of which was lost upon me. For the first time I was, however, able to appreciate the full flower of Pearce's eloquence. His actual words were:

'I shall appeal here and now you big-nosed —ing, bastard, —nt.'

Hoping for some sympathy, I showed this to my ever-loving wife. She commented: 'I don't think that's quite fair. You haven't got a big nose.'

On rare occasions it is sometimes the prisoner who fails to catch what is said. At Bodmin Assizes, in the 1930s, Mr Justice Wright (as he then was) had to pass sentence upon an elderly agricultural labourer who had been found Guilty of deplorable bestiality. In somewhat indistinct tones his Lordship announced:

'Prisoner at the Bar, the jury have convicted you, on the clearest evidence, of disgusting and degrading offences. Your conduct is viewed by all right-minded men with abhorrence. The sentence of the court is that you be kept in penal servitude for seven years.'

It was painfully obvious that this diatribe had not been audible to the prisoner, who had stood with his hand cupping an ear, straining to learn his fate. Therefore the judge said:

'Warder, repeat to the prisoner the sentence of the court.'

The task was beyond the warder's powers, but he did his best, shouting at the condemned felon:

'His Lordship says that you are a dirty old bastard, and he's put you away for seventeen years.'

Whereupon His Lordship observed: 'Warder, I have no objection to you paraphrasing my sentence, but you have no power to increase it.'

302

ONE of the most dramatic court-room moments of which I have personal recollection happened during the last war, when I was prosecuting at the Old Bailey one Nathan Fishberg, a jeweller, and his 30-year-old son Harry Charles, also a jeweller. Both were charged with receiving over a thousand pounds-worth of jewellery knowing it to be stolen. With them in the dock was William Bruce, the alleged thief.

The Fishbergs were defended by Sir Patrick Hastings, KC, who did not seem to enjoy the job much and relieved his feelings by unmercifully bullying his learned friends, Sir John Hutchinson, KC and Derek Curtis-Bennett, who appeared with him. The trial, before Sir Gerald Dodson—Recorder of London—lasted three days. It was not disputed that the stolen jewellery was discovered at Fishberg's shop in Black Lion Yard, Whitechapel; the case for the defence was that it had been 'planted' on the Fishbergs by a detective-inspector of Scotland Yard's Flying Squad who was said to have demanded a bribe of £600 and only received, from Nathan's wife, a mere £60. Sir Patrick thundered, in his final address to the jury:

'The inspector, I submit, is an unprincipled rascal. Such a man is not fit to be in the CID.'

I replied to this tirade as best I could, pointing out that the inspector had taken Nathan to the local police station to be charged, which surely was the last thing an unsatisfied black-mailer would have done.

It was after 6 p.m. when the jury retired to consider their verdict. Forty minutes later they returned with faces of stone. 'Guilty', said the foreman on every charge. A chief-inspector then told the court that Nathan was a Russian. 'He came to Britain in 1911, and has been receiving stolen property for years, assisted by his son. His shop is a regular dump for stolen property; one of the most difficult places in London on which to keep observation. He has no previous convictions.' St John Hutchinson—in the absence of 'Pat'—commented, reasonably enough: 'If the police have been watching the premises for so many years, it seems a little curious that no charges have been brought.'

By this time Nathan had collapsed on the floor of the dock. His son clutched the dock rails and shouted at the jury: 'Why have you done this?' Mrs Fishberg, Nathan's wife, was carried from the court screaming hysterically.

Then suddenly every light in the court went out. As the *Daily Express* reported:

> The court was thrown into darkness. There was pandemonium; something the Old Bailey has never known in all its history. A voice boomed out: 'Black Justice'.

I have a confused mental picture of cigarette lighters flashing, shadowy forms passing swiftly to and fro. A reporter in the Press box turned his light towards the dock, then some electric torches were directed towards the Bench. Unmoved, imperturtable, sitting beneath the ceremonial Sword of Justice, was Sir Gerald Dodson. He rose. 'I will defer judgement until tomorrow,' he said, and the usher recited the proclamation of the adjournment of the court until, 'tomorrow morning at 11 o'clock. God save the King.'

EARL ROGERS (1870–1922)

American Lawyer

303

In the sensational San Francisco graft prosecutions Earl Rogers defended Patrick Calhoun, head of United Railroads. His opponent was Francis J. Heney the fighting prosecutor. The cases proceeded against a background of unparalleled violence. The editor of a paper supporting Heney was kidnapped; Heney himself was shot in the head at point blank range, but survived: the residence and the office of one of the chief prosecution witnesses were both destroyed by dynamite. Inside the court the fireworks were mainly verbal.

BEFORE the trial was many days old the verbal duel between Rogers and Heney had become as deeply interesting to press and public as all the rest of the legal war put together.

'I think it is extremely indecent', said Rogers, 'that as the defendant and counsel for defence are consulting in this courtroom we should have sitting next to us, and listening with all their ears, employees of Detective Burns.'

'I believe', grinned Heney, 'that counsel for the defence should be more specific. That is, he should specify the exact number of auricular organs each employee of Burns is listening with. "All their ears", is very indefinite. Maybe one of them is deaf in one ear.'

Rogers merely glared at him. Heney had won the first round in what one newspaper reporter described as 'the goat-getting contest'.

On another occasion the fiery prosecutor was moved to complain to the court that he objected to the manner in which Rogers was laughing at him while he was conducting the examination of a witness.

'I am not laughing at Mr Heney', declared Earl.

'Well, let's call it smiling insultingly then', answered the prosecutor. 'Anyway I object to the attorney's facial expression during the prosecution's efforts.'

'Well,' conceded Rogers, 'if the eminent and learned counsel will indicate what sort of facial expression he wishes me to assume, I shall be pleased to try to accommodate him.'

Heney knew that Rogers was employing his well-known badgering tactics and kept himself well in hand. Once, when Heney inadvertently stepped behind Rogers the latter whirled about as if greatly agitated and exclaimed in a loud whisper to those near him. 'Never let that fellow get behind you! He's an Arizona gunman. Shot a man to death in Tucson. From the rear.'

Heney only grinned.

304

Two youths, Johnson and Boyd, had been playing poker with a professional gambler called Yeager. Shots were heard. The gambler was found dead. One of the men had done it, but which? Boyd was selected as the murderer. The only witness against him was Johnson, who maintained that when, after shooting the gambler, Boyd had pointed the pistol at him, he had not been alarmed. Earl Rogers, defending Boyd, picked on this single point.

AGAIN and again he queried, 'And you say you were *not* at all alarmed when Boyd pointed his pistol at you after he had just killed Yeager?'

Johnson continued to reply that he had not been in the least frightened.

District Attorney Rives finally complained: 'Why waste the Court's time with silly useless repetition? You have already asked the witness the same question at least twenty times and he has always given you the same answer.'

At this Earl seemed vastly amused.

When the time came for addressing the Jury, Rogers, always the fastidious dresser, appeared in frock coat and white waistcoat. He reviewed the evidence quietly and without passion. He spoke of the youth of the defendant. He deplored the fact that the boy had taken up with bad companions. He made it evident that Johnson was one of them. He argued that any intelligent person, if asked to choose between the stories of both lads, would unhesitatingly say that it was Boyd who was telling the truth.

Suddenly pausing in the smooth flow of his argument, his calm manner underwent a quick transition. Earl backed to a position alongside counsel's table. With an inarticulate cry he stooped over and, in the fraction of a second, rose to his full height, brandishing a huge Colt

45. Several women screamed. Earl turned and pointed the murderous blue barrel directly at the District Attorney and his veteran assistant McComas.

McComas dodged behind a chair and Rives ducked under the table.

The entire court-room was in an uproar. Panic-stricken attorneys thought that Rogers had suddenly become insane from the strain of the trial. Bailiffs rushed towards him. He waved them away.

District Attorney Rives appeared from the shelter of the table.

'Hey, Earl,' he yelled, 'is it loaded?'

'Sure it's loaded.'

'Well then, don't point it this way', roared the District Attorney.

'Put it up, Mr Rogers, put it up', pleaded Judge Smith from the Bench.

Then Earl began to laugh at the the men at whose heads he had been pointing the gun.

He turned to the jury and told them that what they had witnessed was the only possible reaction of normal human intelligence to sudden fear of death.

The State's only direct witness had been so completely discredited by Earl Rogers's dramatic gunplay that Boyd was acquitted on the first ballot.

305

Morrison Buck had shot his employer and benefactor, Mrs Charles A. Canfield, in cold blood, and in front of Mrs Canfield's daughter. His attorney, A. D. Warner, was running the only possible defence: that Buck was insane. On this occasion, most unusually, Rogers was one of the prosecuting team.

MORRISON's brother, William Buck, had come from Arizona to aid his accused relative. He told how Morrison had been severely cut at the base of the skull, by a cleaver in the hands of a drunken Mexican in the Pinal Mountain mining camp of Globe.

A nephew of the defendant told how the latter had been kicked on the head by a horse. Several others testified as to head injuries which Buck had received at different times during his life. Following a long series of such asseverations Attorney Warner dragged Buck over to the jury box, seized him by the hair, and jerked his head down, so that the jurors could view the numerous scars on the cranium of the accused.

But the alert Rogers got hold of Buck's head before Warner could return him to the witness stand and delivered an interesting lecture upon the effects of every variety of head injury known to medical science. The gist of this erudite symposium was that head wounds which affect the brain always *leave scars that are attached to the skull*. And he induced the jurors, severally and collectively, to feel Buck's head so that they might be convinced of the truth of Rogers' assertion that the defendant's scalp was perfectly mobile.

When this last attempt of the defence to establish proof of insanity had failed, Buck fell into a faint. Immediately Earl recalled Dr Cohn, Superintendent of the State Asylum, to the witness stand, and the latter testified that although, in his career, he had observed and examined thousands of insane patients, he had never known one to swoon.

Morrison Buck was found guilty and hanged.

306

The defence was that the deceased woman had brought the fatal shooting on herself by flinging vitriol at the shooter.

WHILE Rogers addressed the Jury he held a vial of sulphuric acid in his hand, occasionally shaking it to keep the jurors' attention upon the deadly chemical. As always he paced pantherlike back and forth.

'Unless you have been burned by the colourless hell's fire, known better by laymen as oil of vitriol, you'll never be able to realise the searing agony it produces upon contact with our flesh', intoned Earl.

As he passed his seated partner, Paul Schenck, he dropped half a teaspoonful of the acid on the latter's leg. It instantly gave off a whiff of blue smoke as it burned a hole in Paul's pants, ruining an expensive fawn-coloured suit, and in the same flicker of an eyelash, seared a hole in his hide.

Earl's horrified associate sprang four feet in the air with a howl of agony that brought all the courtroom to their feet.

'What the hell are you doing?', he yelled.

'You see,' Earl calmly observed to the startled jurors, 'what just a few drops will do to a man's leg. Think of a cup of that hurled in his face.'

Then, as Schenck squirmed with pain and ruefully regarded the ruin of his new $80 suit, Earl, without even a glance in his direction, passed to another phase of the defence case.

307

The narrator is Adela Rogers St Johns, his daughter

IN time he came to have a great reputation. One day I was sitting in Dad's office when a well-dressed high-bred old Chinaman entered. (Dad for many years represented most of the high-class Chinamen in California, and once at least his arbitration settled a tong war. He was a great favourite with the California Chinese and on their holidays our house was always full of lilies and strangely flavoured nuts, of magnificent jade and rich embroideries which had come as presents to 'Mr Rogers'.)

This Chinaman wanted to know how much Dad would charge to defend him for murder. Dad told him. He sat down, began pulling little bags out of his voluminous garments, and finally counted out the money in gold. Then he arose and with a deep bow started out.

'Hey!', said Dad, 'come back here. What's all this? Where are you going?'

'I go kill the man now', said the Chinaman. 'Then I be back.'

STEPHEN RONAN (1848–1925)

King's Counsel and Lord of Appeal

308

STEPHEN had in some ways enraged Judge William O'Brien who took a malicious pleasure in jumping upon Ronan upon the least opportunity. Every time that Ronan offended he was pulled-up by the Judge with a, 'Misther Ronan, Misther Ronan, you know you can't ask that!' And a series of observations about the duty of Counsel and the peril of departure from the strict rule of law would follow.

Stephen chafed; but as the Judge was taking great care to be correct, he could not successfully defend himself. The Junior Bar grinned maliciously at the discomfiture of their leader; this did not prevent them gathering round him in the Bar-room during the luncheon adjournment with hypocritical expressions of sympathy and regret. Stephen sat there in silence, puffing away at his long pipe. At last he rose, hobbled over to the fireplace, knocked out his ashes, and said as he stowed his pipe away: 'If you young gentlemen would care for a little amusement, heh, just be in court after the adjournment, heh.'

The Bar did not ignore this invitation; and it was in a very crowded court that the hearing of the part-heard case was resumed. The Judge was even more overbearing than he had previously been; and there were many more passages at arms in which he appeared to score heavily over counsel. All of a sudden, Ronan interrupted his examination of a witness, and, looking very fixedly at the Judge, said to the witness: 'Now, do not answer this question unless his Lordship permits it'; and he framed a very careful sentence which he put to his witness.

There was an immediate explosion from the Bench, 'Misther Ronan, Misther Ronan, sure you know very well that you can't ask that. Nobody who knew any law at all would ask such a question as that.' Stephen looked at him; an observer might have augured trouble from the light in his eye.

'I propose to argue it', he said tersely. And he framed an argument on first principles, without referring to any authority. The Judge broke in on him: 'I never heard such nonsense; go on with your case and ask some other question.' 'Oh, but I had not finished', cried Ronan. 'I have authority here', and he dived under the table, and from a secret cache produced a volume of the Irish Law Times Reports. 'It is a decision of Baron Dowse, sitting where your Lordship is sitting now; and he was asked to disallow this very question; and, heh, he ruled that it was admissible, heh. He allowed it.' He looked around at the assembled Bar with the nearest approach to a wink he would have allowed himself.

William O'Brien was not in the least perturbed. 'That is a Circuit decision', he said contemptuously. 'It was probably given with one eye on the clock and one on the timetable. I'll not follow his ruling. Get on, now; waste no more time over the matter.'

'Oh, but I haven't finished yet,' cried Stephen, 'I have here a decision of the English Court of Appeal and it turned on the very same point, and here is the decision of a very powerful court that the question is admissible. Does your Lordship admit it now?' And he hopped along the Counsel's row, chuckling to himself and occasionally glancing around to see how the boys were enjoying it.

O'Brien's face clouded; too late he realised that he had been led into a trap; but he was a gallant fighter and determined to go down with his colours flying. 'Misther Ronan,' he said, 'you know well that there is only one transpontine Court that is binding upon me, and that is the House of Lords.'

'Heh! heh! And that's why I brought with me the decision of the House of Lords confirming the Appeal, heh!' And he boldly turned to his audience, to ensure that the Judge would realise how publicly he had been humiliated.

'Ask your question', said O'Brien sulkily. Ronan looked at him sweetly. 'The question seems to annoy your Lordship,' he said, 'and as it is of no importance whatever, I will not ask it.'

EDWARD CAMILLUS RONAYNE (*fl.* 1890–1910)

309

The narrator is Maurice Healy

THE local Bar were once stranded for the night at Kanturk, the Judge having risen early for some reason; and grief and desolation were to be seen on every countenance. The venerable proprietor of Johnson's Hotel was profoundly concerned that his guests should thus be marooned without amusement: he produced the best dinner his house could provide, and that is to be read as a term of high praise. But Edward Camillus Ronayne, Dean of our local faculty, refused to be comforted; he wanted amusement, new faces to look upon, something other than the perpetual discussion of the cases that had just been heard, or the stories of what Tim Doolan had said when Tom Duffy sued him for the price of the house, and such-like. Camillus was in heavy sorrow; even that delectable brew y-clept Guinness seemed to be bringing him slight comfort.

Suddenly in came James Comyn with the news that there was a penny gaff in the town, and that they were playing *Maria Martin* or some such play. Instantly all was confusion, as hats and coats were sought. An eager throng of learned counsel were soon to be seen making their way to the building that had been temporarily turned into a theatre. The play was already under way; a critical moment had arrived, for the villain, a horrible-looking elderly man in a rusty coat, was explaining to the heroine that she was 'be-trrrayed'; for by this deed which he held in his hand all her property had passed under his control, ha! ha! ha! And the beautiful maiden threw up her eyes to

Heaven and wailed, 'What shall I do-oo? What shall I do-oo?' And, the age of miracles not being past, an answering voice, the voice of Edward Camillus Ronayne, rang through the building uttering the unexpected advice: 'Object that the document is insufficiently stamped.'

ELIHU ROOT (1845–1937)

American Senator and Lawyer

310

THE most spectacular case he handled, which gave full play to his powers as a trial lawyer, was the prosecution of James C. Fish, President of the Marine National Bank. For six weeks Root immersed himself in his house, sitting before a big desk on which he had a dozen spindles, a dozen different coloured pencils, and little pads. There he sat surrounded by this enormous mass of undigested documents and, as he worked, from time to time he would make a little note and stick it on a blue spindle; he would make another little note and stick it on a yellow spindle, and when he got through he had a dozen spindles of different colours, and each subject had been analysed and put together, and when he went before the jury with seventeen counts on the indictment, that apparent maze of mystery dissolved into a clear, clean shape of presentation of facts which, like the inevitable columns of the multiplication table, proved themselves one by one, and the jury convicted the defendant on thirteen of the seventeen counts.

311

MANY people expected that President Arthur would offer his friend, Elihu Root, a cabinet post, probably that of Attorney-General. When Root went to Washington on November 13th to argue a case in the Supreme Court the reporters assumed he was making arrangements with the President.

Root was close to Arthur, but neither expected nor desired political office. The President was aware of this feeling, and made no offer to him. Root began to be besieged with requests to recommend candidates for office, from that of New York City Park policeman to Cabinet

Officer. For half a century the siege continued, but when he went to Washington nineteen years later he had learned how to handle the thick end of the stick.

To Daniel G. Rollins, a close friend and then District Attorney, he wrote on January 7th 1881:

My Dear Sir,

May I beg of you the slight favour that you will send for the most accessible reporter from some daily paper published in this City and inform him: that I am your deadly enemy: that you consider me a liar and a horse thief and a scoundrel of the deepest dye and that no person who calls *me* friend can ever receive the slightest consideration at *your* hand.

Thus only will you preserve the sanity of your ever devoted friend from the assaults of candidates for the position of Assistant District Attorney.

Yours wearily,
Elihu Root

CHARLES RUSSELL
(LORD RUSSELL OF KILLOWEN) (1832–1900)
Lord Chief Justice

312

Sir Edward Russell, the Editor of the Liverpool Daily Post, *relates the following incident of Russell's early years at the Bar.*

I WAS always fond of going into law courts, and one day went into one of the Courts of Guildhall when Lord Russell of Killowen—then Mr Charles Russell—was a very young man. The judge on the bench was old Mr Justice Crompton. The plaintiff was a bill-discounter and money-lender. His leading counsel was Mr Edwin James. After a very short time the great advocate threw down his brief ostentatiously before him, and without a word of explicit explanation walked out of court.

The case went on, and the time came when the counsel for the bill-discounter should have replied and put the case finally to the jury. Up stood a junior counsel, when the judge very testily said, 'What do you want, sir?' The young counsel said, 'I am for the plaintiff, my Lord, and I purpose, with your permission, to address the jury.' The veteran judge became more testy than ever. 'Don't you know', said he, 'that your leader has left the court?' 'Yes, my Lord,' replied the young counsel very respectfully, but not flinching a bit, 'I know that Mr James has retired, but I still think there are some points that should be laid before the jury.'

The point of the matter, of course, was that the plaintiff had turned out such a scoundrel that Edwin James would have nothing to do with him, whereas his young junior saw some points that might be made, and felt it his duty to make them.

Mr Justice Crompton threw himself back in his chair, and with an air of vexation not often seen on the bench, said, 'Oh, go on!' And the young counsel went on. He made a clear, emphatic, earnest speech, not disguising the nature of the case or talking any nonsense at all, but putting what could be said in the best possible manner. Before he had uttered many sentences the judge leaned forward again, and still with vexation in his tone, said, 'What's your name?' To which the reply was, 'Charles Russell, my Lord.' And then the young man's speech continued.

By the time it was over, Mr Justice Crompton's wrath had entirely disappeared, and when young Charles Russell—destined eventually to become Lord Chief Justice of England—sat down, the judge said to him very kindly and politely, 'Well, Mr Russell, I thought it was a piece of great impertinence for you to put yourself forward to address the jury when your leader had thrown up the case; but I must say that the ability with which you have spoken, and the skill with which you have made the best points that could be made in a hopeless case, have quite vindicated any presumption there might be in what you did.' And then, with a bow that was very cordial, he turned from the counsel and began to sum up the case before the jury.

313

LORD RUSSELL OF KILLOWEN, the Lord Chief Justice, was, without doubt, the most masterful man in the Law. When he was at the Bar very few counsel or judges could stand up to him. His own clients used to shiver in his presence.

It is said that on one occasion one of his clients, a City solicitor, came into his room in the Temple wearing a fur-lined overcoat with a collar of fur, a garment which Russell abominated.

He glared savagely at it, and barked out, 'Go out of the room and take off that damned coat.'

The solicitor meekly obeyed.

314

Barry O'Brien tells of the dangers of asking a favour of Lord Russell.

Y WENT to Russell's chambers, and came back to me in about three-quarters of an hour. 'Good Heavens!', he said, bursting into my room, 'I have had the devil of a quarter of an hour. Such a man I never met in my life.' 'Well, sit down', I said, 'and tell me all about it.' But Y did not sit down. He was far too excited to sit down. He stood with his back to the mantelpiece and in the most perfect good humour, I must confess, gave me a graphic account of what had happened. Now that he had got out of the lion's den he seemed to enjoy the scene, as I certainly enjoyed his description of it. This is what happened: The clerk took in Y's name, and brought back the message that Sir Charles would be glad if Y would put in writing what it was he wanted. Y wrote a lengthy letter stating his case. The clerk took it in and returned to say, 'Sir Charles will see you, sir'. Y had met Russell once before with Lord — and he thought he would open the conversation by mentioning this fact, so as to produce a favourable impression at the outset. He pulled himself together and entered the room.

SCENE

Y: 'How do you do, Sir Charles? I think I had the honour of meeting you with Lord — at —.'

Russell: 'What do you want?'

Y: 'Well, Sir Charles, I have endeavoured to state in the letter which I . . . '

Russell (taking up the letter): 'Yes, I have your letter, and you write a very slovenly hand.'

Y: 'The fact is, Sir Charles, I wrote that letter in a hurry in your waiting-room.'

Russell: 'Not at all, not at all; you had plenty of time to write a legible note. No, you are careless. Well, go on.'

Y: 'Well, Sir Charles, a vacancy has occurred in . . . '

Russell: 'And you are very untidy in your appearance. . . .'

Y: 'Well, I was travelling all night. I only arrived in London this morning.'

Russell: 'Nonsense, you have had plenty of time to make yourself tidy. No, you are naturally careless about your appearance. Go on.'

Y: 'Well, Sir Charles, this vacancy has occurred and — asked me to see you . . .'

Russell: 'And you are very fat.'

Y: 'Well, Sir Charles, I am afraid that is hereditary. My father was very fat . . .'

Russell: 'Not at all. I knew your father well. He wasn't fat: it is laziness.'

By this time Y (as he assured me) was much more anxious to get out of the room than to get the appointment.

315

On the other hand . . .

ASHEAD ELLIOTT's brother was a solicitor, who had been an articled clerk with Boote and Edgar (well-known Manchester solicitors), and was the hero of a story that was part of the folk-lore of the circuit. Edgar had sent him down to the Assize Courts with an overdue brief to deliver to Charles Russell. He found the great man alone in his room and laid the papers respectfully on the table. Russell looked at them angrily and with several curses and imprecations on the clerk, his chief, the brief and the hour of its arrival, hurled it into a corner of the room.

Elliott walked to the door, turned around and, as if nothing had happened, said in a bland voice, 'Mr Edgar's compliments, and he will be with you at 9.30 tomorrow morning.'

Russell shouted to him to come back saying: 'Pick up the damned papers. I suppose I must look at them.'

Upon which Elliott, following accurately every maledictory precedent set by the great leader, told him to pick the brief up himself or seek a hotter climate for a long vacation.

This pleased Russell vastly. It was a luxury to him to be sworn at. He commended the young man in kindly terms, and paced across the room to where the papers lay. Elliott, relenting and courteous, sought to prevent him. They brought the papers back to the table with hands joined in their support. Russell spoke to Edgar in terms of the highest praise about the ability of his clerk.

316

The narrator is Lord Simon

I WAS told the other day by my colleague Lord Russell that when his father was appointed Lord Chief Justice the Prime Minister, Lord Rosebery, who of course made the appointment, rode over from Epsom to Tadworth Court in order to congratulate Lady Russell.

She said, 'Well, Prime Minister, I had hoped that my husband would be the first Roman Catholic Lord Chancellor since the Reformation.'

Lord Rosebery replied that, though the Woolsack was a dignified position while it lasted, the Lord Chief Justiceship was a far more enviable post, for its occupant did not change with changing governments, 'whereas an ex-Lord Chancellor', he said 'is nothing but a shabby old gentleman with £5,000 a year.'

317

The narrator is Sir Gervais Rentoul

I ONLY saw him once in the flesh but I have never forgotten it, although I was only a boy at the time. The occasion was one November 9th when, as Lord Chief Justice, he had to receive the new Lord Mayor of London, who customarily presents himself at the Law Courts to be welcomed and congratulated by the Chief Justice on behalf of His Majesty's judges. But this time things did not go according to plan.

It so happened that the Lord Mayor in question had been connected with certain financial enterprises which had come in for a good deal of unfavourable public criticism. The grim 'Lord Chief' was not inclined to let this pass. Instead of indulging in the usual compliments he took advantage of the opportunity to deliver a stern homily on the standards of financial and commercial rectitude which ought to animate those elevated to high civic office. Although he did not refer directly to the new Lord Mayor everyone knew to what he was alluding.

It was a most painful scene. The Lord Mayor in his scarlet gown, lace and gold chain turned alternately white and red, and a pin could have been heard drop in the Court.

318

LORD RUSSELL OF KILLOWEN when not practising in the Courts, or presiding, as he afterwards did, with dignity as the Lord Chief Justice of England, seemed to unbend and was the most amiable, good humoured and witty of men. I remember he was once asked by a lady what was the maximum punishment for bigamy. The Lord Chief Justice replied, without any hesitation, 'Two mothers-in-law.'

CYRIL BARNET SALMON (LORD SALMON) (1903–)

319

The narrator is John Mortimer

WHEN I started off my career in defended divorce cases I greatly admired the smooth and elegant advocacy of Lord Salmon, who seemed to me to win his cases with all the noise and bluster of a perfectly tuned Rolls-Royce coasting down hill. Cyril Salmon would take out his more valuable possessions, his gold watch and chain, his heavy gold key-ring and cigarette-lighter, and place them on the bench in front of him. Then he would plunge his hands deep into his trouser pockets and stroll negligently up and down the front bench lobbing faultlessly accurate questions over his shoulder at the witness-box. Here, I thought, was a style to imitate. For my early cross-examinations I would take off my battered Timex watch, lug out my bundle of keys held together with a piece of frayed string and pace up and down firing off what I hope were appropriate questions backwards. I continued with this technique until an unsympathetic Judge said, 'Do try and keep still, Mr Mortimer. It's like watching ping-pong.'

SIR ARTHUR CLAVELL SALTER (1859–1928)

320

The narrator is Sir Edward Parry

CLAVELL SALTER was an earnest and serious student. I heard some lively junior in later days describe him as 'dry Salter'. There is only one recorded *bon mot* of his, and some say it was uttered unconsciously. He was arguing a case before Mr Justice Darling and, intending to criticise some dicta in the Court of Appeal, happened to say, in the course of his argument: 'Your Lordship will no doubt remember what the Lords Justice of the Court of Appeal have said about this point.'

Darling intervened at once: 'Mr Salter, you must not think that I hear very much of the conversation of the Lords Justices, though it is true that I sometimes see them at lunch.'

'Then your Lordship probably sees them at their best', said Salter.

JAMES SCARLETT (LORD ABINGER) (1769–1844)

321

A NORTH country juryman was once asked, after a long assize at Lancaster: 'What do you think of the counsellors in the Northern Circuit?'

'Why,' he replied, 'there's not a man in England can touch that Mr Brougham.'

'But you give all the verdicts to Mr Scarlett.'

'Why, of course. He gets all the easy cases.'

CHARLES KENNETH SCOTT-MONCRIEFF (1889–1930)

322

Order of Service Authorised to be said on the Dissolution of Messrs Hunter and Haynes, Solicitors.

On the appointed day the Minister, wearing a clean linen surplice and accom-

panied by Mrs Pennington-Bickford shall call at 9 *New Square, Lincoln's Inn, and shall say in an audible voice the words here following:*

COLLECT

O LORD, for as much as it pleased Thee in times past to join together these thy servants, Robin Lewis Hunter and Edmund Sidney Pollock Haynes, in a remarkable manner, let it now please Thee to put them lawfully asunder, that foresaking one another they may simultaneously and severally work for their own advancement, and as their union has been singularly fruitless grant that their disconnexion may be rich with increase, and let them avoid all recriminations, neither turning to the other (except in certified sickness) so long as they both shall live according to the promises distinctly conveyed to our forefathers, Abraham and Lot in the Holy Scriptures, Amen.

Hymn

Children of St Clement Danes
Pray for Hunter, pray for Haynes
Doubt of what may be in store
Makes us pray for Haynes the more
And as nothing else will rhyme
(*f*) Pray for Hunter (*ff*) all the time.

Haynes and Hunter in the past
Made a pact that could not last
In the ordinary course
(*p*) Hunter claims a quick divorce
All's arranged behind the scenes
(*f*) No King's Proctor (*ff*) intervenes.

Orange sweet and lemon sour
Lay before them in this hour
Wherein symbolised we see
(*f*) Incompatibility
Lest this prove of time a loss
(*p*) Grant them, Master, their divorce. Amen

At this point oranges and/or lemons will be distributed among the clerks of the dissolving partners. Hunter and Haynes will then be taken to the Old Roman Bath in Strand Lane and partially immersed.

A collection will be made.

Hunter and Haynes will be dried and conducted to their several offices where they will proceed to DISSOLVE.

FREDERICK H. SEDDON (1865–1912)

323

SIR EDWARD MARSHALL HALL had made in his speech for the defence (of Seddon) an effort of such intellectual brilliancy as can have been rarely exceeded in a Court of Law; but it is no disparagement to him to say that, in view of the terrible circumstances that surrounded it, the effort made by Seddon himself was even more remarkable. The instinct which dominated him was that all-powerful one of self-preservation; and if the strength of all his instincts had, in one case, proved his undoing, it was the very strength which, at the last, came near to make amends. It urged him to this gigantic effort, blinded him mercifully to the horror of his position, and gave to his story a ring of truth which was almost unbearable. When, at the end, he lifted his hand in the Masonic gesture and swore by the Great Architect of the Universe that he was innocent, the effect of sincerity produced was a most remarkable tribute to the power of 'selective attention'.

He received his sentence in silence, gathered up his papers, swung sharply round in the dock, and was gone.

PETER SHEILS (Contemporary)

Australian Barrister

324

A MEMBER of the Press Gallery at Parliament House was given a parking ticket when he parked close to the steps. The journalist decided to defend it on the ground that, under the Seat of Government Act, Parliament made its own laws governing its buildings and environment; that no policeman could enter the Parliament unless by invitation; that the Seat of Government extended far beyond the actual building; and that Parliament, and only Parliament, had the right to regulate what took place inside Parliament House and its environs.

Peter Sheils was briefed for the defence, and the case ultimately finished up before a Full Court of the Australian Capital Territory; which, on that day, comprised their Honours Mr Justice Fox, Mr Justice Blackburn and Mr Justice E. Woodward.

Peter Sheils quoted the very old case of *Jay and Topham* (1689) 12 State Reports, where the Master of Arms, Mr Topham, was ordered to remove Mr Jay from the House of Commons. This Mr Topham did, and he was subsequently sued by Mr Jay. Two judges found the Master of Arms guilty of assault, and found that his defence of carrying out the order of the House was not a good plea.

Peter Sheils paused, and first Mr Justice Blackburn, then Mr Justice Woodward, and lastly Mr Justice Fox all interjected with: 'Well, that doesn't appear to help your case', and 'on the surface that would appear very damaging to your case, Mr Sheils.'

Peter waited until they had finished and said, 'I have not finished what I was saying. The House of Commons then ordered the two judges brought before them, *and incarcerated both of them for a lengthy period.*'

SIR NORMAN JOHN SKELHORN (1909–)

Queen's Counsel, Director of Public Prosecutions

325

WHEN I first appeared before Lord Goddard I was twenty-three years old, and he had not long been a High Court Judge, but he was on his old circuit, and it was an intimidating experience to appear before him. I was defending a young man accused of rape. I thought it was common ground that he and the girl had gone out together by arrangement, and that the only serious question was whether what had happened was with her consent; so I did not ask the girl anything about a telephone conversation that the young man said he had with her when they had arranged to meet.

When Goddard came to sum up he said: 'In a case of this sort, as I have already explained to you, you need to have corroboration before you can properly convict. You remember that telephone conversation? Well, this accused is represented by able and experienced counsel. Not a word of that conversation was put to the girl. Not a word. Now if that's the sort of thing you think the young man was making up as he stood in the witness box, that's the sort of thing you can look at to see whether there is corroboration.'

The able and experienced counsel in question, who had not yet been called three years, rose with a deal of trepidation to interrupt the august judge at this stage of the proceedings.

'Well,' Goddard said severely, 'what is it you want?'

'M'Lud,' I managed to get out, 'I must tell your Lordship I had instructions about the telephone conversation. I did not put it to the girl because I did not then think—and with great respect I still do not—that it was material. But he did not make it up as he stood in the witness box. I had instructions and if there is any fault to be found, it must be with me.'

'Very well.' This was the first time I saw the twinkle. 'Well, members of the Jury, I said this young man was represented here by able and experienced counsel. Forget all I've been saying to you.'

My client was acquitted.

FREDERICK EDWIN SMITH (LORD BIRKENHEAD) (1872–1930)

Lord Chancellor

326

THE motion (in the Oxford Union) which he was invited to oppose was on a subject on which F. E., already a heavy drinker, had no need to simulate indignation. 'This house approves of local option.' It was proposed by Lord Balcarres, an undergraduate speaker who had already made his name; and Sir Wilfred Lawson, MP for Carlisle, one of the country's most forceful prohibitionists, was to speak third.

F. E. began conventionally enough, by sticking to the motion, but made the climax of his speech a scathing personal attack on Lawson. After arguing that local option was an unfair and ineffective weapon for extinguishing drunkenness he proceeded, to the huge delight of his audience, to extinguish the honourable member for Carlisle.

'It is a convention in this House, and a right convention, that honourable visitors should be treated with respect and their records and conclusions be challenged only by the courteous denials of debate. But tonight I must deviate from this custom. The honourable gentleman inherited a noble cellar in which the piety of his ancestors had laid to rest delicate clarets, sustaining ports, stimulating champagnes and warm and ancient brandies. What did the honourable gentleman do with his cellar?' (As F. E. and most of his audience knew, on succeeding to the family estate, Lawson had destroyed the total contents of the wine cellars.)

'He destroyed the priceless heritage of the ages, in which was stored the bottled sunshine of the South. He destroyed it in circumstances of such barbarity that even the thirstiest throat in Carlisle was denied participation. I tell you, sir, that if, in years to come, the honourable gentleman comes to me when I am nestling in Abraham's bosom and asks me for a drop of water, I shall say to him, "No, not a drop, you dissipated great liquor." '

327

F. E., who had just begun his career on the Northern Circuit, was on a tram in Liverpool. A young woman sitting opposite him was about to alight when a man boarded the tram and jostled her. F. E. promptly intervened, struck the man on the jaw, and sent him flying into the roadway where he struck his head on the kerb. Instinctively F. E. knew the man was dead. He leaped off the tram and ran as fast as his legs would carry him to a friend in shipping whom he begged to get him out of the country at once. The friend obliged and put him on a boat en route for the Mediterranean. The moral of the rest of this story, said F. E., was, 'Never take your boots off when you're having fun with a woman.' After a fortnight at sea the ship called at Malta where F. E. went ashore and picked up an extremely attractive girl who took him home with her. They went upstairs and he foolishly removed his boots as well as his trousers. Fortunately, as it turned out, he noticed that there was a chamber-pot under the bed. At the crucial moment in came the infuriated husband, armed with knife and revolver. Despite the unpromising circumstances the wife at once began to protest her innocence. F. E. induced her to keep him talking until he located the chamber-pot, which he brought down on the man's head. Then he ran all the way back to the ship in his stockinged feet over the cobblestones, which he described as one of the most agonising experiences of his life. But his escape to Malta had been worthwhile. For on his return to Liverpool he found that though, as he feared, the man on the tram had died, the hue and cry had died also.

328

WE are amazed at this period by his apparent immunity from disaster in his altercations with judges. It defies analysis, but it must be realised that he was far too astute to make a habit of antagonising the Bench, the collisions quoted here being spread out over a considerable period. It is also notable that however offensive he was to a Judge at any given moment, he was usually in the right in the argument. If he was not, he did not force the issue. He was impartial in the insults he addressed to County Court or High Court Judges. When, rising to address the jury in a case before Mr Justice Ridley, the latter had unjudicially observed, 'Well, Mr Smith, I have read the pleadings and I do not think much of your case', stung by this remark he answered: 'Indeed, my Lord, I'm sorry to hear that, but your Lordship will find that the more you hear of it, the more it will grow on you.'

His worst insults were reserved for Judge Willis, a worthy, sanctimonious County Court Judge, full of kindness expressed in a patronizing manner. F. E. had been briefed for a tramway company which had been sued for damages for injuries to a boy who had been run over. The plaintiff's case was that blindness had set in as a result of the accident.

The Judge was deeply moved. 'Poor boy, poor boy', he said. 'Blind. Put him on a chair so that the jury can see him.'

F. E. said coldly: 'Perhaps your Honour would like to have the boy passed round the jury box.'

'That is a most improper remark', said Judge Willis angrily.

'It was provoked', said F. E., 'by a most improper suggestion.'

There was a heavy pause, and the Judge continued, 'Mr Smith, have you ever heard of a saying by Bacon—the great Bacon—that youth and discretion are ill-wed companions?'

'Indeed I have, your Honour; and has your Honour ever heard of a saying by Bacon—the great Bacon—that a much talking Judge is like an ill-tuned cymbal?'

The Judge replied furiously, 'You are extremely offensive, young man'; and F. E. added to his previous lapses by saying: 'As a matter of fact we both are; the only difference between us is that I'm trying to be, and you can't help it.'

329

THIS action (the 'Soap Trust Case') was brought by Mr William Lever MP (afterwards Lord Leverholme) and the well-known firm of soap manufacturers of Port Sunlight against Lord Northcliffe, formerly Mr Alfred Harmsworth and his Associated Newspapers Group, particularly the *Daily Mail*, which had conducted a press campaign over a period accusing Mr Lever of forming a 'soap trust' to exploit the consumer by cornering the raw materials market and raising the retail price of the finished article. As a result of this vindictive campaign Lever Brothers Limited suffered trading losses to the amount of £40,000 while the value of their shares on the Stock Exchange fell by £200,000.

F. E. Smith, who was asked for an opinion at very short notice, is said to have faced a stack of newspapers and other documents nearly four feet high, and after ordering two dozen oysters and a bottle of champagne sat up all night, eventually delivering the following opinion. 'There is no answer to this action for libel and the damages must be enormous.'

330

THE Norman-French statute of Edward III which hanged Sir Roger Casement, and allowed his followers to claim that he had been 'done to death by a comma' was, in fact, highly ambiguous and open to an interpretation which would have acquitted the prisoner.

The point was argued before the Court of Appeal, which upheld the Crown's construction of the Statute and thereafter F. E. remained obdurate, in the face of all pressure, to persuade him to allow a final appeal to the Lords. But this did not end the matter. Four days later the Court of Appeal reconvened on its own initiative, such was its uneasiness that Casement's Counsel had not argued the case adequately at the previous hearing. The Court had been informed that one possible ground for reversal of the verdict (misdirection of the jury) had not been put to them.

It never was. Casement's defenders refused to take advantage of a second resort to the Court of Appeal. As one of Casement's supporters said, in a letter to *The Times*, 'Nothing more is wanted from the Court of Criminal Appeal. What is wanted is that the point of Law already raised should be determined by the highest Court. Sir F. E. Smith, from whom there is no appeal, whose antecedents in Ulster are well known, has refused the certificate and shows no inclination to reconsider his decision.'

Artemus Jones, QC and Professor J. H. Morgan could not believe that F. E. was unshakeable. But when they went to see him the following day they found him totally unmoved by *The Times* letter. He told them that the grounds for appeal were trivial. Undespairing, they then went to call on Sir William Holdsworth. After this interview Morgan wrote to F. E.:

> I am of the opinion that the point of Law is anything but trivial, and your argument against us is anything but conclusive. More than that, I have discussed the point with legal scholars whose reputation in this country stands higher than that of any other lawyer in such matters and they were clearly of the opinion that the matter was one of great doubt and considerable perplexity.

This drew the comment that F. E. was aware of Holdsworth's attainments because Holdsworth had been runner-up to him in the Vinerian Law Scholarship.

Should F. E. have allowed an appeal to the Lords? Whatever he thought of its legal merits, on political grounds the case for granting his fiat was overwhelming. According to Morgan, F. E. himself later admitted that he was wrong, even on legal grounds. 'You had a good point there', he is supposed to have told Morgan in 1918, 'but if I had given my fiat, and the Lords had quashed the conviction on such a technicality, feeling against Casement was so strong it might have brought down the Government.' This story has been denied, but if it is true, it is a powerful argument for removing the responsibility for appeals to the Lords from a party politician.

331

THE silver-tongued Bottomley, whose casuistries had charmed so many unsympathetic shareholders, remained an object of affection to F. E. who realised that Bottomley's resource and genius in oratory matched his own but was warped and perverted. A cynical friendship persisted between the two, surviving Bottomley's imprisonment, and was quenched only by an abortive attempt by Bottomley to blackmail his old friend. It was said, as an indication of the *bonhomie* prevailing between them, that on the night when it became known that F. E. was going to the Woolsack, he was accosted by Bottomley in the smoking-room of the House of Commons and congratulated upon the appointment. Bottomley added, 'Upon my soul, F. E. I shouldn't have been surprised to hear that you had been made Archbishop of Canterbury.'

'If I had,' replied the Lord Chancellor, 'I should have asked you to come to my installation.'

'That's damned nice of you', said Bottomley.

'Not at all. I should have needed a crook.'

332

F. E.'s only later meanness was derived from his early days of horses, and he would never allow one car to make the journey to the station twice in the same day, having an extraordinary idea that motor-cars were subject to the same fatigue as horses. 'I will not have *my* tyres exhausted. Think of the strain on *my* carburetters and magnetoes.' He was assisted in this aberration by Rogers, coachman turned chauffeur, who, when the unfamiliar vehicle became out of control, would rein back heavily on the steering wheel with a cry of 'Whoa!'.

REGINALD SMITHERS (1903–)

Australian Judge

333

The narrator is Kevin Anderson, later himself elevated to the Bench

At a conference the night before a running-down case was to be heard before Mr Justice Monahan and a jury of six, Smithers, then a Queen's Counsel, Anderson, his junior, and the defendant car driver were closeted, with the instructing solicitor, in Smithers's chambers.

Now Reg Smithers always told his clients 'you must tell the truth. It doesn't matter how much it costs you, you have to tell the truth.'

After a few questions Reg realized that his client was rather dumb:

so he said to him, 'Counsel sometimes put two questions into the one question, so, in order to tell the truth, you have to be very careful in answering the question.'

The car driver said, 'What do you mean by putting two questions into one question?'

At this point Reg dived into his bag of awful examples and said, 'I'll give you an example. Let me see. What will we say? Yes, "I said that the plaintiff had his hat on." Now, can you understand the difference between that statement and "He had his hat on." '

'No', said the defendant.

Smithers said, 'In the first instance there was the saying of it, and in the second example there is just the observation that the hat was on.'

'No', said the defendant. 'I don't get it.'

'Well,' said Smithers, 'say Mr Anderson sat, very rudely, through the whole conference with his hat on, and you, having left us, went later to your solicitors, and afterwards met a friend in the street and said to your friend, "I said to my solicitors that Mr Anderson had his hat on." Now, can't you see the difference between saying that and, omitting and deleting all reference to your solicitor, you saying that Mr Anderson had his hat on?'

The defendant said 'I think I get it!'

The next day in Court Hubert Frederico opened the case for the plaintiff and called his witnesses. The plaintiff, who had a broken spine, skull, etc., as a result of the defendant's negligence; the hospital to talk of the pain and suffering; the doctor to say that the plaintiff would never be the same man again; his employer to say that, but for the terrible accident, he would have given the plaintiff another £1,000 a year; and a policeman to say that the defendant was travelling on the wrong side of the road. He asked for £100,000 and closed his case.

Reg Smithers put the defendant in the box. He gave his name, address and occupation and Reg said, 'On the seventh day of April 1960 were you driving your car in a southerly direction along Blank Street?'

'Yes.'

'At what speed were you travelling?'

'Twenty-five miles per hour.'

(All accident cases that I have been involved in have taken place at twenty-five miles per hour—a most dangerous speed.)

'And on what portion of the roadway were you travelling?'

'I was travelling on the left hand side of the road and as close to the kerb as possible, but I couldn't travel too close, because there were cars parked against the kerb.'

'Yes. And now will you tell His Honour and the jury, in your own words what took place as you drove along.'

'Well, as I was saying, I was just driving along when the plaintiff darted out between two parked cars right in front of me. I couldn't avoid him. I couldn't miss him. I had to hit him. And he had his hat on.'

Kevin Anderson became almost sick with laughter, Reg went a peculiar shade of purple, and the judge said to the defendant, 'Why did you say that the plaintiff had his hat on?'

'Because he did have his hat on.'

At this stage Frederico, who had not been attending too well and was half asleep said, 'Excuse me, Your Honour, what was Your Honour's question to the defendant, and what was his answer?'

The Judge looked troubled, scratched his head, and said, 'I said to the defendant "Why did you say the plaintiff had his hat on?", and in answer to my question the defendant said, "Because he did have his hat on." '

Freddie mulled this over a second or two, then said, 'I must object to this on the ground that it is absolutely irrelevant.'

'I'm inclined to agree', said the Judge. 'Mr Smithers, how are you putting this?'

Reg rose to his feet, took a high C, as he could in a moment of stress, and with colour heightened to a deep purple said, 'I'm not putting it at all. I didn't say he had his hat on.'

The defendant leaned out of the box to Reg and said, 'That's what you told me to say last night.'

SIR WINGTRINGHAM NORTON STABLE
(1888–1977)

334

In 1955 Nancy Spain, on behalf of the Daily Express, *attempted, uninvited, to interview Evelyn Waugh at his home at Piers Court. She was ejected. She wrote an article denigrating Evelyn and he wrote one in the* Spectator *which might have been construed as critical of Nancy. The result was an action for libel and a counterclaim, before Mr Justice Stable. Evelyn had the moral support of his parish priest to whom he had promised ten per cent of anything he won.*

MR JUSTICE STABLE, summing up, was not exactly impressed by either of the contending parties. Commenting on Waugh's *Spectator* article he assured the jury, 'If you come to the conclusion that it didn't reflect discreditably on Miss Spain you will dismiss her counter-claim. If, on the other hand, you think it did, you will compensate her accordingly. When Miss Spain said (to demonstrate the influence of her reviews) that the sale of 60,000 copies of Alec Waugh's book *Island in the Sun* was the direct result of the articles she published, she was rather over stating the case. It seemed that she had scraped through it somewhat rapidly in the cocktail bar of the Ritz, and that a rather cursory notice of the book was by no means the most important factor in stepping up the sales.'

In conclusion he indicated clearly his personal attitude, 'It may be that members of the Jury, in this literary atmosphere, may recall one of Shakespeare's earlier works, *Much Ado about Nothing*. Whether this expression applies here is exclusively for you to decide.'

Nevertheless, it took the jury two hours to return a verdict which resulted in Evelyn Waugh being awarded £2,000 damages and costs, the counterclaim against him being dismissed. He was jubilant in his account of it to his friend Nancy Mitford:

> I had a firm solid jury who were out to fine the *Express* for their impertinence to the Royal Family, quite irrespective of any rights and wrongs. They were not at all amused by the Judge. All the £300-a-day barristers rocked with laughter at his sallies. They glowered. That was not what they paid a Judge for, they thought. So Father Collins got £200 and a lot of chaps at Whites got pop.

SIR JAMES FITZJAMES STEPHEN (1829–94)

335

The narrator is Sir Henry Dickens

IT was Mr Justice Stephen who tried the case of Mrs Maybrick. Personally of course I know nothing of that case beyond what is known by the general public, with the exception of one highly dramatic episode which was told me by his brother judge on circuit. He told me that, knowing as he did, that Stephen was a good deal worried over the case, he advised him strongly to get his summing-up completed that day once and for all and not adjourn it over night. Stephen however did not follow that advice. He summed-up all day, apparently in favour of Mrs Maybrick, and adjourned the remainder of what he had to say till next morning. That night his brother judge had a somewhat startling experience. Early in the morning he was awakened by Stephen, whom he found walking up and down his room in a dressing-gown, saying as he did so: 'That woman is guilty. That woman is guilty.' He continued his summing-up next day, but in a manner which was altogether opposed to what he had said on the previous day. So marked and sudden was the change indeed that a crowd almost upset his coach as he left the court.

SEWELL STOKES (Contemporary)

Probation Officer

336

One of Mr Stokes' charges was a boy called Albert Braxton. He received a not very cordial invitation from the boy's father in Brixton. 'Come if you want to. E. Braxton.'

THE roads between Peckham Rye and Dulwich are of interminable length, and, as always in my case, the address I sought seemed to be purposely elusive. But eventually I found myself outside the door of the neat suburban villa I was looking for, and banged on it with what energy I had left. Nothing happened. I banged again, with the same result; and then, gingerly stepping on to a flower-bed, I peered in through the window. As there was nobody inside the room it was absurd of me to knock on the pane, but knock I did, as if half expecting the inmates suddenly to crawl out from under a sofa or come up through a trap-door. And because I refused to believe that I might have made the journey for nothing, I knocked again, more loudly. It was then that a piping voice behind me asked if I was a burglar trying to break into the house. The voice belonged to a boy of about six, who regarded me with obvious suspicion.

'Does Mr Braxton live here?', I asked with a smile, which was not returned.

'You've trodden on my daisy plants', said the boy, in whose small face I now recognized an unmistakable likeness to Albert's. 'Aren't you clumsy!'

Lifting my feet from the crushed flowers, I apologized, and repeated the question.

'Dad's out the back', said the boy and disappeared.

The side entrance of the house led to a strip of back-garden in the centre of which a large man was tinkering with an upturned bicycle. I remember that he had a nearly bald head, and the flattened nose of a bruiser. I remember many other things about him that I wish I could forget, for nobody likes to be reminded of the humiliations he has suffered.

'Are you Mr Braxton?', I asked, with what I'm afraid was something very akin to a Sunbeam's jollity.

'Could be', was the curt reply.

'I'm Mr Stokes. I've come to see you about Albert.'

'Have you now?'

I felt I wasn't going to like Albert's dad, whose identity needed no further proof. *Le style est l'homme même.* And here, unmistakably, was the author of 'Come if you want to. E. Braxton.' I was deciding whether to challenge his impertinence, or ignore it altogether, when Albert's dad said, without turning his head:

'Second puncture I've had this week . . . Kids put tin-tacks on the road . . . If I catch one of them I'll tan the hide off him.'

But I wasn't going to be side-tracked.

'About Albert', I said doggedly.

'What about him?'

'I like Albert.'

'Glad someone does.'

'I understand him.'

'First one who has.'

'He's coming out in two weeks.'

'More's the pity.'

'And he wants to come home.'

'He can want.'

Apart from the locale, we might have been conversing in a comedy by Noel Coward. The bicycle claimed its owner's sole attention. I saw that if I were to get any of it, a provocative note must be introduced.

'After all,' I said, 'was Albert's crime as bad as it was made out to be? Assault on police. Any of us might have done the same thing; in a spirit of fun, of course.'

'Would you?', asked Albert's dad.

'Actually, I wouldn't.'

'No more would I.'

'But I'm inclined to think, Mr Braxton, that the police were just as much to blame as your son. From what Albert tells me, they know him around here and watch out for him. When they see him go into a pub they wait until he comes out. I'm afraid it's a case of *agent provocateur*, you know.'

'Agent my arse', said Albert's dad indignantly; but his attention remained on the bicycle.

Had I known it, then was the moment to give the whole thing up as a bad job, to call it a day so far as Peckham was concerned. The trousers Albert's dad was wearing ought to have warned me that I was playing with fire. But I was not experienced in such matters then. One pair of dark blue legs looked very like another.

'I've nothing against the police, if you understand me?'

'I'm trying to.'

'But I suppose it is a part of their job to get knocked about a bit.'

'And part of Albert's to do the knocking?'

'I don't mean that exactly.'

'Then what the hell do you mean?'

The man's interest was aroused at last. And turning on me a face puce with anger, he said, in the deliberate tone of one who does not intend to be misunderstood:

'Are you aware, Mr Stokes, that when he was brought into the charge-room by the four officers it had taken to arrest him, Albert broke away from them and attacked the station-sergeant? And do you know that when those officers had lifted Albert off the station-sergeant, the station-sergeant had both eyes closed up, his front teeth knocked in—and his nose broken?'

'I didn't know', I said, after quite a long pause.

'I thought not. And there's just one other thing I'd like to tell you: I was the station-sergeant.'

Confusion covered me in a big way. With downcast eyes I noticed, too late, those tell-tale uniform trousers above the sergeant's boots; and I decided to impress upon Albert that in future he must learn to be more explicit in his talk. When I lifted my head it was to find the small boy back again. He clasped a bucket filled with water. I can't think why I remember that Donald Duck's hideous face was on it. I smiled mechanically at the boy. He smiled back at me. And then, taking great care not to avoid his target, he emptied the bucket's entire contents over my shoes.

'That's for treading on my daisy plants', he said, and disappeared.

Squelching my way homewards, I tried to believe in a divine justice that might reveal Albert's brother as the kid who had put the tin-tacks on the road, and that Albert's dad would tan the hide off him for his trouble.

337

Sewell Stokes had become critical of the habit of one of the magistrates of reading aloud to the man in the dock the observations made about him by the prison doctor. Allport is a fictional name which he gives to a real magistrate.

THE flagrant example of Mr Allport's insensitivity which decided me to oppose him concerned a youth named Postlethwaite, whom he asked me to interview when he first appeared in court, charged by his own mother with stealing coins from her gas-meter. Although he was nearly twenty-one he looked far less, and had come voluntarily to the police station with his parent when she gave him into custody. The woman, deserted by her husband, with three small children to bring up, had taken the only step she could think of to cure her eldest son of his thieving habits. He was a good boy in some ways, she said, fond of his brother and sister and willing to do anything for her—except keep his hands off her money.

'He's a regular jackal,' she told me, meaning jackdaw; 'can't keep his hands off other people's cash. Fun-fair mad, that's his trouble. Must have the money to go to them places and loses it when he gets there. Ain't that right, son?'

'Mum's right', her son agreed. 'Right as rain. Don't seem able to keep away from fun-fairs. Never wins anything neither . . . Might do one day, though', he added, half-heartedly.

Postlethwaite was tall and pale, gentle and bemused. To glance at him was to know that his poor brain was only half alive. Yet when he smiled, which wasn't often, he appeared almost sane and encouraged one to believe for a second that some day he might grow up. On the morning when he was to appear in court after his week's remand, I went early to the gaoler's office to have a look at the medical report that had been sent with him from the prison. Officially, nobody was supposed to see these reports before the magistrate had read them. But the gaoler, whose job was to open and attach them to the prisoners' charge-sheets before sending them into court, always obliged me if he was in a good mood. The report on Postlethwaite was about as hopeless as it could be and I went into court depressed; for I knew he was to be put on probation to me and realized how little there was I could do for him.

A few minutes later I was listening to Mr Allport addressing Postlethwaite. Although I knew all along that the old devil would read that hopeless report aloud, I kept telling myself that he might stop at the last minute: that something inside his bald head would warn him of the damage his words could still do to the life of the pathetic creature standing before him. On the boy's face was a look of mild expectation, an expression not exactly of trust, but of belief in the prospect of something being done to clear up the mess that he willingly admitted he had got himself into. It was impossible not to feel desperately sorry for him, knowing what I did of his antecedents. I could very easily have cried. Sentimentality is nowhere more out of place than in court. But in no place is compassion more often felt. And yet for some hidden reason Mr Allport, whose heart turned to mush at the thought of an artful old beggar spending Christmas Day in the cells, calmly said:

'Well, Postlethwaite, did the doctor have a look at you? . . . He did. That's right. There's a report from him somewhere.' A sickening pause while he rummaged among his papers—including the several sketches of prisoners he had already made that morning. 'Ah, I have it.' Adjusting his glasses: 'Here is what he says, "Although nearly twenty-one years old this man's mental age is eleven. He is not at present certifiable as an insane person, but his condition is likely to deteriorate. No reliance can be placed on anything he says, but he knows he has done wrong, and it would be advisable if a probation order is made, to see that he does not frequent fun-fairs, as these appear to be a source of great temptation to him." '

Mr Allport put down the report, removed his glasses, and looked at the boy pityingly, as well he might do. But the boy was not looking at him. Suddenly his lanky body had snapped in two, and he hung over the rail of the dock—sobbing—with his arms dangling loosely in front of him. And his sobs were unbearable to hear, because they expressed a grief that was too private to be shared. Listening to them seemed indecent. Postlethwaite knew at this moment what he may never quite have known before, that he was not as other people; that in fact he was, or must become, an idiot. At school perhaps his dull-wittedness had been made fun of by the other boys: later, almost certainly, men had chaffed him for his odd behaviour; but none of them had had the heartlessness to tell him to his face the truth about himself. Now he had been told it; by someone whose authority left him no longer any comforting doubts to cling to.

'Mr Stokes?', said Mr Allport, nodding in my direction. It was the sign for me to leave my seat, cross the court and take my stand in the witness box. 'I shall make a probation order in this case—for two years. And I shall put in a condition that the boy does not enter a fun-fair during that period.'

'Yes, sir', was all I said. If I'd said all I felt I'd have made the front page of the evening papers.

ALEXANDER MARTIN SULLIVAN (1871–1959)

Serjeant-at-Law

338

In December 1892 I commenced the work of defence of criminal cases at the Winter Assizes. Many years my senior there was then a well-known Cork man engaged as counsel for prisoners in many cases. He had a thousand virtues, but two defects. In the first place he was not more scrupulous than were the minions of the Crown in what might be called the major strategy of the campaign. In the second place he was suffering from a nervous complaint that deprived him of the faculty of moderating his voice. If he commenced addressing a court, his attempts to communicate with his colleague or his solicitor were pitched in the same tone as his speech.

In the particular case he was defending five persons who were charged with a moonlighting outrage. Two of the accused were highly connected in the City of Cork, where the trial was set, and their counsel imprudently announced in the Bar room his intention of carrying on the proceedings over the weekend, when the jury would find themselves in an atmosphere extremely friendly to his clients.

The Crown Counsel were the McDermott and his junior Johnny

Moriarty. The pair recognized the danger of the weekend. They persuaded the Court to sit long hours, cut down their witnesses and closed their case for the prosecution on Wednesday night. This was a heavy blow for the defendants, but their loquacious Counsel rallied. He appeared in the Bar room on Thursday morning with a bulging brief bag and in the best of humours. He uttered a copyright exclamation that sounded like 'Ah-boo-ah' which he used as a stimulant, and announced that his bag contained notes of his speech in which, explaining the details of five different alibis, he expected to revel for more than a day.

What then happened must be considered as doubtful. There was never any legal evidence against either the McDermott or Johnny beyond their joint and several denials, but it was universally believed that the notes were taken from the brief bag by one Crown Counsel at the instigation of the other. Be that as it may, the opening speech for the defence was somewhat difficult to follow as the main discourse and the interlocutory asides were all delivered in identical intonation.

'May it please your Lordship and Gentlemen—Gentlemen, ah-boo-ah is this my bag?—Gentlemen of the jury. I appear with my learned friend—damn it, where are my notes—my learned friend—will one of you fellows see if my notes are in the Bar room?—on behalf of the prisoners at the bar to submit to you—not there, some fellow took them out of my bag—in the first place that the Crown—I know who did it, McDermott—that the Crown has not discharged the onus—you wouldn't do it yourself but Johnny would do it for you.' Here Johnny let fall his monocle, lifted his eyes to Heaven and his lips moved in silent prayer for Divine protection against such defamation. 'Ah-boo-ah. The onus lies upon them but I'll beat them yet.'

He did beat them. The absence of his notes resulted in making him more irrelevant and long-winded than he would otherwise have been. The case went over the weekend, and the jury disagreed.

339

THE peasant's belief in a future existence was vivid and lively. As a train in which I was seated crossed a long viaduct over a Kerry valley, a solicitor in one carriage with me pointed out two farms lying below us and told me that they were the O'Connell and Buckley farms. I had forgotten all about it, but he told me that I had been sent a case to advise the widow O'Connell as to a right of way over her neighbour's land. I had delayed my advice, and the widow, who was in bad health, kept sending in her son to the solicitor's office about it. At last my opinion was delivered, and the young man returned home in great jubilation. At the door he met the doctor who informed him that his mother could not outlive the night. To the youth this appeared a small matter. Bursting into the sickroom he exclaimed, 'Mother, the doctor says you'll die in the night.' The poor woman betook herself to prayer and lamentation. 'Ah, whist now', said her sympathetic child. 'You needn't worry about it, but when you go beyond and see my father I want you to tell him that the Serjeant says we'll beat the Buckleys.'

SIR RIGBY PHILIP WATSON SWIFT (1874–1937)

340

SWIFT's bluff humour, later to be one of his most formidable weapons, was developed during his early days in Liverpool, as was his sensitivity to the atmosphere of a tribunal and his adaptability to whatever its peculiar requirements might be. An instance of this trait is seen in his tactics before the Liverpool Court of Passage. That venerable court was then presided over by the octogenarian Judge Baylis. White bearded and not a little deaf, the judge had, long before, written a book about the Law of Servants, and if Swift found himself unable to rouse him by other methods, he would cite, as loudly as he could, 'Your Lordship's well-known codification of the law relating to domestic servants'.

This would invariably enlist the judge's attention, and may have had some bearing on Swift's signal success in that court. The skill with which he contrived to pray-in-aid a passage about housemaids in a case relating to a bill of exchange or a tram-car collision was remarkable.

341

JOSEPH GRADWELL, the father of Leo Gradwell the well-known Metropolitan magistrate was a solicitor who practised in Liverpool when Rigby Swift was a member there of the Junior Bar.

On one occasion Mr Gradwell found himself, as many solicitors do, out of time with a pleading in a piece of litigation in which he had instructed Rigby, who had settled the Statement of Claim. The reply was due to be delivered next day and Gradwell had been unable to obtain an extension of time.

Realizing, late in the evening, that he had no reply ready for delivery he set out by train for St Helens, where Rigby lived, and arrived at Counsel's home at about 11.30 p.m. His knock at the door was answered by Counsel at a first floor window inquiring who was there.

'It is I, Mr Swift,' said Gradwell. 'I have come out from Liverpool to ask a favour. I know it's very late, but I must deliver that reply tomorrow, and I wondered if you could oblige me by settling it now.'

Rigby's reply was not reassuring.

'Go away', he said. 'I am a Barrister. Not a — midwife.' His son, Leo, who tells this story, was a guest, many years later, during the Manchester Assizes at one of Rigby's lunch parties, which were always held in the rooms behind his court, when another guest, the High Sheriff's Chaplain, misjudged the suitability of the occasion to the extent of embarking, or trying to embark, upon a religious discussion.

Rigby's reaction was prompt and typical. 'Chaplain,' he said, 'I think there is a proper time and place for everything, and I do not think my lunch table is a proper place for a religious discussion. You know, when Gradwell and I are conducting a little criminal business in my court it would be a dreadful thing if we were saying our prayers all the time, wouldn't it, Gradwell?'

'One of us is', said Gradwell.

342

ON the Monday of Ascot week in 1920 Swift found himself in Mr Justice McCardie's court, briefed to defend an action over the ownership of a racehorse. The horse was 'Happy Man' and belonged, or had belonged, to Swift's client Mr Fred Hardy, the well-known owner. The plaintiff, Mr John Joyce, also well known on the turf, said he had bought the colt, and he employed the advocacy of that rising young silk, Mr Patrick Hastings, to argue his contention.

The case commenced in the afternoon, and Hastings had barely concluded his first speech by the time the court rose. The next morning a feverish note crept into the proceedings. It was the opening day at

Ascot and Happy Man was entered for the Ascot Stakes to be run at 2.30. Suppose he were to be placed; whose horse was he? Could the case be finished by then?

The morning dragged on. The first witness went into the box. Hardy slipped out of court, beckoning Swift to follow.

'I can't stand it,' he said. 'You must settle this case on the best terms you can. I'm going to Ascot.'

Swift consulted with the other side, and presently was able to announce to the judge that the action had been settled upon terms that Hardy would retain the horse, paying to Joyce the sum of £1,000 and costs.

As his client was hurrying away, Swift stopped him. 'Put a pound on Happy Man for me.'

Hardy put on a considerably larger sum on his own account and arrived at Ascot to see his colt come in first—at twelve to one. His winnings sufficed to defray the entire expenses of the law suit.

The next day Swift received two messages. One took the form of a letter from Hardy accompanied by a cheque for £12. The other was conveyed by the Lord Chancellor's secretary, who called to announce that the Lord Chancellor proposed to recommend Swift's appointment to be one of the Justices of the King's Bench Division.

'Happy Man' was the watchword of that memorable day.

343

A YOUNG and inexperienced Counsel who did not have many cases, found that he had two for trial on the same day. One was a case in the County Court: the other a case in the High Court which was likely to come on before Mr Justice Swift. The Young Hopeful decided to apply to Swift for an adjournment, basing his application on his personal difficulty having regard to the County Court case. The application was refused.

Whereupon a well-known and busy Silk rose to make a similar application on behalf of a plaintiff, basing *his* application on the grounds that the plaintiff's original solicitor had died necessitating the belated instructing of a new solicitor; that the plaintiff himself was ill; and that three witnesses essential to the plaintiff's case were abroad.

Rigby: 'And I suppose you are engaged at the Blankshire Assizes.'

Silk: 'Well, as a matter of fact, my Lord, I am: but I can assure your Lordship that that has no bearing on this application.'

Rigby allowed the application and then, with a smile, turned to the Young Hopeful. 'You see, Mr Hopeful, that's the way to do it: *wrap it up*.'

As Swift grew older, he grew a little more tolerant of such requests. It is recounted that on one occasion at Northampton Assizes a woman plaintiff in an action for damages alleged that one of the results of an injury to her head was that she suffered from double vision. Her Counsel was Mr Arthur Ward who was then still at the Junior Bar, and the possessor of a very large practice which frequently demanded his presence in two courts at the same time.

As the plaintiff was giving evidence Ward's clerk entered the court to speak to him.

Rigby (to the plaintiff): 'Tell me more about this double vision. Does it mean you see two of everything?'

Plaintiff: 'Yes, my Lord.'

Rigby: 'Do you see two of me?'

Plaintiff: 'Yes, my Lord.'

Rigby: 'Do you see two of the Usher there?'

Plaintiff: 'Yes, my Lord.'

Rigby: 'Do you see two of Mr Arthur Ward?'

Plaintiff: 'Yes, my Lord.'

Rigby: 'Well that's very fortunate, because one of him is wanted in the other court.'

344

MR J. C. JACKSON KC was in court at Manchester one day while a young barrister was making his concluding address to Mr Justice Swift. Everyone, except this barrister, appreciated that Swift was in his favour. Counsel droned on until Jackson, whose case came next in the list, passed him a note saying:

'Sit down you b— fool. Can't you see the old —— is with you?'

Counsel glanced at the note and sat down.

Swift: 'May *I* see that note?'

Counsel (embarrassed): 'It is a personal note to me, m'Lord from Mr Jackson'.
Swift: 'Mr Jackson, have you any objection to me seeing the note?'
Jackson: 'None at all, my Lord.'

In tense silence the note was handed up. The judge read it and passed it back.

'A very proper note. I quite agree with it.'

[*There are a number of versions which elaborate this story. In one of them the barrister concerned disregards the note, and continues his address. Swift extracts the note from him, casts an eye over it, and hands it back to him saying: 'Excellent advice. You should take it.' However, Mr Jackson insists that his version is the only authentic one.*]

SIR GEORGE JOHN TALBOT (1861–1938)

345

MR JUSTICE TALBOT was one of the old school and a high churchman. He was about to try a really sordid case at Liverpool Assizes and he invited the ladies to retire.

Some did, but about half a dozen or so in the public gallery remained. So he then said:

'The ladies having retired, I now give the women remaining in Court an opportunity to do likewise.'

But the indomitable six who were left made no movement and there was nothing the old gentleman could do about it.

FREDERICK THESIGER (FIRST BARON CHELMSFORD) (1794–1878)

346

The Dictionary of National Biography *says, 'Thesiger had a fine presence and handsome features, a beautiful voice and a pleasant, if too frequent, wit.'*

SIR ALEXANDER COCKBURN said he was sitting next to Thesiger during a trial before Campbell, Chief Justice, in which the judge read some French documents and, being a Scotsman, it attracted a good deal of attention. Cockburn, who was a good French scholar, was much annoyed at the Chief Justice's pronunciation of the French language.

'He's murdering it,' said Cockburn, 'murdering it.'

'No, my dear Cockburn,' answered Thesiger, 'he's not killing it, only scotching it.'

ROBERT TRAVER* (1903–)

American Judge

347

When a prisoner is brought into Court upon a plea of Not Guilty he is entitled, under the laws of the United States, 'to make his appearance free of all shackles or bonds'.

I'LL never forget 'Crazy Matt'. His hearing was before Circuit Judge Glenn W. Jackson, a fine judge and my esteemed friend. Now Crazy Matt had previously escaped from every prison in the State. He had once held the entire parole board as hostages during an attempted escape. We *knew* all this and when the prison guards delivered him into our hands they solemnly urged the sheriff and me to be sure to keep him both manacled and leg ironed. 'Bad, *bad* actor', they warned darkly. So Crazy Matt was brought clanking into Court and propped in place in the witness chair sagging under his burden of armour.

Judge Jackson observed all this and frowned.

'Why all the medieval hardware?'

'Real dangerous customer, Judge.'

'I don't like it. Remove the hardware.'

Allah had spoken, so we shrugged and the sheriff went out and got a prison guard to unlock Crazy Matt—a ritual almost as elaborate as opening a bank in the morning. This done, Crazy Matt sat back, flexing his cramped wrists and looking down at me with the pent fury and detached malevolence of a caged lion—or worse yet, a lion whose cage door has carelessly been left open. Then his darting eyes began casing all the exits in the court room.

The Judge nodded to me to begin and I cleared my throat to gain

* Pseudonym of Judge Voelker.

Crazy Matt's attention. Again his eyes locked with mine, again flecked and aglint with a kind of cold impersonal fury. 'When will it happen?', I asked myself.

'Proceed', said the Judge.

'Yes, your Honor.'

I barely got to ask Crazy Matt his name when all hell broke loose. He leaped from his chair and stunned us into inaction with a swift hypnotic flow of rich old Anglo Saxon invective. This included some trenchant advice on what all of us might forthwith proceed to do with ourselves. Then he leaped nimbly over the front rail of the witness box and dashed by me at full speed. Hurling a farewell obscenity over his shoulder he darted out the main front door and clattered on down the wide marble stairs.

Meanwhile the sheriff was tugging away at his hidden shoulder holster like a man frantically scratching himself. Finally he produced a pistol and lumbered out a rear door plaintively muttering to himself like a reproachful scoutmaster, 'Hold on there, now. Just you hold on there.'

In the distance we could hear the sounds of running feet and muffled, barking shouts. Presently there was a quick series of pistol shots. I ran out the sheriff's door only to meet the sheriff and prison guards coming back with Crazy Matt, sheepish looking and unharmed. The sheriff had shot at his legs, and Matt had rapidly got the message and deferred any escape plans until another day. I hurried back to report all this to His Honor.

I found the judge sitting very still up on the bench in the deserted courtroom. He seemed a little pale. I went around to the side and saw that he had lifted, and was still holding, his black silk gown off the floor—daintily with two fingers of each hand—and that his feet were also at least two inches off the ground, like those of a maiden lady being terrorized by a mouse.

'Got him', I announced.

'Dead?'

'Nope, surrendered. Not a scratch.' I affected a calm I did not feel. 'Ah—shall we proceed with the hearing?'

Color and confidence were returning rapidly to the Judge. He lowered his feet and his gown, 'Of course, of course', he said gruffly. 'Go tell 'em fetch him in.'

I paused at the courtroom door and turned back. 'Hardware this time, your Honor?'

His Honor pondered a moment and then smiled at me ever so faintly. 'Hardware this time', he ruled. '*All* of it.'

WILLIAM HENRY UPJOHN (1853–1941)

King's Counsel

348

The narrator is Sir Patrick Hastings

I HAVE known many great lawyers, many of whom have received not only my admiration but affection, for, strange though it may seem, to be a great lawyer is not necessarily to be a bore. There are exceptions, especially among men of the older school, as for instance, the famous Mr Upjohn. Undoubtedly a great lawyer, as a man I found it usually took him two days to say what anyone else could have said in an hour.

I well remember a young solicitor who was instructing Upjohn in an important case, when the exigencies of war removed the young man to military service in France during the First World War. Such was the importance of the action that he received formal notification that he had been granted fourteen days' special leave to return to England for the purpose of the trial.

To that notification he sent the following reply:

I am now on military duty engaged in the task of shifting manure. I prefer that duty to that of instructing Mr Upjohn for fourteen days in the Privy Council.

BAILIE WALLACE OF TAIN (*fl. c.*1900)

349

The administration of justice in Tain.

ON the bench was Bailie Wallace, tall, white-bearded, aged eighty, and a senior partner in Wallace and Frazer, a firm of large iron-mongers in the town.

The Bailie's shop was opposite the court-house, and he was working at his ledger when a policeman entered.

'Could you come over to the court-house, Bailie, for minute. We've got a case.'

'Tut, tut. You see I'm busy. Can you not get one of the others?'

'No, no Bailie. You're the only one.'

'Well, well', and the Bailie carefully removed his spectacles, put them in their case, took his silk top-hat from its peg, and walked across the street.

In the dock was Jeannagh, an old crofter, with a face like a witch. She was charged with stealing a sheep. She had not killed the sheep, but it was found in an out-house on her croft. She pleaded guilty and the Bailie addressed her.

'You've pled guilty to stealing a sheep, a crime for which no more than a hundred years ago you would have been hanged.'

'Ay, Bailie, and wouldna that have been a fine disgrace to the town of Tain?'

'Hold your tongue, woman. You're fined half a crown.'

'Then ye can pay it yersel' Bailie.'

'I'll do no such thing. There's an account of two and sixpence against you for two years in our books for a new broom.'

In the dock stood Davy.

'Well, Davy. What's it this time?'

'Drunk and disorderly', answered the gaoler.

'Tut, tut', said the Bailie. 'This will never do. Ye'll be fined half a crown, or a day in prison.'

'All right, Bailie. And you can pay the fine yersel.'

'You dirty trouster', shouted the Bailie. 'How many times have I paid your fines. If you can't afford to pay your fines, you've no business to get drunk.'

A lecture on temperance followed, but towards the end of his remarks the Bailie thrust his hand into his pocket, pulled out half a crown, placed it on the bench, and walked back to his shop. It may be it was out of consideration for his own pocket that the Bailie seldom fined anyone more that half a crown. He died at the age of a hundred.

EARL WARREN (1891–1974)

American Chief Justice and Statesman

350

IN the summer following his junior year, young Warren worked for the Southern Pacific as a call-boy. He was paid twenty-two cents an hour to corral the crew when a train was scheduled to start its run. He put in a twelve-hour day, covering the town on his bicycle, flushing crewmen from a front-porch swing, a neighbourhood bar, a floating crap game, or a crib in Jap Alley, where Japanese girls smiled at male passersby from windows hung with colorful paper lanterns.

A few blocks away, John Withington's saloon near Nineteenth and K streets was a hangout for the town's politicians. On election day party workers would round up the hobos strung out along the Southern Pacific tracks and herd them to the polls, where they cast ballots in the name of dead men still listed as registered voters. A dormant propriety awakened in the saloon keeper one day when he called out to a derelict about to palm himself off as a dead Withington: 'No, you can't vote in the name of my father!'

'It was a wild, wild town', Omar Cavins recalls. 'There was always a poker game going on in the back room at the Arlington saloon. I've seen twenty-dollar gold pieces stacked on the table as high as a player's head. There were three dance halls—the Owl, the Standard and the Palace. They charged two-bits a dance, and the Johns were encouraged to buy the Janes a glass of colored water—cold tea, I suppose. I used to stuff myself on the free lunches, and if I had a nickel, I'd buy a beer. They didn't pay any attention to kids. You could help yourself.'

Barging in and out of saloons and poker parlors, tracking down an elusive engineer, young Warren was soon on the best of terms with local dealers and croupiers. They took professional pride in demonstrating the technique of dealing from the bottom of the deck and slipping a pair of loaded dice into a friendly crap game. This technical information was filed away in the boy's memory, to be drawn on later when he started tidying up Alameda County.

EDWARD HENRY WARREN (1873–1945)

American Jurist

351

ON one occasion a student made a curiously inept response to a question from Professor Warren. 'The Bull' roared at him, 'You will never make a lawyer. You might just as well pack up your books now and leave the school.'

The student rose, gathered his notebooks and started to leave, pausing only to say, in full voice, 'I accept your suggestion, Sir, but I do not propose to leave without giving myself the pleasure of telling you to go plumb straight to hell.'

'Sit down, Sir, sit down', said the Bull. 'Your response makes it clear that my judgement was too hasty.'

RICHARD EDWARD WEBSTER (LORD ALVERSTONE) (1842–1915)

Lord Chief Justice

352

SOME amusing and curious evidence was given at the trial. Among other witnesses who were called for the plaintiff was a doctor, who alleged quite seriously that the distance to which infection would extend depended entirely upon the number of patients collected at one spot, and that it would travel in exact proportion to that number. I had to cross-examine him, and his answers were both amusing and instructive as showing the extent to which a person can bring himself to believe in a theory.

I said: 'I understand you to say, Doctor, that if with one patient there would be risk of infection at a distance of, say, ten yards, with two at twenty yards, and so on, it follows that if there were a thousand patients there would be risk of infection several miles away.'

'Exactly, that is my meaning.'

'Well,' I put to him, 'it has nothing to do with the case, but for the satisfaction of his lordship and myself, will you tell me some place in

London where we should be comparatively safe from infection from smallpox?'

He replied: 'The middle of Hyde Park and 29, Pembroke Gardens'—which was his own house.

HENRY WYNDHAM WEST (1848–90)

Queen's Counsel

353

The narrator is Sir Edward Parry

WHEN I first joined the Northern Circuit, I remember Louis Aitken giving me a graphic account of an encounter between West and Lord Chief Justice Coleridge. He used to say it was the most exciting contest he had ever witnessed between Bench and Bar. Every word uttered by the combatants was charged with venom, yet spoken with honeyed courtesy and, on West's part, with an almost reverent respect for the Bench, if not for its immediate occupant. All this was heightened by the tense stillness of the Court during the few minutes the battle lasted.

West was defending some men for assault upon a woman. Nash and Aitken were his juniors. He had put up some men in the Court and asked the woman questions about them. He did not call the men as witnesses.

After West had made his speech to the jury, during which there had been several skirmishes between Coleridge and himself, the Lord Chief Justice began the summing up. West went out of the Court. The Chief commented severely upon West omitting to call the men who had been shown to the jury. Nash jumped up to remonstrate, but Lord Coleridge swept him aside. Aitken went out for West, who returned and made an endeavour to intercept the judge for which he was strongly rebuked, and the summing up continued to the end, and the jury retired.

Then West, with aristocratic humility, but in the tone of a schoolmaster who is going to administer punishment at the end of the lecture, began:

'My Lord, I understand your Lordship commented unfavourably on my action in not calling as witnesses the men who were put up in court for identification by the prosecutrix.'

'I did, indeed, Mr West', replied Coleridge in his silkiest manner. 'Very unfavourably. Indeed, I regretted to feel compelled to make such strictures on the conduct of counsel.'

'I felt sure your Lordship would, and it is with equal regret, and only because it is my duty to the prisoners and your Lordship, that I must call your Lordship's attention to the case of the *Queen against Holmes* reported in 1871 in the first volume of the Law Reports Crown Cases Reserved, at page 334. This case overruled the case of the *Queen against Robinson* which doubtless your Lordship remembers.'

'And what does the *Queen against Holmes* decide, Mr West?'

'It decides that such witnesses cannot be called', said West, handing up the volume with a grave bow. 'Your Lordship will find that the Court of Crown Cases Reserved had exactly the same point before them that your Lordship referred to in this case, and the court overruled your Lordship's learned father for the same error that your Lordship has fallen into this morning.'

Coleridge did not lose his head, but replied with a charming bow and sweet smile, 'I am much indebted to you, Mr West.'

West bowed low, and the duel was over.

Coleridge had to send for the jury and tell them his mistake, which he did, of course, amply and thoroughly, and the men were acquitted.

JAMES ABBOTT McNEILL WHISTLER
(1834–1903)

354

In the famous case of Whistler v. Ruskin the artist had sued the critic for a criticism of one of his 'nocturnes' so outrageous as to amount to a libel. Ruskin had written, 'I have seen and heard much of cockney impudence before now but never expected to hear a coxcomb ask two hundred guineas for flinging a pot of paint in the public's face.' 'Coxcomb' was unkind, but Whistler, known to his disciples as 'the Master', was undoubtedly extravagant in his dress and behaviour.

SIR JOHN HOLKER, the Attorney-General (appearing for Ruskin) perhaps intended Whistler to betray his extravagances to the jury, as Buzfuz hoped to do with Sam Weller, but history repeated itself, and the witness was the victor.

'How long', asked Sir John, 'did it take you to knock off that nocturne?'

'About two days, perhaps', replied the artist.

'Oh, two days! The labour of two days, then, is that for which you ask two hundred guineas?'

'No: I ask it for the knowledge of a life time.'

There you have one of those brilliant impromptus which followers of 'the Master' boasted of, and sometimes used as their own. It was a crushing reply to a fellow-man-of-art who was sitting with a hundred guinea brief in front of him 'knocking off' a day's work.

But his final blow to Holker left him dead upon the field. The advocate asked him: 'Do you think now that you could make make *me* see the beauty of that picture?'

Whistler gazed at the picture and at the Attorney-General attentively, several times, scanning his face carefully. At the end of a long silence he said, with judicial gravity, 'I fear it would be as hopeless as for a musician to pour his notes into the ear of a deaf man.'

SIR WILLIAM WIGHTMAN (1784–1863)

355

The narrator is Serjeant Ballantine

MR WIGHTMAN afterwards became one of the Judges of the Court of Queen's Bench, and a very efficient and useful one. He had a certain amount of dry humour, an instance of which I remember upon a trial at the Maidstone Assizes. A very excellent and learned friend of mine, not famed for his brevity, had been for some considerable time enforcing his arguments before a Kentish jury. Mr Justice Wightman, interposing, said Mr — you have stated that before': and then, pausing for a moment, added, 'but you may have forgotten it. It was a *very* long time ago.'

JAMES PLAISTER WILDE (LORD PENZANCE) (1816–99)

356

MR WILDE (afterwards Lord Penzance) when a Queen's Counsel was a remarkable advocate, with the advantage of a good presence, and unlike many eminent leaders generally took a favourable view of a case before it came on, instead of suggesting difficulties. If he lost the verdict he would say: 'We can't always win.' On one occasion he adopted a remarkable course with great success. It was an action against a shipowner for alleged negligent damage to the cargo. The plaintiff, who did not enjoy a very good reputation, had given evidence and been cross-examined at length by Mr Wilde, with the result that it clearly appeared that at all events the claim was grossly exaggerated, and in fact fraudulent, but that did not necessarily preclude the plaintiff from recovering something. When the plaintiff's counsel said in the usual way on the conclusion of the evidence, 'That is the plaintiff's case', Mr Wilde, instead of proceeding in the ordinary way to address the jury, repeated, 'That's the plaintiff's case', and paused. The jury looked puzzled, and Mr Wilde repeated with emphasis, 'That's the plaintiff's case', and again paused. The jury thereupon began to talk to each other, and for a third time Mr Wilde with increased emphasis said: 'THAT'S the plaintiff's case', and paused. The foreman of the jury then got up and said: 'My lord, we think there is no case', and thus the defendant had the verdict. Had the trial proceeded the plaintiff would probably have obtained a verdict for small damages, for I doubt whether our witnesses would have been able to justify the way they had treated the cargo. Chief Baron Pollock, who tried the case, made no remark.

When at the Bar Mr Wilde frequently said he would never accept a judgeship, but he married when in extensive practice as a prominent leader, and then was appointed a Baron of the Exchequer. When reminded of what he had said when at the Bar he replied: 'Marriage is, as you know, a revocation of a man's will.'

SIR JAMES SHAW WILLES (1814–72)

357

WHEN Mr Justice Willes was made a judge he suggested to many of his clients that they should send their papers to Mr Vernon Harcourt. In consequence Mr Harcourt was, at that time, constantly referred to as 'the Codicil'.

MONTAGUE STEPHEN WILLIAMS (1835–92)

Queen's Counsel

358

ONCE, at the Old Bailey, a tradesman, apparently of the highest possible respectability, was placed upon his trial upon a charge of fraud. I forget now who prosecuted him, but I was counsel for the defence. He had been in very large business as a florist, nurseryman, and fruit-grower, in the neighbourhood once famous for the Cremorne Gardens; and, yielding to the general feeling in favour of joint-stock enterprises, he had turned his business into a company, and secured one or two of the nobility as directors.

The company was eventually wound up; and the charge against the prisoner was that, when he knew perfectly well that matters were coming to a crisis, he had represented to a lady, desirous of investing a small capital to advantage, that the concern was in a most flourishing condition and likely to pay a good dividend. It was alleged that, in consequence of those false representations, a number of shares which he had received as part payment for the good-will of the business had been taken over by the lady.

Lord Suffield was one of the directors. He appeared in Court, being accommodated, as they say in the newspapers, with a seat upon the bench. He had come prepared to be called as a witness by me, if necessary, to depose that, to the best of his belief, at the time the defendant made the representations, they were justified by the condition of the company.

On reading my brief I was convinced of the bona fides of my client. I was, and always shall be, of opinion that he had intended no fraud. It is natural, therefore, that I looked upon the case as what is termed familiarly among us as a 'galloping acquittal'.

It so happened that I had been principally engaged during the week in the Court in which this case was tried. This was the last day of the sittings, and I had therefore been addressing the same jury two or three times on each of the preceding five days. As was so often the case, having been in the company of this particular set of men from ten in the morning to five or six in the evening, I was on excellent terms with them—that is, of course, from a distance. I had, indeed, been more fortunate than usual in my verdicts with this jury.

At the end of the case for the prosecution, I looked, with a shrug of the shoulders, towards my twelve friends, as much as to ask the question in dumb show, would they like me to address them? To my astonishment, they all, and more particularly the foreman, met me with severe looks. I therefore proceeded to address them, and, having argued upon the merits of the case, stated that, if they were not satisfied with the observations I had made, Lord Suffield and another director would enter the box, to give their opinion of the defendant's character, and of the position of the company at the time the alleged false representations were made. I looked at the jury again, expecting to get some expression of opinion; but once more was I grievously disappointed. I called my witnesses, and among them, his lordship, who bore out precisely the contentions I had urged on behalf of my client. The Judge summed up, and the jury turned round in their box to consider their verdict. They consulted together for some considerable time, and I confess that I soon began to lose my temper. What on earth could it mean? In a little while the foreman turned round and said, 'My lord, we can't agree—we should like to retire and talk it over'; and retire they accordingly did. Hours passed by, and when at length the ordinary time arrived for the rising of the Court, the jury were sent for. They stated that there was not the smallest prospect of their coming to a unanimous conclusion, and they were accordingly discharged.

As I was picking up my papers with, I am afraid, a somewhat fiendish expression upon my face, the foreman of the jury, accompanied by one or two of his fellows, approached me on the way to the corridor. Pausing for a moment, he said:

'Very sorry, Mr Montague, couldn't vote for you in the last case. We always like to give you a verdict when we can; but we really couldn't do it this time.'

'What on earth do you mean?' I said. 'I never heard of such stupidity in the whole course of my life. The man is as much guilty as you are.'

'Ah,' was the reply, 'he's your client, of course, and we know you're very staunch. But not a bit of it—I hate them d . . . d lords. What business, sir, has a lord turning shopkeeper? What right have they to become tradesmen? Let 'em be lords, or let 'em be tradesmen. I don't like 'em as lords, but when they combine the two, you may depend upon it there's fraud somewhere, and they don't have no vote of mine'; whereupon, looking at me with a knowing wink, he passed from the Court into the corridor.

[*At the re-hearing the judge, without calling on the Defence, directed the Jury that there was no case to answer.*]

359

THE Chairman of a Bench of County Magistrates was a large landed proprietor. He had among his labourers a very useful man who was somewhat of a favourite of his. This person had taken a fancy to some of his neighbour's fowls, was arrested, and was brought before the local Bench. They sent him to take his trial at the Quarter Sessions over which his master presided. Upon the case being called on, the prisoner, in answer to the charge, pleaded 'Guilty'. The chairman, nevertheless, went on trying the case, and had the prisoner given in charge of the jury, just as though the plea had involved a denial of the accusation. Knowing that the chairman was very deaf, a counsel present jumped up, and, as *amicus curiae*, ventured to interpose, and to remind his worship that the prisoner had confessed his guilt. Upon this, the presiding genius flew into a tremendous passion, begged that the learned counsel would not interrupt him, and exclaimed:

'Pleaded guilty! I know he did; but you don't know him as well I as I do. He's one of the biggest liars in the neighbourhood, and I wouldn't believe him on his oath.'

360

Williams had lost his loved dog, Rob.

ABOUT three weeks after the date of my dog's departure, I was sitting in my chambers reading briefs. My clerk entered, and announced that a man had called who stated that he wished to see me on urgent private business, but that he must decline to give his name. The man was shown in, and the moment he entered I had a correct presentiment as to the nature of his business.

'Lost a dawg, sir, I believe?', said he, 'collie dawg, valuable dawg, sir. I've heard of one which answers the description from nose to tail. If it's all square and right, guv'nor, I knows a pal of mine as might be able to work the hanimal back.'

So anxious was I to recover Rob that I was willing to agree to any terms, and gave in without further parlance. It was arranged that I was to bring the money (£20) in gold to Shoreditch Church at half-past seven o'clock that night.

At the right time I sallied forth to keep my appointment. I don't think I was ever out on a worse evening. The wind was blowing a hurricane, and a mixture of snow and hail was falling. It was certainly not a fit night to turn a dog out—but I was going to try and bring one home. Passing from King's Bench Walk across the Temple Square, and through Serjeants' Inn into Fleet Street, I hailed a hansom, jumped in, and, in about five-and-twenty minutes, was standing on the pavement outside the railings of Shoreditch Church.

For some time I stared anxiously through the snow and mist without seeing a soul. Presently, however, a man, with a peculiarly halting gait, emerged into sight, and came shambling up to me.

'Dawg, sir?', said he, touching his hat, 'come about a dawg lost in Upper Brook Street, £20 reward? Are you the gentleman?'

It was not a night to stand arguing, so I quickly gave the stranger to understand that I was the gentleman, that I wanted my dog, and that I was quite prepared to hand him over the money.

'Wait a minute, sir', he said. 'Business can't be done in that sort of way. You are not on the cross, sir? By yourself? No coppers about, eh?'

I hastened to assure him that he had nothing to fear from me, that I had given the necessary promise to his agent in the morning, and that my word was my bond. To my astonishment and disgust, he then informed me that the dog was not in his possession, but that, if I followed him to the second-class refreshment-room at Bishopsgate Station, the transaction should be completed. It was, I confess, with great difficulty that I kept my temper. Muttering something not very complimentary to my guide, I told him to lead the way, and that I would follow.

When we were close to the station, my companion was joined by another man. We all three then proceeded down the platform, to a dark corner near the second-class refreshment-room.

'Now, sir,' said the man whom I had encountered outside the church, 'give us the quids, and in five minutes you shall have the dawg.'

I thought this rather a cool request, and explained that the proposal would not suit me at all. I was not such a fool, I said, as to hand him the money before he handed me the dog. A good deal of haggling then took place between us, and it was finally arranged that he should go and fetch the dog, while his friend remained by my side with the twenty sovereigns in his hand.

In a few minutes the man returned with Rob. The sagacious creature, on catching sight of me, nearly broke away from the rope by which he was led. The transaction was now duly completed; I took the dog, and the man who had restored the animal took the money.

It was bitterly cold, and wishing (for reasons I will presently explain) to know something more about my companions, I invited them to come into the refreshment-room and have something to drink. Needless to say, the offer was promptly accepted. Standing beside the bar, we had a tolerably long chat. My Shoreditch friend, after partaking somewhat liberally of hot whisky and water, described, in answer to my questions, the manner in which the dog had been abducted. He explained that he and his companions waited for days before they could capture Rob, and that, on being enticed from the street-door on the Sunday morning, he was bundled into a covered baker's barrow in waiting round the corner.

I ventured to remark to my two acquaintances that they must be doing a thriving business, £20 being a large sum to receive for the restoration of one dog. The answer I received was that it was 'only two quid apiece, as there are ten of us in it, and it is share and share alike'. I then somewhat modestly remarked that, knowing who I was, I thought it rather too bad of them to steal my dog.

'Ah! that's the best of it,' said one of them, 'Lord, sir, you should have seen how my pal Bill here did laugh. "Ain't it rather hard", says I, "to take the counsellor's dawg?" "Not a bit, Jim," says he; "he's had a good lot out of us, and why shouldn't we get a little out of him?" '

The two scoundrels went into a fit of laughter, and I am very much afraid that I joined in the merriment. As I said before, however, I had my own reasons for prolonging the interview. The truth is, a friend and neighbour of mine, living in Norfolk Street, Park Lane, had lately lost her collie for the fourth time. For weeks she had been endeavouring in vain to recover the animal. I now introduced the subject of my neighbour's loss, and was not long in discovering that the collie was in the hands of these Philistines. After ordering some more whisky and water for the party, I offered half the sum I had paid for the recovery of my own dog, for the recovery of my friend's. This they seemed to regard as an excellent joke, and on my venturing to remind the Shoreditch gentleman that the collie in question was an old one and not so valuable as mine, the scoundrel replied:

'Quite true, sir; he's an old 'un, and not so much value in the market as the other. He wouldn't do for exportation like yours' (here was a fate my poor friend had been saved from!); 'but he belongs to a lady. She's so fond of him; and the gents, too, they dotes on him. He's a reg'lar old family relic. You must spring a good deal more on him before you can expect to get him back.'

This was rather more than I could stand, and feeling that there was no chance of the negotiations coming to a successful issue, I proceeded, in rather forcible terms, to give the speaker a piece of mind.

'Not going to round on us, guv'nor?', he replied; 'not going to round? We knew that we could take the counsellor's word, and he ain't a-going to break it?'

I at once put his mind at rest on that score. I added that though, according to the treaty, he was safe for that night, it was not likely I should forget the features and appearance of the man who had helped to deprive the 'counsellor' of his favourite dog.

The interview was over. Muttering something, the two men hurried off. Rob and I jumped into a hansom, and within an hour, both of us were at home, asleep before the fire.

Two years passed away, and once more it was clear the 'Forty Thieves' were at work. They levied contributions from the public with more daring than ever. Things came to such a pass, indeed, that the authorities had to take the matter up.

In my official capacity as Counsel to the Treasury for the County of Middlesex, I was instructed to prosecute various dog-stealers who had been arrested by the police. The very first case of this description was that of a man who had frequently been convicted for the offence. By statute, the maximum punishment for dog-stealing, even after previous convictions, is only eighteen months' hard labour; a dog, for some reason or other which I never could understand, being, by the law of England, regarded as not a chattel. On reading the depositions before drawing the indictment, I found that the dog, when stolen, had a collar on. I resolved, therefore, to draw two indictments: one for felony (stealing the collar); the other for the statutable misdemeanour of stealing a dog, after previous convictions for the same offence. I determined to try the man for the misdemeanour first, and then, if he were convicted, to proceed with the charge of felony. The truth is, I had not forgotten the £20.

The indictments were preferred and found, and the prisoner came up to plead. Judge of my astonishment and delight when I found myself face to face with my old Shoreditch friend. He recognised me at a glance, and the expression of the rascal's face was most ludicrous. From start to finish of the trial, he never took his eyes off me once. During my opening of the case his face grew longer and longer. He seemed not to pay the slightest attention to his own counsel, Mr Thorne Cole.

The jury returned a verdict of 'Guilty'; and when I expressed my intention of trying the prisoner again, for the theft of the collar, he seemed to give a long, low kind of whistle.

The second trial took place, and the man was again convicted. He was sentenced to eighteen months' imprisonment for the misdemeanour, and twelve months' for the felony, the terms of confinement to run consecutively. It is a known fact that habitual criminals prefer penal servitude to two years hard labour; and it was clear that the prospect of thirty months on the latter condition somewhat staggered the prisoner. He put his hand up to his head, and, looking very hard at me, muttered, as he was hurried off to the cells: 'Thought he'd have me some day. He's made me pay d . . . dear at last for those pieces.'

SIR JOHN EARDLEY WILMOT (1709–92)

361

SOMEWHERE about 1760 there was a strange affair at an Assize at Worcester. Sir Eardley Wilmot, then Judge of the King's Bench, and later Chief Justice of the Common Pleas, writes thus to his wife:

I send this by express, on purpose to prevent your being frightened, in consequence of a most terrible accident at this place. Between two and three, as we were trying causes, a stack of chimneys blew upon the top of that part of the hall where I was sitting, and beat the roof down upon us; but as I sat up close to the wall, I have escaped without the least hurt. When I saw it begin to yield and open, I despaired of my own life and the lives of all within the compass of the roof. Mr John Lawes is killed, and the attorney in the cause which was trying is killed, and I am afraid some others: there were many wounded and bruised. It was the most frightful scene I ever beheld. I was just beginning to sum up the evidence, to the jury, and intending to go immediately after I had finished. Most of the counsel were gone, and they who remained in court are very little hurt, though they seemed to be in the place of greatest danger. . . . Two of the jurymen who were trying the cause are killed, and they are carrying dead and wounded bodies out of the ruins still.

In another letter he says,

It was an image of the last day, when there shall be no distinction of persons, for my robes did not make way for me. I believe an earthquake arose in the minds of most people, and there was an apprehension of the fall of the whole hall.

Lord Campbell adds:

His safety is supposed to have been entirely owing to his presence of mind, which induced him to remain composedly in his place till the confusion was over—a circumstance which, with his usual modesty, he suppresses.

(MOSES) WISNER (1815–64)

District Attorney in, and Governor of, Michigan USA

362

In combating the defence of Act of God set up by an American advocate who was defending a client on a charge of arson, Governor Wisner, for the prosecution, disposed of the theory of spontaneous combustion, and succeeded in satisfying the jury of its absurdity.

'It is said, gentlemen, that this was Act of God. It may be, gentlemen. It may be. I believe in the Almighty's power to do it. But I never knew of His walking twice round a stack to find a dry place to fire it, with double-nailed boots on so exactly fitting the ones worn by the defendant.'

ALEXANDER WOOLLCOTT (1887–1943)

363

How to influence a jury.

IN 1920 a certain Carl Wanderer, wishing to dispose of his wife, picked up a tramp in the street, hired him as an accomplice, and planned a bogus hold-up, spinning into that luckless ear a tall tale about the great roll of bills which his stingy wife always carried in her purse. It was arranged that after the hold-up the two were to meet down the street and divide the proceeds. What eventually hanged Wanderer, in addition to his using two guns both of which could be traced to himself, was the fact that during the excitement he lost his head, such as it was, and killed his wife and the tramp *with the same gun*.

The word 'eventually' is used advisedly, for when he was tried for the murder of his wife, Wanderer was defended by foxy lawyers who were capable of maintaining—in one breath—that the confession which Wanderer had made to the police had been extracted by brute force; that Wanderer was crazy as a coot; and that anyway it had all been done by a couple of other fellows. These forensic didoes so bemused the jury that, after deliberating for twenty-three hours, they brought in a verdict of guilty but—as is the privilege of juries in Illinois—so limited the penalty that he need only behave himself in prison to be turned loose after thirteen years.

As a comment on this verdict the Hearst morning paper came out next day with a photograph of those jurors under the caption 'A Dozen Soft-boiled Eggs'. It also published the names, addresses and telephone numbers of each, together with a broad hint that any disapproving citizen might do well to call them up. Thanks to these tactics a second jury arrived in court freshly admonished as to its duty. For Wanderer was not out of the woods yet. He could not be tried again for the offence of killing his wife, but he stood accused of another. That was the killing of his forlorn accomplice, the tramp, who still lay unidentified on a slab in the morgue. It took the second jury less that half an hour to reach a verdict which sent him to the gallows.

WILDEY WRIGHT (1840–1910)

364

A CHAPTER would be needed for Wildey Wright. When were ever such splendid periods—such flights of oratorical fancy? In the hands of Wildey Wright a County Court case became a State trial. Before the midday adjournment he was magnificent; after that interval, stupendous. Johnsonian in the morning, he was Demosthenic in the afternoon. No pen could describe, no mimic could reproduce, the rich fruitiness of his language or the overwhelming pomp of his manner. 'I am convinced', he said to Mr Justice Lawrence while opening an 'Order XIV' case in which he represented the holder in due course of a bill of exchange, 'that your Lordship will not sully your hitherto unspotted ermine by giving effect to the preposterous defence foreshadowed in the defendant's affidavit.' 'Well and bravely spoken, like a high-minded and generous opponent!', he remarked to a fierce member of the Bar, who had just concluded a violent attack upon him. Nor was he readily rebuffed. After he had secured from a jury in the City of London Court a verdict of which the Judge strongly disapproved, his application for various items of costs requiring the certificate of the Judge was received in stony silence; 'I gather,' said Wildey Wright, 'from your Honour's genial nod that my application is granted.'

It was in answer to Mr Justice Day that he explained how the lady he represented was able accurately to fix the vital date. His client had purchased an expectant cow, and immediately after the purchase had been made, 'there sprang up', said Wildey Wright, 'as between my lady client and the cow, a species of friendly rivalry as to which should add to the population. So it was that she was able to speak with precision on the point'.

SOURCES AND ACKNOWLEDGEMENTS

1. Edward Abinger, *Forty Years at the Bar* (Hutchinson, 1930).

2. C. P. Harvey, *The Advocate's Devil* (Stevens & Sons, 1958). Reprinted by permission of Sweet & Maxwell Ltd.

3. Sergeant A. M. Sullivan, *The Last Sergeant* (1952). Reprinted by permission of Macdonald & Co. (Publishers) Ltd.

4. James Agate, *Ego 2* (Gollancz, 1936). Reprinted by permission of A. D. Peters & Co. Ltd.

5. *James Agate Anthology*, ed. Herbert Van Thal (Rupert Hart-Davis, 1961). Reprinted by permission of Granada Publishing Ltd.

6. *Reminiscences of Sir Henry Hawkins*, ed. Richard Harris (London, 1904).

7. Gilchrist Gibb Alexander, *Temple of the Nineties* (William Hodge, 1938).

8. *Felix Frankfurter Reminiscences, Recorded Talks with Dr Harlan B. Phillips* (1960). Copyright © 1960 by Harlan B. Phillips. Reprinted by permission of William Morrow & Company.

9. Sir Gervais Rentoul, *Sometimes I Think* (1940). Reprinted by permission of Mrs Rentoul and Hodder & Stoughton Ltd.

10. Bernard Botein, *Trial Judge* (1952). Copyright © 1952, 1980 by Bernard Botein. Reprinted by permission of Simon & Schuster, Inc.

11. A. S. Gillespie-Jones, *The Lawyer Who Laughed* (1978). Reprinted by permission of Hutchinson Australia.

12. *A Lawyer's Notebook*, Anon. (Secker & Warburg, 1933).

13. Fredrick Trevor Hill, *Lincoln the Lawyer* (New York, 1912).

14. Serjeant Robinson, *Bench and Bar* (London, 1889).

15. Barry O'Brien, *Lord Russell of Killowen* (London, 1901).

16. Gordon Lang, *Mr Justice Avory* (Herbert Jenkins, 1935).

17. G. D. Roberts, *Law and Life* (W. H. Allen, 1964). Reprinted by permission of Mrs G. D. Roberts.

18–19. Sydney Aylett, *Under their Wigs* (1978). Reprinted by permission of Methuen, London and the Estate of Reginald Crutchley.

20–2. J. H. Balfour-Browne, *Forty Years at the Bar* (London, 1916).

23. Serjeant Robinson, *Bench and Bar* (London, 1889).

24. F. W. Ashley, *My Sixty Years in the Law* (John Lane, 1936).

25. Sir Edward Chandos Leigh, *Bar, Bat and Bit* (London, 1913).

26. *Memoirs of Edward Vaughan Kenealy* (London, 1898).

27. F. D. MacKinnon, *On Circuit* (1940). Reprinted by permission of Cambridge University Press.

28. A. S. Gillespie-Jones, *The Lawyer Who Laughed* (1978). Reprinted by permission of Hutchinson Australia.

29–30. Max Beerbohm, *Yet Again* (Heinemann, 1922). Reprinted by permission of Mrs Eva Reichmann.

31. J. B. Atlay, *Victorian Chancellors*, vol. 2 (London, 1908).

32. Iain Adamson, *The Old Fox* (Frederick Muller, 1963). Reprinted by permission of the author.

33. *Reflections and Recollections by His Honour J. D. Crawford* (London, 1936).

34. H. Montgomery Hyde, *Lord Justice: The Life and Times of Lord Birkett of Ulverston.* Copyright © 1964 by H. Montgomery Hyde. Reprinted by permission of Random House, Inc, and Hamish Hamilton Ltd. Published in the UK with the title *Lord Birkett.*

35. Sydney Aylett, *Under their Wigs* (1978). Reprinted by permission of Methuen, London and the Estate of Reginald Crutchley.

36. H. Montgomery Hyde, *Lord Justice: The Life and Times of Lord Birkett of Ulverston.* Copyright © 1964 by H. Montgomery Hyde. Reprinted by permission of Random House, Inc and Hamish Hamilton Ltd. Published in the UK with the title *Lord Birkett.*

37. *The Black Book,* An Exposition of Abuses in Church and State (London, 1832).

38. *Boswell's London Journal, 1762–1763,* ed. Frederick A. Pottle (New York, 1950).

39. From the preface by Christopher Morley to the Yale Edition of *Boswell's London Journal.* Printed with permission of Yale University and the McGraw-Hill Book Company (William Heinemann Ltd.).

40–1. Bernard Botein, *Trial Judge* (1952). Copyright © 1952, 1980 by Bernard Botein. Reprinted by permission of Simon & Schuster, Inc.

42. G. D. Roberts, *Without My Wig* (Macmillan, 1957). Reprinted by permission of Mrs G. D. Roberts.

43. J. D. Casswell, *A Lance for Liberty* (1961). Reprinted by permission of Harrap Ltd.

44. Gordon Lang, *Mr Justice Avory* (Herbert Jenkins, 1938).

45. J. D. Casswell, *A Lance for Liberty* (1961). Reprinted by permission of Harrap Ltd.

46. Sir Henry Stewart Cunningham, *Lord Bowen* (privately printed, 1896).

47. Montague Williams, *Leaves of a Life* (London, 1890).

48. Theobald Mathew, *For Lawyers and Others* (William Hodge, 1937). Reprinted by permission of T. D. Mathew.

49. Lord Alverstone, *Recollections of Bar and Bench* (London, 1914).

50–1. Sir Henry Stewart Cunningham, *Lord Bowen* (privately printed, 1896).

52. Lord Simon, *Retrospect* (1952). Reprinted by permission of Hutchinson Publishing Group Ltd., and Viscount Simon.

53. Ernest Bowen-Rowlands, *In the Light of the Law* (Grant Richards, 1931).

54. J. D. Casswell, *A Lance for Liberty* (1961). Reprinted by permission of Harrap Ltd.

55–6. Sir John Hollam, *Jottings of an Old Solicitor* (London, 1906).

57. W. Forbes-Gray, *Some Old Scots Judges* (London, 1914).

58. Serjeant Robinson, *Bench and Bar* (London, 1889).

59. A. S. Gillespie-Jones, *The Lawyer Who Laughed* (1978). Reprinted by permission of Hutchinson Australia.

60. J. B. Atlay, *The Victorian Chancellors* (London, 1908).

61. *Memoirs of Edward Vaughan Kenealy* (London, 1898).

62. Robert Graves, *They Hanged My Saintly Billy* (Cassell, 1957). Reprinted by permission of A. P. Watt Ltd. for the author.

63–5. George S. Hellman, *Benjamin N. Cardozo* (1940). Copyright 1940 George S. Hellman. Reprinted by permission of McGraw-Hill Book Company.

66. Gilchrist Gibb Alexander, *Temple of the Nineties* (William Hodge, 1930).

67. Edward Marjoribanks, *The Life of Lord Carson* (Gollancz, 1932). Reprinted by permission of A. D. Peters & Co. Ltd.

68–9. Edward Abinger, *Forty Years at the Bar* (Hutchinson, 1930).

70. Joseph S. Auerbach, *The Bar of Other Days* (Harper & Row, 1940). Copyright © renewed 1968 by Mrs Helen D. Emmet.

71. J. Alderson Foote, *Pie-Powder* (John Murray, 1911).

72–5. Iain Adamson, *A Man of Quality* (Frederick Muller, 1964). Reprinted by permission of the author.

76. Sir Edward Chandos-Leigh, *Bar, Bat and Bit* (London, 1913).

77. Hailiday Sutherland, *A Time to Keep* (Geoffrey Bles, 1934).

78–9. Theron G. Strong, *Joseph H. Choate* (1917). Reprinted by permission of Dodd, Mead & Company, Inc.

80–5. Edward G. Parker, *Reminiscences of Rufus Choate* (New York, 1860).

86–7. Sir Edward Clarke, *The Story of my Life* (London, 1918).

88. W. Forbes-Gray, *Some Old Scots Judges* (London, 1914).

89. Lord Alverstone, *Recollections of Bar and Bench* (London, 1914).

90. Gilchrist Gibb Alexander, *Temple in the Nineties* (William Hodge, 1938).

91. Ernest Hartley Coleridge, *Life and Correspondence of Lord Coleridge* (London, 1904).

92. Anthony Mockler, *Lions Under the Throne* (1983). Reprinted by permission of Muller, Blond & White Ltd.

93. J. Alderson Foote, *Pie-Powder* (John Murray, 1911).

94–6. J. B. Atlay, *The Victorian Chancellors*, vol. 1 (London, 1906).

97. *Memoirs of Edward Vaughan Kenealy*, ed. Arabella Kenealy (London, 1898).

98. Edmund D. Purcell, *Forty Years at the Criminal Bar* (London, 1916).

99. John D. Crawford, *Reflections and Recollections* (London, 1936)

100–1. William Charles Crocker, *Far from Humdrum* (1967). Reprinted by permission of Hutchinson Publishing Ltd.

102–7. Roland Wild and Derek Curtis-Bennett, *Curtis*. Originally published by Cassell & Co. Ltd. (1937). Reprinted with the permission of Macmillan Publishing Company.

108. J. D. Casswell, *A Lance for Liberty* (1961). Reprinted by permission of Harrap Ltd.

109. Sir Henry Dickens, *Recollections* (Heinemann, 1934). Reprinted by permission of the descendants of Sir Henry Fielding Dickens.

110–11. Sir Edward Parry, *My Own Way* (Cassell, 1932).

112–14. Derek Walker-Smith, *The Life of Charles Darling*. Originally published by Cassell & Co. Ltd. (1930). Reprinted with the permission of Macmillan Publishing Company.

115. Edward Maltby, *Secrets of a Solicitor* (London, 1929).

116. Derek Walker-Smith, *The Life of Charles Darling*. Originally published by Cassell & Co. (1938). Reprinted with the permission of Macmillan Publishing Company.

117. Edward Maltby, *Secrets of a Solicitor* (London, 1929).

118. C. P. Harvey, *The Advocate's Devil* (Stevens & Sons, 1958). Reprinted by permission of Sweet & Maxwell Ltd.

119–23. Irving Stone, *Clarence Darrow for the Defence* (1941). Copyright 1941 by Irving Stone. Reprinted by permission of Laurence Pollinger Ltd., and Doubleday & Company, Inc.

124. Theobald Mathew, *For Lawyers and Others* (William Hodge, 1937). Reprinted by permission of T. D. Mathew.

125. *Anecdotiana*, collected by an Eminent Literary Character (London, 1841).

126. Barry O'Brien, *Lord Russell of Killowen* (London, 1901).

127–8. Lord Denning, *The Family Story* (1981). Reprinted by permission of Butterworth Law Publishers Ltd.

129. A. S. Gillespie-Jones, *The Lawyer Who Laughed* (1978). Reprinted by permission of Hutchinson Australia.

130. Edward Abinger, *Forty Years at the Bar* (Hutchinson, 1930).

131–2. Sir Henry Fielding Dickens, *Recollections* (Heinemann, 1934). Reprinted by permission of the descendants of Sir Henry Fielding Dickens.

133. Lord Simon, *Retrospect* (1952). Reprinted by permission of Hutchinson Publishing Group Ltd. and Viscount Simon.

134. *Insurance Counsel Journal*, no. 25.

135. Sir Norman Skelhorn, *Public Prosecutor* (1981). Reprinted by permission of Harrap Ltd.

136. Ernest Bowen-Rowlands, *In the Light of the Law* (Grant Richards, 1931).

137. Edmund D. Purcell, *Forty Years at the Criminal Bar* (London, 1916).

138–9. Sir Travers Humphreys, *Criminal Days* (Hodder & Stoughton, 1946). Reprinted by permission of the Executors of the Estate.

140. Lord Elwyn-Jones, *In My Time* (1983). Reprinted by permission of George Weidenfeld & Nicolson Ltd.

141. Kylie Tennant, *Politics and Justice* (1970). Reprinted by permission of Angus K. Robertson (UK) Ltd.

142. *The Diary of John Evelyn* (Oxford University Press, 1959).

143. John Pugh, *Goodbye for Ever* (1981). Reprinted by permission of Barry Rose (Publishers) Ltd.

144. W. Forbes-Gray, *Some Old Scots Judges* (London, 1914).

145–6. J. Alderson Foote, *Pie-Powder* (John Murray, 1911).

147–9. *Felix Frankfurter Reminiscences: Recorded Talks with Dr Harlan B. Phillips* (1960). Copyright © 1960 by Harlan B. Phillips. Reprinted by permission of William Morrow & Company.

150–1. Muriel Box, *Rebel Advocate* (1983). Reprinted by permission of Victor Gollancz Ltd., and Eric Glass Ltd.

152. Frank Owen, *Tempestuous Journey* (1955). Reprinted by permission of Hutchinson Publishing Group Ltd.

153. F. W. Ashley, *My Sixty Years in the Law* (John Lane, 1936).

154. A. Wilson-Fox, *The Earl of Halsbury* (Chapman & Hall, 1929). By permission.

155. J. Alderson-Foote, *Pie-Powder* (John Murray, 1911).

156. A. Wilson-Fox, *The Earl of Halsbury* (Chapman & Hall, 1929). By permission.

157. Cecil Whiteley, *Brief Life* (1942). Reprinted by permission of Macmillan, London & Basingstoke.

158. A. S. Gillespie-Jones, *The Lawyer Who Laughed* (1978). Reprinted by permission of Hutchinson Australia.

159–60. Arthur Smith, *Lord Goddard* (1959). Reprinted by permission of George Weidenfeld & Nicolson Ltd.

161. Glyn Jones and Eric Grimshaw, *Lord Goddard* (Allan Wingate, 1958).

162. Joseph S. Auerbach, *The Bar of Other Days* (Harper & Row, 1940). Copyright © renewed 1968 by Mrs Helen D. Emmet.

163. Lord Simon, *Retrospect* (1952). Reprinted by permission of Hutchinson Publishing Group Ltd., and Viscount Simon.

164. Sir Edward Parry, *My Own Way* (Cassell, 1932).

165. Serjeant Robinson, *Bench and Bar* (London, 1889).

166. Theobald Mathew, *For Lawyers and Others* (William Hodge, 1937). Reprinted by permission of T. D. Mathew.

167–168. Edward Marjoribanks, *Sir Edward Marshall Hall* (Gollancz, 1929). Reprinted by permission of A. D. Peters & Co. Ltd.

169. John Mortimer, *Clinging to the Wreckage* (1982). Reprinted by permission of Weidenfeld & Nicolson Ltd., and A. D. Peters & Co. Ltd.

170. E. C. Bentley, *Those Days* (Constable, 1940). Reprinted by permission of Curtis Brown Group Ltd.

171. F. D. MacKinnon, *On Circuit* (1940). Reprinted by permission of Cambridge University Press.

172. Sir David Napley, *Not Without Prejudice* (1982). Reprinted by permission of Harrap Ltd.

173. George Lyttelton and Rupert Hart-Davis, *The Lyttelton/Hart-Davis Letters*, Vol. 1, (1978). © 1978 Sir Rupert Hart-Davis. Reprinted by permission of John Murray (Publ.) Ltd., and Academy, Chicago.

174. C. P. Harvey, *The Advocate's Devil* (Stevens & Sons, 1958). Reprinted by permission of Sweet & Maxwell Ltd.

175–6. Sir Patrick Gardiner Hastings, *Autobiography* (1948). Reprinted by permission of William Heinemann Ltd.

177. Sir David Napley, *Not Without Prejudice* (1982). Reprinted by permission of Harrap Ltd.

178. *Felix Frankfurter Reminiscences: Recorded Talks with Dr Harlan B. Phillips* (1960). Copyright © 1960 by Harlan B. Phillips. Reprinted by permission of William Morrow & Company.

179. Sir Patrick Gardiner Hastings, *Autobiography* (1948). Reprinted by permission of William Heinemann Ltd.

180. Reginald L. Hine, *Confessions of an Un-Common Attorney* (1945). Reprinted by permission of J. M. Dent & Sons Ltd.

181. *Reminiscences of Sir Henry Hawkins*, ed. Richard Harris (London, 1904).

182. Serjeant Robinson, *Bench and Bar* (London, 1889).

183. Sir Henry Dickens, *Recollections* (Heinemann, 1934). Reprinted by permission of the descendants of Sir Henry Fielding Dickens.

184. Edmund D. Purcell, *Forty Years at the Criminal Bar* (London, 1916).

185. *Reminiscences of Sir Henry Hawkins*, ed. Richard Harris (London, 1904).

186. Sir Travers Humphreys, *Criminal Days* (Hodder & Stoughton, 1940). Reprinted by permission of the Executors of the Estate.

187. Gordon Lang, *Mr Justice Avory* (Herbert Jenkins, 1935).

188. Arthur Garfield Hays, *City Lawyer: Autobiography of Arthur Garfield Hays* (1942). Copyright 1942 by Arthur Garfield Hays. Reprinted by permission of Simon & Schuster, Inc.

189–90. Maurice Healy, *The Old Munster Circuit* (1939). Reprinted by permission of Michael Joseph Ltd.

191. J. D. Casswell, *A Lance for Liberty* (1961). Reprinted by permission of Harrap Ltd.

192. Lord Alverstone, *Recollections of Bar and Bench* (London, 1914).

193. F. W. Ashley, *My Sixty Years in the Law* (John Lane, 1936).

194–5. H. A. Taylor, *Jix* (Stanley Paul & Co., 1933).

196. George Lyttelton and Rupert Hart-Davis, *The Lyttelton/Hart-Davis Letters* (1978). © 1978 Sir Rupert Hart-Davis. Reprinted by permission of John Murray (Publishers) Ltd., and Academy, Chicago.

197. Francis L. Wellman, *Day In Court* (New York, 1910).

198. Reginald L. Hine, *Confessions of an Un-Common Attorney* (1945). Reprinted by permission of J. M. Dent & Sons Ltd.

199. W. Forbes-Gray, *Some Old Scots Judges* (London, 1914).

200. A. E. Bowker, *Behind the Bar* (Staples Press, 1951). Reprinted by permission of Granada Publishing Ltd.

201. Henry Cecil, *Just Within the Law* (1975). © 1975 by Henry Cecil. Reprinted by permission of Hutchinson Publishing Group Ltd., and Curtis Brown Ltd. on behalf of the Estate of Henry Cecil.

202–5. Richard H. Rovere, *Howe and Hummel* (New York 1947).

206. *Memoirs of Edward Vaughan Kenealy* (London, 1898).

207. Richard H. Rovere, *Howe and Hummel* (New York, 1947).

208. Sir Travers Humphreys, *Criminal Days* (Hodder & Stoughton, 1946). Reprinted by permission of the Executors of the Estate.

209. G. D. Roberts, *Law and Life* (W. H. Allen, 1964). Reprinted by permission of Mrs G. D. Roberts.

210. Gervais Rentoul, *Sometimes I Think* (Hodder & Stoughton, 1940). Reprinted by permission of Mrs Rentoul.

211. *Rufus Isaacs* (Hutchinson, 1942). Reprinted by permission of the Marquis of Reading and A. P. Watt Ltd.

212. H. Montgomery Hyde, *Lord Reading* (New York, 1967).

213. G. D. Roberts, *Law and Life* (W. H. Allen, 1964). Reprinted by permission of Mrs G. D. Roberts.

214. *Rufus Isaacs* (Hutchinson, 1942). Reprinted by permission of the Marquis of Reading and A. P. Watt Ltd.

215. P. J. Helm, *Jeffreys* (T. Y. Crowell, 1966). Reprinted by permission of Harper & Row Publishers, Inc., and John Johnson (Author's Agent) Ltd.

216–17. Richard O'Connor, *Courtroom Warrior* (Little Brown, 1963). Copyright © 1963 by Richard O'Connor. Reprinted by permission of McIntosh and Otis, Inc.

218. *Life of John, Lord Campbell*, ed. Mrs Hardcastle (London, 1881).

219. F. Tennyson Jesse, *The Trial of Samuel H. Dougal* (1928). Reprinted by permission of William Hodge & Company Ltd.

220. Serjeant A. M. Sullivan, *Old Ireland* (Thornton Butterworth, 1927). By permission.

221. Iain Adamson, *A Man of Quality* (Frederick Muller, 1964). Reprinted by permission of the author.

222. A. E. Bowker, *Behind the Bar* (Staples Press, 1951). Reprinted by permission of Granada Publishing Ltd.

223. J. B. Atlay, *The Victorian Chancellors*, vol. 2 (London, 1908).

224. Lord Alverstone, *Recollections of Bar and Bench* (London, 1914).

225. *Memoirs of Edward Vaughan Kenealy* (London, 1898).

226. Sir Frank MacKinnon, *On Circuit* (1940). Reprinted by permission of Cambridge University Press.

227. Edmund D. Purcell, *Forty Years at the Criminal Bar* (London, 1916).

228. F. W. Ashley, *My Sixty Years in the Law* (John Lane, 1936).

229. A. S. Gillespie-Jones, *The Lawyer Who Laughed* (1978). Reprinted by permission of Huthchinson, Australia.

230. Ernest Bowen-Rowlands, *In the Light of the Law* (Grant Richards, 1931).

231. Anthony Mockler, *Lions Under the Throne* (1983). Reprinted by permission of Muller, Blond & White Ltd.

232–3. Fred D. Pasley, *Not Guilty: The Story of Samuel S. Leibowitz* (1933). Reprinted by permission of Putnam's, New York.

234. Henry Cecil, *Just Within the Law* (1975). © 1975 by Henry Cecil. Reprinted by permission of Hutchinson Publishing Group Ltd., and Curtis Brown Ltd. on behalf of the Estate of Henry Cecil.

235–8. Frederick Trevor Hill, *Lincoln the Lawyer* (New York, 1912).

239–40. Augustine Birrel, *Sir Frank Lockwood* (London, 1898).

241. Edward Abinger, *Forty Years at the Bar* (Hutchinson, 1930).

242. Lord Simon, *Retrospect* (1952). Reprinted by permission of Hutchinson Publishing Group Ltd., and Viscount Simon.

243. Sir Travers Humphreys, *Criminal Days* (Hodder & Stoughton, 1946). Reprinted by permission of the Executors of the Estate.

244. Sir Frank MacKinnon, *On Circuit* (1940). Reprinted by permission of Cambridge University Press.

245. Sir Gervais Rentoul, *Sometimes I Think* (1940). Reprinted by permission of Hodder & Stoughton Ltd., and Mrs Rentoul.

246–7. F. D. MacKinnon, *On Circuit* (1940). Reprinted by permission of Cambridge University Press.

248. Maurice Healy, *The Old Munster Circuit* (1939). Reprinted by permission of Michael Joseph Ltd.

249–50. W. Forbes-Gray, *Some Old Scots Judges* (London, 1914).

251. Arthur Garfield Hays, *City Lawyer: The Autobiography of a Law Practice*. Copyright 1942 by Arthur Garfield Hays. Renewed © 1970 by Jane Hays Butler. Reprinted by permission of Simon & Schuster, Inc.

252. Edward Maltby, *Secrets of a Solicitor* (London, 1929).

253. Sir Henry Fielding Dickens, *Recollections* (Heinemann, 1934). Reprinted by permission of the descendants of Sir Henry Fielding Dickens.

254. Sir Edward Parry, *The Seven Lamps of Advocacy* (T. F. Unwin, 1923).

255. Francis L. Wellman, *Day in Court* (New York, 1910).

256. Sir Henry Fielding Dickens, *Recollections* (Heinemann, 1934). Reprinted by permission of the descendants of Sir Henry Fielding Dickens.

257–8. Sydney Aylett, *Under their Wigs* (1978). Reprinted by permission of Methuen London and the Estate of Reginald Crutchley.

259. Sir Travers Humphreys, *Criminal Days* (Hodder & Stoughton, 1946). Reprinted by permission of the Executors of the Estate.

260. Lord Simon, *Retrospect* (1952). Reprinted by permission of Hutchinson Publishing Group Ltd., and Viscount Simon.

261. Frederic H. Maugham, *At the End of the Day* (1954). Reprinted by permission of William Heinemann Ltd.

262–4. Serjeant Robinson, *Bench and Bar* (London, 1889).

265. *The Reminiscences of Sir Henry Hawkins*, ed. Richard Harris (London, 1904).

266. Serjeant Robinson, *Bench and Bar* (London, 1889).

267. Ernest Bowen-Rowlands, *In Court and Out of Court* (Hutchinson, 1925).

268. Sir Robert Menzies, *The Measure of the Years* (Cassell, 1970). © R. G. Menzies 1970. Reprinted by permission of Macmillan Publishing Company and the Executors of the Estate of the Right Honourable Sir Robert Menzies KT, CH, FRS, QC.

269. Sir Frank D. MacKinnon, *On Circuit* (1940). Reprinted by permission of Cambridge University Press.

270. Sir Robert Menzies, *The Measure of the Years* (Cassell, 1970). © R. G. Menzies 1970. Reprinted by permission of Macmillan Publishing Company and the Executors of the Estate of the Right Honourable Sir Robert Menzies KT, CH, FRS, QC.

271. J. W. Goldman, *Cricketers and the Law* (published privately, 1958). Reprinted by permission of A. I. F. Goldman of Isadore Goldman & Son, Solicitors 1885–1985.

272. Sir Gervais Rentoul, *This is My Case* (1944). Reprinted by permission of Hutchinson Publishing Group Ltd.

273–5. Claud Mullins, *Fifteen Years Hard Labour* (Gollancz, 1968). Reprinted by permission of A. M. Heath & Co. Ltd. for the author's estate.

276. Edmund Heward, *Lord Mansfield* (1979). Reprinted by permission of Barry Rose (Publishers) Ltd.

277. Michael A. Musmanno, *Verdict* (1958). Copyright © 1958 by Michael A. Musmanno. Reprinted by permission of Doubleday & Company, Inc.

278. Serjeant A. M. Sullivan, *Old Ireland* (Thornton Butterworth, 1927). By permission.

279. *The Reminiscences of Lord O'Brien* (London, 1910).

280. Gervais Rentoul, *This is My Case* (1944). Reprinted by permission of Hutchinson Publishing Group Ltd.

281. Robert Walton, *Random Recollections of the Midland Circuit* (privately printed, 1869).

282. Serjeant Ballantine, *Some Experiences of a Barrister's Life* (London, 1882).

283. Theobald Mathew, *For Lawyers and Others* (William Hodge, 1937). Reprinted by permission of T. D. Mathew.

284. Morris Salem, *Reflections of a Lawyer* (New York, privately printed, 1911).

285–6. Sir Edward Parry, *My Own Way* (Cassell, 1932).

287. J. Alderson Foote, *Pie-Powder* (John Murray, 1911).

288–9. Bellamy Partridge, *Country Lawyer* (McGraw Hill, 1939). Reprinted by permission of Mrs Bellamy Partridge.

290. Randolph S. Churchill, *What I said about the Press* (1957). Reprinted by permission of Weidenfeld & Nicolson Ltd.

291. Lord Alverstone, *Recollections of Bar and Bench* (London, 1914).

292. J. H. Balfour-Browne, *Forty Years at the Bar* (London, 1916).

293. A. M. Sullivan, *Old Ireland* (Thornton Butterworth, 1927). By permission.

294. Edmund D. Purcell, *Forty Years at the Criminal Bar* (London, 1916).

295. W. Forbes-Gray, *Some Old Scots Judges* (London, 1914).

296. Sir Gervais Rentoul, *Sometimes I Think* (1940). Reprinted by permission of Mrs Rentoul and Hodder & Stoughton Ltd.

297. Sir Gervais Rentoul, *This is My Case* (1944). Reprinted by permission of Hutchinson Publishing Group Ltd.

298–302. G. D. Roberts, *Law and Life* (W. H. Allen, 1964). Reprinted by permission of Mrs G. D. Roberts.

303–7. Alfred Cohn and Joe Chisholm, *Take this Witness* (New York, 1934).

308–9. Maurice Healy, *The Old Munster Circuit* (1939). Reprinted by permission of Michael Joseph Ltd.

310–11. Philip C. Jessup, *Elihu Root* (1938). Reprinted by permission of Dodd, Mead & Company, Inc.

312. Barry O'Brien, *Lord Russell of Killowen* (London, 1901).

313. Gilchrist Gibb Alexander, *Temple of the Nineties* (Wm. Hodge, 1938).

314. Barry O'Brien, *Lord Russell of Killowen* (London, 1901).

315. Sir Edward Parry, *My Own Way* (Cassell, 1932).

316. Lord Simon, *Retrospect* (1952). Reprinted by permission of Hutchinson Publishing Group Ltd., and Viscount Simon.

317. Sir Gervais Rentoul, *This is My Case* (1944). Reprinted by permission of Hutchinson Publishing Group Ltd.

318. Edward Abinger, *Forty Years at the Bar* (Hutchinson, 1930).

319. John Mortimer, *Clinging to the Wreckage* (1982). Reprinted by permission of Weidenfeld & Nicolson Ltd., and A. D. Peters & Co. Ltd.

320. Sir Edward Parry, *My Own Way* (Cassell, 1932).

321. Sir Edward Parry, *The Seven Lamps of Advocacy* (T. F. Unwin, 1923).

322. *A Lawyer's Notebook* (London, 1933).

323. Dr Harold Dearden, *The Mind of the Murderer* (Bles, 1930).

324. A. S. Gillespie-Jones, *The Lawyer Who Laughed* (1978). Reprinted by permission of Hutchinson Australia.

325. Sir Norman Skelhorn, *Public Prosecutor* (1981). Reprinted by permission of Harrap Ltd.

326–7. William Camp, *The Glittering Prizes* (Macgibbon & Kee, 1960). Reprinted by permission of the author.

328. *The Life of F. E. Smith, First Lord Birkenhead*, by his son (1959). Reprinted by permission of Eyre & Spottiswoode.

329. H. Montgomery Hyde, *Lord Reading* (1967). Reprinted by permission of William Heinemann Ltd.

330. William Camp, *The Glittering Prizes* (Macgibbon & Kee, 1960). Reprinted by permission of the author.

331–2. *The Life of F. E. Smith, First Lord Birkenhead* (1959). Reprinted by permission of Eyre & Spottiswoode.

333. A. S. Gillespie-Jones, *The Lawyer Who Laughed* (1978). Reprinted by permission of Hutchinson Australia.

334. Muriel Box, *Rebel Advocate* (1983). Reprinted by permission of Victor Gollancz Ltd., and Eric Glass Ltd.

335. Sir Henry Fielding Dickens, *Recollections* (Heinemann, 1934). Reprinted by permission of the descendants of Sir Henry Fielding Dickens.

336–7. Sewell Stokes, *Court Circular* (Michael Joseph, 1950).

338–9. Alexander Martin Sullivan, *Old Ireland* (Thornton Butterworth, 1927). By permission.

340. E. S. Fay, *The Life of Mr Justice Swift* (Methuen & Co., 1939). By permission.

341. F. E. Pritchard, *Rigby* (W. & J. Mackay & Co., 1968).

342. E. S. Fay, *The Life of Mr Justice Swift* (Methuen & Co., 1939). By permission.

343. F. E. Pritchard, *Rigby* (W. & J. Mackay & Co., 1968).

344. E. S. Fay, *The Life of Mr Justice Swift* (Methuen & Co., 1939). By permission.

345. Arthur Smith, *Lord Goddard* (1959). Reprinted by permission of George Weidenfeld & Nicolson Ltd.

346. *Reminiscences of Sir Henry Hawkins* ed. Richard Harris (London, 1904).

347. Robert Traver, *The Jealous Mistress* (1967). Reprinted by permission of the author.

348. *The Autobiography of Sir Patrick Hastings* (1948). Reprinted by permission of William Heinemann Ltd.

349. Halliday Sutherland, *A Time to Keep* (Geoffrey Bles, 1934).

350. John D. Weaver, *Warren: The Man, the Court, the Era* (Gollancz, 1968).

351. *Harvard Law Review*, Vol. 58, p. 1136. Copyright 1944 by the Harvard Law Review Association.

352. Lord Alverstone, *Recollections of Bar and Bench* (London, 1914).

353. Sir Edward Parry, *On My Way* (Cassell, 1932).

354. Sir Edward Parry, *The Drama of the Law* (London, 1924).

355. Serjeant Ballantine, *Some Experiences of a Barrister's Life* (London, 1882).

356–7. Sir John Hollam, *Jottings of an Old Solicitor* (London, 1906).

358–9. Montague Williams, *Leaves of a Life* (London, 1890).

361. Sir Frank MacKinnon, *On Circuit* (1940). Reprinted by permission of Cambridge University Press.

362. Sir Edward Parry, *The Seven Lamps of Advocacy* (T. F. Unwin, 1923).

363. *The Portable Woollcott*, ed. Joseph Hennessey (1946). Copyright 1946, renewed © 1973 by the Viking Press Inc. Reprinted by permission of Viking Penguin, Inc.

364. Theobald Mathew, *For Lawyers and Others* (Wm. Hodge, 1937). Reprinted by permission of T. D. Mathew.

While every effort has been made to secure permission, we may have failed in a few cases to trace the copyright holder. We apologize for any apparent negligence.

INDEX OF NAMES MENTIONED

(References are to page numbers)

INDEX OF TOPICS

(References are to page numbers)